Treating Couples

The Intersystem Model of the Marriage Council of Philadelphia

Contents

    Clients and Therapists............................ 215
        Terry Marek

11. Relational Therapy with Lesbian Couples 236
        Virginia J. Swartz

12. Effects of Parental Separation and Divorce on Children 258
        Sherry Farmer

PART III. THEORY

13. The Relationship Life-Cycle 287
        Edward P. Monte

14. An Intersystem Approach to Treatment 317
        Gerald R. Weeks

    Name Index 341

    Subject Index 344

Preface

In some ways the development of the theory and practice of marital therapy seems like a relative newcomer to those clinicians who practice systems therapy. Most of the books in the field stress the total *family* as the unit of treatment in terms of understanding the dynamics of family interactions and intervention techniques. For the past 15 to 20 years, clinicians interested in systems work sought training in "family" therapy programs and at "family" therapy workshops. This training led to a dramatic shift in the practice of psychotherapy away from the individual as the unit of treatment to the family. Much less emphasis has been given to the marital dyad or couple as the unit of treatment.

Although there has been an increasing interest in and focus on the couple, those who practice marital therapy still do so in a context which is dominated by family systems therapy. This phenomenon is puzzling given that one of the axioms of family therapy is that children who are presented as identified patients are suffering from the projection of unresolved marital difficulties. The family therapist, who has been traditionally trained to deal with family problems, frequently stops short of working exclusively with the couple. The failure to develop sharply focused skills for dealing with the marital subsystem may contribute to the inability of the therapist to enable the total family system to make necessary or desired changes.

This is not meant to imply that the marital subsystem is more important than the total family system (including the intergenerational subsystem). Rather, the emphasis is on the belief that the quality of the marital relationship greatly influences, and may in fact determine, the quality of the total nuclear family relationship. It is our belief that marital and family therapists need skills for assessment and intervention in the total family system and in each of the subsystems.

The purpose of this book is to help fill the gap between individual and family therapy. Our focus is on the couple-as-a-couple. This focus of study has a very long tradition at the Marriage Council of Philadelphia, which was founded in 1932 under the direction of Emily Mudd.

The early work of Marriage Council consisted of premarital counseling and providing sex information and education to couples. The need for marital therapy quickly emerged within this context. During the period from 1932 to the 1950s, Dr. Mudd published several books on marital therapy and hundreds of scholarly articles and lay articles. From a historical perspective, marital therapy was well established in the early days when the field of marital and family therapy was developing.

This book represents the latest thinking of the staff of Marriage Council, which is a freestanding training institute accredited by the American Association for Marriage and Family Therapy and affiliated with the University of Pennsylvania School of Medicine. It is also a major treatment center for couples in the northeast. All of the core faculty at Marriage Council teach, supervise, and practice marital and family therapy. The majority of the clinical work is couple therapy. Because our name is Marriage Council, couples and professionals who refer to us tend to be highly selected. This process has created a unique environment in which to study the couple and refine the practice of marital therapy.

The emphasis of this book is clearly on the couple and the special problems presented by couples such as extramarital affairs, conflicts, violence, sexual problems, and divorce. One purpose of the book is to help the clinician understand the couple as a system unto itself and the principles and techniques which we use daily. Another purpose is to foster a belief in the value of integrative approaches as opposed to singular and unidimensional approaches which are so often presented in a dogmatic and parochial fashion.

Since the early 70s, the staff has been striving to develop an integrated approach. Today, a number of writers in our field have started to stress the need for integration. Unfortunately, the majority have sought to integrate only two approaches, such as object-relations and systems theory, or psychodynamic theory with behavioral theory or systems theory. Our approach to integration is much more encompassing. We believe the clinician must simultaneously consider the individual (e.g., intrapsychic dynamics), interactional (e.g., communication deficits), and intergenerational (e.g., unresolved family triangle) aspects of the couple relationship. We call the integration of these systems/approaches the Intersystem Approach. Indeed, this task is ambitious and complex. A master therapist for us is not someone who has mastered a particular approach to treatment. The master therapist has a current knowledge base in the theory and practice of all three approaches and can systematically and effectively integrate them in treating any client unit. This volume will reveal the complexities of our thinking in weaving together these approaches with couples.

OVERVIEW OF THE BOOK

Chapter 1 describes the early and ongoing issue of assessment and treatment planning for the married couple, marital inventories, individual development and personal lifestyles, couple dynamics, communication skills, marital contracts, and the multigenerational context.

Chapter 2 shows how goal setting in the intersystem model provides the basis for intervention into the interactional, intergenerational and individual aspects of a couple presenting in therapy. It explores some general assumptions and principles of goal setting through the use of clinical material. It also highlights how goals set within the intersystem model allow ongoing therapy to touch upon deeper issues and solutions.

Chapter 3 presents the basic structural principles of the Intersystem Approach. The structural elements include engaging the couple, individual sessions, the initial contract, stages of treatment, the intake session, and the evaluation stage.

Chapter 4 details a clinical approach to patients in which every attempt is made to focus on intrapsychic dynamics and events as well as on the interpersonal, systemic frame of reference. The author examines the currently accepted diagnostic nomenclature, noting the advantages and disadvantages of diagnostic concepts and the evolution of the American Psychiatric Association's Diagnostic and Statistical Manual.

Chapter 5 discusses the basic process principles of the Intersystem Approach. The process elements include the evaluation of the therapeutic agenda, maintaining balance, facilitating communication, modifying the system, and heightening affect. Intervention strategies are discussed in terms of systemic change and the profound effect on the relationship.

Chapter 6 directs our attention to the final phase of therapy, ending the therapy. The chapter addresses both appropriate and premature termination, deals with resistances to termination, and suggests a model for the successful termination of couple or family therapy.

Chapter 7 compares the styles of three therapists who operate within the framework of intersystem therapy. Differences in style are illustrated through the use of excerpts from therapy sessions which focus on similar content. A three-dimensional model of therapeutic focus is used to analyze how each therapist targets different levels of the system.

Chapter 8 offers a clinical guide to the marital/family therapist working with the problem of extramarital sexual relations. It begins with a brief consideration of definitional issues, followed by a review of pertinent empirical studies, before moving on to more clinical material. The importance of careful assessment is emphasized, as well as the skillful management of the extramarital crisis. Special problems posed by the secret affair and the continuing affair are discussed. The process of recovery and its complications are traced. Finally, the author presents a multilevel explanatory model of extramarital sex to be used with client couples.

Chapter 9 addresses the concern of physical abuse between partners. There is a context in which abuse can be successfully treated without challenging the integrity of the dyad. The approach put forth combines behavioral, educational, and psychodynamic interventions within a systemic perspective.

Chapter 10 describes a therapeutic model for separation and divorce. This model highlights specific guidelines for treatment including: criteria of a constructive separation-divorce; the composition of sessions; the tasks and role of the therapist; a typology of separation-divorce cases; and the complex feelings evoked in both clients and therapists.

Chapter 11 reviews the literature on lesbianism and the psychological health of lesbians. Implications for relational therapy with lesbian couples are discussed. Different types of lesbian dyads are identified and common concerns of these couples are illustrated via case examples. Therapist characteristics and training needs are examined.

Chapter 12 examines ways in which the child's response to parental separation/divorce-related events may be influenced by his developmental level in cognitive, emotional, and social skills at the time the events occurred. Examples are given of how to use a developmental perspective to decide what can, should and should not be said to the child about these events. These include ways to help the child: (a) on a one-to-one basis; (b) in a family context; (c) as a member of a children's support group. A model for a children's support group, developed and in use at the Marriage Council of Philadelphia, is described.

Chapter 13 offers a theoretical framework from which to view life-cycle stages and issues of the committed relationship. The author presents an integrative perspective encompassing the individual, interactional and intergenerational components of experience and development. Additionally, a model of specific relationship life-cycle stages, with primary emergent issues, is presented. Corresponding clinical issues in each of these stages are discussed and clinical approaches suggested.

Chapter 14 provides the theoretical understanding of the intersystem approach to therapy. The author establishes a metatheoretical foundation for this approach to treatment and then develops both a general theory of psychotherapy and a specific theory of marital therapy. The approach to marital therapy is based on both theoretical and empirical social-psychological principles — not on systems theory.

This book is best read cover to cover. However, some readers may prefer to read the theory section first in order to understand our theoretical conceptualizations before returning to earlier sections of the text which deal with more practical matters.

The insights described in this book are based primarily on clinical experience. Marriage Council provides approximately 1,000 clock hours of marital therapy per month. Over a period of years, the authors of this text have accumulated thousands of hours of experience which have been integrated and processed through teaching, supervising, participating in weekly case conferences, and working with couples directly. We hope these insights will benefit other therapists, whether novice or experienced, who work with couples.

Contributors

JAMES M. BAHR, M.S. Ed.
Research Assistant, Marriage Council of Philadelphia.

SHERRY FARMER, M.C.A.T.
Senior Staff Therapist and Supervisor, Marriage Council of Philadelphia; Clinical Associate in Psychiatry, University of Pennsylvania School of Medicine.

MARTIN GOLDBERG, M.D.
Director, Marriage Council of Philadelphia; Clinical Professor of Psychiatry & Director, Division of Family Study, University of Pennsylvania School of Medicine.

EVELYN R. GROOME, M.S., M.S.Ed.
Senior Clinical Therapist and Supervisor, Marriage Council of Philadelphia; Clinical Associate in Psychiatry, University of Pennsylvania School of Medicine.

LARRY HOF, M.Div.
Director of Clinical Development, Marriage Council of Philadelphia; Lecturer in Psychiatry, University of Pennsylvania School of Medicine.

BEA HOLLANDER-GOLDFEIN, Ph.D.
Senior Clinical Therapist and Supervisor, Marriage Council of Philadelphia; Clinical Associate in Psychiatry, University of Pennsylvania School of Medicine.

RICHARD N. MACK, M.Div.
Senior Staff Therapist & Supervisor, Marriage Council of Philadelphia; Clinical Associate in Psychiatry, University of Pennsylvania School of Medicine.

TERRY MAREK, M.S.W., A.C.S.W.
Formerly Senior Clinical Therapist and Supervisor, Marriage Council of Philadelphia; Clinical Associate in Psychiatry, University of Pennsylvania School of Medicine.

EDWARD P. MONTE, Ph.D.
Director of Clinical Services, South Jersey, Marriage Council of Philadelphia; Clinical Associate in Psychiatry, University of Pennsylvania School of Medicine.

VIRGINIA J. SWARTZ, M.S.W., A.C.S.W.
Clinical Associate and Staff Therapist, Marriage Council of Philadelphia; Doctoral Candidate, School of Social Work, University of Pennsylvania.

STEPHEN R. TREAT, D.Min.
*Senior Clinical Therapist and
Supervisor, Marriage Council of
Philadelphia; Clinical Associate in
Psychiatry, University of
Pennsylvania School of Medicine.*

GERALD R. WEEKS, Ph.D.
*Director of Training, Marriage Council
of Philadelphia; Clinical Associate
Professor of Psychology in Psychiatry,
University of Pennsylvania School
of Medicine.*

APRIL WESTFALL, Ph.D.
*Director of Clinical Services, Marriage
Council of Philadelphia; Clinical
Assistant Professor in Psychiatry,
University of Pennsylvania School
of Medicine.*

Treating
Couples

The Intersystem Model of the
Marriage Council of Philadelphia

PART I

Principles of Marital Therapy

Chapter 1

Marital Assessment: Providing a Framework for Dyadic Therapy

*Larry Hof
and
Stephen R. Treat*

Thorough and accurate assessment is crucial to the practice of marriage and family therapy. Without assessment, treatment plans can be ill conceived and the therapist could be approaching his/her work with a couple on a moment-by-moment basis. If such is the case, therapy can be prolonged, even harmful to the client couple.

The assessment process itself is ongoing and not limited to the information gathered in the first few sessions. The treatment plan is based upon the initial assessment, but as that plan unfolds, the assessment process continues, with confirmations and disconfirmations of initial hypotheses and treatment plans. The approach and substance of marital therapy are then affirmed, revised, modified, tuned, or changed dramatically as the ongoing assessment process continues. The result is that assessment affects treatment, and treatment affects assessment, and so on.

Thorough assessment of the marital relationship must be systemic in nature. While fault may seem to rest with one partner, there is always some complementary behavior demonstrated by the other. These behaviors interact, often in a repetitive and circular fashion, creating a systemic and not a solely individual problem. With an understanding of each partner's contribution to the marital difficulty, the therapist can intervene to break the destructive cycles of behavior and replace them with more constructive and healing interactions.

Furthermore, accurate and systemic assessment contributes to several initial goals of therapy. As the therapist communicates verbally and nonverbally, his/her comprehension of the couple's difficulty, of the dyad's fears and anxieties, their commitment to the therapeutic process increases. Joining is facilitated as the couple feels that the therapist cares and understands. Accurate assessment then leads to on-target intervention.

When evaluating the marital relationship, five specific areas of focus are indicated: (1) psychometric indicators of marital adjustment; (2) individual development and personality styles; (3) assessment of the current relationship style of the couple; (4) identification and assessment of the original and current marital contract; and (5) exploration of the extended family/multigenerational context.

PSYCHOMETRIC INDICATORS OF MARITAL ADJUSTMENT

A variety of inventories and scales are available to enable the therapist to assess marital adjustment.

The use of brief, valid, and reliable instruments such as the Locke-Wallace Marriage Inventory or the Dyadic Adjustment Scale can give the therapist a good overall sense of the clients' perceptions of marital adjustment and satisfaction (Locke & Wallace, 1959) and dyadic adjustment (not necessarily marital), the latter with a focus on dyadic satisfaction, dyadic cohesion, dyadic consensus, and affectional expression (Spanier, 1976). The Marital Satisfaction Inventory (Snyder, 1979) focuses on a variety of relationship issues, including effective communication, problem-solving communication, quality of leisure time together, etc.

Proper use of such inventories by a marital therapist is essential. The inventories should not be used as a task-oriented substitute for the therapist's relating to the couple. Often, anxiety-laden therapists will use inventories to exert control, to provide a structure to the session, or to arrive at a premature diagnosis. Accurate assessment needs to be done on several levels at the same time. Individual psychopathology, psychopharmacology, social history, and present context all need to be considered. Marital inventories should be only one of many assessment tools and not the final word. Assessment results are not facts, but indicators which can focus the structure, definition, and direction of therapy. Sharing the results of inventories with the marital couple, if done caringly and discriminately, can often pinpoint issues quickly, raise serious concerns, and generally guide therapy in proper healthful directions.

INDIVIDUAL DEVELOPMENT AND PERSONALITY STYLES

Although the primary focus of marital therapy is the marital relationship, the therapist must still be well acquainted with personality development theory and psychopathology. The dynamics which contribute to the formation of each individual lead to the development of identity and a personality style which directly affects the way an individual relates to other people. Needless to say, identity development and personality styles impact greatly upon a marital relationship.

Sager (1976) has done a great deal of work developing personality typologies and discussing how they interact in marital relationships. His discussion of parent, child, romantic, rational, companionate, parallel, and equal-partner styles has provided helpful guidelines for therapists wanting to blend individual personality theory with marital theory and counseling.

The marital counselor must have a thorough knowledge of individual psychopathology, so that she/he may be aware of significant individual issues which impact greatly upon a marital relationship. Familiarity with and understanding of the five axes in the *Diagnostic and Statistical Manual of Mental Disorders (DSM-III-R)* will give the therapist knowledge of the diagnostic criteria of the various forms of emotional illness. With such knowledge, the therapist can preliminarily assess the nature and severity of individual issues, e.g., chronic anxiety, mood disorder, thought disorder, personality disorder, etc. This will increase the likelihood that the marital therapist will work within his/her limits of training and experience and be able to assess accurately. If the assessment process reveals significant psychopathology, specialized treatment plans can be made or appropriate referral facilitated.

ASSESSMENT OF THE CURRENT RELATIONSHIP
STYLE OF THE COUPLE

The assessment of the current relationship style of the couple enables the therapist to identify positive forces and processes within the relationship which could facilitate treatment, as well as identify relationship-diminishing forces and processes which could disrupt or block desired growth and change in therapy. When evaluating the current relationship style of the couple, the therapist seeks information via questioning and direct observation regarding the following issues:

1) How are the inclusion, control, and affection/intimacy issues handled within this relationship?
2) What is the balance between feelings, rationality, and behavior in this relationship?
3) How effectively do the partners communicate with each other?
4) How effective is the couple's problem-solving and decision-making process?
5) How effectively do the partners manage conflict?

Inclusion, Control, and Affection/Intimacy Issues

Schutz (1966) has stated that all individuals have three basic interpersonal needs which are manifested in various behaviors and feelings in the individual's relationships with other people: the need for inclusion, the need for control, and the need for affection/intimacy. Berman and Lief (1975), Hof and Miller (1981), and Doherty and Colangelo (1984) have discussed and developed the relationship of Schutz's concepts to marital and family functioning, emphasizing that these are perhaps the three core issues in relationship functioning.

The key "inclusion" question in a marriage is: What is the extent of each partner's commitment to the other and to the relationship? A continuum from noncommitment or disengagement to overcommitment or extreme enmeshment expresses the various possibilities. The therapist can inquire directly regarding the extent and nature of commitment (e.g., high versus low level of commitment; commitment out of duty, fear, religious values, financial realities, for the sake of the children or maintaining a family unit versus commitment based on love, shared values, interests, and intimacies). In addition, further insights can be gained as the couple's communication and interaction are observed (e.g., to what extent do they speak of a future together?).

It is important that each partner have a sense of personal identity (versus enmeshment); a sense of togetherness, commitment, belonging, or membership (versus disengagement); and a belief that the other person is committed to the relationship at a somewhat similar level. Without some sense of parity in this area, trust will remain relatively low, as will the willingness to risk self-disclosure in potentially vulnerable areas. Without a sufficient level of self-identity and commitment to the relationship, many partners are unable or unwilling to expose their pain, embarrassment, shame, etc., or to risk trying to change behaviors when failure could possibly lead to feared ridicule or abandonment.

Some key "control" questions in a marriage are: How equitably is power distributed and what is the level of satisfaction with the power distribution? To what extent does each partner see him/herself and the other as a responsible person? The therapist can inquire directly regarding these issues and can observe the interaction of the couple when a decision is required in the therapeutic process on even such a small issue as the day and time of the next appointment. Does each express opinions? Do they consult each other in the decision-making process? Do they value each other's ideas? Can they compromise?

When one partner feels somewhat powerless or resents the other's unilateral decision-making or role definition, the situation is ripe for a control struggle, usually characterized by anger, aggression, withdrawal, or passive aggressiveness. Couples struggling for control rarely remain peers, but seem to act out more parent-to-child behavior. On the other hand, when both partners feel powerful and responsible, mutual and satisfying problem-solving, decision-making, and role renegotiation become real possibilities.

The key "affection/intimacy" question in a marriage is: What is the degree of intimacy experienced between the partners, and to what extent are they each satisfied with it? Intimacy here refers to the in-depth sharing of core aspects of oneself with one's partner. As with the inclusion and control issues, direct questioning in this area can yield significant information. For example, "What is each partner's perception of the quantity and quality of physical and nonphysical affection expressed in the relationship?" "What types of intimacy do they share and what is their satisfaction level with each type?" Direct observation can also give important clues (e.g., to what extent they employ touch during the sessions and to what extent supportive, warm, and caring expressions are exchanged during the sessions).

Like Clinebell and Clinebell (1970), the authors believe there are at least 12 varieties or facets of intimacy: sexual, emotional, intellectual, aesthetic, creative, recreational, work, crisis, commitment, spiritual, communication, and conflict. Since no one can be intimate with all people in all ways, it is important that a couple mutually define for themselves in what ways they desire intimacy and work to achieve those goals. When intimacy in one area is desired by one partner to a certain degree, but to a lesser degree or not at all by the other, the potential for deep hurt, diminished satisfaction, and feelings of rejection in the relationship is obvious. When core intimacy needs are not addressed satisfactorily, the potential for marital and sexual dissatisfaction increases dramatically.

Many individuals fear being intimate with another. It is important to assess the depth and organization of such fears. As mentioned above, intimacy requires vulnerability and self-disclosure. If fears in one or both individuals of a couple are considerable, an "intimacy dance" can be created by the dyad to protect each person from hurt and rejection. Neither will then be willing to be vulnerable enough to openly disclose his/her honest desires, wishes, fears, hopes, etc. Instead, the protective "dance" will substitute for genuine intimacy.

A couple's dance will evolve out of a lack of personal differentiation and of social skills, which in turn heightens fears of intimacy. An undifferentiated person has difficulty defining who he/she is and what he/she needs. Often, boundaries with others are poorly formed, manifested by a person being too needy or too disengaged. When a significant other seeks closeness, fears of losing the self definition one has and of being overwhelmed are common. The dance protects each person from such vulnerability, and becomes necessary for effective sexual expression.

The "intimacy dance" is a metaphor for the means by which each member of a couple maintains a safe distance from the other, protecting each partner's vulnerabilities. Often, as one partner will step toward the partner, the other will collusively step back. For example, a couple complained to a therapist that their sexual relationship had been unsatisfactory for nine years. During the first four years, the woman pursued her husband and he withdrew. During the past five years, the husband played the pursuer role and his wife rejected him. Both dynamics of rejection and intrusion (Napier, 1978) were manifested by the partners for the maintenance of a "safe" distance in the relationship. If the therapist does not comprehend and assess this "intimacy dance," one partner will appear to be sexually dysfunctional and the other sexually adjusted when, in actuality, both individuals of the dyad are exquisitely working together to maintain distance and protect each other.

The initial content of each evaluation session can be given far too much attention if the couple's "intimacy dance" is not understood. For example, a couple came into a second session feeling argumentative and hopeless. The session was unsatisfactory for everyone. The therapist became exasperated and was confused because during the initial session the couple had demonstrated more warmth and intimacy. The therapist failed to realize that the couple's argument and hopelessness were "dance" steps to balance more vulnerable feelings of intimacy and emotional closeness which were felt during the first therapeutic hour. The "intimacy dance" of this couple protected the relationship homeostasis — the tendency toward maintenance of balances within a dyad to keep a certain established equilibrium in the relationship (Jackson, 1957).

The intimacy dance is designed to avoid fears associated with intimacy. Fear of intimacy can include fear of hurt, abandonment, rejection, intrusion, and loss of self. These fears can be increased or decreased based on the level of differentiation attained by each individual. A poorly differentiated person will often feel more susceptible to being overwhelmed. The "intimacy dance" can be comprised of sometimes obvious or, more often, subtle steps established for the maintenance of a protective shield for the individual and the couple, such as the following two dances illustrate.

Dance 1

John and Susan have been married for 7 years. John's mother is able to intrude into their married life in various ways and he cannot or will not stop the intrusion. In part, he fears confronting his mother because she will withdraw, as she has historically, and he will consequently feel guilty. John complains that Susan invades in the same way. Susan is secretly questioning her own femininity and helps to create an environment in which femininity or vulnerability never needs to be addressed. She fears that if she were not in control she would not be loved. Both partners have colluded in a "dance" to remain separate and to limit the threats of intimacy.

Step 1　John comes home from work and goes directly to the mail. Susan comes home from work and begins to make dinner.

Step 2　They begin to recount the day. If there is any sense that one might want to be close to the other, a fight starts. Susan says, "I am really glad you are home." John responds, "Why isn't dinner ready?"

Step 3　After dinner, John does the dishes and Susan leaves the kitchen.

Step 4　Both watch TV in the evening but do not like the same shows. They watch in two separate rooms.

Step 5　John goes to bed earlier than Susan, and when she comes to bed, she undresses in the bathroom.

Step 6　They give each other a habitual kiss and go to sleep.

This dance is for the purpose of avoiding being close and vulnerable to each other. Sexual expression is limited and thus feelings of rejection and hurt are masked. The dance is designed with complex steps to limit intimacy. Sensitivity to this dance will allow the therapist to be balanced in approaching and supporting both, while confronting their fears. Each partner will need the help of the therapist to support his/her partner's movement, because their individual fears suggest neither partner will be able to initially support the other's growth and will often attempt to undermine it. In the assessment period, the therapist must analyze the "dance," and remain balanced in approaching each partner of the dyad, attributing equal responsibility for the "dance" steps.

Dance 2

Alice and Mark come to an initial session remarking that both are very dissatisfied with their sexual relationship. Mark constantly pursues Alice, asking for holding, intimate conversation, and sexual intercourse. Alice resists all of Mark's advances. The consequence is that Mark consistently experiences feelings of rejection and Alice feelings of being intruded upon.

Step 1 Mark chose Alice for his spouse unconsciously knowing that she was sexually inhibited and fearful.

Step 2 He then opened his arms to Alice, desiring intense intimacy at every turn.

Step 3 Because his wife was fearful of sexual intimacy in the first place, the invitations for intimate expression were/are threatening. His open arms cause hers to close.

Step 4 Mark solidifies the dance by continually having his arms open wide, enabling Alice to consistently withdraw and defend herself.

Step 5 Mark chooses a therapist who would be inducted into thinking that he was open and Alice had the sexual problems.

This dance fits Napier's (1978) classic description of a "rejection-intrusion" pattern. It appears that one partner is devoid of sexual interest and seeks to avoid engulfment and intimacy, while the other partner appears open to, desirous of, and actively pursuing sexual intimacy. In actuality, both partners are fearful of being close to the other and both fear rejection. While their behaviors appear to be for different purposes, the outcome is the same, and the key dynamic for the therapist to watch is the avoidance of intimacy.

It is apparent from this perspective that the therapist working to enhance marital relationships must be process-oriented and perceive these elaborate dances in which couples are involved. Most couples have perfected some dance that is uniquely their own and it is the role of the therapist to learn the steps, anticipate the turns, and to confront the process within the therapeutic hour.

Feelings, Rationality, and Behavior

In order for an individual and a relationship to function at its optimal potential, it is necessary that there be a balance between feelings, rationality, and behavior. Many therapies emphasize one of these dimensions of the self to the virtual exclusion of the others, encouraging the development of skills in one area as the so-called "key" to effective interpersonal functioning. Thus, we have Behaviorists, Cognitionists, and Affective Expressionists. All, in the authors' view, err to the extent that they do not seek a balance between all three of these areas of the self.

Egan (1970) has expressed the need for "total human expression" in relationships, the blendings of "thought-full" and "feeling-full" expression in effective communication processes. L'Abate and Frey (1981), with their E-R-A (Emotionality-Rationality-Activity) model, make the same point.

Unfortunately, in many couples, one partner is deemed more cognitive and rational and the other more emotional. In a reciprocal pattern, both of these forms of expression may become more polarized. The cognitive person, fearing the emotion of his/her partner, becomes even more rational and controlled. The more emotional person, feeling the distance and withdrawal of the cognitive partner, often becomes more emotional to vent frustration and also to "reach" his/her often rational spouse. Assessment of the level of organization of this pattern and emphasizing the undeveloped part in each partner are keys to change.

When evaluating the marital relationship with regard to these imbalances, the therapist seeks to ascertain the extent to which each partner is aware of the full range of human emotions—joy, love, hurt, loneliness, pain, anger, etc., and to what extent each is able to express those feelings effectively and appropriately to the other. When lack of affective awareness or ineffective or inappropriate expression blocks effective relationship bonding or functioning, skill training may be needed (see Hof & Miller, 1981; L'Abate & Milan, 1975 for specific exercises). For example, the effective expression of and empathic response to pain, fear, or anger frequently remove blocks to intimacy by diminishing defensive responses or passive-aggressive gambits.

In the area of rationality, the therapist can be most helpful in looking for cognitive distortions and irrational beliefs (Burns, 1980; Epstein, 1982; Epstein & Eidelson, 1981). Cognitive distortions such as the following can be very destructive: (a) overgeneralizations (e.g., "Since it happened once before between us, it will happen over and over again!"); (b) all-or-nothing thinking (e.g., "Since we have this one problem area that is really destructive, our whole relationship is bad!"); (c) magnification of the negative and disqualifying the positive (e.g., "This one problem area has got to be worked on at all costs, because it impacts tremendously on everything we do and makes all the good things between us meaningless!"); (d) personalizations (e.g., "The fact that you have this problem proves that you don't love me, that there's something wrong with me, and that I am probably responsible in some way for your problem!"). When applied to oneself, to one's partner, or to the marital relationship, these attitudes can distort reality, leading to erroneous conclusions and contributing to the development of hurt or angry feelings and defensive postures.

Virtually every marital therapist has assigned a behavioral task to a couple, only to have them report that it was an unmitigated disaster. Yet, after close scrutiny, the clients and therapist discovered that it was really 80% positive, but the couple had cognitively distorted the evaluation of the experience by overemphasizing the negative and discounting the positive.

Perhaps the most common irrational belief encountered in marital therapy is that "My partner should know what I need and how I feel without me having to tell him/her." This idea leads to what is commonly known as mind reading. Other examples include the following: if you loved me you would do what I want, always; if I know what you feel, I must do what you want; I should be able to fix anything that is wrong between us; a man should never be weak or vulnerable; a woman should never be sexually aggressive or too opinionated; if we get too close, one of us will lose control, and that will be bad or destructive.

If the marital evaluation can identify the presence of these unhelpful cognitions, appropriate steps can be taken to correct them before the advent of specific therapeutic interventions which may be blocked by such distortions. Or, at the minimum, the clients can be forewarned regarding the potential negative consequences of continuing to use such irrational or distorted cognitive processes. Frequently, the assigned task of specifying strengths regarding oneself, one's partner, and the relationship can point up cognitive distortions rather quickly, as the process is observed and monitored by the therapist. Clients frequently have difficulty with this task if there are significant distortions in their cognitive processes.

In the area of behavior, the marital evaluation focuses on communication skills, problem-solving and decision-making skills, conflict utilization skills (all discussed in subsequent sections), and behavior exchange skills. The therapist needs to know to what extent each partner is able to express positive and specific requests for behavioral change in the other, and to what extent the couple is able to create and carry out appropriate "partitive" (*quid pro quo* or tit-for-tat) contracts or "holistic" (good faith) contracts (Stuart, 1980). Where these skills are absent, their development frequently becomes part of the treatment process, facilitating the expression of behavioral requests in a positive manner and the creation of behavior exchanges.

Communication Skills

In the area of communication, the interviewer is endeavoring to assess the ability of each partner to express clearly and effectively his/her thoughts and feelings in self-responsible "I" statements; to use both verbal and nonverbal means of communication; to confirm/clarify what was heard; to give selective, specific, and timely feedback; and to make constructive and positive requests (Stuart, 1980). When these basic skills are missing, skill training will be needed to overcome the deficits in social learning in this area. (For specific communication exercises, see Guerney, 1977; Hof & Miller, 1981; Miller, Nunnally, & Wackman, 1979.)

When these skills are present, partners are more likely to be aware of the total person, what is being said verbally and nonverbally, and what is not being said, such as unexpressed feelings, hidden messages, etc. They are better able to listen to their partner with ears, eyes, and sometimes touch, and they can listen and attend to the impact of the other upon themselves, their thoughts, feelings, and bodies.

There are numerous communication skills which are imperative for the therapist to understand and assess. Besides rules for the expressor and listener referred to above, there are three other communication topics deemed to be important for assessment and early intervention. These are: (a) the ability of the dyad to differentiate reaction and response, (b) the level of intensity of the couple communication, and (c) the various nonverbal messages given and responded to by both partners.

Responsivity vs. reactivity. A couple's ability to change is a function of their responsivity (response-ability) vs. reactivity (re-activity).

The act of being responsive means maintaining a balance between one's intellect and emotion for the purpose of building a more productive and satisfying relationship (Egan, 1970; L'Abate & Frey, 1981). Dynamically, such balance gives one's partner permission to express fears, hurts, needs, etc. A person who responds will inquire, share feelings nonjudgmentally, and encourage elaboration. On the other hand, a reaction, a defensive posture designed to protect the self by attacking the other, limits the freedom of a partner to express feelings and needs. Reaction contributes greatly to the loss of the balance of intellect and emotion, thus producing exchanges that are mostly emotional and defensive posturing.

In intimate communication, a speaker must share both intellect and emotion directly, using "I" statements, followed by a feeling or a thought, sensitively and empathetically demonstrating a desire to understand. A responder needs to demonstrate the ability to listen accurately and empathetically by asking appropriate questions and not contradicting or giving one's opinion prematurely. When the responder is too emotional, with either hysterical crying or anger bordering on rage, or too intellectual, with no sign of affect or empathy, the result will often be that the person sharing a feeling will feel misunderstood.

The following are examples of reacting and responding between partners.

1) Person A: "I really felt hurt by what you did."
   Person B: "You hurt me worse." *(reaction)*
               "How did I hurt you?" *(response)*
2) Person A: "I would like to be hugged this way."
   Person B: "You never hug me." *(reaction)*
               "You mean like this?" *(response)*

A relationship will rarely be enhanced if a couple is reacting too frequently to each other. Reaction for the most part blocks the ability to listen. Neither partner, therefore, feels understood or appreciated. A reactive couple is enmeshed, undifferentiated, and diffuse. The therapist's task is to assess and control early a reactive process and support and teach responsivity.

Levels of affect. Assessment of the levels of affect is important. Marital relationships will be negatively affected with both too little intensity or too much. In general, anger and aggressive tones of voice show neither. If relationship intimacy is requested aggressively, a partner will most likely withdraw, feeling attacked or vulnerable. If the affect is too emotional as in, "I can't live without you!" or "Why can't you just love me!!" the listener will similarly be repelled. The therapist needs to initially assess levels of affect and teach clients how to communicate with a level of affective intensity that can be advantageous to building intimacy.

Some couples show so little affect that emotional bonding is very difficult. However, this type of disengaged dyad, a "rational partner with a rational partner" (Sager, 1976), is less likely to enter therapy. A type of couple more likely to enter therapy is one which communicates with such intensity that each partner constantly feels either rejected or invaded, as is often the case with "childlike and childlike" partnerships (Sager, 1976).

Nonverbal communication. The therapist needs to assess many of the nonverbal communications which can affect marital relations. Often these communications are symbolic representations of each partner's intrapersonal process. Folded arms and legs, facial expressions, and positions of the body are obvious considerations. Less obvious ones might be subtle movement of the chairs (e.g., forward or backward) or types of clothing worn (e.g., inhibiting, seductive, etc.). In one couple complaining of intimacy problems, the wife expressed that she felt she had no space or personal integrity in the relationship. During each session, her partner would move the chair 4 or 5 inches closer to her as he sat down; she would then move back. This was a metaphor for their entire relationship.

Awareness of the role of touch is also important. Does the couple touch each other during, before, or after the session, and with what sensitivity? How sensual is each individual? Does the client's clothing suggest an openness and vulnerability, or the opposite? Equally important as the therapist's assessment of the nonverbal behavior is the manner in which each partner interprets the communication of the other. The therapist's role is to ascertain what meanings each individual draws from the nonverbal messages. This is done by asking each client, for example, "What does this behavior mean to you?"; "What do you think that your partner is trying to say?"; "How do you interpret this message?"

Problem-Solving and Decision-Making Processes

In this area of the relationship, the therapist assesses the ability of the couple to define a problem, to explore alternative solutions and the possible positive and negative consequences of each, to reach an effective decision regarding which alternative(s) to explore provisionally, to create an action plan, and to carry out the plan and evaluate it when completed. (The "power" aspects of the decision-making process were discussed above, under *Inclusion, control, and affection/intimacy issues.*) Without sufficient problem-solving and decision-making skills, the likelihood of maintaining the ability to change various aspects of the marital relationship without the aid of third-party intervention is minimal. However, with these skills, partners become effective change agents for themselves.

Conflict Management

In the marital evaluation, the practitioner needs to assess how the couple manages conflict. Can each partner "own" and accept his/her feelings and not blame the partner for the way she/he feels? Can they identify the "real" issue? Can they maintain a present orientation, avoiding the dragging up of past history to "prove a point?" Can they use polarization constructively, to get away from each other when anger has escalated beyond manageable limits, or just to think more clearly, for the purpose of figuring out how to move closer together on the issue at hand? Can they identify areas of mutuality regarding the issue (i.e., what they have in common)? Do they have an effective problem-solving process? Can they celebrate the resolution of a conflict and, where needed, at least agree to disagree?

Destructive marital conflict can result from deficits in social and skill learning regarding conflict utilization, conflict management, and problem-solving. In addition, dysfunctional intrapsychic-interpersonal processes can lead to and contribute to dysfunctional conflict spirals. Narcissistic vulnerability, which can lead to destructive parental transferences upon one's partner and the use of projective identification, can wreak havoc in a relationship.

During the marital evaluation, the therapist needs to assess the amount of narcissistic vulnerability within the system. Feldman (1982) defines this vulnerability as "a weakness or deficiency in the structural cohesiveness, temporal stability, and/or affective coloring of the self-representation" (p. 417). It can lead a person to respond to real or perceived disapproval or rejection with "conscious or unconscious self-fragmentation, identity diffusion, and/or diminished self-esteem"

(p. 417). The amount of narcissistic vulnerability present within the system can be gauged by assessing the relative strength and weakness of positive and negative introjects within each partner. Where significant vulnerability and sensitivity are present, narcissistic expectations, unemphatic behavior, narcissistic rage and anxiety, projective identification, and cognitive distortions can flourish, leading to destructive conflict spirals (Feldman, 1982).

Feldman's (1982) thorough paper on this subject highlights the need for genuine empathy on the part of the therapist to enable individuals and couples to resolve narcissistic vulnerability. In addition, he explains how emotional awareness training, dream work, empathy training, cognitive awareness training, relationship strength specification, self-instruction training, problem-solving training, and behavioral contracting can be utilized to overcome the more destructive outgrowths of narcissistic vulnerability and enable couples to develop more constructive conflict styles.

Without the ability to manage conflict effectively, angry and resentful feelings have a way of remaining unresolved and ever present, serving as effective means for undermining therapy. Yet with such skills, hope and trust are increased as issues are addressed constructively and resolved.

IDENTIFICATION AND ASSESSMENT OF THE ORIGINAL AND CURRENT MARITAL CONTRACT

Much of the information gathered in the aforementioned areas gives the interviewer and the couple insight into various dimensions of the current relationship contract (i.e., what each person desires and expects in a variety of areas in the marriage; what each is willing to give; what agreements — verbal, conscious but nonverbalized, unconscious — have been made with oneself and one's partner) (Sager, 1976). Open discussion regarding the current and original marital contract enables the therapist and clients to get as much as possible "on the table," where it can be carefully examined, affirmed where it is helpful, and changed where it blocks current desired personal or relational growth and change.

Sager's (1976) "Reminder List for Marriage Contract of Each Partner" provides a helpful means for exploring the marital contract via (a) categories based on expectations of marriage (e.g., to create a family, to provide sanctioned and readily available sex, etc.), (b) categories based on psychological and biological needs (e.g., independence-dependence, activity-passivity, closeness-distance, etc.), (c) categories that are derivative of the externalized foci of other problems (e.g., energy level, interests, friends, values, etc.). By writing out a summary of what each partner wants in relationship to these areas, and what each is willing to give in exchange, personal responsibility and clarity of expression are likely to increase. (A more popular and very readable trade version of Sager's contract theory and process is available in Sager & Hunt, 1979.)

EXPLORATION OF THE EXTENDED
FAMILY/MULTIGENERATIONAL CONTEXT

The origins of difficulties in a marital relationship can often be found in relationships outside the marriage. Therefore, the evaluation of the marital relationship must also include at least a brief look at the extended family/multigenerational context of the couple and the problem. The therapist examines where each person "fits" in his/her extended family, what "messages" have been transmitted as "legacies" across the generations with regards to inclusion, control, and affection/intimacy issues (including messages related to sexuality), and what impact those messages have had upon the person as she/he lives within the current relationship.

The extended family/multigenerational context also includes the identification of where each partner and the relationship fit with regard to the individual and family life-cycle (Carter & McGoldrick, 1980). Life-stage transitions (e.g., midlife transition) can be traumatic. Normative events (e.g., marriage, birth of a child, retirement, etc.) and paranormative events (e.g., miscarriage, divorce, job loss, etc.) in the family life-cycle can generate pronounced effects, especially with the first occurrence of an event (e.g., the birth of a first child). Life-style changes, anxieties, resentments, and fears triggered by such transitions and events can impact directly upon the marriage. By being sensitive to such possibilities, the interviewer can often enable the couple to discover previously unrealized forces at work within or beneath the presenting complaint. These forces may be triggered by current life-cycle issues, or may be the result of "unfinished business" from the couple's past. The therapist can help the couple explore this area by focusing on how each partner and the couple handle transitions from one life-stage to another and cope with the normative and paranormative events of the family life-cycle.

EVALUATING THE MARITAL
RELATIONSHIP PROCESS GUIDELINES

As the practitioner conducts the marital evaluation, several process guidelines need to be present in his/her mind. First, the amount of information to be gathered may appear to be overwhelming at the outset. Yet, when one realizes how much of it can be gathered through the assignment and discussion of one or two small tasks, it can be placed in a proper perspective. An effective evaluation can be accomplished in two to four sessions.

We frequently assign the Marital Pre-Counseling Inventory (Stuart & Stuart, 1972) and the Sexual Adjustment Inventory (Stuart, Stuart, Maurice & Szasz, 1975) to clients presenting with marital difficulty. These positively-oriented, data-gathering devices are filled out and discussed by the partners. The results are then discussed with the therapist (who observes the clients' interaction in the office setting, attending to his/her own feelings as they are evoked in the interview), giving precise information in virtually all of the areas discussed above in *Assessment of the current relationship style of the couple.*

Simple questions such as "What expectations did you have of each other when you married?" open up the discussion of the marital contract. Similarly, questions regarding "How did you learn that?" or "What was it like in your family of origin in that area?" lead into a discussion of the extended family/multigenerational context.

Second, the marital evaluation, like all aspects of the total assessment process, is ongoing. It continues throughout treatment, is affected by the treatment process, and contributes to the ongoing adjustment of the treatment process. The therapist continually scans the couple and the relationship with reference to marital adjustment, current relationship style, the marital contract, and the extended family/multigenerational context. An individual session with each partner can be very helpful in identifying or uncovering relationship secrets (such as a previous or current extramarital affair) and in giving the therapist a sense of how each person's style of interaction is affected by the presence/absence of the partner. Similarly, a total family session or two may reveal new information regarding interactional styles, family secrets, and potential supports of or blocks to the therapeutic process.

Third, the marital evaluation is, in fact, part of the treatment process insofar as it enables the clients to gain insights, diminish anxiety, increase hope, and plan for change.

Fourth, the marital evaluation process is with the clients, not just by the therapist. Preliminary impressions are elicited from the clients, as well as shared by the therapist. Provisional hypotheses regarding how behaviors have been learned, what purpose they have served in the relationship, etc., are suggested by both the clients and the therapist, and discussed openly more often than not. (Of course, speculations regarding the nature of unconscious motivations are treated very cautiously.) This demystifies the therapeutic process, increases the sense of a "treatment team" approach to the marital problems, and is likely to increase the responsible involvement of the clients in the resolution of their difficulties and enhancement of their relationship.

Fifth, the therapist should realize that indications and contraindications are not to be rigidly imposed. They are not rigid rules to be adhered to without flexibility. For example, the presence of severe narcissistic vulnerability is a contraindication for marital therapy. However, if the "facts" are discussed with the couple and all agree on a provisional try of marital therapy, with the possible positive and negative consequences considered in advance, several benefits may occur. Success of the therapy in such an instance is often based on the therapeutic skill in balancing couple issues and responsibility, i.e., understanding that severe narcissistic vulnerability in one partner says something equally strong about the other. The clients may, somewhat paradoxically, succeed and attain their goal. Or they may not succeed, and having given it a try, may then be willing to do some individual work needed to provide a firmer base for the future resolution of the marital problems.

A significant part of the art of marital therapy involves assessing when relationship issues can be or need to be bypassed, and when they need to be confronted or resolved. Answers to questions of what to address and when and how to confront or bypass relationship issues frequently emerge as the assessment and treatment process evolves, and they just as frequently change along the way. The ability to maintain a flexible and open stance vis-à-vis these issues would appear to be a helpful attribute for any clinician.

In conclusion, the therapist needs to proceed with acceptance and respect, moving slowly with incremental steps, accentuating the positive and managing anxiety along the way. Active involvement of the clients as therapeutic partners in all phases of the assessment and treatment processes and viewing everything as a provisional try are key. In therapy grounded in such an assessment process, the likelihood of the clients being able to resolve their difficulties and enhance their marital relationships is greatly increased.

REFERENCES

American Psychiatric Association (1987). *Diagnostic and Statistical Manual of Mental Disorders* (3rd ed., rev.). Washington, D.C.: Author.

Berman, E., & Lief, H. I. (1975). Marital therapy from a psychiatric perspective: An overview. *American Journal of Psychiatry, 132,* 583–592.

Burns, D. (1980). *Feeling Good: The New Mood Therapy.* New York: New American Library.

Carter, E., & McGoldrick, M. (1980). *The Family Life Cycle.* New York: Gardner.

Clinebell, H. J., & Clinebell, C. H. (1970). *The Intimate Marriage.* New York: Harper & Row.

Doherty, W. J., & Colangelo, N. (1984). The family FIRO model: A modest proposal for organizing family treatment. *Journal of Marital and Family Therapy, 9,* 19-29.

Egan, G. (1970). *Encounter: Group Processes for Interpersonal Growth.* Belmont, CA: Brooks/Cole.

Epstein, N. (1982). Cognitive therapy with couples. *American Journal of Family Therapy, 10,* 5-16.

Epstein, N., & Eidelson, R. J. (1981). Unrealistic beliefs of clinical couples: Their relationship to expectations, goals and satisfaction. *American Journal of Family Therapy, 9,* 13-22.

Feldman, L. B. (1982). Dysfunctional marital conflict: An integrative interpersonal-intrapsychic model. *Journal of Marital and Family Therapy, 8,* 417-428.

Guerney, B. G., Jr. (1977). *Relationship Enhancement.* San Francisco: Jossey-Bass.

Hof, L., & Miller, W. R. (1981). *Marriage Enrichment: Philosophy, Process and Program.* Bowie, MD: Brady.

Jackson, D. (1957). The question of family homeostasis. *Psychiatric Quarterly Supplement, 31,* 79-90.

L'Abate, L., & Frey, J. (1981). The E. R. A. model: The role of feelings in family therapy reconsidered: Implications for a classification of theories of family therapy. *Journal of Marital and Family Therapy, 7,* 143-150.

L'Abate, L., & Milan, M. A. (Eds.) (1975). *Handbook of Social Skills Training and Research.* New York: Wiley.

Locke, H. J., & Wallace, K. M. (1959). Short marital adjustment and prediction tests: Their reliability and validity. *Marriage and Family Living, 21,* 251-255.

Miller, S., Nunnally, E., & Wackman, D. B. (1979). *Talking Together.* Minneapolis: Interpersonal Communication Programs.

Napier, A. Y. (1978). The rejection-intrusion pattern: A central family dynamic. *Journal of Marriage and Family Counseling, 4*(1), 5-12.

Sager, C. J. (1976). *Marriage Contracts and Couple Therapy.* New York: Brunner/Mazel.

Sager, C. J., & Hunt, B. (1979). *Intimate Partners.* New York: McGraw-Hill.

Schutz, W. C. (1966). *FIRO (The Interpersonal Underworld).* Palo Alto: Science and Behavior.

Snyder, D. K. (1979). Multidimensional assessment of marital satisfaction. *Journal of Marriage and the Family, 41,* 813-824.

Spanier, G. B. (1976). Measuring dyadic adjustments: New scales for assessing the quality of marriage and similar dyads. *Journal of Marriage and the Family, 38,* 15-28.

Stuart, R. (1980). *Helping Couples Change.* New York: Guilford.

Stuart, R., & Stuart, F. (1972). *Marital Pre-Counseling Inventory.* Champaign, IL: Research Press Co.

Stuart, F., Stuart, R., Maurice, W., & Szasz, G. (1975). *Sexual Adjustment Inventory.* Champaign, IL: Research Press Co.

Chapter 2

Goal Setting and Marital Therapy

Evelyn R. Groome

One of the purposes of evaluation is setting goals for treatment. Regardless of the therapeutic model used to shape the course of therapy, goals are a necessary aspect of the therapeutic process. Without goals, the path of therapy can only be circuitous, confusing, and irrelevant. A lack of goals can result in problems seeming hopeless, therapy feeling leaderless, and change being serendipitous. The formulation of goals makes a powerful statement about a couple's potential for change. For the therapist using the Intersystem Model, goals provide the basis for intervention into the interactional, intergenerational, and individual aspects of a couple presenting in therapy. Establishing goals gives a couple hope that change is possible. Within the Intersystem Model, this change has the potential to be profound, because goals become operationally translated into a multidimensional framework.

CONTROL, RESPONSIBILITY AND
MOTIVATION THROUGH GOAL SETTING

For the couple and the therapist, the goal-setting process clearly establishes a sense of control and structure, provides the underpinnings for sharing responsibility, and enhances motivation, especially if the goals are viewed as being fair and achievable. Several assumptions are inherent in such a process: that problems have solutions, that therapy has a structure and direction, and that change is a shared responsibility.

The therapist initially takes the lead in setting goals in order to establish an atmosphere of confidence and security in the therapeutic process. Goals are set by asking questions, such as, "How would you like your situation to be different?", by making suggestions, such as, "I would like to suggest that one goal for you is to communicate more directly with each other," or by reflecting statements, such as, "From what I'm hearing, you're ambivalent about separating and would like to explore the relationship before making a decision."

The ultimate aim, however, is for the couple to eventually share the responsibility in formulating common, achievable goals. For example, the couple will be as likely as the therapist to say, "It seems we expect mind reading from each other. We need to learn how to be more direct in our communications." This kind of statement shows the couple's motivation for therapy, reflects a shared sense of responsibility, and demonstrates they can begin to structure and control the resolution of their own problems. This kind of change indicates to the couple they can eventually leave therapy, and feel confident they can solve their own problems.

Initially, however, many couples come into therapy feeling overwhelmed and hopeless. This chaos can appear unmanageable for both the therapist and the couple. The couple needs to feel that the process of therapy involves an agreed-upon direction, so that the hard work necessary to continue will seem worthwhile. The therapist needs to take control from the beginning, so that feelings of confusion change to hopeful feelings, and become manageable for the couple. Paradoxically, the therapist's task is to create control in order to give it back to the couple. Control is given back to the couple by the clinician reflecting, interpreting, probing, and synthesizing in an effort to focus the couple's statements on the development of workable, problem-oriented goals. These statements help the couple turn what they experience as the uncontrollable and involuntary into the controllable and voluntary. When the couple has a sense of control, they are better able to accept mutual responsibility for both the problems and the necessary changes.

A sense of responsibility increases for couples as they see their problems can be broken down into more manageable components. Couples often wait before seeking therapy until every aspect of life seems negatively affected by their problems. They are unable to sort out what changes they want, which symptoms stem from which problems, where and when difficulties began, or in what order they should be examined.

This presentation is not unusual, because dysfunction in any relationship tends to highlight a marked imbalance between cognitive functioning and affective functioning. Often, one partner is extremely emotional, while the other is cut off from feelings. The therapist can be barraged with either intense affect or a pronounced lack of it. In the former, there is a problem of gathering factual information and the accompanying perceptions. In the latter, it can be hard to know what emotional reactions are permeating the couple environment, and how each partner is being affected by the difficulties. This imbalance makes it hard for a couple to articulate what they want from therapy. It is important, therefore, to work toward distinguishing thoughts, feelings, and behaviors.

This involves the clinician helping to establish rationality by aiding the couple in gaining control over emotionality—sometimes by decreasing the affect, or in devitalized situations by increasing it. Rationality requires a balance of thoughts and feelings. When a couple has had some success identifying and integrating thoughts and feelings, they are better able to express realistically what changes need to take place. For instance, if a couple or partner is flat and seems overly businesslike, there is a need to stimulate some affective responses to the situation and to each other. This might include the therapist's use of self by reacting personally to what's heard, thus providing a model of a wider range of expression for the couple. On the other hand, if someone is highly anxious and in a runaway emotional state, it is necessary to focus on thought processes. Recollection and the sequencing of events, attempted solutions, consequences of actions, etc., all help to focus the client on thinking rather than feeling. When people have access to both cognitions and affect, they are better able to establish goals for themselves.

As couples experience the beginnings of control over their once overwhelming situation, they invariably become more motivated to negotiate goals and pursue solutions. They see that they have already changed, which means expectations can be met, and further work may pay off.

The couple's motivation to continue to work on change can also be generated by the influence of the therapist. If the therapist indicates that things do not appear so terrible, that seemingly disconnected pieces do fit together, or that certain feelings are understandable, she/he is showing there is a different way of viewing the problem. A change in perspective allows the couple to experience something different. With affirmation and hopefulness, the couple can now begin to trust their own perceptions and their sense of self. The fact that the couple see that the therapist is not mired down by their difficulties in the same way they are allows them to place some degree of hope in the therapist.

There are times, however, in the early phases of therapy when a partner or couple are unable to negotiate goals. They will flounder and feel the process is not in their best interest. Feeling unsure and hopeless, couple members may intensify resistance to any attempts toward the development of control, responsibility, and motivation. Some ways couples set up roadblocks in therapy include denying problems, blaming, shutting down, trying to seduce the therapist to join as a fellow warrior, and digressing. Oftentimes, in their apparent phase of confusion and resistance, the therapist must sit tight and allow the couple to realize that the therapist is "just there" for the two of them by encouraging both to discuss their resistance. Doing nothing can sometimes be doing something.

Allowing the partners to play out their resistance can be difficult. Eager to overcome and push through the resistance, a therapist can often respond prematurely. As a result, the therapist either reacts nonsystemically, perpetuating aimlessness and increasing frustration for all involved, or else the therapist unilaterally sets the agenda and risks sacrificing mutual cooperation, responsibility, and motivation. The couple can feel overpowered and manipulated by either of these moves and believe they cannot trust the therapist. Therefore, allowing the therapeutic process to develop at its own rate and tolerating ambivalence and confusion can at times be the most helpful stance for the therapist to take. The therapist who has a feel for pacing and a realization that there is a time for the development of control, responsibility and motivation is practicing the art of therapy.

GENERAL PRINCIPLES OF GOAL SETTING

There are some important general principles that apply to setting goals for therapy. We propose: 1) that goals lend themselves to relieving symptoms and promoting health; 2) that they structure the ensuing therapy; 3) that they are achievable, understood, and agreed upon by the couple and therapist; and 4) that they stem from the problems presented.

These essential characteristics emphasize the importance of realism, relevance, and negotiation. The following are examples that show how some couples present with unworkable goals:

> A woman requested that her husband be interested in art, change his sense of humor, and be more sophisticated. She was asking him to be another person. This was an unachievable goal. Instead, when she eventually was able to state a desire for them to develop some common interests, therapy had a direction.

> A man, trying to lessen the anxiety in his life, decided the way to go about this was to create a friendship between his wife and his lover. This was not a realistic goal. He was encouraged to work on making a decision between the two.

> A man complained, "She and I are having violent fights because her son drives me crazy. I want to get him out of the house and have him live with his father in Boston." This was not a mutually negotiated goal for therapy. "We want to see if there are some ways her son and I can stop driving each other crazy," more clearly suggests mutuality and agreement.

It can be a positive experience for all involved when the general principles of goal setting are achieved in the early phases of therapy. Even when couples present in a severely deteriorated state, are embittered and blaming, and complain in all or nothing terms, they can experience a rare moment of cooperation and relief by agreeing upon goals. This process should begin in the first session. If it does not, then it must evolve as therapy continues, helping to bond the couple in a common purpose.

Goal setting can best be viewed as evolutionary. Even though people may present as knowing what they want, it may take time and work to uncover, listen to, and clarify material well enough so that the principles of goal setting can be adequately adhered to. Sometimes the content merely suggests or hints at the issue(s) needing attention. For instance, the statement, "He's never on time for anything," once explored, can really mean, "I can't trust or rely on him, and it scares me."

Besides careful exploration and probing, the therapist can uncover an underlying issue by working at a process level and pointing out what is implicit in the couple's interaction. An example of this might be the statement, "When you tried to answer your husband, you seemed nervous and afraid." In stating this observation, the therapist highlights a basic incongruity in the couple's relationship and focuses attention on it. The couple can then decide whether or not to formulate a goal that addresses the therapist's observation.

Goals Relieving Symptoms and Promoting Health

Whether the couple look directly at their dynamics, or are more focused on concrete material, the therapist must be able to understand which dynamics are being played out, and how, in order to formulate goals that are relevant and consistent with a hypothesis. For instance, the symptom of continual arguing can be addressed through the goal of improving communication skills, or through the goal of negotiating the power structure in the relationship. Which definition appears to be more meaningful and relevant for the couple depends on the therapist's assessment of the couple's interactional, intergenerational, and individual material, and of how this couple will experience change in the most effective way.

The process of defining goals must be congruent with the clients' conceptual framework of the problem and its solution. For example, a couple who believes that insight is a must should not be directed toward formulating strictly behavioral goals. On the other hand, goals must allow enough room for the therapy to move from the more concrete, surface level to a deeper exploration of the problem. This means goals should be inclusive enough so that the definition of the problem can be expanded. It does not mean they should be vague and meaningless.

The content of problems can make them appear very different, while in fact the impaired underlying dynamic is the same. For example, an engaged couple presented feeling ambivalent about getting married and wanted to know why; a newly married couple felt anxious and distressed around their sexual response; a working couple with children were angry and found themselves arguing all the time; a middle-aged couple were depressed and complained of loss of interest in each other; a remarried couple were exhausted because all their emotional energy was spent on problems of the children. All these cases, as it turned out, had the same underpinning — that of lack of trust in the relationship. Though the symptoms described were different, the central dynamic needing repair was the same.

The therapist attempted to draw attention to the deeper issue, with questions and statements about trust in the relationship. The responses from the couples gave valuable information about how best to word and formulate the goals of therapy for each of them. For instance, the second couple stated their goal as wanting to increase their trust in each other by more freely expressing their feelings and fears around sex.

It cannot be forgotten that it is ultimately the ongoing decision of the clients as to how to view their problems and what depth of exploration feels meaningful to them. Clients usually demonstrate this decision through their responses to the therapist's remarks. The therapist, however, can help move them toward a deeper level of viewing their problem if the couple will allow this kind of exploration. The potential for such movement implies that promotion of health may extend beyond the removal of apparent symptoms. The symptoms may be eliminated by using techniques which reach to various depths. In most cases, couples who wish to explore more individual and intergenerational material will spend more time in therapy and share more of themselves than those who wish to focus exclusively on the interactional material.

Goals Structuring Therapy

An important way in which goal setting seems to create structure for the ensuing therapy is through the introduction of process observations. The initial understanding of the couple is primarily concerned with the content of their story: who does what to whom, when and how, etc. The therapist must be able to move beyond the content to the process: how they interact with each other, what feelings are being alluded to, who protects whom, when and why, etc. At this point, the therapist may wish to change the content by introducing the idea of process. This skill of the therapist in understanding the process may help the couple change their goals of therapy away from specific content toward altering the patterns of their interaction. It is at such a juncture that goal setting and intervention tend to merge. When such a change has been accomplished, the couple will not get stuck in the same way again, because their perceptions of the problem have been altered.

Moving to the process level is important, but it can be difficult for both the couple and the seasoned therapist. However, therapists who have greater knowledge and experience are better able to move to this level. Understandably, beginning therapists tend to focus more on the content of the sessions.

For instance, it may be difficult for the therapist when a couple wants the therapist as a referee, pronouncing righteousness on one or the other of them. The therapist must keep a wide-angle lens so as to view the symptom as it relates to the couple system, and not get pulled into the role of referee. This neutrality can be a challenge. It involves staying focused on nudging the couple towards recognizing their process and avoiding the seduction of their story.

An example of a process statement would be: "From the situations you two describe, it sounds as if you're in a stiff competitive race with each other. A race like yours must be exhausting." Such a statement lifts out the issue and feelings underlying the couple's story. It makes room for them to begin to work beyond rehashing the "facts."

When a couple can eventually view their own process, they become more aware of what they do as a couple and what each does individually. Their shift in perception creates a greater sense of personal responsibility. It is only when each partner is willing to accept responsibility that change is possible.

Equally important to attending to process in setting the stage for ongoing therapy is creating a strong therapeutic relationship. This happens as the couple realize that the therapist is not without some ideas and hope, does not take sides, does not single one out as bad, does not blame, reject, or put down, and *does* bring a different perspective to the problem. Setting goals strongly demonstrates the collaborative nature of therapy. This inevitably creates trust in the mutual goodwill which is essential to ongoing therapy. Abiding by the principles of goal setting enhances this trust and increases motivation for the duration.

Goals Agreed Upon and Achievable

Whether attending primarily to content or process, both therapist and couple want to work toward setting goals that reflect the element of mutuality in the problem. In other words, both partners must become involved in the process of change by taking responsibility for their part in the problem and for changing self. There is a basic systemic assumption implicit in this principle: Both people are in pain, regardless of who seems to be carrying it for the couple. Oftentimes, one partner will express or show evidence of pain and anguish, while the other will appear unaffected and denying of the problem. The uninvolved partner states that he/she is coming to therapy as a favor to the other and has nothing to do with the unhappiness. A therapist viewing this couple from a systemic perspective would not accept this view, but instead would want to encourage the uninvolved partner, in a safe, supportive way, to move beyond the denial of responsibility and feelings about the marriage.

Real understanding and agreement in goal setting can come only as a result of this kind of mutual involvement. Any change that occurs must affect both people and each must be aware of this phenomenon. Therefore, a goal cannot be designed to relieve symptoms and focus on the positive development of one partner without having an effect on the other partner. Such an unrealistic goal is seen in the following situation: "I want it arranged so that we are officially and publicly separated, but that I live in our house with you and come and go as I please." This is a goal which benefits one partner at the expense of the other. Goals must be designed to benefit each individual, as well as the couple system.

Other, not unusual situations which can make arriving at mutually agreed upon, achievable goals difficult are when the partners' wishes are in conflict, are peripheral to the central issue, or call for another form of therapy (i.e., individual or group). The success of therapy depends on clarifying, negotiating, and focusing on a direction. For instance, it is not uncommon for two opposing agendas to be presented by a couple: "Help me get out of this relationship," vs. "Help me keep him/her in this relationship." It is the therapist's role to point out that this is an unworkable situation, and to make a statement about how it is the couple's responsibility to work with the therapist to come up with a common goal. In this instance, it could be either to recognize ambivalence and decide to explore the potential in the relationship, or to deal with the realities of separation. When it is clear that the partner who wants to leave feels the situation is irreconcilable, then the therapist needs to acknowledge this fact in order to help both people agree to work on the realistic goal of separating.

Goals Relevant to Presented Problems

Sometimes, the symptoms presented by a couple are the result of forces outside the relationship, although initially the couple may identify them as relational. Through history taking, questions about key life events, and probes for reactions and perceptions, the therapist should be able to pinpoint the locus of the presented problems as being primarily inside or outside the couple system. For example, a remarried couple presented feeling tension and experiencing disagreement between them. As they described their situation, they discovered that they were reacting to the behavior of an acting-out child testing the loyalty of his parent. The child's behavior seemed to be the trigger for conflict, rather than something intrinsic in the couple relationship. The therapist had some hunches about the dynamics of the couple, but did not feel it necessary to explore these in order for the couple to set workable goals. The goals changed from focusing on the couple's relationship dynamics to family therapy and dealing with parenting skills.

Besides identifying the primary source of the problem, the therapist should be ready, in cases where there is a multitude of problems, to develop priorities or establish a hierarchy of concerns, in order to set achievable goals: "It looks as if you first need to work on better ways of speaking to each other before you can tackle negotiating some of the major issues you refer to."

This can involve seeing and accepting the interrelatedness of goals: "You two are finding yourselves in lots of arguments and want your relationship to be less adversarial. You also want Mrs. X's child to stop acting out. Let's first see what kind of connection there might be between the two problems."

Sometimes it is clear that, after creating a hierarchy of goals and interrelating them, the therapist may suspect that couple therapy is not the most appropriate form of therapy at this time:

> A remarried couple presented having stress in the relationship. As the evaluation progressed, it became apparent that the woman was distracted and anxious over the issue of child custody from her former marriage. The therapist saw that the woman had very little energy left to focus on the problems in her second marriage, and suggested she seek individual therapy first, and then at a later time, reengage in couple therapy with her husband. The couple goals were not achievable for her until she was able to deal with her individual issues.

THE INTERSYSTEM MODEL AND GOAL SETTING

The Intersystem Model supplies the breadth and depth to account inclusively for the interactional, intergenerational, and individual components of the couple's relationship. It is this comprehensiveness that allows the therapist to tailor the goals of therapy to the client system, and serves as the foundation for a richness not found in other models. Other models of therapy tailor the goals of treatment to a unidimensional model, thus limiting the scope and the profundity of change. For instance, the behaviorists might define the goal of treatment exclusively in communications/behavioral terms (Jacobson & Margolin, 1979). Sager's Contract Model (1976) focuses its expression of goal formulation on the conscious, open and hidden, and unconscious expectations of each individual, and how these change over time. Such insight enables change. Lastly, Family of Origin models help the clients understand their family histories and their implicit obligations and legacies, in an effort to identify what is maintaining and influencing the couple's current pattern of behavior (Boszormenyi-Nagy & Ulrich, 1981). Change occurs through the understanding of projections, object relations, and "ledgers of merit," occurring within the family of origin.

The language used to formulate goals and contracts differs significantly from one school to the next. A goal expressed in behavioral terms might include, "to increase and reinforce positive behaviors." One expressed in the language of the contract theorists would involve "uncovering original, hidden notions about one's gender role." The family of origin school might define the goal of treatment as being a journey toward the discovery of self as seen differently than by family members.

Although there are sharp differences between the various schools, there are also some fundamental and common preliminary steps involved in assessment and the formulation of goals. It is important 1) to procure a clear statement about the current problem and what each member wants from each other and from therapy, 2) to hear what solutions have been attempted so that a couple's problem-solving abilities are integrated into realistic, success-promoting goal setting, and 3) to formulate problem areas into some kind of meaningful organization of information.

The Intersystem Model first assumes a systemic interpretation of the presented problem. The basic tenet of this systemic view is that a symptom represents dysfunctionality in a system, not in an individual. The couple system often keeps its painful dance going by viewing its problems from the perspective of individual pathology. Partners may deny, blame and externalize in order to escape from taking responsibility for problems:

> "We haven't had sex in over six months because I'm just not a very sexual person."
>
> "If he'd just get his head together and stop flying off the handle, we'd be fine."
>
> "It's all those radical feminists where you work, putting strange ideas in your head, that's causing this mess."

The couple focuses a great deal on describing the "causes" of the problem in order for the therapist to help them work out changing the rules of the system. Understandably, the couple tends to think in terms of, "If he'd/she'd stop doing such and such or be more . . . , the marriage would be fine, so please change him or her." The therapist, on the other hand, wonders such things as what this level of emotionality gets for each of them (individual), what role each plays for the other (interactional), what shrouded expectations from the past are being expressed in their communications (intergenerational). Using the Intersystem Model, the therapist usually thinks in terms of the symptom being part of the interactional sequence. The symptom keeps the roles and the organization of the couple intact, and further calls upon each individual's defenses and motivations. Couples collude with each other to keep the symptoms, because change can be more frightening for both than the pain of the dysfunction.

For instance, a commonly seen couple dynamic involves an emotional, overadequate woman trying to elicit more involvement and openness from a remote, underadequate man. This couple colludes to keep her in the controlling position. When in control, she does not have to experience the intolerable fear and anxiety involved with feeling dependent. He does not have to risk engulfment if he remains aloof. They collude to keep a distance that allows them to avoid their profound fears of intimacy.

The therapist can begin to help the couple break this kind of collusion through the goal-setting process. This is done first by identifying the dysfunctional behavioral patterns, i.e., her bossy, critical statements followed by his withdrawing and "mistake" making; next, by asking each member what changes each would have to make to alter this pattern. Another important question to ask is how partners see themselves preventing themselves from getting what they want. The questions highlight for the couple how each member is responsible for the behaviors that keep their situation from changing. They both behave in a way that avoids intimacy, and they maintain these behaviors because each has real fears involved with increased closeness.

Goal Setting in a Case Study Using the Integrated Model

The following case shows how the goals of a distressed couple incorporate this multidimensional perspective. The goals are specific enough to address the problems directly and concretely, and expansive enough to permit each individual to grow within the system.

> Harry Smith came into therapy, complaining that his wife, Valerie, was not sexual enough. Valerie saw Harry as uncooperative and self-absorbed, so she felt sexually disinterested. Both were angry and felt defeated. The therapist observed several patterns: The husband was angry and demanding; the wife, retreating and whiney. The distress each was feeling was being maintained by strong individual beliefs having to do with what husbands should be, what wives should be, what men should be like, what women should be like. The therapist suspected a strong family of origin influence for each partner in playing out these beliefs. The therapist wanted to organize clear goals with the couple from a systems perspective.
>
> The first goal was to see if they could all work together to find several behaviors which would demonstrate caring in order to increase the goodwill and lessen the tension between them. As they began to work on this goal of being more positively responsive to each other, they were able to include another goal: to gather enough insight and understand-

ing in order to own their individual contributions to the problems between them.

The individual issue that emerged for Harry was low self-esteem, primarily coming from work-related stress. As for Valerie, she showed extreme self-imposed pressure to be "super mom." By recognizing and owning these individual issues, they were ready to explore how they had developed distorted expectations toward each other, stemming from their individual unhappiness, and to create ways they could feel better about themselves. As a result, each felt greater personal control and understanding, and felt able to move on to identify other current interactional problems. Their spontaneous, good feelings were exclusively directed toward their child, whom they kept with them constantly. They established the goal of restructuring the family in a way that would allow them time for each other. The next goal they established was to work on exploring their families of origin to see how they had been scripted in their sex roles. This work eventually freed each partner from the past and allowed both to rethink the kinds of roles that seemed more appropriate to their relationship.

Careful assessment of the difficulties brought to light the interactional, intergenerational, and individual components of the Smith's situation. The goals reflected these components. The goal-setting process allowed the therapist to take into account the full range of the couple's experience — how their interactions had become rigid and hostile, how their feelings were ones of hurt and isolation, and how each was unable to behave in any other way.

This perspective illustrates other multidimensional features. The presented problem set the stage for all the goals decided upon. By addressing the problem as it was presented by the Smiths, the therapist helped reduce anxiety, and promoted thinking and calm discussion as opposed to feeding into the emotional reactivity of their system. As the Smith's anxiety and feelings of hopelessness were reduced, the therapist promoted thinking rather than feeling, and began the first step toward helping the couple take individual responsibility for the relationship problems.

The second step involved encouraging both Harry and Valerie to express what their behaviors meant to each other. The therapist was then able to reframe both their expressed feelings and their behaviors. She did this in the following way: "In some ways, you're perhaps indicating to each other how much you each count. If you didn't care, you couldn't hurt each other, and, in turn, you wouldn't need to protect yourselves by withholding. But you would agree that you need more positive ways of showing caring." In the reframe, withholding was protection, not punishment, as originally understood by the Smiths. Self-protection now related to caring, rather than to an act of aggression. The Smiths, in turn, were in a better position to feel less vulnerable and to take a risk to suspend their blaming. The reframe lead to a shift away from a recapitulation of their old feelings and behaviors to a feeling of better control of their situation. By reframing the problem in new terms that brought out unrecognized feelings, the therapist challenged the Smith's original definitions and made room for a new expression of desired goals.

The goal changed from "She needs to be more sexual" and "He needs to do more to help me" to "We need to figure out more effective ways to show each other we care." Furthermore, by accepting mutual responsibility, each gained rather than lost power. The problem now seemed somehow solvable, because both laid claim to it. The Smiths could put their original complaints in perspective without feeling they were being neglected as individuals. They were able to see how their symptoms were connected to the larger issue of intimacy.

The objective of goal setting is to have the therapeutic goals take into account behaviors, thoughts, and feelings as they relate to the individual, interactional, and intergenerational dimensions of the relational system. To do this, the therapist organizes, expands, or contracts the goals in collaboration with the couple. But first the therapist needs to accept the problem focus, indicate concern for each individual, as well as for the livelihood of the couple, and get across a professional intent to work in the couple's behalf. If the process is successful, there usually is enough trust instilled either to expand the goal, i.e., "I see your problem as being more complicated, and feel we must first explore other related issues before we can more directly confront this problem," or to contract the goal, i.e., "Let's identify some specific ways you will feel you are being cared for, and see if you both can exchange these behaviors to relieve the tension between you."

In establishing goals with a couple, it is helpful for the therapist to have a sense of what constitutes marital health. Hofling and Lewis (1980) state it is "an open, growing system, capable of responding in innovative ways to outside challenges." Couples come to therapy when their relationship no longer holds this promise.

In some cases, however, the breakdown has been so severe and extensive in so many areas that the hopes to regain the promise are neither realistic nor congruent with the capabilities of the couple. The price for unbalancing the system to bring about the requested changes may be too great, and ultimately catastrophic for the system. Sometimes the therapist becomes fully aware of the inflexibility of the couple system only after an attempted intervention, and must renegotiate new goals.

In contrast to the above case, the following one illustrates that movement from goal setting to goal accomplishment does not necessarily proceed in a forward direction. Sometimes, something different from what the client expects must happen when one considers what is best for each partner.

> George was threatening to leave his marriage of 20 years, but wanted to give one more try at saving it. Helen had a long, complex psychiatric history, with frequent hospitalizations. George felt he no longer could contend with the chronic stress. Helen depended very strongly on her husband, but was constantly angry at him. He was withdrawn and secretive toward her. In therapy, she requested that he become more involved and more open with her. He said he wanted her to stop criticizing. These requests seemed to set up reasonable goals for treatment.
>
> The therapist began to focus on communication skills with them. As George attempted to communicate slightly more frequently and actively with Helen, she became distressed and ultimately suicidal. She had to be rehospitalized. She apparently did not have the capacity to include George in her life to any greater degree and felt intolerably pressured by his increased presence. His new responsiveness overwhelmed her and reactivated hopeless and helpless feelings. The couple system had proven to be too severely deficient in healthy qualities to tolerate any shift in its balance.
>
> Instead of continuing couple therapy, the therapist recommended outpatient individual and group therapy for Helen, so that she could have a support system outside the couple system. The recommendation for George was to seek individual therapy in order to provide him with help in working out his ambivalence around the future of the relationship.

CONCLUSION

The goal-setting process in the Intersystem Model is the bridge between assessment and intervention. How couples manage this process gives the therapist valuable information with which to formulate a hypothesis and develop a comprehensive, multidimensional treatment plan. The goal-setting process itself is an intervention into the system. It is an inclusive and wide-angled process, and therefore it allows the therapist latitude and freedom to access a variety of treatment approaches. The process involves the therapist and the couple working as equal members of a team designed to alleviate symptoms in the system and provide for the health and growth of each individual.

The goals may be expansive enough to incorporate the multidimensional, complex aspects of a couple system, and specific enough to reflect small behavioral changes. The process of setting goals creates structure, control, clarity, direction and collaboration within the therapeutic environment, and produces the beacon and reference point for the ensuing therapy.

BIBLIOGRAPHY

Boszormenyi-Nagy, I., & Ulrich, D. (1981). Contextual family therapy. In A. Gurman & D. Kniskern (Eds.), *Handbook of Family Therapy.* New York: Brunner/Mazel, pp. 159–186.
Hofling, C., & Lewis, J. (1980). *The Family: Evaluation and Treatment.* New York: Brunner/Mazel.
Jacobson, N., & Margolin, G. (1979). *Marital Therapy: Strategies Based on Social Learning and Behavioral Exchange Principles.* New York: Brunner/Mazel.
Sager, C. (1976). *Marriage Contracts and Couples Therapy.* New York: Brunner/Mazel.

Chapter 3

Basic Principles: Structural Elements of the Intersystem Approach

Bea Hollander-Goldfein

INTRODUCTION

As a member of the senior staff of the Marriage Council of Philadelphia, I find it a humbling task to attempt to present the general principles that underlie the work of my colleagues. I am at great risk of leading the reader to assume either homogeneity in the staff or that my position on an issue represents the majority view; neither of these is necessarily true. We have much in common as clinicians, but diverge in many ways within the framework of the Intersystem Approach. Perhaps the differences among us reflect the nature of an integrated model. Being faced with this dilemma, I will describe in this chapter our points of convergence, and, in so doing, hopefully present with greater clarity those elements which bind our clinical work into an integrated, albeit complex, whole.

Systemic therapy and individual psychotherapy are often viewed as opposite ends of the therapy continuum. They can, in fact, represent diametrically opposed approaches to psychological and relationship problems, depending on the theoretical school of thought. Utilization of the Intersystem Approach in marital therapy requires that the clinician not only grasp the differences between such divergent approaches, but also understand where they converge. For the systemic therapist, the points of convergence are more than just theoretical intersections where different terms are utilized by varying schools to label the same phenomenon. They represent different facets of the human experience, all of which have clinical relevance.

Integration requires a breadth of conceptualization that views problems as multifaceted and treatment intervention as multidimensional. A specific problem may be addressed in many different ways and a therapeutic intervention may impact many different problems, or many levels of one problem. A therapist working within an integrated theoretical framework keeps the multifaceted problem and multidimensional intervention in constant focus and moves between facets, dimensions, and levels in a systematic way. To label this ability "eclecticism" is to miss the essential point.

Integration is not just a matter of being facile enough to view a problem as having a specific etiology or function and choosing the appropriate technique from a broad range of possibilities. It is a process that involves viewing a problem in the broad context of its many etiologies, choosing techniques that impact on many levels, and fluidly shifting when the optimal opening for change presents itself. This may mean reframing the problem to change its meaning, restructuring cognition to facilitate acceptance of the new meaning, setting up a behavioral contingency to reinforce change, improving communication about the problem, fostering affective expression, enhancing closeness, and challenging an intergenerational legacy, all done concurrently through a series of coherently planned interventions. At any moment in time these varied levels may not all be in clear focus, but as focus shifts in the mind of the therapist the impact on each level can be perceived.

The practice of the Intersystemic Approach requires the therapist to sustain a broad view of the multifaceted nature of the problems addressed in treatment and to move flexibly between varied change strategies. Subsumed within this general framework are basic principles which govern the structure and process of therapy. The adherence to these principles maximizes the potential of the Intersystem Approach to achieve movement, change, and growth. How these operating principles determine the structural elements of the Intersystem Approach is the focus of this chapter. The process elements will be discussed in Chapter 5.

OVERVIEW

Engaging the couple is the first critical task during the early stage of treatment. This requires the initiative of the therapist to enlist both partners to be present and involved in the therapeutic process. Once the couple is present, engagement depends on joining with the individuals and the system in a balanced fashion. Over the course of treatment, it may become necessary to assess whether or not the use of individual sessions is indicated as an adjunct to conjoint marital therapy.

Establishing the initial contract is the next important task for the therapist. This includes defining problems, assessing what is being requested by the couple, and establishing goals. In conjoint marital therapy there is an additional essential element in contracting for treatment. The therapist needs to foster a working alliance with the partners by enlisting commitment, not necessarily to the relationship, but to the therapeutic process that will address the relationship. If the therapy is effective, the couple will be able to work with the potential for positive change that exists within the marriage. In an open-ended process, with a broadly defined therapeutic contract, the movement towards change occurs in stages. When time is limited by the nature of the case, the therapeutic contract becomes more narrowly focused on what can be accomplished within the available time frame.

The task of gathering the history of the couple and each partner's family of origin is crucial for a comprehensive understanding of the marital relationship. This principle is based on the idea that the interaction patterns of couples cannot be fully understood without knowledge of 1) the historical context of the relationship, and 2) the multigenerational influence on both intrapsychic and interpersonal dynamics. This information, in addition to the therapist's assessment of the current functioning of the relationship, provides the basis for the intersystemic conceptualization of the case and for the generation of hypotheses about strategies for change.

The following discussion will explore each of these basic principles in greater depth. Case examples are used to explicate applications to clinical practice.

ENGAGING THE COUPLE

The most obvious fundamental principle in the Intersystem Approach is working with the partners conjointly. Effective conjoint therapy is based on engaging the couple as a system in a balanced manner, with parallel processes of joining with each partner. This principle has been repeatedly affirmed by the clinical experience of the senior staff at Marriage Council. Engaging the couple has come to be considered essential for marital therapy to be optimally effective. Supporting evidence for this principle has come from the contrast between conjoint marital sessions and individual sessions for marital problems. Even when one is seduced by the effectiveness with individuals (and there is successful marital treatment with individuals), the sobering reality that there is still only one half of the relationship in the office becomes clear when the opportunity to meet with the partner presents itself. Marital problems, when seen in context, always take on different and more complex meanings.

The effort to engage the couple begins with the first contact, usually on the phone. When both partners agree to come in together, initiating the therapeutic contact can be fairly straightforward. It is when this option is resisted or refused that the therapist needs to pursue, in direct discussion with the partner who is present, the reason for the other partner's absence and the meaning of this absence for the relationship. The therapist needs to pursue engagement of the absent partner before the therapy proceeds too far. This is first done through the partner who is in the office, by explaining the importance of working together and by challenging the one present to engage the one absent. This early interchange will reveal the reasons for the resistance to conjoint therapy. The reasons may range from the direct refusal of the absent partner to the ambivalence of the partner who is present. Discovering the reasons for one partner's absence offers information about the interactional dynamics of the couple, providing a glimpse into the broader context of the marital problems. Often, the way a couple enters treatment is a metaphor for the entire relationship.

The clinical example that follows is an unusual case because of the relatively long period of time before the absent partner entered conjoint therapy and because of the early focus on family of origin material.

Despite these elements, this case poignantly depicts how the couple's dynamics were evidenced by the way they entered treatment.

A woman in her late 30s requested individual therapy because she felt depressed and unhappy and was experiencing marital and family problems. Although critical of her husband, she expressed doubts about her perceptions and guilt about her contribution to the marital difficulties. She described her husband as unwilling to come in and/or unable because of scheduling conflicts with work. Besides, she was not really sure if she wanted him to join her. She saw him as having nothing to say. Moreover, it felt important to her to "fix" herself first.

There was a strong message during these early sessions that active, unresolved issues with this client's parents, especially with her father, were interfering in the marriage. In this case, the initial contract was made for brief family of origin work, with the understanding that the possibility of conjoint therapy would be raised again when she was ready to address the marriage.

The client expressed an overwhelming feeling of depression for which she had no explanation. Through the exploration of her complex relationship with her parents, it was revealed that their bitter and painful divorce had left her closer to her mother, with whom she always had a conflicted relationship, and alienated from her father, with whom she always had a close, supportive relationship. When her relationship with her father was rebuilt, her depression lifted. The realization that the "loss" of her father had set up the impossible expectation that her husband would fill the void allowed her to redirect her anger toward her father. Feeling less angry at her husband enabled her to invite him into therapy and he came willingly. Not surprisingly, once allowed in, he had a lot to say and she began to listen to what he was saying.

This couple's entrance into treatment was a clear portrayal of their marital dynamics. The wife entered therapy and shut her husband out. She felt that he wasn't interested. He felt rejected. At home, her anger and rejection perpetuated his passivity and withdrawal. His passivity and withdrawal fueled her anger and dissatisfaction. She was present and he was absent, in therapy and in their marriage.

Whatever the reason for the resistance to conjoint marital therapy, this becomes the first item on the therapeutic agenda. The initial step is to provide encouragement to bring in the partner. If this request is resisted, the next step can be the request for a consultation session with the absent partner, once again through the partner who is present. Another possibility is to make a direct request for the absent partner to call the therapist, or to gain permission to call her or him. In most cases, where the partner has not definitively refused to participate in therapy, there is a good chance of successfully engaging the couple.

During the exploration of resistance to conjoint involvement in marital therapy, the therapist needs to examine the possibility of colluding with the resistance. There are many possible motivations for a therapist's collusion. For example, the therapist's transition from individual to conjoint therapy is often difficult and anxiety producing. A therapist attempting to shift models may be all too willing to accept any reason for the partner's absence. Also, gender issues may play a role if the therapist feels more comfortable working with men or women. Further, the absent partner may have been presented in such negative terms that it may feel more comfortable for the therapist to keep her/him out. Additionally, the marital dynamic as conveyed by the client may trigger unresolved relationship issues for the therapist. Unquestioned acceptance of the spouse's absence from therapy may be an avoidance of the countertransference issues experienced by the therapist. Finally, specific problems, such as physical abuse, may frighten the therapist into joining with the victim to keep the abuser out of therapy for their "mutual" safety. Whether these factors are conceptualized as induction into the system or countertransference, the therapist needs to be as vigilant about self and internal motivations as she or he is about the motivations and hidden agendas of clients.

The therapeutic positions among Marriage Council staff range from the refusal to see one partner without the other to the agreement to see one partner alone until the absent partner joins the process. The latter position represents the predominant clinical approach. The major consideration when seeing one partner alone is the timing of the absent spouse's entry into therapy. Beyond a certain point, too great an alliance develops with the partner who is present for the therapist to develop a balanced relationship with the partner who would be just entering the process. As a general guideline, it is optimal to involve the absent partner by the third or fourth session, which is the length of time typically defined by Marriage Council staff as the evaluation stage. When the number of sessions goes beyond the time frame determined by the therapist, conjoint marital therapy becomes impossible.

If the other partner becomes involved before the cut-off, individual sessions with the partner just entering the process are used to "catch up," in order for the therapist to attain a balanced position in the conjoint sessions. After the cut-off point, individual therapy with the partner who initiated treatment may continue. However, if conjoint work is requested past this point, the couple should be referred to another therapist who can engage them as a system. Shifting to the couple, once too strong an individual relationship and too biased a view of the absent partner have developed, is extremely difficult and often blinds the therapist to the interactional dynamics that perpetuate the problems.

It should be apparent that conjoint therapy is much more than just having both partners present in the therapist's office. Whether the partners enter treatment together or the absent partner is brought in at a later point, the marital therapist must relate to the couple as a system, maintaining at all times the broad perspective of the interactional dynamics and joint contribution to the marital problems. This task is often difficult when couples enter treatment blaming each other from polarized positions. Joining with the system gives each side credibility while exploring the mutually reinforcing dynamics of the problem. At the same time that the therapist is both relating to, but standing apart from the marital system, she or he needs to join empathically with each partner and enlist each in the therapeutic process. It is almost as if three therapeutic relationships are developed at the outset of treatment: those with each partner, and that with the system. In both thinking about the case and interacting with the couple, the therapist needs to be warm and caring, while preserving balance and therapeutic distance.

Determining an effective treatment strategy depends on knowing the parameters of differing therapeutic modalities and how each can address the multidimensional nature of the human experience. Conjoint marital therapy is an effective therapeutic approach for most couples, but there are clinical situations that require the therapist to consider the advisability of individual sessions or the need for individual therapy. In the next section, the role of individual sessions in marital therapy will be explored.

INDIVIDUAL SESSIONS

While acknowledging conjoint therapy as the treatment of choice for marital and relationship difficulties, the Intersystem Approach recognizes the occasional necessity and advisability of individual sessions. To refresh the reader, it is a basic structural premise of the Intersystem Approach that marital therapy has a much greater probability of success when both partners are involved. However, as the therapeutic process emerges, interactional and intrapsychic dynamics may block the process, challenging the therapist to reevaluate the most effective approach to treatment, thereby raising the question of the usefulness of individual work.

The decision regarding the use of individual sessions must be guided by flexibility, clinical judgement, and an understanding of the relevant structural and process issues. Individual sessions are most typically utilized when the therapeutic process in conjoint therapy is stalemated. When the structure of therapy is modified, it becomes feasible to get past the block and move forward. Therapeutic stalemate can result from many divergent factors. Individual sessions become a consideration when 1) resistance is excessive, 2) a hidden agenda is operating, 3) the therapist has been inducted into the marital system, 4) unresolved issues from family of origin block movement in the couple, 5) traumatic events have blocked normative development, or 6) individual sessions are requested.

Excessive Resistance

A stalemate resulting from excessive resistance on the part of a couple may be the result of rigidified interactional dynamics or deep-seated intrapsychic problems that remain unresponsive to therapeutic intervention. Having attempted creative conjoint therapeutic strategies that are consistently unsuccessful, the therapist may have no alternative but to break through the impasse by disrupting the marital system. Seeing the partners individually for a limited number of sessions gives the therapist the latitude to explore the problems from different vantage points. This format also provides an opportunity to rejoin with each partner and thus enhance the force for change imbedded within the therapeutic relationship itself.

Individual sessions may introduce new perspectives, different language, alternative frames of meaning, deeper self-knowledge, and greater expressiveness on the part of each spouse. These gains are then incorpo-. rated into the conjoint therapy, thus enabling the couple to work together more effectively. The experience of individual sessions introduces new elements which challenge the marital system and aid the therapist in adopting a fresh perspective and in repositioning herself or himself in reaction to the couple. When this approach to a therapeutic stalemate is effective, the therapist gains greater latitude to effect change in the dysfunctional marital system.

Hidden Agendas

A similar therapeutic impasse occurs when there is a hidden agenda on the part of either or both partners. Individual sessions are indicated when the therapist senses the presence of a hidden agenda and is unable to foster its revelation in session. Individual sessions provide another route for unearthing the hidden agenda that may be "safer" for the clients. Once made explicit, the previously hidden material can be addressed in conjoint sessions. However, opting for this approach raises complications for the subsequent therapy similar to those to be discussed in the section about secrets.

Although the content of the hidden agenda may be readily revealed in individual sessions, the reasons for keeping the material hidden might not be so easily resolved. This situation raises the issue of confidentiality and leaves the therapist in an imbalanced position with the couple. The resolution of this dilemma will depend on the specific nature of the hidden agenda and the skill of the therapist in eliciting its open expression between the partners. If the previously withheld material is addressed directly, the therapeutic impasse can be worked through successfully. However, if the hidden agenda becomes a "secret," the therapy remains stalemated and the therapist is left in an untenable position.

As will be described in the section on secrets, the therapist must reestablish the parameters of the therapeutic contract with the spouse who is the bearer of the secret. The contract may include a condition about the possible discontinuation of treatment if keeping the secret threatens the viability of the therapeutic process and the therapist's position vis-à-vis the couple. In most cases, the hidden material does emerge in the couple sessions, leaving the therapist free to help the partners work towards resolution. The complexities of the hidden agenda are illustrated in the following case example.

> In a couple, the husband no longer loved his wife and wanted a divorce. However, he was unwilling to be honest about these feelings because he feared the blame that would be heaped upon him. His motivation for "marital therapy" was to find a way to vindicate himself by convincing his wife that, despite their best efforts, the marriage was unworkable.

Induction of Therapist into the Marital System

Another type of therapeutic stalemate results from the induction of a therapist into the marital system. This stalemate is not as easily assessed as are the two situations described above. By the very nature of this problematic dynamic, the therapist is unable to objectively assess the factors contributing to the stalemate because she or he is part of the problem and has lost an objective stance. For a variety of reasons, the therapist who has been inducted into the system behaves in ways that sustain the dysfunctional interactional patterns as opposed to fostering change. The reasons may include: 1) a powerful rigidified marital

system that pulls the therapist in because of its tenacity and the therapist's vulnerability, 2) transference in the individual partners that pulls
for a particular set of responses from the therapist and imbalances the
therapeutic relationship, 3) transference in the therapist whereby one
or both partners take on aspects of other relationships and trigger
unresolved issues that get played out in the current therapy, and/or 4)
countertransference responses to the transference elements.

In the case of possible induction into the system, the use of individual
sessions should be preceded by supervision and possible consultation
with a colleague in order to aid the therapist in regaining a more objective position. If the induction is due to transference and/or countertransference dynamics, the shift to individual sessions may serve only
to reinforce the transference and further avoid unresolved issues. Conversely, an understanding of the transference and countertransference
dynamics should assist the therapist in pulling out of the induction,
thus providing the necessary leverage for the therapist to regain an
appropriate therapeutic posture to continue the conjoint sessions without interruption. If the induction results in the therapist losing control
of the therapy, individual sessions may be an appropriate treatment
alternative to assist the therapist in regaining control. By splitting up the
marital system temporarily, the therapist has the opportunity to reassess
the case and reestablish an effective working alliance with the couple.

Family of Origin Issues

In a totally different situation, the therapeutic stalemate results from
unresolved family of origin issues, in one or both partners, which are
unresponsive to systemic approaches. In this case, the couple's rigidified
interactional dynamics are driven by the compulsive repetition of family of origin dynamics in the current marital relationship (Stewart,
Peters, Marsh, & Peters, 1975). Although the Intersystem Approach
addresses family of origin material, the format of conjoint therapy may
be ineffective in resolving deeply imbedded intrapsychic issues. The
option of time-limited individual therapy offers the therapist an opportunity to explore, uncover, and rework unresolved issues with parental
figures and significant others from the client's past, enabling the couple
to renegotiate their relationship in the present.

The negotiation of individual sessions should take into account the
importance of sustaining the therapeutic balance necessary for conjoint
therapy. It is often the case that one partner is in greater need of
individual work than the other. This presents a dilemma because the
engagement of one partner individually may upset the therapeutic

alliance with the couple. In order to preserve the delicate balance, it is best to engage both partners in concurrent individual sessions. The exception to this principle is in rare cases where the couple's issues have been addressed openly and are understood by both partners, and a strong commitment to the relationship and trust in therapy exist. In these cases, it may be possible to engage just the partner in greater need of individual therapy, while the other partner serves as a support system until conjoint therapy is resumed.

Even in these cases, referral of the one partner to another therapist for individual treatment while continuing conjoint sessions is an option worthy of serious consideration. In order to make this determination, an assessment of the intrapsychic issues and the context in which they can best be addressed is crucial. It is also important to consider the willingness, readiness, and response of the clients to the treatment alternatives. There is a greater likelihood for cooperation and success when the therapeutic options are discussed by the clients and therapist and a decision emerges from this process of joint exploration.

Traumatic Events

In a similar but more specific case, therapy may be blocked because traumatic events in one partner's life may have blocked her or his psychological development. Some examples of traumatic life events that fall into this category are: physical abuse, sexual abuse, incest, rape, surviving a war, natural disasters, witnessing a fatal accident, and losing a child. In such cases, the victim/survivor may not have healed psychologically from the devastating experience. The ego defense mechanisms that enable the individual to cope often impede growth in other areas of the person's life. By being blocked personally, the partner is blocked in her or his ability to grow and change within the relationship.

In some cases, it is feasible for the couple to discuss the traumatic material in conjoint therapy. More commonly, though, the traumatized partner feels threatened by exposure, fearing the partner's response, the feelings of shame, and the recurrence of pain. If the trauma was particularly severe and the mechanism of repression was used to cover up the painful material, it is to be expected that the individual will feel threatened by the possibility of bringing the memory of the traumatic event back into consciousness. The uncovering of this material requires a safe and supportive therapeutic environment.

Treatment of victims and survivors of trauma requires careful and sensitive consideration. From among the various alternatives, the therapist must seek the best therapeutic course for both the individual and the couple, balancing the needs of both and assessing the most constructive sequencing of psychological work. Sequencing refers to the stages of resolution and healing that occur in the context of varied therapeutic involvements. For one individual, safety and security may need to be established in the marital relationship before the difficult journey of individual therapy can begin. For another individual, the residual effects of the traumatic experience may make it impossible to address the marriage before healing on a personal level takes place. Selection of the appropriate treatment strategy requires consideration of these factors.

There is great benefit to be derived for a couple who can discuss the painful events and provide a support system for each other. However, it is commonly accepted that the victim/survivor must be psychologically ready for disclosure, and her or his partner must be ready to hear. Most couples are not ready for the joint exploration of traumatic material; therefore, conjoint therapy is not typically the treatment of choice. It may or may not be constructive to engage in conjoint and individual therapy concurrently. This will depend on the client's level of functioning and psychological stamina. Group therapy is another treatment alternative that has been shown to be extremely helpful to abuse victims, and serves as an excellent adjunct to conjoint and individual modalities. Assisting clients in making informed choices about treatment alternatives, as well as making appropriate referrals to qualified professionals, can help ensure a successful therapeutic experience.

Request for Individual Sessions

A less complex clinical situation is one in which a partner requests an individual session. It is often beneficial to follow the emotional agenda of clients in order to join with them and avoid frustrating their needs, thereby circumventing resistance. Nonetheless, the request for individual sessions in the context of couple work requires exploration. It is important for the therapist and spouse to understand the reason for the request. If the request is seen as a form of resistance, the skill of the therapist is required to foster greater trust, comfort, and openness in conjoint sessions. If the request stems from the need to discuss something personally while maintaining commitment to the framework of conjoint therapy, compliance with this request can be very constructive. The issues addressed in individual sessions should be directed back to the conjoint sessions in order to foster a shared experience that enables the couple to more freely address their varied individual and mutual concerns with each other.

The six therapeutic situations described above challenge the therapist to assess the clinical usefulness of individual sessions as an adjunct to intersystemic marital therapy. In each case, the pros and cons of utilizing this therapeutic strategy must be weighed, both in terms of the needs of the clients and the impact on the therapy. In order not to undermine the conjoint work and the effectiveness of interventions on a systemic level, the following potential difficulties need to be taken into account: 1) maintaining confidentiality, 2) preserving neutrality and balance, 3) the use of individual sessions as a weapon or as a way of splitting the therapeutic relationship, 4) labeling one partner as "sick," and 5) losing the systemic structure and focus on conjoint goals (Berman, 1982). When the utilization of individual sessions is a viable clinical choice, the therapist must work through each of the potential difficulties outlined above. The use of individual sessions can be an effective, powerful, and sometimes essential adjunct to conjoint therapy when the case is appropriate, the clients amenable, and the potential difficulties worked through.

THE INITIAL CONTRACT

Once engaged with the couple system, the next task is the establishment of a therapeutic contract. Although the contract is typically renegotiated over the course of treatment, the realistic and sensitive negotiation of a meaningful initial contract is a major contributing factor to the ongoing commitment to treatment and an extremely important therapeutic task. It is a much different process than in individual psychotherapy. When working with an individual, there is one person to join with and one agenda to address. When a couple is present, there are two, often opposing agendas to address and three relationships to nurture. If the therapist is not successful in fostering a sense of therapy as a joint effort towards agreed-upon common goals, the couple may terminate before the work has begun. There are several considerations when establishing the initial contract.

Couples usually enter treatment in great distress. It is rare for marital therapy to be initiated with the goals of relationship growth and self-understanding, although premarital counseling is often prompted by these uncomplicated motivations. In the most difficult cases, the couple is in crisis, either on a purely emotional level or complicated by thoughts, threats, or acts related to separation or divorce. What the partners are seeking from therapy is often unclear or contradictory to the therapeutic process. There is great impatience and an intense need for relief. The attempt to establish an initial contract must take this into account.

Blaming, polarization, defensive self-protection, anxiety, and despair are common starting points for marital therapy. It is not uncommon for partners to seek a pronouncement from the therapist about who is right or who is in the most pain. One partner may express the attitude that the other partner is the one who needs help or needs to be "fixed" for all to be well in the marriage. The therapist is often asked to determine whether or not the marriage is worth attempting to save. Complicating therapy further is the common occurrence that the partners enter treatment with differing levels of commitment to, and emotional readiness for, the therapeutic process. Finding the common ground upon which to contract for therapy requires the therapist to establish herself or himself as the ally of the marriage that has bound the partners together before they entered therapy. By focusing on the relationship as a joint enterprise, the therapist conveys to the couple that only by working together can they determine the future of the marriage, be it positive or negative.

The fundamental element of the initial contract is an agreement between the partners about commitment. To some extent, this is simply the commitment to the relationship, which is a barometer for the commitment to therapy. The commitment can be stated in positive terms (i.e., to make things better), in negative terms (i.e., to explore what went wrong), or in terms labeled confusion (i.e., to determine whether or not there are the potential and willingness to try to improve the relationship).

Commitment

Whatever the apparent leanings of the individuals, there needs to be an explicit commitment to "hang in there" with each other while the future of the marriage is being addressed and the problems are being treated. Commitment is important for many reasons. In the midst of the pain and the turmoil, the verbalization of commitment is an important reaffirmation, even if stated in negative terms. It relieves the pressure for immediate resolution and allows the therapist to enlist the partners as allies in a therapeutic process that takes time and does not offer immediate answers. Finally, it offers a sense of direction for the first stage of treatment.

Implicit or explicit in the initial contract is the therapist's communication to the couple that she or he will not take sides, nor fix one partner, nor invest more in the relationship than the couple is willing to invest. It is also important for the therapist to convey confidence that the problems are not too overwhelming to address and that the couple can move beyond the current impasse. However, this form of reassurance should neither be a promise of success, nor a prediction about the future. It should convey the therapist's commitment to helping the partners come to grips with their relationship.

The therapeutic agenda of the first stage of treatment is based on the initial contract. When the couple agrees to commit to the relationship by "hanging in there," the sense of immediate threat is alleviated and the therapist is then able to focus the agenda on the problem areas of the marriage. When this agreement is made, exploration can occur because the partners are reassured that no one is leaving, even if the couple are already separated. If the couple is unwilling to make the commitment directly to each other, they can be asked to make it to the therapist and the therapeutic process. Three months is the recommended time period to request the couple for a contractual commitment to therapy. Clinical experience has shown that by the end of the three months most couples have a sense of the direction of their relationship. They either make a commitment to ongoing work on the relationship or they decide to break up.

The initial contract provides direction for the early stage of therapy. Without direction, the therapy will flounder in the same way that the marriage is floundering. Most important, the commitment elicited by the initial contract gives the therapy time to work, that is, improve communication, foster conflict resolution, and facilitate a wider range of emotional expression. The following are examples of structuring statements that focus the early stage of treatment based on the initial contract. "Help me understand the problems so that we can work towards making things better." "What has brought the relationship to the point of viewing a break-up as inevitable?" "Let's explore what has gone on in the marriage to evaluate whether or not a reconciliation is feasible." "What part did each of you play in the relationship developing to this point?"

STAGES OF TREATMENT

Couples often ask how long therapy will take. Clinical experience has shown that it takes approximately three months to get down to the core issues of the marital problems, and for the couple to experience a real sense of working together. It is this observation that forms the basis for the recommended three-month time period for the initial contract.

Core issues refer to the reciprocal dynamics underlying the presenting problems. As gains are achieved for the more malleable marital problems, and those that remain unchanged are explored in terms of their multilevel, multifaceted meanings and etiologies, the basic nature of the problems is better understood by the therapist and the couple. There develops a growing sense, for couples aware of the underlying reciprocal dynamics fueling their ongoing difficulties, that they are finally working on what is really wrong in the marriage.

The early gains in treatment are important. They provide hope, relief, and, often, new skills and new ways of relating. Most importantly, partners develop a sense of mutual responsibility. Movement during the initial stage of treatment is real but, depending on the case, the changes may be at the content level and not central to the operation of the marital system. In the same way that clients in individual therapy are vulnerable to defense mechanisms that protect the self from anxieties generated by change, couples in marital therapy are subject to restabilizing mechanisms that protect the system from the perceived threat that change engenders. In other words, there is a tendency for couples to retreat to the old, familiar patterns of relating. During the initial stage of therapy, defined here as approximately three months, the improvements in a marital relationship are challenged by the need to return to familiar patterns until a fundamental change in the system fosters a reintegration of the relationship at a more functional level.

The next stage of therapy reworks the clinical material that was addressed during the initial stage and fosters the emergence of new material. This is described as a deepening process because the underlying interactional and intrapsychic causes of the presenting problems are more readily revealed. This is due, in part, to the increased level of trust that has developed in the therapeutic relationship and the establishment of a working alliance between therapist and clients.

Built upon the foundation of the initial stage, the second stage typically involves a reexamination of insights that were only taken in on a superficial level, the reiteration of reframes that were comforting yet not fully accepted, and the reevaluation of assumptions that formed the basis of the dysfunctional patterns of relating. New information emerges, in response to the probing of the therapist, due to the increased ability of clients to handle greater personal vulnerability in the therapeutic process. In other words, as therapy progresses, it becomes safer to be more honest and more real.

At approximately the six-month mark, there appears to be another turning point. Couples who decide to break up terminate therapy, while couples who are making progress and feel invested in the therapeutic process commit to longer-term treatment. In a case going well, the six-month point in therapy is characterized by the experience of change as lasting and integrated into the relationship dynamics. Based on the sense of progress, there can be a reaffirmation of commitment to the relationship and to therapy. By this stage in treatment, the fundamental issues have been explored to the extent that a direction for the relationship can be articulated. Even if the couple is not in concert, and the decision to end the relationship is made by one partner, the other partner is typically stronger and better able to accept the breakup than she or he was at the outset of treatment. At this point, a new contract is negotiated with the couple.

The new contract puts a greater emphasis on the therapeutic agenda and goals. Commitment to the relationship has typically been resolved one way or the other and commitment to therapy, at this point in treatment, is usually clear. The contract redefines the problems and issues to be addressed and refines the goals sought by the couple. The negotiation process may involve an explanation by the therapist of what can be gained by longer-term therapy and by deepening the exploration of the issues. The established working alliance between therapist and clients facilitates a smooth transition between the renegotiation of the therapeutic contract and the continuation of treatment.

Clinical experience indicates that during the middle stage of treatment, there is another dramatic turning point occurring somewhere between nine months and one year. For cases going well, there seems to be a "breakthrough," when much of the therapeutic input takes hold and the therapy takes on an accelerated pace. The couple begins to work more independently of the therapist, and the issues raised earlier in therapy are reworked once again to more satisfying and successful resolutions.

The preceding description of stages and time frames in the Intersystem Approach is based on common clinical experience across a variety of cases. This generalization does not address the complexity of clinical practice, of course. There are many exceptions, including couples who terminate prematurely, who never adapt to the therapeutic process, who move more slowly or more quickly, or who stay in therapy to foster an illusion of change while never modifying the core dynamics of the relationship. Another category of couples who follow a different course than that described above includes those who tend to replay the stages due to repetitive crises such as the revelation of secrets, wounds that will not heal (e.g., extramarital affairs, former drug use, gambling), and unresolved family-of-origin issues. These cases are characterized by repetitive periods of regression, renegotiation, and recompensation.

Obviously, each case is different and works within its own time frame. But, irrespective of differences in pacing, what each case has in common is the movement through therapeutic stages that build upon each other. When therapy works, as the couples move through the stages and experience breakthroughs, the presenting problems are broadened to include the exploration of underlying dynamics and core issues, communication skills are improved, new ways of relating are fostered, a wider range of emotions is expressed, and the partners work more effectively together and more independently of the therapist.

LONG-TERM VERSUS SHORT-TERM THERAPY: ISSUES OF TIME

Notwithstanding the previous discussion of therapeutic stages, distinctions between long-term and short-term therapy are not integral to the Intersystem Approach presented here. Length of treatment is determined by the nature of the problems and the goals presented by the couple. Long-term and short-term approaches to treatment are integrated into the broad framework of this approach. Just as the flexibility of this therapeutic system enables the therapist to utilize treatment strategies that can most effectively address the presenting problems and treatment goals, the therapist is free to work within the time frame that is best suited for a particular case.

The discussion of stages in the preceding section was a descriptive presentation of how couples progress in therapy within an open-ended time frame. The observation that stages occur in approximately three-month intervals is based on cases in which the couples were experiencing serious difficulties and entered therapy seeking intensive intervention to resolve their problems and to achieve broadly defined goals. These cases, of necessity, would be engaged in longer-term treatment. Even within a long-term framework, there are couples who move more quickly and those who move more slowly toward the successful resolution of the therapeutic agenda.

In contrast to the type of case described above, there are couples who initiate treatment in order to work on problems within a limited time frame, toward circumscribed goals. Marital therapy in these situations is often shorter term and focused on a limited agenda. Even if the problems are serious, there are couples who seek treatment as a means for getting through a particular crisis, choosing to work on their other difficulties without the assistance of a therapist. Also, practical considerations such as moving, work schedules, limited finances, and insurance constraints often impose a predetermined time limit. Under these circumstances, the goal of therapy is to help couples achieve the goals that can be realistically attained within the time that is available.

Although neither the Intersystem Approach nor the therapist imposes a time structure on the therapy, couples often raise the issue of time. As discussed earlier, the negotiation of the initial contract may include the commitment to a minimum defined period of time in therapy. But, even with this agreement, the therapist needs to assess how important the time factor is in a particular case. Therapy proceeds differently when there is a commitment to an open-ended, versus a closed-ended process. In an open-ended process, the therapeutic agenda is more flexible, allowing for additional problems and issues to be incorporated into the therapeutic domain. In this situation, the tacit understanding between therapist and clients is that therapy is over when the work is done. In a closed-ended process, the therapeutic agenda needs to be limited to the problems and issues that can be effectively addressed within the prescribed time limit. Therapists need to be sensitive to the fact that clients enter treatment with varying levels of tolerance for the amount of time they are willing to give therapy to work. Issues of time should be discussed explicitly between the therapist and clients in order to reach a common understanding of the time frame for therapy.

How much time the therapist has will determine the focus of sessions, the issues addressed, and the pacing, especially during the initial stage of therapy. Sensitivity to the issue of time is as crucial as the sensitivity the therapist should have about any need or expectation that clients bring in with them when they enter treatment. If the time frame presented by clients is unrealistic, then the therapist should address this issue honestly and directly and negotiate for something workable.

As recommended previously, three months is clinically indicated as a reasonable period of time for the initial contract. After this period of time, clients have a better understanding of the timing and pacing of therapy and the potential for gain from the therapeutic process. At that point, the negotiation of time can occur on a more realistic basis. Clients tend to become more flexible about time once they have experienced the positive effects of therapy and can point to the progress they have already made.

THE INTAKE SESSION AND EVALUATION STAGE

During the initial sessions, the therapist establishes the foundations for ongoing treatment. Two primary tasks during the initial stage are the engagement of the couple and the negotiation of the initial contract.

These tasks are essentially structural in nature, establishing who will be involved in treatment and the commitment to the therapeutic process.

The intake session and evaluation stage of therapy present three other fundamental tasks for the therapist. The first task involves building the therapeutic relationship. Joining with clients begins during the initial phone contact and the first meeting in the waiting room. The second task involves getting to know the clients and letting them know the person of the therapist. This occurs through a process of gathering information and reflectively feeding back to clients what the therapist understands of what is being shared. The third task involves evaluating the clinical data and formulating hypotheses about the nature of the problems and the most appropriate therapeutic approach. These three tasks are not finite in nature, but in fact represent functions that the therapist engages in over the entire course of therapy.

Marriage Council staff employ varied approaches during the evaluation stage of treatment. A commonly utilized approach in clinical practice and training is the model of a three-session evaluation period (Berman, 1982). The intake session involves both partners; the subsequent two sessions involve each partner individually. The fourth session brings the partners back together. The particular nature of this model has implications for the processes of information gathering and relationship building that will be discussed later.

The intake session begins a process of information gathering and joining with the couple. The focus of information gathering is on the presenting problem(s). The individual sessions continue the process of assessment and facilitate the process of joining with each partner. By spending a session exclusively focused on each individual, joining with the couple during the subsequent conjoint sessions is made easier. There seems to be less blaming and polarization when each partner feels she or he has been heard and understood by the therapist. The sense of comfort gained by the individual contact helps decrease the competition for the therapist's attention, approval, and sympathy which typically takes place during the first stage of marital therapy. Aside from gathering individual histories and joining, the opportunity to view a partner alone at least once is extremely informative.

The contrast between the individual and conjoint sessions provides a unique insight into the system. Through this simple format, differences between individual functioning and interactional dynamics become apparent in ways that the therapist can utilize in later sessions. For example, an apparently quiet partner may be rather talkative in an individual session. Raising the perception of this discrepancy with the couple can elicit an exploration of the couple's view of their dynamics. Since the quiet partner has been engaged, it becomes easier to invite her or him to talk in conjoint sessions.

The fourth session brings the couple back in together, marking the transition from the evaluation stage to direct intervention in problem areas. The therapeutic match should also be addressed at this point. Therapeutic match refers to the comfort level, compatibility, and trust between therapist and clients. These are essential components of a strong working alliance. If any component is absent, the therapeutic process will be less effective. When these issues are raised, clients are given the responsibility to explore their experience of the therapist and to affirm working with the therapist as a choice. The therapist needs to convey a clear message to the couple that they are entitled to explore the compatibility of the therapeutic relationship over the course of treatment and that they should address issues of discomfort as they arise. This is a reciprocal responsibility; the therapist must also assess her or his capability of working with the couple. Once these tasks have been accomplished, the working stage of therapy is initiated by determining what problem or issue the couple wishes to address first.

As with all models, there are variations and exceptions in clinical practice. A number of Marriage Council staff utilize conjoint sessions exclusively during the evaluation stage. The therapists who operate within this format consider joint history gathering, wherein partners hear each other's histories, as very productive and constructive. This approach asserts that bonding occurs on both the individual and couple level without the necessity of individual sessions. Adherents of the three-session evaluation format utilize this approach flexibly.

Two types of cases typically require modification of the evaluation format so that it can respond to the emotional demands of the couple. These are marriages in crisis, and chronically conflicted couples.

In starting therapy with marriages in severe crisis, it is advisable to begin therapeutic intervention immediately, postponing history gathering and the scheduling of individual sessions to a later stage. Couples in crisis require a period of stabilization before they can settle into the pacing of ongoing therapy. For these cases, negotiating the initial contract in conjoint sessions can serve to mediate the urgency of the crisis. In cases where conflict dominates the intake session to the extent that the therapist has difficulty controlling the therapeutic process, it also becomes necessary to modify the evaluation format. Once again, it is advisable to postpone history gathering, but in these cases individual sessions are used to mediate the level of hostility and conflict. This can be contracted with the couple, until such time when the therapist determines that a modification in the rigid conflictual patterns achieved on an individual basis can be used to facilitate constructive engagement between the partners in conjoint sessions.

The Intake Interview

Within the broad framework of tasks and processes that comprise the initial stage of conjoint marital therapy, it is important to conduct the intake interview in a manner that effectively elicits specific kinds of information about the couple. The primary focus of inquiry is on the presenting problem(s). The primary goal is to understand, with as integrated a perspective as possible, the difficulties experienced by the partners. In concert with the exploration of the problems that brought the couple into therapy is the exploration of the positive aspects of the relationship. In addition to helping the therapist assess what mechanisms work well within the relationship, eliciting verbalization of the positive can also help the couple to regain perspective about what is good in their marriage and about the positive reasons for being together. This can help mediate the escalation of negative feelings which limit the focus of the couple to the failings of the relationship. Also, a reminder about the strengths of the marriage can generate hope and positive feelings. Both responses are potentiating forces in the therapeutic process.

Guidelines for the areas of inquiry and style of approach that should be incorporated in the intake interview follow. The opening question, as well as other open-ended questions, should be addressed to both partners in a manner that clearly invites both to respond. Who answers first, the nonverbal messages between the partners, the style, pacing, and affective expression are all essential bits of information. As the discussion of problems unfolds, the primary goal of the therapist is to understand each partner's view of the marital difficulties and how each one perceives the other. This task is accomplished by the therapist's moving back and forth between the partners, while letting the couple's natural process emerge as much as possible.

The duration of the problems needs exploration, as does the point in time when each partner perceived deterioration in the relationship. As couples discuss what is wrong, what went wrong, why, and when, it is crucial to assess whether the problem dates back to the beginning of the relationship, or if it developed at some later point. It is also crucial to assess whether the desired change represents something new for the couple or a return to a more satisfying past. Two other essential questions are: 1) why the initiation of therapy at this particular point in the life of the relationship, and 2) who initiated the contact? The answers to these questions provide meaningful insights into the current interactional dynamics of the couple, the antecedent events, and the historical context of the ongoing difficulties.

In most cases, couples report that the relationship was good during some period of time, before the emergence of the problems that brought them into treatment. The implicit or explicit request by the couple is to regain the way of relating that made them happy in the past. Other couples may enter treatment requesting a totally new way of relating to each other. Clearly, this represents a very different therapeutic agenda than helping couples regain what they were once able to share.

Gathering History

There are three histories important to the Intersystemic Approach: the history of the relationship and the individual history of each partner. This information is crucial for understanding the couple as two individuals, each with her or his own psychological makeup, who bond to form an interactional system that functions within an intergenerational framework. The basic principle underlying adherence to this model of evaluation is the assertion that the present relationship cannot be fully understood without knowledge of its historical context and the interpersonal dynamics cannot be fully understood without knowledge of the multigenerational impact upon intrapsychic dynamics. From these data, a conceptualization of the case emerges and the therapist determines the level at which to address the current problems and which issue will provide the greatest leverage for change.

The conjoint intake interview begins the process of information gathering and assessment by focusing on the present and the immediate concerns of the couple. Gradually, the historical context of the presenting problems is constructed from the information gathered during the evaluation stage and over the course of treatment. The history of the marriage paints the scene before which the current relationship dynamics are enacted. It is important to discern how the couple met, the bases for initial attraction, the evolution of commitment, the emotional underpinnings, and the conscious and unconscious expectations, deals, bargains, and trade-offs. Were the current issues present in the beginning of the relationship? If so, how were they viewed, and when and why did they become problems? If not, when did the difficulties develop? The answers to these questions form the bases for conceptualizing the etiology, function, and role of the current marital difficulties.

The fourth session marks the return to conjoint sessions and serves as a transition between the evaluation stage and the working stage. As a transitional session, the therapist must provide a bridge between the presenting problems, the information that was elicited, and the initial focus of therapy. The content that helps establish the bridge is gained through the exploration of how the couple met, the bases for their mutual attraction, and their early expectations of each other. This material provides the historical context within which the restatement of presenting problems takes place. During this session, the problem areas of the relationship are reexamined and broadened to include the information shared during the evaluation process. The sense of where to begin emerges from this expanded perspective. But, before the transition into the working stage can take place, there needs to be agreement about the initial contract and the goals of treatment.

History gathering is a very different process within an intersystemic framework from that in individual psychotherapy. In addition to the information traditionally obtained, there needs to be a careful exploration of the varied significant relationships in each spouse's life, both in terms of dyadic involvements and constellations of significant others. Both cognition and emotion are crucial bits of information. Circular questioning (Penn, 1982), and probing perceptions of others, as well as the perceptions of how others perceived oneself, provide insight into family of origin interactional processes. The role of the partner in the current relationship gains meaning when viewed with this information as the backdrop.

Parallels between past and present relationships alert the therapist to the existence of unresolved family of origin issues that are being reenacted in the marriage. The repetition of relational patterns stems from a psychological predisposition to create a relational world that is familiar to the partners, even though what is being created is usually painful. The intrapsychic mechanisms by which this occurs are driven by a conscious or unconscious wish to satisfy unmet needs and thereby resolve the unfinished business from the past through the current relationship. However, this is an impossible task because the marriage that is built upon the past is condemned to relive it. In spite of the wish for resolution and change, the drive to recreate the familiar keeps the individual and the couple psychologically stuck in the repetition of relational patterns which trigger the reemergence of deeply imbedded emotional issues, and vice versa. In order to address the multigenerational patterns, the couple needs to engage in the direct exploration of family of origin material. The current relationship can be renegotiated only on its own terms, in the present, when the repetitive relational patterns are understood in terms of their roots in the past (Paul & Paul, 1975; Sager, 1976; Scarf, 1987).

Gathering information about life-stage and significant life events has clinical relevance for the assessment of a case (Carter & McGoldrick, 1980). Each stage of the family life-cycle challenges the members to perform certain tasks and move to another developmental level. A significant life transition for one family member requires concomitant shifts for every other member (Weeks & Wright, 1979). If the family does not adapt to the demands of the new stage, symptoms often develop that signal trouble in the system. The assessment of a couple in treatment requires knowledge of the family's life-stage and whether or not previous developmental tasks have been successfully negotiated. If tasks preceding the current stage remain unresolved, the couple needs to work through the prior stage in order to address the demands of the current stage.

It is also important to discriminate between response patterns that are normative during transition periods in the life-cycle, usually reaching resolution on their own, and problematic patterns that do not resolve spontaneously and persist over time irrespective of circumstances. For example, it is normative for couples having their first baby to experience sexual difficulties. The same difficulties unrelated to life-stage transitions and protracted over time represent problems endogenous to the functioning level of the couple. The context of clinical intervention is different in each of these cases.

Significant life events are major contributors to the vicissitudes of marriage. These include the death of an important person; illness of loved ones; changes in jobs, geographic location, or finances; children leaving or returning home; the occurrence of accidents; the divorce of parents, relatives, or friends; loss of a pet, etc. Very often the impact of a significant life event is not apparent until a period of time after the event has taken place. The time between a significant life event and the reaction may span many years. The therapist needs to help the couple understand the relationship between their current difficulties and the precipitant cause, which may have occurred a while ago. Once again, by maintaining an historical perspective, the therapist can aid the couple to recognize that the source of the difficulty lies outside of the marriage and does not represent a failure in the relationship. The relationship and each partner can be supported and strengthened to cope with the problems imposed by the demands of life. The following example demonstrates how significant life events and the demands of a shifting life stage can threaten an otherwise strong marriage.

A couple in their 50s initiated treatment for marital problems described as constant arguing and increasing feelings of dissatisfaction and incompatibility. Prior to this period, the couple had always seen themselves as best friends and very compatible. They had gone through two significant life events within the three-year period prior to initiating therapy, and were now facing a new life-stage.

Three years before, the husband had undergone surgery for a potentially life-threatening brain tumor. They reported coping well with this crisis, and feeling grateful that the tumor was operable and that he was now well. A year before, the wife lost her mother, with whom she and the entire family had been very close. Once again, they coped well; they pulled together for mutual support and accepted the death as inevitable. Concurrently, their college-age daughter was planning to move to her own apartment, which would propel them into the empty nest stage. The mother was extremely supportive of the move. However, the father didn't want to pay the bills for their daughter's "independence." This was a source of intense conflict. Another source of conflict was the husband's recent experimentation in business and financial investments. The wife was against the risks taken by the husband and, for the first time, he began to make decisions without her.

This couple, with an apparently strong relationship, had lost perspective of the enormous impact of the recent life and death crises and life transitions. They had displaced the emotional repercussions onto the marriage. With the marriage in trouble, the parents had triangulated the daughter, thus making the launching of this young adult very difficult. The husband, going through a mid-life crisis, turned away from his wife when he received no support. The wife, having lost a very significant person in her life, her mother, turned her grief, which she thought had passed, into anger at her husband and enmeshment with her daughter. The son, who was living away at college, and the daughter attended two therapy sessions. Both felt, especially the daughter, that they were caught in the parents' struggle and couldn't be themselves for fear of being disloyal to their mother and grandmother and perceived as allied with the father. It was more acceptable in this family to acknowledge the mother's depression than the father's. In great emotional need, the mother had moved closer to the children and was viewed as the "good guy." Equally as needy, but adopting a defensive posture, dad was out in the cold and viewed as the "bad guy." The harder dad fought to regain his prior position in the family, the more authoritarian he became and the more rejected by the family.

Treatment focused on the following clinical issues: 1) communication and problem-solving strategies within the marriage, 2) normalizing the husband's attempts to change and revitalize his life, 3) viewing the husband's changes as part of the age 50 mid-life transitional stage, 4) fostering the expression of the intense grief over the loss of the wife's mother, 5) allowing the wife to assume her mother's role in the extended family, 6) helping the children understand the pain and vulnerability of each parent and establish closeness with both, 7) fostering the partnership of the couple in new business pursuits, 8) helping the daughter leave home, and 9) acknowledging the mother's fear of the empty nest. In brief, for this couple, there was death to grieve, life to celebrate, and life stages to master.

In addition to variations in evaluation formats, Marriage Council staff vary in their approach to gathering historical information. At one end of the continuum, history gathering is not structured into any particular stage of therapy. The past is explored only as it seems relevant to the work on present issues. Historical information is shared as part of the unfolding process of therapy. On the other end of the continuum, the examination of family of origin material is approached as an essential circumscribed task for the first stage of treatment. Whether or not individual sessions are utilized, the therapist engages both partners to report, record, and react to historical information through the structured use of genograms (McGoldrick & Gerson, 1985; Sauber, L'Abate, & Weeks, 1985). The genogram can be assigned as homework or drawn in session, often on large newsprint with colored magic markers indicating relationships, themes, and patterns in bold and creative ways. Utilization of this technique can lead to spontaneous and meaningful insights that are then applied to the current situation.

Secrets

There is one type of information that places the therapist in an extremely difficult position — the "secret." A secret may take many forms. It may relate to the past or the present and may involve anything from finances to extramarital affairs. Obviously, the nature of the information not available to the other partner can present various degrees of dilemma for the therapist and represent various degrees of threat to the marriage. There is general agreement that secrets are harmful to the marital relationship and should be shared with the partner. But even this principle does not apply under all circumstances.

In some cases, the secret is about something embedded in the past, the revelation of which would not help the couple and may cause unnecessary hurt. There are various circumstances under which this may be true. For example, a couple may be engaged in destructive conflict unrelated to the secret information. The revelation of the secret would only serve as ammunition for the ongoing battle. In a totally different circumstance, such as in the case of an adult survivor of child abuse, the bearer of the secret may barely be able to accept, face, and speak the truth to a therapist, much less to anyone else, especially the partner. Premature revelation to a partner may cause decompensation in the abuse survivor and a retreat from dealing with the painful material. By sharing the secret with the therapist, the client can unburden herself or himself and thus move on with the partner. Individual work can help the partner grapple with the secret and prepare to bring it to the partner in a constructive fashion.

The therapist must be clear at the outset with the client about his or her position as the recipient of the secret information. The client needs to understand the predicament of the therapist and the potential damage that could result from maintaining secrecy. The therapist may agree to keep the confidence for a time-limited period with the understanding that the secret should eventually be revealed within the therapeutic context. If the client is not forthcoming, and the therapist is left feeling bound or in a harmful alliance, an individual session may be necessary to confront the bearer of the secret with the necessity for revelation.

In the most extreme cases, the therapist may be in the position of having to propose the termination of treatment if the information isn't shared, especially if the secret is directly related to the current difficulties in the marriage and serves to maintain the dysfunctional system. It is impossible for a therapist to be balanced in conjoint therapy if there is a collusion with one partner to keep a secret from the other. The most damaging collusion of secrecy is about an ongoing extramarital affair. In this situation, as a prerequisite for the continuation of treatment, the therapist must stipulate either that the affair be terminated, or that it be openly shared with the partner. If one of these conditions is not met, conjoint therapy becomes unworkable.

For those clinicians who work with couples only in conjoint sessions, there is significantly less opportunity for secrets to triangulate the therapist. When partners are seen together for all sessions, there may be a secret but, because it is unknown to the therapist, she or he is free to probe whatever suspicious information is shared during the session. This lack of information is an advantage in one respect, because the therapist is not vulnerable to collusion. On the other hand, the secret may be having a negative effect on the marriage and the therapist will be limited in her or his effectiveness by not knowing an important piece of information. For those therapists who utilize individual interviews as part of the evaluation process, balance and leverage can be maintained by a clear message to the bearer of the secret of what the therapist expects and how keeping the secret binds the therapist.

Clinical experience suggests that a secret is rarely withheld for more than a few sessions when the therapist adopts the clear position that it is necessary to share the information. Typically, the improved communication that results from therapeutic intervention during the early stage of treatment leads to greater honesty in general and ultimately to the disclosure of the secret, if needed. In order for clients to share freely in session, it is important for the therapist to sustain an open environment that fosters sharing, trust, and safety.

The Battle for Truth

A common dynamic of couples entering treatment is to engage in a battle for ownership of the truth. As each partner states her or his perceptions of the marriage, the overt or covert battle over who is right is played out. In response, the therapist needs to dispel the illusion of an absolute truth and validate each partner's experience. The battle can then subside as each partner feels accepted and understood in his or her separate experience. This aspect of therapy is as important in couple work as it is in individual psychotherapy, although more difficult to attain with a dyad. Eventually, even polarized viewpoints need to be framed and accepted as different facets of the same interconnected reality.

Language can be one of the most useful tools to aid the resolution of the battle for truth. Clients engaged in this battle will speak in dichotomies — right versus wrong, good versus bad, crazy versus sane. The therapist may actually play into this type of thinking by asking for each partner's "side" of the story, thereby implying that each holds some truth. Since each side contradicts the other, the therapist would be hard pressed to find a middle ground. The therapist must emphasize, through her or his own language and direct statements to the couple, that what matters is "what works." That is, each partner has perceptions, opinions, and differences about the problems of the relationship, neither bears the truth. What works is attempting to reconcile differences of opinion; truths are not as flexible.

How readily couples come to share an inter-subjective view of their experience is diagnostic of the course of treatment. Partners who can more easily hear each other's points of view can better accept the common ground in their shared experience and can be more empathic to each other. Couples with this capability make greater gains earlier in therapy. With couples for whom this is more difficult, the first stage of treatment moves more slowly and is characterized by repetitive engagement in an adversarial battle. Obviously, in consideration of the therapeutic necessity of balance, the therapist needs to avoid taking sides. From an intersystemic viewpoint of joint responsibility, there are no sides to take. An effective approach with conflict-habituated couples is to probe with each partner the vulnerability underlying their hostile affect. By fostering the direct communication of hurt, need, and caring, the therapist can facilitate a more constructive process, beginning with the abandonment of the struggle for truth and self-vindication.

Prior Treatment

It has been fascinating to note how many couples come in reporting dissatisfaction with their prior involvement in marital therapy. There seems to be a disproportionate number of false starts for couples seeking marital therapy as compared with individuals seeking individual therapy. Many couples drop out of prior therapy because of the vicissitudes in the relationship, the ambivalence of one or both partners, or dissatisfaction with the therapist or treatment approach.

Information about previous therapy is invaluable in setting the stage for the current therapy. The therapist maximizes the potential for a positive therapeutic connection by respecting and working with the couple's agenda. This agenda is incorporated into the negotiation of the initial contract. The Intersystem Approach allows the therapist to utilize an approach compatible with the couple's style and stated needs. Very often, these early messages from clients, which appear controlling and resistant, are accurate signals about where the work should start if it is to be successful. The case examples that follow present two situations where previous negative experience in marital therapy set the parameters for the early stage of treatment in the subsequent therapeutic relationship.

A couple in their late 30s entered therapy with two caveats based on their prior frustrating experiences in marital therapy: no "wasting time" with family of origin material and no assignments to go out on Saturday nights. When the therapist accepted these limitations, it was possible to avoid initial resistances, gain trust, and promote change. Later in the process, because of the positive therapeutic relationship that had developed, it became much easier to introduce the material that they had earlier stated was taboo.

A woman in her mid-30s was referred for individual psychotherapy. Her presenting problem was her failing marriage. Her primary objective was to find a way to make the marriage work. Her contact was preceded by four years of a series of unsuccessful marital therapies. She and her husband had worked unsuccessfully with a nationally famous therapist. Since that therapy hadn't worked, they believed that conjoint marital therapy couldn't work for them. The husband was the first to seek a therapist for himself and the wife then followed suit by finding her own therapist. Early in therapy, it became clear that the past attempts at conjoint therapy hadn't worked because of the secret of her husband's extramarital affair. Yet, even with this out in the open and the affair ostensibly over, the door was closed to conjoint work, based on their prior experiences. The client's request for marital therapy in individual sessions was accepted with reservation.

As the therapy progressed, it became apparent that the prior treatments failed partially because of the intense ambivalence and lack of differentiation in the marriage. By working with their drive to be together, the conjoint therapies paradoxically drove them apart at home. By working in individual therapy, as a means of being separate, they were able to come together at home. After six months marked by improvement in the marriage, the husband decided to get a divorce, and the wife could see more clearly that, in fact, the marriage wasn't working for either one of them. Only with support to increase her investment in trying to make things better in the marriage was she able to become aware that she was clinging to a man who offered her little and did not make her happy.

SUMMARY

The basic principles described in this chapter comprise the fundamental structural elements of the Intersystem Approach. The structural elements address the questions of who, what, and when.

The structure of therapy is built on who is involved in treatment, the nature of the therapeutic contract, the progression of stages that deepen the clinical material, and the time frame. The first basic principle of marital therapy is engaging the couple. The second basic principle is negotiating a workable contract that fosters a sense of joint effort and commitment on the part of the couple. The progression of therapy through stages is marked by the sequential movement of clients from the partial resolution of problems on one level to increased sharing and the resolution of problems on a deeper level. The basic time frame of this therapeutic framework is the time it takes to finish the work. Depending on the case, this may involve short-term or long-term therapy.

During the evaluation stage of therapy, the therapist has three basic tasks. The first task is the elicitation of presenting problems. The second task is gathering history. The third task is forming a systemic conceptualization of the case. The information upon which the therapist assesses a case is derived from what is heard verbally (CONTENT) and from what is observed interactionally (PROCESS). Presenting problems are explored and broadened so that their meanings and functions for the couple can be ascertained. Three histories are gathered, one for the relationship and one for each partner. From these data, the therapist formulates a conceptualization of the couple as an interactional system that operates within an intergenerational framework based on intrapsychic dynamics. From these early hypotheses, the therapist devises a treatment strategy that changes and evolves over the course of treatment. The structure established during the initial stage of therapy forms the foundation upon which the therapist and clients proceed to the working stage.

REFERENCES

Berman, E. M. (1982). The individual interview as a treatment technique in conjoint therapy. *American Journal of Family Therapy, 10*(1), 27-37.

Carter, E. A., & McGoldrick, M. (Eds.) (1980). *The Family Life Cycle: A Framework for Family Therapy.* New York: Gardner.

McGoldrick, M., & Gerson, R. (1985). *Genograms in Family Assessment.* New York: Norton.

Paul, M. L., & Paul, B. B. (1975). *The Marital Puzzle.* New York: Norton.

Penn, P. (1982). Circular questioning. *Family Process, 21,* 267-280.

Sager, C. J. (1976). *Marriage Contracts and Couple Therapy.* New York: Brunner/Mazel.

Sauber, R., L'Abate, L., & Weeks, G. (1985). *Family Therapy: Basic Concepts and Terms.* Rockville, MD: Aspen.

Scarf, M. (1987). *Intimate Partners: Patterns in Love and Marriage.* New York: Random House.

Stewart, R. H., Peters, T. C., Marsh, S., & Peters, M. J. (1975). An object relations approach to psychotherapy with marital couples, families and children. *Family Process, 14*(2), 161-178.

Weeks, G., & Wright, L. (1979). Dialectics of the family life cycle. *American Journal of Family Therapy, 7,* 85-91.

Chapter 4

Individual Psychopathology from the Systems Perspective

Martin Goldberg

In order to conceptualize and understand psychotherapy and psycho-dynamic theory, one must be able to deal with ambiguities. There is, for example, the ambiguity inherent in the very nature of psychotherapy: the requirement for coexistent empathy and detachment. Thus, an effective psychotherapist must somehow be able to *feel into* patients — to get inside their skins — while still retaining some degree of objectivity. In the ultimate sense, it is an impossible task, of course. But the skilled therapist is able to tolerate the ambiguity and to repeatedly perform split-second shifts from empathy to detachment which approximate a simultaneous achievement of the two qualities. Moreover, the dilemma cannot be resolved by retreating to one pure and unsullied position. Empathy without objectivity is a useful commodity, but it can be furnished by any good friend and does not require the services of a professional. And objectivity without empathy, sad to say, is worse than useless for the resultant observations will fall on deaf ears and will never be accepted by the patient.

When we come to consider the topic of this chapter, we promptly encounter another striking ambiguity. The term *individual psychopathology* surely has reference to those phenomena which have much of their expression, as well as their genesis, within the individual. One thinks of conditions such as bipolar affective disorder (manic-depressive disease), panic states, alcoholic addiction, dementias and deliriums, etc. These can all easily be visualized as occurring within the patient.

As an example, we can accept the premise that the alcoholic has a disease in which he is quite unable to control his intake of alcohol and/or to metabolize it properly after ingestion. This is the view in terms of the individual. With a little more difficulty, we may say that a particular alcoholic uses his lack of control and the result of his drinking as a way to "get at" his wife and family — to reach them, to displease them, to provoke them, and mobilize them into attempts to care for him or rescue him. And we may realize that his disease gradually excludes him from his family in such a way as to establish a vicious circle. Such a circle has no beginning, but in it we find one member of the family (the alcoholic) drinking, behaving badly, being gradually excluded, resenting this, and drinking all the more in an effort to retaliate and to reverse the exclusion, and evoking yet more exclusion as the process goes on and on. This is the view in terms of the family system. Either view alone is probably grossly inaccurate and oversimplified, so we must strive again for the impossible — to somehow have both views simultaneously.

The plight of the biology student learning to use a microscope is a related one. There are three objectives on the microscope, housing low-power lens, high-power lens, and oil-immersion (even higher-power) lens. In order to study a microscopic slide, the student needs to examine it first with the naked eye, then scan it under low power, then high power, and then possibly under the oil-immersion lens. You will note, however, that at no moment is the student viewing the slide simultaneously by low and high power, for indeed that is impossible. But what the student does learn to do, in short order, is to rotate the microscope objectives rapidly *back and forth, back and forth*, so as to obtain the next best and closest imitation possible of the simultaneous, integrated view.

In just such a manner, the family therapist must learn to rotate back and forth, back and forth, his own "lenses" which allow him to focus on what is happening within the individual (the biologic and the intrapsychic), on what is happening between a couple (the interpersonal), and on what is taking place in the family, group, subculture, and society (the systemic). Since we lack anything as concrete as actual microscopic lenses to play with, we face the far more difficult task of performing these complex shifts with only our own beings, our own minds, our own experiential involvement.

It is virtually certain that no therapist ever performs this task in anything like a perfect fashion. Therapists whose early training and experience are largely or entirely in one-to-one psychotherapy are always in danger of dwelling too much on the intrapsychic view. Equally, therapists trained first and foremost in the systemic approach are more apt to become enamored of the system and to neglect what is within the individual. And all of us who consider ourselves psychotherapists are far too likely to ignore the underlying biology and genetic endowment of our patients.

Those of us who handle this task the best are, consequently, those of us who remain alert to its magnitude and its inherent difficulties. Proper semantics may be helpful. The term *biopsychosocial* accurately describes the viewpoint needed to understand psychopathological concepts and entities. Once embedded in our thinking, our talking, our writing, it should help to eliminate such concepts as the "schizophrenogenic mother." (That concept is long since discredited and discarded, and yet it crops up repeatedly and distressingly in the discussions and writings of students as well as professionals in family therapy.)

Concern with proper semantics and proper nosology must also lead us to concern about the volume which sets much of our standards in this respect, the Diagnostic and Statistical Manual of Mental Disorders, published by the American Psychiatric Association. The DSM III (1980) and its successor, the DSM III-R (1987) have their advantages and disadvantages. Among the former are the general, wide acceptance of these volumes in the scientific community, and the fact that they attempt (with great success) to be highly specific while at the same time being atheoretical. (The benefits of this latter characteristic have been questioned, however [Faust & Miner, 1986].)

The drawbacks of the DSMs are considerable. There are very few unifying concepts in these diagnostic classifications. The old tripartite division of mental disorder into neuroses, psychoses, and personality disorder (utilized in DSM I and DSM II) has been abandoned and the resulting concepts may be more accurate, but there is a notable overall lack of cohesion which makes the new classifications difficult to learn and to use. Any real orientation to systemic thinking is, of course, quite lacking in both DSM III and DSM III-R, and family therapists must wait for another day to see this incorporation take place.

Most distressing of all may be the tendency of the DSMs to purchase clarity at the expense of accuracy. Nowhere is this illustrated better than in the handling of the schizophrenic disorders. The chapter on these disorders in DSM III starts out well in that it is titled — quite accurately — in the plural form, *Schizophrenic Disorders*. But there is a footnote to the very first sentence which reads as follows: "Although Schizophrenia is most likely a group of disorders of differing etiologies, common usage refers to 'Schizophrenia' rather than the technically more accurate term, 'Schizophrenic Disorders'" (APA, 1980, p. 181). DSM III then goes on to completely ignore the technically more accurate term and to adopt what is "common usage," evidently forgetting that the task of a DSM is to *establish* what should be common usage rather than to go along with existing errors in it.

DSM III-R does correct its predecessor's inconsistency. Unfortunately, it does so by the simple expedient of changing the title of the section to the singular, "Schizophrenia." Common usage has carried the day, evidently.

The results of this are unfortunate. Considerable confusion and argument result from the misconception of the schizophrenic disorders as being a single entity, "Schizophrenia." We have known it as clearly a *syndrome* — a set of symptoms that may reflect one of a number of different and as yet largely undescribed conditions which in all probability have very differing etiologies.

The situation can well be likened to that which pertained some years ago for a disorder called Bright's disease of the kidney. In the 1800s and early 1900s, many, many patients suffered and many died from this disease. The etiology was unknown and the treatment, needless to say, was unreliable and unsatisfactory. Today, no one suffers from Bright's disease — for indeed there is no such entity. We now recognize that the diagnosis was given to a dozen or so conditions — subacute glomerulonephritis, chronic glomerulonephritis, acute tubulointerstitial nephritis, chronic tubulointerstitial nephropathy, toxic nephropathies, acute glomerulonephritis, immune renal disease, nephrotic syndrome, etc. — which have different etiologies, different pathophysiologies, different courses, different treatment, and different prognoses.

As little as we know about the schizophrenic disorders — and that is indeed quite little — we are aware that the course and prognosis of illness are markedly different in different subgroups of patients so diagnosed. For example, individuals suffering from the catatonic type of schizophrenic disorder have a prognosis which is considerably better than those suffering from the disorganized type, and indeed they have markedly different symptomatology as well as markedly different courses to their illnesses. Under these circumstances, lumping the two types of disorder under the term schizophrenia is inexcusable and can serve only to further confuse our guesses about etiology. Attempts to explain a schizophrenic disorder only in terms of the *individual's* psychology, biology, and genetics are certainly questionable in catatonic or paranoid schizophrenia, but may have far more merit for the disorganized schizophrenic. And attempts to explain a schizophrenic disorder largely in terms of family or social interaction can become absurd if they are applied to the disorganized schizophrenic rather than to the paranoid or catatonic.

Yet another feature of the DSMs has considerable impact on the marital and family therapist. This is the use of so-called *multiaxial evaluation*, in which an individual is evaluated on each of five axes. Axis I consists primarily of the so-called "clinical syndromes," whereas Axis II consists of Personality Disorders (seen chiefly in adults) and Specific Developmental Disorders (seen chiefly in children and adolescents). It seems strange and arbitrary that the Axis II conditions are somehow separated off from Axis I; is a Passive-Aggressive Personality Disorder any less of a clinical syndrome than a Multiple Personality? Nonetheless, this distinction is made and is explained thus: "This separation ensures that consideration is given to the possible presence of disorders that are frequently overlooked when attention is directed to the usually more florid Axis I disorder" (APA, 1980). We will skip over the question of what Axis I disorders are more "florid" than Borderline Personality Disorder or Histrionic Personality Disorder and simply note that if the DSMs aimed to ensure consideration of Personality Disorders and Specific Developmental Disorders, they have in fact produced no such result. There is a natural, human tendency to emphasize whatever is number one to the exclusion of number two. Consequently, the overwhelming majority of diagnoses are formulated only in terms of Axis I, and the Personality Disorders and Specific Developmental Disorders continue to be frequently overlooked. (Axis III provides for a listing of Physical Disorders and Axis IV and Axis V deal with the Severity of Psychosocial Stressors and the Highest Level of Adaptive Functioning in Past Year. These last two are totally ignored in the great majority of clinical settings.)

One result of the system of multiaxial evaluation (which provides no axis at all for indication of marital or family functioning) is that a very sizable percentage of patients seen in marital or family therapy are diagnosed as suffering from Adjustment Disorder, including Adjustment Disorder with Depressed Mood; Adjustment Disorder with Anxious Mood; Adjustment Disorder with Mixed Emotional Features; Adjustment Disorder with Disturbance of Conduct; Adjustment Disorder with Mixed Disturbance of Emotions and Conduct; Adjustment Disorder with Work (or Academic) Inhibition; Adjustment Disorder with Withdrawal; Adjustment Disorder with Physical Complaints; and Adjustment Disorder with Atypical Features. Obviously, there are enough diagnoses in this category to fit almost any patient and since the connotations of Adjustment Disorders are quite nonpejorative and nonjudgmental, the temptation to use these diagnoses becomes almost irresistible for the family therapist.

The connotation of the concepts involved in defining the Adjustment Disorder seems to be that they do not involve deep-seated and/or considerable intrapsychic pathology but result, rather, from interactional or interpersonal causations. These causations, designated as *stressors* in the DSMs, specifically include many situations which bring patients into marital and/or family therapy. In describing Adjustment Disorder, DSM III-R states, "The stressors may be single, such as divorce, or multiple, such as marked business difficulties and marital problems. . . . They can occur in a family setting, e.g., in discordant intrafamilial relationships" (APA, 1987, p. 329).

What we have, then, is a diagnostic category which can be interpreted or stretched to fit most of our patients, and this is precisely how we use it. But there is real doubt that this is how the authors of the DSMs intended it to be, since the entire description of *all* the forms of Adjustment Disorder listed in DSM III-R takes up a grand total of less than three pages! (Compare this, for instance, to 11 pages devoted to the category of sleep disorders.)

The gravest danger in the overdiagnosis of Adjustment Disorders is that by not making more accurate diagnoses we may be less than alert to possible complications and pitfalls for our patients. A man whose wife has left him may become very depressed thereafter and may continue to be quite depressed during the four to five months that he is seeing a marital/family therapist. The latter may consider it reasonable to diagnose him as suffering from an Adjustment Disorder with Depressed Mood. However, careful questioning may reveal that the patient is also experiencing associated symptoms such as loss of appetite, weight loss, severe insomnia, difficulty in concentration, lack of energy, feelings of worthlessness, and diminution of personal interests and pleasures. Under these circumstances, the patient is probably suffering from a Major Depressive Episode and it is of more than academic interest to diagnose him properly, since doing so will alert the therapist and other concerned parties to the definite suicidal potential present in such a situation. This, of course, should be very carefully explored and evaluated with the patient. *Careful* use of the DSM might prevent misdiagnosis in this situation. DSM III-R lists five diagnostic criteria for Adjustment Disorders, the very last of which requires that "the disturbance does not meet the criteria for any specific mental disorder" (APA, 1987, p. 330). In practice, very few clinicians pay much attention to this insufficiently emphasized disclaimer.

A salutary approach for the marital/family therapist is to restrain the tendency to overdiagnose Adjustment Disorder by careful attention to all five of the criteria required to make such a diagnosis. In addition, where Adjustment Disorders are diagnosed, careful attention should be paid to the Axis II diagnostic evaluation. This Axis can be used not only to diagnose Specific Developmental Disorders and Personality Disorders, but also "to indicate specific personality traits or the habitual use of particular defense mechanisms. This can be done when no Personality Disorder exists or to supplement a Personality Disorder diagnosis" (APA, 1987, pp. 16-17).

Defense mechanisms are defined in DSM III-R as "patterns of feelings, thoughts, or behaviors that are relatively involuntary and arise in response to perceptions of psychic danger. They are designed to hide or to alleviate the conflicts or stressors that give rise to anxiety" (APA, 1987, p. 393). Examples cited include projection, splitting, acting out, suppression, and denial.

In defining *personality traits*, DSM III-R states, "Personality traits are enduring patterns of perceiving, relating to, and thinking about the environment and oneself, and are exhibited in a wide range of important social and personal contexts. It is only when personality traits are inflexible and maladaptive and cause either significant functional impairment or subjective distress that they constitute Personality Disorders" (APA, 1987, p. 335). This definition is considerably less than crystal clear but the implications of all this are that, for example, some mild degree of passive-aggressive or schizoid behavior could and should be noted under Axis II. If such behavior is regarded as a trait it should *not* be given a DSM code number since this would imply the existence of a Personality Disorder.

There is little question that a sizable percentage of the patients whom we see for marital/family therapy could well be diagnosed as having either personality traits or Personality Disorder on Axis II. Moreover, recognition of these traits or Disorder could be helpful to the therapeutic process in many instances.

Case Example

Burt and Ann, a couple in their mid-30s, came to Marriage Council of Philadelphia asking for help with their troubled marriage and saying that their communications had broken down almost totally. They had been married for seven years and had two young children whose care was a major issue between them. In early interviews Burt proved to be a highly perfectionistic individual who was very wrapped up in his career as a dentist. He spent so much time on his professional work that he was rarely home and, even on weekends, had little time or energy to devote to Ann or the children. He also had difficulty in showing affection to family members or indeed to anyone else.

Ann complained that every morning Burt presented her with a list of tasks he expected her to accomplish that day. These lists paralleled similar ones which Burt compiled for himself, but he was invariably disappointed because Ann managed to avoid doing anything on the lists given to her.

For her part, Ann was an intense, moody woman who had brief periods of marked depression and/or anxiety and repeated episodes of intense anger, directed at Burt, the children, or anyone else who happened to be around. All these episodes were short-lived and Ann could best be described as mercurial. In a given therapy session she could be — unpredictably — furious with Burt, madly in love with him, mildly euphoric, nicely contented, or desperately depressed. Not infrequently, she managed to be all of these in one brief session.

Her relationships with other family members and friends also fluctuated wildly, between great affection and profound hostility. She complained repeatedly of feeling bored with Burt, of feeling tied down with the children, and of having no real interests. On more than one occasion, she physically abused her husband and on more than one occasion she made suicidal threats. In one particular sequence of events, she made a suicidal gesture by swallowing 10 Valium tablets and then promptly called Burt at his office to tell him what she had done and demand his help.

Needless to say, the therapist working with this couple had no easy task. About a dozen conjoint sessions were held. They were far from dull and at times seemed highly encouraging, as the interactions in the system were brought to light. However, every good session or good week was invariably followed by a horrendous one. Meanwhile the case was subjected to diagnostic review and the following DSM diagnoses were made:

(1) For Burt:

Axis I: 309.28 Adjustment Disorder with Mixed Emotional Features

Axis II: 301.40 Obsessive Compulsive Personality Disorder

(2) For Ann:

Axis I: 309.28

Axis II: 301.83 Borderline Personality Disorder

These diagnoses indicated the recognition of the intrapsychic pathology occurring within the individual even as the marital and family system was being observed. The Axis II diagnoses were of particular importance in this respect and once these diagnoses had been established, they led to the next therapeutic move. Burt and Ann were each referred for individual psychotherapy with the aim of giving them sufficient help with their intrapsychic problems to then permit a future resumption of the marital therapy with more chance of real progress occurring. (The therapist who had seen the couple conjointly did *not* attempt to see either of them in the individual psychotherapy, but referred them to two other therapists. Failure to do this often results in blurred boundaries between the individual therapy and the marital therapy. Such blurring is seldom helpful and would certainly not be appropriate for someone with a Borderline Personality Disorder, in which one of the cardinal features is a difficulty in establishing and respecting boundaries.)

Careful scrutiny of the diagnoses made in the above situation could raise some question about the Axis II diagnosis made on Burt. Should he be regarded as having an Obsessive-Compulsive Personality Disorder or would it be more accurate to call it a *personality trait?* The distinction is made on the question of whether the pattern of behavior is "inflexible and maladaptive and causes either significant functional impairment or subjective distress" (APA, 1987, p. 335). In this instance, the marital therapist felt that Burt's behavior did meet these criteria. It is also true that diagnosing one spouse as having a Personality Disorder and the other as having a personality trait could lead to some imbalance in the therapeutic approach, which is generally undesirable.

Indeed, the whole matter of formulating individual diagnoses or even of recognizing individual psychopathology within a marital system leads to some serious quandaries for the therapist. When couples seek help, so often one (or both) of the spouses is certain that the problem lies entirely with the other. "I'm here because my wife is a mental case," or "I only came because my husband needs help so badly." Such statements bombard us all the time and necessitate great vigilance on our part. Any action by the therapist which seems to label only one person as disturbed or upset has the potential to be interpreted as a clean bill of health and a personal vindication by the other spouse. This happens quite often when, for example, psychotropic medication is prescribed for one of the two individuals who is in marital therapy.

Such an outcome is hardly desirable and certainly upsets the balance of our therapeutic efforts. Moreover, there is a considerable body of thought to support the idea that "psychopathology seeks psychopathology" (or "psychopathology seeks its own level"), meaning that many or most people have equivalent degrees of mental health or mental disturbance to the spouses they choose. Consequently, most marital therapists appear to stay with the idea that in any marital dilemma there is equal involvement and equal contribution by both spouses. That idea may or may not be true. The following episode, which occurred in the author's practice, seems relevant.

Betty and Al, both in their 50s, came for marital therapy after many years of storm and strife. Betty previously had some relatively brief individual psychotherapy, which seemed to be helpful. Al had undergone eight or nine years of rather intense psychoanalytically oriented treatment, with little apparent result. In addition, they had jointly consulted with a number of marital and family therapists, all of whom had insisted that both spouses were making equal contributions to the marital discord. Betty indicated, early on in the present therapy, that she did not buy this viewpoint. She emphasized the overwhelming importance of Al's passive-aggressive behavior, which was indeed both extreme and pervasive, and of his problems with recurrent episodes of transvestite fetishism. Despite this, it seemed to emerge in the therapy that the marital problems were indeed shared and circular, and the therapist repeatedly pointed this out to both spouses.

In this setting, when the couple appeared for their session one day, Betty handed the therapist a copy of the *New Yorker* magazine, requesting that he read a very short story in it, which she felt had bearing on the situation. The story was a fictional, tongue-in-cheek piece about Dr. X, "The World's Greatest Expert in Sex Therapy," and included an account of Dr. X's initial interview with a couple. This couple came into the office and Dr. X asked them to describe their problems. "Well," said the man, "it's our sex life. When we first met it was wonderful — absolutely all I could ask for. But over the years it's gradually diminished in quality and quantity and now we just don't have the interest or anything like the satisfaction we had. The passion is gone, the romance is gone, the spark is gone. I only hope and pray that you can help us." "All right," replied Dr. X, "as I understand it, your perception is that a previously satisfactory relationship has somehow gotten off the track and you would like to restore what you had." "How about you," he asked, turning to the woman. "Me!" she exploded, "I'm a waitress in the diner across the street from your office! I never met this kook before in my life, until 10 minutes ago when he grabbed me and hustled me up here, saying it was a matter of life or death." "I see," said Dr. X, "you perceive that this man is not your husband and you somehow view the situation quite differently than he does. Now, you two do have a problem!"

Betty made her point with this story, and if it needs any spelling out it is simply this: Anything—including the systemic approach—can be overdone at times, and there certainly are some situations in which one partner's pathology overshadows the other's.

ADVANTAGES AND DISADVANTAGES OF DIAGNOSIS

Given the fact that a systemic orientation is almost totally lacking in DSM III and DSM III-R, one could well question whether there is any reason for the marital/family therapist to utilize the diagnosis of individual psychopathology. In many ways, matters would be neater, cleaner, and more in balance if we could just ignore such labelling. Not infrequently, our therapeutic endeavors are adversely affected by a diagnosis, as is the case when an overly pessimistic diagnosis carrying a glum prognosis causes us to limit our goals or reduce the energy put into the therapeutic process. Moreover, although diagnoses are confidential, they are frequently seen or heard by outsiders, with negative effects for the patient. For example, a diagnosis of Schizophrenia or Major Depressive illness may raise questions on a patient's medical and health records, leading to the loss of a job opportunity (ask Senator Tom Eagleton!), to a higher rate for life insurance, or even to the denial of insurance.

And yet the merits of individual diagnosis may outweigh all of this—particularly if we are able to regard diagnoses as always tentative, flexible, and subject to change, and never fixed, rigid, and static. Diagnosis should help us in the recognition and assessment of a patient's potential for suicide, homicide, or other self-destructive behavior. The patient with a major depressive episode is always plagued by such dangers, and this is equally true of the patient who is addicted to alcohol, other drugs, and/or gambling. And we need to diagnose the patient in a manic state promptly and accurately, for he or she can do tremendous damage to self, to spouse, and to family with inappropriate, uncontrolled behavior such as wild spending or promiscuity.

Marital and family therapists have also shown some fascination over the years with the exercise of formulating "diagnoses" not just on individuals but on marriages. Thus, the sociologist Cuber described in his studies of American marriages: the vital marriage, the chronically conflicted (or conflict-habituated) marriage, the passive-congenial marriage, and the devitalized marriage (Cuber & Haroff, 1963). These "diagnoses" are indeed systemic in that they describe the nature of the relationship rather than the characteristics of the spouses.

Peter Martin has been a pioneer in describing "marital patterns" which reflect more of the individual psychopathology in the system (Martin, 1976). His description of the "love-sick wife" and the "cold-sick husband" is in fact a description of the marriage most often encountered in white, middle-class Americans. This is a pairing of a husband with Compulsive personality trait or disorder and a wife with Histrionic personality trait or disorder. It is not surprising that such marriages are extremely common among successful American couples. For years our society has indoctrinated us with the positive value of these traits, in a gender-specific manner. That is, we have raised our boys to work and *perform* in a cold, unemotional, impersonal, detached manner (the Gary Cooper or John Wayne image) and have raised our girls to be "warm," i.e., emotional and fragile, with great emphasis on appearance and physical attractiveness (the Marilyn Monroe image).

Those boys have grown up to be compulsive, workaholic men who achieve a good deal in the competitive world of business or the professions but do so at the price of distancing their emotions and their personal contacts. They are apt to seek out and choose as mates histrionic women, mistaking the volatility, easy emotion, and self-dramatization of these women for genuine warmth and tenderness.

And the histrionic women, in turn, have been attracted to compulsive men by the mistaken notion that the latter's coldness, detachment, and work orientation somehow equate with strength, solidity, and protectiveness. (In recent years, the impact of feminism may well have changed this sort of classical male compulsive-female histrionic pairing, but that remains to be seen. One somewhat chilling thought is that we may now have more marriages in which both husband and wife are predominantly compulsive in type, since society has prepared both of them for the demands of the marketplace.)

People with compulsive personality trait or disorder often attract as potential mates another group of individuals who have a need for order and structure and boundaries in their lives: those with borderline personality trait or disorder. The case of Burt and Ann, previously described, is an example of this sort of pairing in which the appeal for the compulsive seems to lie in a misidentification of the borderline's volatility and emotional turmoil as representing warmth and tenderness.

Another pattern first described by Martin (1976) under the unfortunate and pejorative label of "The Double Parasitic Marriage" consists of those ill-fated unions in which both husband and wife suffer from Dependent personality trait or disorder. Neither spouse has much ability to take care of self, let alone of the other, and the inevitable result is that such couples fill the rolls and waiting lists of our public clinics, agencies, and family services.

Yet another easily recognized type of marriage is the Paranoid marriage in which the marital relationships and system whirl around in a vortex of suspicion and jealousy. This paranoia may be shared, as in a *folie à deux*, in which case it may be a major unifying factor in the marriage. Or cohesion in the marriage may result from a dovetailing of personalities, as when a paranoid, jealous husband marries a flirtatious, histrionic wife. Such a couple will be forever provoking and evoking each other's pathology. When one spouse is paranoid and the other spouse will have no part of it, however, the virtually inevitable result is that the marriage will split.

Describing married couples in terms of the individual psychopathology of each spouse leads to an inevitable question: How much of this psychopathology was there before the marriage and how much developed later, as a reaction to the marital relationship? The most likely answer, in the majority of cases, is that both factors play a significant part. Nowhere is this better demonstrated than in marriages wherein one spouse is addicted. There was a period some years ago in which various authorities and writers on addiction described the sort of person who was likely to become the spouse of an alcoholic. More recently, alcoholic marriages and families are described in terms of their *effects* on the "sober spouse" and other nonaddicted family members. The most enlightening approach, in fact, may result from emphasizing and combining both viewpoints and both sorts of descriptions.

Most alcoholic addictions start early in life, not infrequently with patterns of heavy teenage drinking. Consequently, the person who marries an alcoholic individual usually does know about the addiction—at some level of consciousness. That knowledge is often denied, needless to say. Nonetheless, it is reasonable to postulate that in some (not a few) cases, people choose alcoholic spouses because of their own complementary needs: needs to nurture, to control, to reform, etc. What subsequently happens to such people, as they are affected and shaped by their marriage and their families, is another matter.

A fairly common script is that of Betty, a woman in her early 40s who is married to Steve, a chronic alcoholic. Betty married Steve when they were both just a year or two out of high school. At the time, he appealed to her in terms of his apparent strength and protectiveness. A rugged, strapping young man, he was working in a construction job and earning good wages at the age of 19. Betty dismissed his frequent heavy drinking as something that went with the territory for construction workers and their life-style. She also enjoyed Steve's tendency to rely on her good sense and judgment, which were unusually sound for a youngster.

Over the course of some 20 years of marriage and the birth and growth of three children, Betty's sense and judgment have remained excellent. And Steve has continued to drink heavily, but with increasingly negative results. He has long since left construction work and is now a rather successful realtor who owns his own sizable company. But neither his change in occupation nor Betty's attempts to reform him have changed his addiction. Meanwhile, Betty has withdrawn more and more of her love and attention from Steve and focused them on the children.

In a pattern common to many addictive families, Steve has succeeded in excluding himself and/or has gradually been excluded by the other family members. Today, Betty is clearly the dominant force in a family in which Steve, who is making an effort at recovery through Alcoholics Anonymous, is a very distant and emotionally absent member. Is this the sort of family Betty wanted and opted for when she married? Very probably not; very probably it is largely the result of the impact of addiction on the family system. And yet, some element of personal need, personal desire, and even personal choice has led Betty into this and kept her functioning within the system, rather than allowing her to withdraw from it.

Most families wherein one parent is addicted function in fact as single-parent families. And in a fair number of such systems, the sober "single parent" gets a great deal of inner satisfaction out of that role and sooner or later begins to thrive on it. Consequently, one of the keys to aiding the recovery of an addict is the readiness of the sober spouse to give up the role of single parent and return to (or take on for the first time) the role of marital partner and co-parent.

Scripts such as this are not confined to families wherein one parent is addicted, but may be encountered also in families wherein one parent is chronically depressed, schizophrenic, phobic, etc.

What is almost totally lacking in our knowledge of individual psychopathology from the systems perspective is evidence of the beneficial effects of a benign marital interaction on the individual psychopathology.

As just one such example, consider the case of Rob, a terribly heavy drinker from a family of alcoholics, who drank his way through a first marriage at age 20 and a divorce several years later. He was still drinking at age 28 when he met a woman with whom he fell madly in love. At her insistence, he reduced his drinking to very small proportions and they were married in short order. But over the course of the next year or two, Rob made the inevitable slide back into more drinking, albeit at a level greatly reduced from his previous patterns. Nonetheless, his new wife packed up bag and baggage and moved out one night, leaving a note to the effect that she would return when and if he gave up drinking totally and permanently. In a surprise ending to a familiar story, Rob did just that and his reunited marriage has continued for over 20 years in a very sober and sound fashion.

This is a concrete instance of a maritally induced (i.e., systemically induced) change for the better in individual psychopathology. Unquestionably, there are other more abstract or diffuse examples which occur not uncommonly but which fail to come to our attention simply because they do not require clinical intervention.

CONCLUSIONS

In the final analysis, the view of individual psychopathology from the systems perspective remains a clouded one. It is clouded by ambiguity, by complexity, and by lack of sufficient knowledge. But it remains richly interesting and rewarding for the clinician who is willing to attempt it without resorting to oversimplification, arbitrary formulations, or reassuring dogma.

In the absence of these roadblocks, the dedicated therapist can maintain relatively steady contact with the patient's intrapsychic dynamics as well as with the interpersonal and systemic setting and events. The interplay between these forces can then be estimated and allowed for, and appropriate therapeutic measures can accordingly be designed and employed.

REFERENCES

American Psychiatric Association (1987). *Diagnostic and Statistical Manual of Mental Disorders* (3rd ed., rev.). Washington, D.C.: Author.

American Psychiatric Association (1980). *Diagnostic and Statistical Manual of Mental Disorder* (3rd ed.). Washington, D.C.: Author.

Cuber, J. F., & Haroff, P. B. (1963). The more total view: Relationships among men and women in the upper middle class. *Marriage and Family Therapy, 25*, 140-145.

Faust, D., & Miner, R. A. (1986). The empiricist and his new clothes: DSM-III in perspective. *American Journal of Psychiatry, 143* (8), 962-967.

Martin, P. (1976). *A Marital Therapy Manual.* New York: Brunner/Mazel.

Chapter 5

Basic Principles:
Process Elements of the
Intersystem Approach

Bea Hollander-Goldfein

INTRODUCTION

Psychotherapy is a structured interpersonal process. The fundamental *structural* elements were discussed in Chapter 3. This chapter will discuss the fundamental *process* elements that operate over the course of treatment. Simply stated, process is how therapy works. The process of therapy involves tracking the content verbalized by clients and the interactional dynamics manifested in their behavior. From these two sources of information, the therapist constructs a conceptualization of the interactional and intrapersonal dynamics, generates hypotheses about the etiology, role, and function of the presenting problems, and formulates a treatment strategy. However, as the word "process" implies, these functions are not static.

The therapist is constantly engaged in conceptualizing the case, generating hypotheses, and formulating treatment strategies. Therefore, in order to operate effectively, the therapeutic process should be fluid and open to feedback, flowing back and forth between therapist and clients. As clients reveal more about themselves, the therapist reformulates the case based on the emerging information. As the therapist implements a treatment strategy, the reactions of the couple provide feedback about its effectiveness. The new information is integrated into an evolving conceptualization of the case, and new hypotheses are formulated. The therapist may use this information to shift to another focus or a different level of intervention into the system.

This type of fluidity is essential to the Intersystem Approach because it enables the multifaceted and multidimensional nature of relationships and individuals to unfold and permits the therapist to probe each facet as it emerges. The metaphor of a diamond captures this experience. The appreciation of a diamond's beauty stems from the perception of the whole and its many facets. So too, the therapist must experience the diversity of the couple's experience in order to understand, join, and intervene.

OVERVIEW

The actual work of marital therapy rests on a number of fundamental principles, five of which will be discussed in this chapter: Evolution of the Therapeutic Agenda, Balance, Facilitating Communication, Modifying the System, and Heightening Affect. When working with a couple, the therapist must interact with, yet remain outside of the marital system. From this position, the therapist sustains leverage for change. The therapist's ability to work with the dysfunctional interactional dynamics is compromised if she or he is inducted into or triangulated by the system. While maintaining a position outside the system, the therapist needs to maintain a warm and empathic connection with the couple. In order to achieve this, the self of the therapist must be open and resonant to the interpersonal and intrapsychic processes unfolding in therapy.

In addition to the therapeutic posture vis-à-vis the couple system, the therapist needs to maintain a balanced posture vis-à-vis the individual partners. Balance is an essential principle of conjoint marital therapy. It stems from a conceptualization of a case that incorporates assessments of individual and joint responsibility for the dysfunctional relationship. The interactions of the therapist with each partner should be equidistant and equally aligned. By keeping the interactional process in constant focus and working with each partner's contribution to the ongoing problems, the therapist achieves the balance that is essential to systemic change.

Working from a posture that is empathically connected to the couple, outside the system, and balanced between the partners enables the therapist to have a positive impact on the problems and dysfunctional patterns of the marriage. It is a basic principle of the Intersystem Approach that lasting change results from the modification of the processes occurring within the system; the resolution of problems on a content level is necessary but insufficient. Content serves as the vehicle for the modification of process.

There are two major process levels underlying the manifest content. These levels are: 1) patterns of verbal and nonverbal communication, and 2) emotional expression. Facilitating effective communication on cognitive, behavioral, and emotional levels is a powerful force in the change process.

EVOLUTION OF THE THERAPEUTIC AGENDA

The evolving therapeutic agenda is a fundamental aspect of the therapeutic process. The statement of the presenting problems represents one level of the couple's relationship. As stated in Chapter 3, the initial content shared with the therapist reflects the material that is most easily revealed, most accessible to consciousness, and most representative of the couple's rigidified view of their current reality. The difficulties that brought the couple into therapy are typically discussed before trust in the therapeutic relationship has been established. As therapy progresses, clients share deeper levels of their joint and individual experiences, revealing more facets of their relationship. The descriptions of problems are broadened, clarified, redefined, expanded upon, and sometimes changed. The therapeutic agenda is constantly evolving as part of this process. The following example illustrates this process.

> A couple complained about a total lack of communication. However, this did not seem accurate based on their interactions in sessions. They were given the directive to speak to each other only when necessary over the coming week and otherwise not to speak to each other. During the next session, the couple reported that the homework was very difficult. By complying, they were surprised to realize how much they actually did verbally communicate. They redefined the "presenting" problem as "how" they spoke to each other, and acknowledged that they had initially reported a distorted perception.

In this example, the couple redefined their problem and the focus of therapy as a consequence of changing perceptions and greater honesty fostered by the therapeutic process. Over the course of treatment, the definition of problems expanded and changed many times as they achieved deeper understanding of their interactional dynamics.

In many ways, both subtle and direct, the therapist challenges the couple's perceptions of their problems. The previous example describes how directives to enact the problematic behavior provide experiential feedback to the couple that their perceptions are inaccurate or incomplete. The reformulation of presenting problems can be described as recontextualization. This term accurately defines the process because it links the redefinition of a problem with the reevaluation of its meaning and function within the context of the relationship. The process of recontextualization begins even before the implementation of specific interventions in the problem areas. The therapist is influencing clients' views of their difficulties from the outset of therapy.

How problems are perceived and defined is crucial to the effectiveness of treatment strategies. When problems are viewed in exclusively negative and accusatory terms, it is difficult to facilitate movement. By blaming each other, the marital partners place the responsibility for change outside of themselves, that is, on the other partner and on the therapist. The rigidity of this position functions as a contributing factor in the dysfunctional marital system and serves to perpetuate the problems. In order to create a constructive therapeutic environment, the therapist must foster a shift from a position of blame to a position of joint responsibility . When blame is removed, there is less of a need for the partners to be adversarial and defensive. Therefore, the probability increases that each partner will make a personal investment in the therapeutic process for the sake of a more satisfying relationship.

If therapy is to be successful, the couple must broaden their view to include the context of the problem and its meaning in their relationship. An apparently withholding and uncaring partner may be frightened or hurt, may be protecting the partner from her or his anger, may be protecting self from being engulfed by the partner, etc. Whatever the "interpretation," the couple need a framework within which to adapt alternate views of their difficulties. As these views change through a deeper understanding of their current reality, the potential for change emerges and the therapist can then work with the individuals and their interactional system.

In the field of marital and family therapy, one strategy by which the therapist recontextualizes problems is called reframing. This strategy involves relabeling or redefining a perception of reality with the intention of giving it a slightly different and more constructive perspective. By reframing the meanings ascribed by clients to thoughts, feelings, behaviors, or situations, the therapist helps to create a problem definition that appears solvable (Haley, 1976; Watzlawick, 1978; Weeks & L'Abate, 1982).

The exploration of how the presenting problem operates within the marital system elucidates the role each partner plays in the interactional dynamics. With the aid of reframing, the therapist facilitates a process by which the couple can explore the complementarity within their relationship and the function served by the problem. As a context of joint responsibility and the culpability of interactional patterns are posited, the view of the problems is recontextualized by the couple. The focus shifts from "his" or "her" problem to "our" problem. This fundamental shift of focus, resulting from the couple recontextualizing the problem, is a powerful force for change.

In the following example, problem redefinition and deeper exploration of issues are described. The process took place over approximately one year. The evolving redefinition of the presenting problem and the shifting of focus between a number of interpersonal and intrapsychic issues were at points explicitly stated and at other points not explicitly stated until the couple could articulate for themselves their changing perspective.

> The couple stated that their presenting problem was the wife's recurring anxiety about the husband's potential involvement with another woman. This symptom was precipitated by an incident when their daughter overheard a telephone conversation between her father and a woman making arrangements to meet. The husband claimed that this was a playful conversation and that he had no intention of getting involved with someone else. His disclaimer did not allay his wife's anxiety.
>
> History taking revealed many unresolved issues in the marriage, which were due to ineffective communication in an otherwise strong and committed relationship. Most significant was the wife's intense unexpressed anger at her husband for not working, while she felt burdened with the financial support of the family in a very pressured job.
>
> Therapy initially focused on current conflicts related to the presenting problem. With a straightforward problem-solving strategy, they successfully negotiated resolutions to these conflicts. They felt relieved and encouraged by these small successes. Having experienced effective problem-solving communication, they could now shift the focus to the general issue of their ineffective communication.
>
> Their increased self-awareness, openness, and trust in the therapy made it possible to challenge a dictum that they had taken from a prior therapeutic involvement. The position they had adopted was to avoid conflict "at all cost" because of the negative impact of the husband's

temper. In this therapy, conflict was reframed as a necessary experience for the growth of their relationship. This concept was met with resistance, but was taken seriously because of the benefits already attained from direct communication.

The wife eventually began to express her stored-up anger at her husband for a 10-year-old role reversal. Shortly thereafter, the wife's anxiety dissipated. At this point, a connection between the wife's anxiety and the couple's conflict avoidance was articulated. This opened the door for both partners to express thoughts, feelings, and attitudes about the marriage, past and present.

The increased openness facilitated the expression of deeper emotional issues. From this work, they were able to say "I need you," both verbally and nonverbally. The wife's anxiety and husband's frustration could then be explored in the broader context of their entire relationship and family of origin messages about vulnerability, intimacy, and dependency. Once closer, more secure, and more caretaking of each other, the couple could argue about the role reversal in their marriage. In spite of several painful interactions, they each felt that the foundation of their relationship was stronger and more secure.

At this stage in the therapy, the couple returned to the problem of the husband's temper. They had progressed to a point where the angry outbursts had significantly decreased in frequency and duration, but their periodic recurrence would send the couple into a period of regression. Through the utilization of their improved communication skills, and based on the enhanced trust and openness in the marriage, the couple was able to discuss the angry outbursts.

The therapeutic task was to depersonalize the outbursts. It was acknowledged that the husband was struggling to bring them under control, but, until that time, they were reframed as "altered states." With this reframe of the problem, the wife was able to find a way not to take what was said personally and to stay in contact with her husband. They devised a strategy whereby she would signal him that he was in an "altered state," which was what he needed in order to regain control. The couple experienced the negotiation of a solution to this problem as a victory over a significant emotional wedge in their marriage.

The preliminary hypothesis, based on the information gathered during the evaluation stage, was that the anxiety reported by the wife, although precipitated by a real incident, was symptomatic of suppressed anger and that the husband was indirectly expressing the marital dissatisfactions of both partners. Although the problem was reframed in incremental steps, the couple did not articulate the redefinition of the problem as suppressed anger until the wife was able to express her anger directly in the session. Once experiencing the gains from effective communication of negative feelings, the couple could make their own connection between the symptom of anxiety and their unaddressed problems. The reader will note from this vignette how the problem was reconceptualized in stages timed to the couple's readiness to integrate the new and emerging view. It was only later in the therapeutic process that the redefinition of the presenting problem was made explicit. The seed for this perspective was planted during the intake session, when it was first proposed that perhaps the anxiety was a symptom of other problems in the marriage.

Problem redefinition and the evolution of the therapeutic agenda are processes that involve the shifting of content and areas of focus in the Intersystem Approach. No matter what content areas are being addressed in the ongoing sessions, the following process elements are operating and require the therapist to interact with the couple as a system, in order to maximize the potential for change.

BALANCE

Balance is a major therapeutic principle of conjoint marital therapy. Balance has two essential elements. The first prescribes that the therapist relate to and interact with both partners of the couple in a balanced way: understanding both, challenging both, speaking to both, inviting both, and involving both partners. This aspect of balance describes an interactional process between the therapist and the couple which is essential to building the therapeutic relationship and to the successful implementation of intervention strategies targeted to change the dysfunctional system. The therapist must achieve an alliance with the couple as a system, and maintain a constant focus on their interactional dynamics.

Successful balance of the interactions between therapist and clients has a strong impact on the "experience" of therapy. The therapist feels equally joined with the partners as individuals and as a couple. The discussion flows easily between the three participants, as the therapist is not bound by an unbalanced alliance with one partner. The clients experience therapy as a joint endeavor. Each partner feels heard, understood, and accepted. The therapist is perceived as fair, unbiased, and impartial, irrespective of the content and the particular issues addressed. During a recent termination session, the husband reported, "You were tough on me, but always fair." This is a great compliment for a marital therapist who has the difficult task of sustaining positive contact with two people who are in conflict with each other. The achievement of balance is a crucial element of effective marital therapy.

The second basic element of balance prescribes that the problem, issue, situation, dynamic, and process be viewed by the therapist in a systemic way. That is, the case must be conceptualized in terms of the contribution, input, and responsibility of both partners in association with each other. At whatever point in therapy, during whatever stage, within whatever interactional sequence, the therapist must maintain a balanced view of the couple's interactional dynamics and probe for the complementary piece of what is occurring or being described in the session. In the same way that the therapist engages the partners on a verbal interactional level by moving back and forth between them and probing for the other side of the experience, so too the thought processes of the therapist shift between the partners and across levels, probing for workable hypotheses and systemic conceptualizations of the case.

The two basic elements of balance are concurrent, interrelated processes. As the therapist interacts with clients and gleans more information about their interpersonal relationship and intrapsychic functioning, the data are integrated into an evolving conceptualization of the marital system, which then influences how the therapist will interact with the couple.

Sustaining balanced interaction in therapy raises the issue of timing and other fundamental questions. In clinical practice there is great variability in how systems therapists handle the timing of balance and the extent of engagement with the couple versus the individual partners. There is common agreement that overall balance is essential to systemic therapy, but there are differences of opinion on how this is to be attained. Approaches range from balancing the interaction with clients from moment to moment, to balance attained over a number of sessions.

Balancing from moment to moment requires the therapist to consistently engage the couple, either by requesting that the partners speak only to each other, or by probing each partner in quick succession about the issues being discussed. The therapist poses questions to the couple and interpretations are consistently framed in interactional terms. Balance attained over a number of sessions requires the therapist to sustain a broad perspective, but affords greater flexibility within a session. Questions and interpretations can be individual or couple focused, since balance is experienced over time. The therapist can engage with one partner, in order to deepen the understanding of a particular interactional or intrapsychic issue, and then shift to the other partner. The material explored by the partners individually in the context of conjoint sessions is then directed back to the couple for joint discussion. Rather than utilizing one consistent approach, most therapists integrate these divergent approaches and adapt their style to the demands of the case. Balance, like many other elements of the Intersystem Approach, is negotiated differently with each couple.

Sustaining a balanced view of the interactional dynamics of a case raises the issue of the extent to which the therapist needs to share the hypotheses and conceptualization of the case with the clients. Once again, there is great variability in clinical practice. Approaches range from explaining the therapist's thinking to the couple, in order to establish a common frame of reference, to intervening on a process level, in order to facilitate new experiences. Here again, most therapists will integrate the elements of these divergent approaches into a therapeutic style that best suits the case.

The previous case example demonstrates that there are varying ways to handle this issue, even within a case. There were times over the course of therapy when the systemic conceptualization of the problem was posed to the couple in order to establish a shared view of the problem. There were other times when change was fostered on a process level, and only then, after there was improvement in the problem area, was the understanding of the underlying dynamic articulated for the couple. How this is handled by the therapist will often depend on the couple's readiness to integrate alternate views of their relationship.

As change occurs, couples begin to view their relationship in a more balanced, equitable way and clients and therapists evolve toward a more congruent view of the interactional dynamics. No matter how much the nature of relationships and change processes can be verbalized on a cognitive level, there are still elements of relating and change that are beyond articulation, operating on unconscious, emotional, and nonverbal levels.

Loss of balance can have a deleterious effect on the therapeutic relationship and the effectiveness of change strategies. The experience of taking sides, allying with one partner and/or blaming the other, whether perceived by the clients or by the therapist, is a clear warning signal that there is an imbalance in the therapy. When treatment is stalemated, possible contributing factors include imbalances in the therapeutic process and/or in the conceptualization of the case. Often the imbalances are not apparent, prompting the therapist to experience the frustration of being stuck as stemming from a host of possible causes, including client resistance, ineffective change strategies, transference, countertransference, etc. These factors need to be carefully considered in conjunction with an exploration of a possible therapeutic imbalance. The therapist may not be equally joined with the partners of the couple and may be missing a critical element in the interactional system.

In order to regain balance, the therapist needs to realign with each partner and probe for the hidden element of the system. A blind spot in the therapist's conceptualization of the case may result from something as yet not revealed by the couple or not yet perceived by the therapist. Regaining balance requires a change in the therapeutic system that frees the therapist to probe for more information or to consider an alternate view of the couple dynamics.

FACILITATING COMMUNICATION

Whether or not on the list of presenting problems, communication is the essential interactional dynamic addressed in conjoint marital therapy. Early in treatment, a major task for the therapist is to direct the couple to speak to each other, not to or through the therapist. This process is crucial in order for the therapist to learn about and understand the marital system as it truly operates.

By speaking through the therapist, couples avoid addressing the systemic nature and emotional impact of their problems. This dynamic, termed triangulation, detours the emotional material away from the couple. Each partner sustains a safe distance from difficult issues by talking to the therapist about the problems as opposed to bringing their dysfunctional dynamics into their immediate experience of the session. Whether it is the clients who try to keep the therapist triangulated between them or the therapist who interacts with the couple in such a way as to be triangulated, the result is the same: no change.

Direct verbal communication between the partners brings the problems into the session and enables the therapist to intervene directly in the interactional system. Certainly, there is material that is appropriately communicated to the therapist, but once past the initial evaluation stage, more and more of the interactions should be occurring between the partners. Learning to remain separate from the couple's relational system while actively intervening to foster change in their process is the most difficult task for a systemic marital therapist. All of the principles discussed in this chapter are component parts of this task.

Before implementing specific treatment strategies which target the communication patterns of the couple, the therapist must evaluate the pattern of communication, that is, its role, function and meaning within the relationship. The assessment process involves the exploration of multiple levels of clinical material. What does verbal communication represent to the couple? Is it a means of sharing information,

engaging, or disengaging? Do the couple consider verbalization important, or do the partners assume that what they need to know about each
other should be intuited without words? How do the communication
patterns operate and how rigidly determined have they become? Do the
partners take on circumscribed roles, such as the devil's advocate, the
problem solver, the victim? To what extent are verbal dynamics based
on multigenerational relational patterns? Are emotions expressed directly or indirectly? How are other types of relationship problems
sustained by faulty communication? How are the personal needs of
each partner conveyed? Are the communication difficulties symptomatic of emotional blocks, or are they the result of skill deficits?
The answers to these probing questions and others inform the therapist
about the nature of marital communication and the specific aspects of
the verbal interchange that require intervention.

The evaluation of patterns of communication is conceptually similar
to the evaluation of presenting problems. The difference lies in the level
of focus. In the former case, the focus is on the verbal interactions
between the partners, while in the latter case the focus is on the verbal
content shared by the partners. In other words, the assessment of
communication patterns is primarily based not on what is said, but on
how it is said.

By directing the partners to speak to each other about a problem or
other content area, the therapist sets up an enactment of what occurs
when the couple attempts to discuss issues at home. It is to be expected
that the couple will exercise some measure of social monitoring in the
session. Nonetheless, the dysfunctional elements of the couple's communication style become apparent. Clinical experience reveals that no
matter how clients describe their communication style outside of therapy,
they cannot help but reveal their basic communication difficulties
when they present in session. Even with a set of socially approved
standards for verbal communication, most couples will fall back into
their habitual patterns of verbal interaction. Given latitude and time to
interact when asked to speak to each other, especially about emotionally
charged issues, couples will generally demonstrate their typical communication patterns. In addition, by using probing questions, the therapist can further explore with the clients how similar their in-session
communication style is to their communication style outside of session.

The exceptions to the therapeutic dynamic described above are couples with extreme forms of communication difficulties, for example,
couples who are verbally abusive versus those who are non-communi-
cative. The first such exception is the couple engaging in verbally

abusive forms of arguing. The extent of the actual verbal abuse that occurs at home may never be brought into session, either because of the couple's collusion to keep this embarrassing reflection of themselves secret from the therapist, or because of one partner's fear of the other partner's anger if the verbal abuse is exposed in therapy. Once the information is made available to the therapist, increased sensitivity to issues of timing, readiness, and potential retribution are crucially important.

Verbal abuse is usually difficult to handle therapeutically, especially if it is easily triggered and experienced as being out of control. However, it is often possible and helpful to utilize contracting as a means of facilitating more open communication of the real issues in session, while mitigating the verbal abuse that may follow. This situation requires creative problem solving. In one case, where the wife feared the hour-and-a-half barrage of blame, accusations, and cursing that occurred during the car ride home if she said anything in session that upset the husband, the couple was directed to be absolutely silent during this period of travel time. This allowed for an effective cooling off period. In another case, the partners themselves opted to go out to eat after sessions, knowing that they would avoid verbal confrontations in restaurants. In this case as well, the result was an effective cooling off period that served to circumvent the use of verbal abuse as a deterrent to honestly addressing the marital problems in therapy. By use of such creative problem solving, the therapist helps to create a safe environment for the couple to discuss their painful communication problems along with the other issues that brought them into therapy.

Along the same continuum is the case where the couple repeatedly engage in destructive arguing in session, almost as if the therapist does not exist. This pattern is counterproductive for the couple and sabotages the effective utilization of therapy. When faced with this situation, the therapist needs to actively intervene to assert her or his authority and to establish the therapeutic contract. Once again, creative solutions are necessary. In extreme cases, a rule could be imposed that the session will be terminated if the couple persist in their destructive arguing and remain unresponsive to therapeutic intervention. If the argumentative pattern is so rigidly set that the couple are unresponsive to intervention, a possible treatment strategy is the utilization of individual sessions to break the rigidified pattern. In less extreme cases, an effective approach is to purposefully detour discussion through the therapist until such time that the couple is better able to address the conflictual material in a more constructive fashion. The goals of this strategy are to: 1) disrupt the interactional system; 2) clarify the individual issues; 3) deepen the emotional material; and 4) model constructive communication. When this approach is successful, the therapist facilitates a process by which the couple can reengage in the emotional battle, but on a different basis that allows for movement and conflict resolution.

By using the self of the therapist as the channel of communication, control of the process can be regained and the devastating emotional impact of the persistent arguing can be modulated. The therapist should not use this procedure for conflict avoidance, but for the constructive modification of a destructive process. The task is to help the partners get in touch with the painful, needy feelings underlying the anger or rage. Once expressed within the relatively safe context of therapy, these feelings can be communicated directly between the partners.

Dealing with anger and conflict in marital therapy is a difficult and challenging task. For many marital therapists, anger is the most difficult affect to work with in therapy, as its presence in a session may trigger countertransference reactions that limit the effectiveness of the therapy. A therapist working with couples in conflict needs to work through her or his own issues about anger in order to work from a balanced therapeutic position with these cases. The therapeutic task in such a case is not to diminish the emotional intensity, but to broaden the emotional expression to include other salient emotions and to foster constructive expression of even the most rageful feelings so that the couple can achieve greater understanding of each other and resolution of emotional issues.

On the other end of the continuum is a situation where verbal communication between the couple is almost nonexistent. Here the therapist is working to create new behavior, not to change old behavior. This task requires a different therapeutic focus, which will be discussed in greater depth later. In therapy, the partners may demonstrate appropriate verbal communication and when directed to talk to each other they will comply. Taken at face value, it appears that the couple verbally communicates and that what is occurring in session is an enactment of what takes place generally. In fact, the session may be the only context in which the partners address these issues to each other. The therapist may never know the extent of the communication deficit unless she or he asks directly. If the verbal interchanges that occur in therapy do not generalize to the relationship outside of the session, the result is an illusion of change in a situation that is in fact at a therapeutic stalemate.

At another point along this continuum lies the more typical case. It is common for clients to report that they have already discussed a problem at home, implying that there is no need to rehash the incident in therapy. The therapist who concedes this point falls victim to a collusive process that protects the couple from exposing their ineffective communication, and allows the couple to remain at the level of talking *to* the therapist *about* what they had discussed with each other. The therapist needs to encourage the couple to reopen the conversation in the session. In so doing, the partners are helped to confront their communication difficulties and to understand the extent to which the issues between them remain unresolved. When partners are encouraged to bypass their resistance and readdress an issue in the session, new information emerges which takes the couple to another level of problem resolution. So much of what partners think they have said to each other, in fact, was never said out loud or communicated clearly.

Directing couples to speak to each other, as opposed to through the therapist, is a fundamental technique of all marital therapies. It accomplishes two important goals as described above. First, it provides essential information about couple dynamics and communication patterns for the therapist. Second, it actually recreates the conditions in which the partners are experiencing their relationship in the present, as opposed to just talking about it. This technique enables the therapist to impact at both process and content levels.

The content discussed in therapy may be more or less meaningful for the couple, but the tracking of process is always important for the therapist. The case of the "Yellow Tie" is a good example of the distinction made between content and process, that is, what is said versus how it is said.

> Lack of communication was the primary presenting problem of this couple. By the fourth session it was clear that the couple consistently blocked their communication, leaving issues, disagreements, and arguments unresolved. As a diagnostic and therapeutic strategy, during the fifth session the couple was assigned the task of finishing a "fight." The couple came in with an unfinished argument about whether or not the husband should wear a yellow tie after Labor Day.
>
> In the session, they blocked in their typical fashion, but at each point they were encouraged to go on until they were finished. The husband was encouraged to speak up for himself and modify his tendency to placate. The wife was encouraged to stay engaged and not retreat. On a content level the couple reached agreement about how to handle the wife's feedback about the husband's choice of wardrobe, instead of settling for their typical solution of withdrawal. On a process level they had the positive experience of resolving a conflict. The changes that began during this session were useful as the couple addressed more meaningful con-

tent over subsequent sessions. They experienced something different happening between them even though the content they were discussing was simply that of a "yellow tie."

Operationalizing the fundamental technique of having partners talk to each other varies according to the style of the therapist, the needs of the case, and the creative interface between the two. Some therapists foster more consistent engagement while others allow for more flexible movement back and forth between the couple talking to each other and talking to the therapist. These differences are based on the therapist's clinical judgment of what salient content and process issues need to be addressed through the couple versus through the therapist. The readiness of the couple to work in this fashion is an essential factor. The great variability among cases requires the therapist to be flexible and to work in the manner that is best suited for each couple. Irrespective of the variations in style that do exist, it is common in clinical experience that as treatment progresses there is an increasing proportion of time over sessions that the couple engages in direct dialogue with less and less therapeutic intervention.

The therapist's verbal instruction and nonverbal gestures socialize the couple to speak to each other. The sense of therapeutic movement stemming from direct contact between the partners becomes self-reinforcing. Therapy begins to flow when the therapist can direct the couple towards each other by a slight body movement. Clients often respond with humor as one partner talking to the therapist will shift to the other partner and instinctively change pronouns in response to a small gesture from the therapist that is clearly understood to mean "talk to each other." The therapy reaches a new stage when couples entering the office automatically readjust the chairs to face each other without prompting from the therapist.

In addition to timing and engagement, there is also variability in how therapists communicate these expectations to couples. Styles range from actively interventionist to passively facilitative, depending on the demands of the case and the personality of the therapist. An approach which combines both of these styles is to let couples go on for a period of time in their natural interchange and then to limit interventions to succinct directives or comments to either both partners or one partner. The interventions are not intended to direct the conversation back to the therapist, but to keep the interchange between the partners going while introducing elements of change. It is as if the therapist serves as an alter ego speaking into the ears of the partners, guiding the process while not engaging in it directly. This style is based on the intention to change the communication process while not disrupting the emotional momentum and the flow of content between the couple.

As this process unfolds, the clients hear the therapist and address the modified responses directly to the partner. The changes are experienced by the couple as part of their interactive process. Impacting upon the marital system while the couple is engaged in the system generates change that is experienced in the present on behavioral, cognitive, and emotional levels. When the therapeutic intervention is successful and fits the dynamics of the case, the change becomes self-reinforcing as each partner accommodates to the more effective pattern of communication. Change accomplished in this manner represents a fundamental shift in the system because it is based in the experience of the couple and not in a discussion about their experience. This process is the essential therapeutic principle of the Intersystemic Approach.

How couples communicate and their responses to the therapeutic attempts to modify verbal interactional behavior provide important information about the meaning and etiology of their communication difficulties. These data are crucial for the therapist in determining therapeutic strategy. It is never sufficient just to direct a couple to talk to each other. They are in a therapist's office because their communication has been dysfunctional. Working through the blocks that have made direct verbal communication difficult is an essential component of directing couples to engage.

Communication Strategies

There are many approaches to working with marital communication. Within the Intersystem Approach, the particular approach utilized with a case is geared to the needs of the clients and the style of the therapist. The options range from structured to unstructured techniques. The discussion of specific communication programs is outside the purview of this chapter. For more information about communication therapy, the reader is referred to Gottman, Notarius, Gonso, and Markman (1976), Hansen and L'Abate (1982), Levant (1984), and Nichols (1984).

Whatever communications approach is utilized, there are two basic therapeutic goals. One goal is to foster direct communication between the partners, which was discussed earlier; the other is to improve communication skills. Teaching the couple to talk to each other can occur within the context of skill building exercises incorporated in a structured program, or during the course of unstructured therapy. Both approaches can be equally effective, depending on the skill of the therapist. When the therapist is choosing a therapeutic approach and communication strategy, it is important to assess the couple's communication deficits. Different treatment strategies are utilized if the partners are deficient in skills as opposed to their being unable to utilize their skills due to rigidified patterns and emotional blocks.

Very often, by working through emotional barriers or interactional blocks, effective communication skills emerge. It is also the case that the utilization of structured communication exercises can serve to reveal underlying dysfunctional dynamics. The clinical judgment of the therapist, based on the evaluation of a case, determines which route will be most effective at differing points in the therapy. When basic communication skills are absent, the therapist must first help the couple learn the basic skills and then utilize them to address the marital problems. In most cases, the task of the therapist is to help couples utilize the skills they already have. Many apparent communication problems stem from sources other than lack of skill. The therapist must determine the therapeutic approach that has the greatest likelihood of addressing the level of the problem that provides the best leverage for change.

Communication techniques are not limited to traditional talking therapy. A powerful adjunct is the use of audiovisual aids. Playing back a segment of audiotape or videotape can accomplish more in five minutes than five sessions of unaided therapy. These adjuncts allow the clients to see themselves as they are viewed by others and to begin to view self more objectively. Most clients are surprised to watch or hear themselves communicate in ways they can clearly recognize as counterproductive, but were unable to perceive within the experience itself. Obviously, the use of audiovisual aids will depend on the readiness and willingness of the clients and, as with any other technique, should be used judiciously.

This technique is especially helpful with clients who resist feedback and do not perceive or take responsibility for their role in problematic interactions. It is also precisely this type of client who is most threatened by this approach. The therapist needs to prepare clients for audiovisual feedback, taking precautions to prevent the use of taped materials as an additional source of ammunition for blaming the other partner and further avoiding personal responsibility. When open to the personal feedback that audiovisual taping can offer, partners can learn a great deal about themselves and each other.

A modified version of this technique is to direct couples to tape verbal interactions at home and bring them into session. This assignment is often met with great reluctance and embarrassment. However, if the couple complies, much can be learned from this form of feedback. Clinical experience has shown that even if couples refuse to comply with this suggestion, there is sometimes an interesting phenomenon of spontaneous improvement. It seems that the threat of exposure stimulates a flight into health whereby couples begin to utilize more effective communication skills in order not to be embarrassed by the truth. Although the motivation is to avoid exposure, the resulting improvement is positively reinforcing and can lead to real change. In difficult cases the therapist is challenged to intervene creatively in order to break through persistent negative communication patterns.

> In this case, the husband engaged in persistent monologues of accusations, blame, recriminations, and demands for information after finding out that his wife had kept secret the fact that she had been sexually abused as a child. The wife was directed to write down the husband's statements verbatim. This served to slow down the process. The husband had to speak more slowly, which enabled him to gain perspective on how he was punishing his wife for keeping this terrible secret, thus victimizing her again. The wife could gain self-protection from the emotional onslaught by having the role of "recording secretary." After other therapeutic attempts had failed, this was the only technique that managed to arrest the emotional runaway of verbal assaults. The result was improved communication and a cessation of the husband's obsessive need to interrogate his wife and blame her for betraying him. The couple was then better able to utilize therapy.

In this case, therapy was stalemated because of a destructive pattern that was unresponsive to therapeutic intervention. The creative use of homework targeted the problematic communication pattern in such a way as to slow down and change the process. Thereby, the partners were able to experience their roles in the patterns differently, facilitating the emergence of a more constructive communication pattern. Once this occurred, the issues were addressed more directly and effectively. By creating a different experience, the couple could move beyond their rigidified pattern of interaction. By changing the process, the therapist enabled the couple to more effectively address their problems on a content level.

MODIFYING THE SYSTEM

In each of the preceding sections, the organizing principle of working with the relational system was examined from various vantage points. This section looks at the relational system of the couple as the focus of change. The field abounds in theoretical frameworks and treatment approaches for working with couples. However, the ultimate purpose of the techniques and strategies utilized in conjoint therapy is to bring about change in the fundamental dynamics of the relationship.

Changing the nature of a relationship is no small task. It requires both problem resolution and system modification. Problem resolution refers to the effectiveness of treatment strategies that target specific aspects of the marital relationship. These strategies include facilitating communication, restructuring cognition, expressing affect, modifying behavior, negotiating conflict, fostering trust, clarifying family of origin issues, and other change processes. Change due to problem resolution is conceptualized as the cumulative effect of improvements in specific aspects of the relationship on the couple's experience of satisfaction in the marriage. Symbolically, this change can be depicted by the equation, $1 + 1 = 2$. This indicates that the resolution of any two problems has an additive effect on the experience of satisfaction in the marriage.

System modification refers to the effectiveness of treatment strategies that target the fundamental dynamics of the relationship. The treatment strategies are the same as those outlined above, but the therapeutic goals are different. Instead of targeting a problematic aspect of the relationship, the target is the very nature of the relationship itself. The goals are to modify the basic functioning of the relational system and to establish new ways of relating. Change due to system modification is conceptualized as a profound shift in the relationship. Symbolically, this can be represented by the equation, $1 + 1 = 3$. This indicates that the modification of the interactional dynamics plus the establishment of new ways of relating yields a profoundly different experience of the marriage.

In other words, the principle derived from systems theory that the whole is greater than the sum of its parts is applicable to the conceptualization of change. Systemic change yields positive effects that reverberate throughout the relational system. When the fundamental dynamics of a relationship are modified, the blocked potential of the couple to grow, learn, and change is released. The powerful effects of systemic change make it unnecessary for therapy to address each and every problem area. By targeting key relational dynamics, the therapist maximizes the leverage for change in broad areas of the relationship. The modified system will then take on "a life of its own," continuing to evolve and change (Watzlawick, Weakland, & Fisch, 1974; Weeks & L'Abate, 1982), as in the case below.

In this case, the wife was raised by an overbearing, intrusive mother, and the husband grew up in a large, impersonal family. Before the couple's presenting problem of inhibited sexual desire could be addressed, their ineffective communication required therapeutic intervention. After experiencing the benefits of improved communication the couple reported their sense that they could never again react to each other in their old ways, thereby laying the foundation for continued change. On one level, the change came about because the partners learned to communicate directly, but, more to the point, the dynamics maintaining the dysfunctional patterns had been resolved, modified, redirected, and changed. Their new style of relating felt so comfortable and positive that it became a new level of organization for the couple system. Their response set of avoidance was successfully replaced with the response set of connection.

In a telling segment of a therapy session, when the therapist intervened prematurely, the wife indicated that she wanted to hear from her husband not the therapist. Recalling that this woman had not been able to express her feelings openly, much less address her husband directly, without going through the therapist, the profound nature of the change is quite apparent. Yet, even more importantly, the systemic change provided the basis for growth in other areas of their relationship.

System modification and problem resolution are concurrent processes that complement each other. The progress that couples experience in addressing their problems creates a fertile environment for systemic change, while the modification of relational dynamics enables couples to more effectively resolve their difficulties. These processes operate on different levels — system modification focuses primarily on the process level and problem resolution focuses primarily on the content level. As explained in Chapter 3, tracking cases on content and process levels is a necessary skill for the intersystemic therapist. From the description of problems on a content level, the therapist gleans an understanding of the interactional patterns. The first step towards modifying the system is to conceptualize how the relationship operates and why it operates in the ways that it does. Based on this conceptualization of a case, the therapist intervenes directly or indirectly to "push" the system towards change.

In most marital therapy cases, the partners present as polarized, their interactional patterns involving extreme positions. In order to modify the system, the therapist is faced with the challenge of enabling the couple to achieve a healthy balance. Some approaches advocate bridging the gap by bringing couples together. Other approaches advocate an intensification of the polarization in order to foster a paradoxical effect of rebalancing the couple. Whatever the approach, finding the balance is essential. Conflict avoiders need to fight, overcommunicators need introspection, hard workers need vacations, the serious need fun, the easygoing need anger, and saints need to fall from grace.

While polarized marital relationships present the therapist with a clear-cut therapeutic task, these cases are often the most difficult to work with because of the rigidity of the system. When the attempt to modify the system and rebalance the couple is successful, the theoretical basis of the Intersystem Approach is translated into a powerful therapeutic experience for the clients and therapist. It is a profound experience to watch a system unfold in response to intervention strategies that target the fundamental nature of the relationship. The vignette that follows attempts to describe the essence of the systemic change that occurred for the couple. The couple initiated therapy at the brink of separation. Their hard work and commitment to the therapeutic process enabled them to rebuild a satisfying marriage, based on the new way of relating to each other that emerged.

> A couple reporting inhibited sexual desire as their primary complaint initiated treatment seeking a straightforward cure for what they viewed as a clearly defined problem. The husband was dynamic, talkative, somewhat controlling, and critical. The wife, who matched her husband as a dynamic person, would uncharacteristically retreat in response to her husband's criticisms. The husband raged outwardly at her withdrawal, while she raged inwardly at his attempts to intimidate her. His anger, insecurity, and disappointments seemed to be related to his use of sexual expression as a means of making contact. Her internalized anger had the effect of shutting down her sexual interest. Because of these underlying dynamics, traditional sex therapy approaches were ineffective and the stalemate seemed interminable, bringing the couple to the brink of separation.
>
> A significant shift occurred when the husband cried for the first time in a session when talking about the isolation and pain of his childhood. Once she was able to experience her husband's anger as stemming from his own vulnerability rather than from her real and perceived inadequacies, the wife could free herself of the prison of her own childhood created by the violent warfare of her parents' destructive marriage. As she emerged from her withdrawal, she experienced greater entitlement to express her anger directly and set her own limits. The husband, experiencing this change as the contact he so desperately needed, became less angry and less obsessed with the sexual relationship. The wife, experiencing greater validation for herself as a person, became more angry and more expressive sexually. Once this balance was achieved, the sexual relationship

blossomed, the wife pursued her life-long goal of going to art school, instead of just keeping house, and the husband felt that he was finally able to make a relationship work after two failed marriages.

The couple experienced a new way of relating to each other. The changes in the interactional system were first initiated in the therapy sessions, then generalized to the ways they related to each other outside of the therapeutic context. The changes were profound and meaningful, enabling the couple to resolve their presenting problems, affirm their marriage, and move on in their lives. Toward the end of therapy, the couple reported that the relationship "would never be the same."

HEIGHTENING AFFECT

The importance of emotion in marital therapy would seem obvious since the feelings of love, intimacy, trust, satisfaction, and happiness are fundamental to the therapeutic agenda. But, as evidenced by the writings in the field, it is not obvious. It has only been in the past five years that the role of affect in psychotherapy in general and in marital therapy in particular has received increased attention (Fincham & O'Leary, 1982; Greenberg & Johnson, 1986a, 1986b, 1986c; Greenberg & Safran, 1984a, 1984b; Johnson & Greenberg, 1987; Margolin & Weinstein, 1983). Still, in most accounts of therapeutic approaches, the utilization and intensification of affect in marital therapy have been largely ignored. This omission is unfortunate in light of the role emotion plays as a powerful force for change. It is for this reason that the therapeutic use of emotion receives special attention in this chapter.

While varying models of marital therapy differ in their emphasis on behavior, emotion, or cognition as the primary target of therapeutic intervention, the Intersystem Approach considers these modes of relating as equally important and interconnected. It is the premise of this chapter that it is the synergistic effect of modifying behavior, evoking emotion, and restructuring cognition that serves to maximize change. A change in one mode sets off a chain reaction that affects other levels of the relational system. When choosing a treatment strategy, the therapist needs to assess which of these three basic modes of human functioning would be most amenable to intervention. An intervention that targets change on a behavioral level will invariably influence cognition and emotion. Of course, the reciprocal is also true. Heightening the emotional intensity of a couple's interactions breaks through the rigidity of the emotional system, much as directing behavioral change breaks through the rigidity of the behavioral system. Therefore, the Intersystem

Approach necessitates conceptualization of the emotional life of a couple as an integral part of their relational system.

The therapist is *always* impacting on the emotional relationship of the couple. The implementation of the basic principles described in this chapter results directly or indirectly in the intensification of affect. Moreover, the principle of heightening affect is actually an extension of the two preceding principles, facilitating communication and modifying the system. Although separated into three discrete principles for the sake of discussion, these are overlapping functions, which often occur simultaneously during stages of the therapeutic process. By operationalizing these principles, the therapist facilitates a process that shifts the couple away from talking about their feelings towards experiencing their feelings in the session. The intensity created by these techniques brings the couple to a heightened state of emotional arousal that fosters experiential change. Neglecting this element of the couple's relational dynamics closes off an important avenue for growth. Conversely, when one works with affect, the emotional connection between the partners can be directly explored.

The complex and multidimensional nature of emotion necessitates that the therapist develop a conceptual framework regarding the nature and function of affective expression. The objective of heightening affect is not ventilation, nor is it catharsis. The goal, as for all of the principles discussed in this chapter, is change in the relational system. The theoretical model of Greenberg and Johnson (1986a; 1986c) describes emotion as a relational dynamic that serves to connect people with objects in their environment. Based on this conceptualization of emotion as action tendencies and relationship mediators, the rationale for eliciting and redirecting emotional expression in marital therapy is even more compelling.

A brief review of the model proposed by Greenberg and Johnson (1986a; 1986c) will serve as a framework for the discussion of the role of emotion in the Intersystem Approach. They divide emotions into three categories: primary, secondary, and instrumental. Primary emotions are the deeper biologically adaptive feelings that form the bonds of human relationships (e.g., need for closeness). Secondary emotional states are typically defensive coping strategies (e.g., anger when the need for closeness is frustrated). Instrumental emotions serve an interpersonal function and are used to influence the reactions of other people. They are manipulative in nature and are often expressed as roles (e.g., being helpless in order to get one's needs met).

It is important to integrate an understanding of these divergent emotional states in order to determine which emotional material to elicit in therapy and how to intervene. The experience and expression of primary emotions are the major objectives of heightening affect. These feelings form the foundation upon which the partners, as individuals, experience their world, and, as spouses, experience their marriage. When the affective relationship is highlighted, the emotions that bring the partners together and those that drive them apart are brought into conscious awareness. The direct expression of these emotions enables the couple to confront the true nature of their relationship.

Primary emotions are usually not fully in awareness when clients initiate therapy. Because these feelings trigger deeply imbedded vulnerability, there is a great need in couples to prevent them from entering consciousness. The psychological mechanisms that keep these emotions out of awareness serve to maintain the dysfunctional system (e.g., blaming, denial, and projection instead of expressing needs). When the couple are able to "get in touch" with these feelings (i.e., bring them into conscious awareness and express them in the context of the session), a reorganization of the emotional system of the couple can occur. The process of evoking and expressing primary emotions enables the couple to empathize with each other. Empathy leads to greater understanding, positive reactions, and increased responsiveness to each other's needs.

Heightening the affect enables the couple to "engage," develop trust, and feel close in ways that few other treatment strategies can achieve. The heightening of affect in the session, by helping couples get in touch with their primary emotions, is experienced as intense, real, and "moving." Moving refers to being touched by the other person in such a way that a new mode of relating emerges. Movement in other areas results from the release of positive forces that were constrained by the unacknowledged emotions and the rigidified system that was set up to protect the partners from their emotional vulnerability.

Progress is gauged by the constructive processes utilized to reach an understanding of the relationship and its ultimate course, not by the ultimate disposition of the relationship. By accessing and expressing deeper emotion, clients achieve a better understanding of self, other, and the relationship. As a result, couples experience either an affirmation of their relationship, which leads to productive resolution of their difficulties, or a negation of the relationship, which leads to the decision to break up. Either outcome may be considered successful if the partners have been engaged in the constructive process of accessing and expressing their deeper emotions.

Secondary emotions are usually conscious to clients and are most typically the feelings expressed during the early stage of treatment. These feelings may also serve as defensive coping strategies and therefore represent the emotional states that fuel dysfunctional interactional systems. The intense emotions that result from the frustration of personal needs (e.g., anger, resentment, guilt, jealousy, fear, anxiety) serve to polarize the couple by maintaining the cycle of blame. Although secondary emotions serve a negative function in the life of the couple, these feelings constitute the partners' experience of their relationship when they enter therapy. Clients need to ventilate these emotions in order to be heard, understood, and supported by the therapist. The therapist needs to validate the couple's feelings in order to join and form a working alliance. Therapy provides the safe environment in which the therapist helps the couple move beyond their secondary emotions toward greater awareness and expression of their primary emotions.

Instrumental emotions are expressed through the roles that spouses assume in their marriages. The roles function as fixed elements of the dysfunctional system. It is as if each partner has a script to follow that determines how she or he will behave in the relationship. The expression of instrumental emotions by one partner is intended to manipulate the other into taking care of her or his needs. This manipulation does not occur through direct communication, but by means of the enactment of circumscribed roles. An example would be the attempt to fulfill the emotional need for intimacy by playing the role of helpless victim to one's partner's role of caretaker. The couple draw closer to each other through the enactment of their roles, but the result is only pseudo-intimacy because the partners are not relating to each other as whole human beings.

Exploration of the roles which characterize the marital relationship facilitates the expression of instrumental emotions, which in turn are probed to elicit the expression of the underlying primary emotions. Through this process of exploration of the previously mentioned "helpless victim-caretaker" dynamic, the partners would gain insight into how one partner uses feelings of helplessness and dependency to trigger the other partner's feelings of competency and counterdependency in order to establish intimacy. Fear of abandonment may be the underlying primary emotion that drives each partner to keep the other in close contact. Unfortunately, the fear of abandonment stemming from family of origin experiences cannot be assuaged by emotional manipulation. Only by drawing the underlying fear into conscious awareness can the couple express their emotional needs directly and learn to take care of each other.

Evoking primary emotions varies in difficulty depending on the dynamics of the case and the level of integration of each of the partners. Probing questions can be very effective in the exploration of underlying feelings when coupled with the directive for the partners to speak to each other. The intensification of affect is a natural outgrowth of the convergence of these intervention strategies. The heightened affect experienced in the session brings feelings into greater awareness and creates internal pressure to express them. As the therapist intervenes to increase the level of intensity, the couple are compelled to engage emotionally. There is a variety of techniques that can be utilized to "shake up" the system and evoke deeper emotions. These include reframing, paradoxical prescriptions, strategic "no change" messages, role playing, gestalt exercises, and others. The evocation of primary emotion through the utilization of techniques which heighten affect brings the emotional life of the relationship into the therapeutic domain.

Once again, the case of the "yellow tie" earlier in this chapter illustrated the powerful effect that heightening affect through engagement can have on the relational system. An entire session was spent encouraging the couple to finish the argument about the yellow tie, instead of acting out their characteristic pattern of withdrawal. The rationale for this approach stemmed from the hypothesis that the conflict over the tie was symbolic of the deeper struggle between autonomy and connection. The reenactment of the argument was utilized as a conduit for exploring their underlying dynamics. The content of the argument was not important. The focus was to keep the couple engaged. The directive to finish the fight in the session, along with the implementation of interventions that succeeded in helping the couple resolve the conflict, generated a high level of emotional intensity. The heightening of affect forced the expression of anger, resentment, hurt, and fear as each partner's attempt to withdraw was frustrated by the therapist's insistence that they remain engaged. By repeatedly complying with the therapeutic demand for engagement over the course of therapy, the couple were able to adopt a new way of relating to each other. The changes on the behavioral and emotional levels of the relationship enabled them to engage more naturally and more spontaneously. Eventually, it became easier and more satisfying for the couple to explore the remaining issues in the marriage.

When a couple's resistance, vulnerability, and rigidity are too great to effect change in the present, the therapist must take a detour to find another way to access the underlying emotional dynamics of the relationship. An effective approach under these circumstances is to focus the content on family of origin material, which serves to diffuse the vulnerability experienced in the current relationship. By exploring the emotional experiences of childhood, clients can often be less defensive and more open. When deep-seated emotional reactions from the past can be addressed on a personal level within the context of couple sessions, it becomes less threatening to make the connection between the past and the same emotions that are operating in the current relationship. The impasses previously sustained by the expression of secondary (defensive) emotions can be removed by the direct expression of primary emotions.

Heightening affect is often the only approach capable of breaking through emotional barriers. Accordingly, it is the most difficult change process to effect in marital therapy, because of the intangible nature of emotion and the perceived threat to self and other. It is common to hear clients express their concern that emotional expression will hurt their partner, make things worse, or reveal weakness. These statements are made even when the relationship is already in serious trouble, or the couple are already hurting each other in so many different ways. If the therapist accepts these rationales out of her or his own need to protect and be protected, a collusion against affective expression may develop that leads to a therapeutic stalemate. By its very nature, successful intervention on this level is harder to attain and requires greater emotional availability and vulnerability on the part of clients and therapist than do other approaches. The intensity can be very great, but the emotional "heat" can melt a system frozen by its own inertia and forge new ways of relating.

The emotionally volatile cases described in the section on facilitating communication would seem to demand an approach that constrains affect. While this is true insofar as the therapist must manage the affect in order to maintain control of the therapy and modify destructive interchanges, it is still an essential task of the therapist to facilitate the constructive expression of emotion. The goal, therefore, is not the constraint of emotional expression, but the constraint of the destructive use of emotion. It is still the therapist's task to foster the direct expression of primary emotions, including anger, in order to bring the couple to greater mutual understanding and increased interpersonal contact.

Heightening affect is mediated by the level of intensity experienced between the therapist and the couple. The therapist needs to be direct and focused in the attempt to access deeper feelings and needs to circumvent the use of content as a distraction. A question asked intently and then repeated to deepen the answer increases emotional intensity. A statement made slowly and softly draws attention to the emotional message. Asking partners to repeat emotionally laden interchanges brings their emotional experiences into greater awareness. The therapist can coach, guide, and, by taking on the role of alter ego, rephrase client content messages into emotional messages.

A very powerful technique involves rephrasing a statement for a client with the emotion that the statement intends to convey. The therapist fosters congruence between the content and emotion of what is being said by then directing the partners to repeat these statements to each other with the appropriate feeling. If the partners achieve emotional congruence in their direct communications, the interactional system shifts in response to this new mode of relating. The impact of this shift then generates changes in behavior and cognition that reinforce the improved emotional communication. It is striking how often couples begin to utilize their latent skills for constructive interaction once an emotional barrier has been bridged.

In order to heighten affect, something different is required of the therapist than is typically required by the utilization of other techniques. The self of the therapist must always be present as a feeling human being, "in touch" with her or his own emotional experiences. This requires self-awareness, comfort with strong affect, and the resolution of personal barriers to the expression of emotion. The therapist needs to move closer to the couple in order to resonate with the clients' emotions.

By intensifying the emotional interaction between the partners, the therapist can push the couple over their emotional threshold. This intensification of affect may trigger fears of vulnerability. Therefore, it is essential that the therapist create a safe environment, convey confidence in the usefulness of affective expression, and work with the emotional intensity to bring the couple to a different experience of themselves. The treatment strategy involves raising the emotional thermostat, but it can go only as high as the therapist can bear. A therapist's emotional block can inadvertently block the couple. Clients will often conceal their emerging emotions when they sense the therapist's discomfort. The therapist's confidence in handling the emotional intensity is necessary so that clients can take the risk of delving into their primary emotions and expressing them directly.

Implementing the approach outlined above represents, in its most basic form, the principle of therapist use of self. The therapist must be comfortable with a broad range of emotion, must join the couple without being inducted into the system, and must sustain an observing piece of the self that monitors and guides the emotional expression on a constructive course. This is a difficult skill to master and confronts the therapist with her or his own unresolved issues. When applied appropriately and sensitively, heightening affect serves to maximize the effectiveness of other treatment approaches. The direct expression of emotion creates a fertile environment for experiential learning and growth.

INTEGRATION

Dissecting the therapeutic process in order to expose the basic principles of the Intersystem Approach has been a challenging task. In order to present the principles clearly, it was necessary to highlight particular elements while relegating other elements to the background. The experience was reminiscent of Gestalt images, whereby figure and ground shift to reveal differing percepts. While this is a necessary approach when analyzing multidimensional processes, it conveys, by its very nature, an unrealistic picture of actual therapy. The basic principles discussed in this chapter are not discrete constructs. They are interconnected and operate synergistically. Similarly, the clinical material for the case examples was distilled in order to present the aspects of the case that were most illustrative of the principle being discussed. The other aspects of the case were not addressed for the sake of brevity and clarity. The result is the inevitable simplification of a complex human process.

In order to gain a better understanding of therapeutic components, the chapter has broken the whole down into its parts. Integrating the information from this chapter into an effective therapeutic style requires the reconstruction of the parts back into the whole. A three dimensional model was devised in order to aid the reader in conceptualizing the therapeutic focus of the Intersystem Approach (see Figure 5.1).

The model is based on three dimensions that comprise common elements between therapeutic interventions. Treatment strategies, which are operationalized through a series of interventions, have a time orientation, either past, present, or future, focus on either content or process, and address a mode of functioning, either behavior, emotion, or cognition. Each block in the model represents an intersection between the elements of each dimension. The diagram makes it feasible to schematically describe the level of the system targeted by therapist interventions. It also allows one to visualize the impact that treatment strategies can have on other levels of the system.

Three blocks of the model have been offset in order to illustrate how the basic principles target varying aspects of the therapeutic domain.

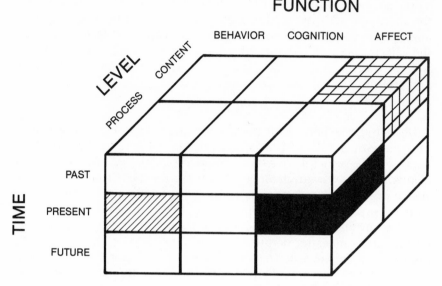

Figure 5.1. Three-dimensional model of therapeutic focus.

For example, the shaded block represents the operationalization of the principle of heightening affect. From the three dimensional view, the shaded block indicates that the therapist is targeting the emotional relationship of the couple, by focusing on the present, and intervening on the process level. A representation of the approach of facilitating the expression of emotion by focusing on family of origin material is depicted by the block filled in by checkerboard lines. This block indicates that the therapist is targeting the emotional experiences of the partners (AFFECT) by focusing on family of origin material (PAST) and interacting with the couple on a content level (CONTENT) (see example on page 89).

In contrast, the directive to talk to each other while the therapist attempts to modify the couple's behavior is represented by the block with diagonal lines. The case of the yellow tie is a perfect example (see page 98). The couple were directed to talk to each other and finish the fight (PROCESS) that was left unresolved from the morning (PRESENT) while the therapist intervened to keep them engaged and to facilitate communication (BEHAVIOR).

The reader will note that the distinction between individual, interactional, and intergenerational foci is not depicted on the model. This is partially due to the practical limitations of graphic representation. The predominant reason for leaving out this distinction is based on the premise that all interventions are ultimately aimed at relational systems. The blocks, although drawn with solid lines, should be conceptualized as having semipermeable boundaries. A particular therapeutic focus characterized by a time dimension, level of intervention, and targeted mode of functioning is simultaneously affecting other aspects of the system. The therapist, while working with one part of the system, must sustain a view of the whole. This skill becomes second nature to a systems therapist who keeps the whole and its parts constantly in view.

The transition from an individual to a systems orientation, from a linear to a circular model, and from content to process focus occurs as therapists immerse themselves in this type of therapy. Training programs provide the didactic and supervisory input that facilitates this process, but they cannot make the transition happen. The shift is experiential and occurs through the work with clients. Once the systemic perspective "clicks in," therapists report a dramatic change in their frame of reference. Similar to the couple who report that they can never go back to the old way of relating, the systems therapist can never go back to a linear, unidimensional approach to therapy. It is like a window to the human experience that, once open, can never again be shut.

The model represents the entire domain of therapy. The process of therapy is a journey through various levels as the therapist and couple work together to discover the roads to change. The sequential movement from one aspect of the relationship to another builds a momentum for change that profoundly affects the interactional patterns. The resulting sense of movement and growth is based partially on therapeutic intervention and partially on the emergence of strengths in the couple that were blocked from expression by the dysfunctional system.

The shifting focus of the therapeutic process can be tracked by use of this model. It can be a useful tool in the integration process, enabling the therapist to shift percepts while sustaining the view of the therapeutic whole and its component parts.

SUMMARY

The multifaceted nature of human experience and the multidimensional impact of therapeutic intervention are presented as the overarching framework of the Intersystem Approach. The task of a therapist working within the Intersystem Approach involves viewing a problem within the broad context of its many etiologies, choosing techniques that impact on many levels, and fluidly shifting when the optimal opening for change presents itself. The effectiveness of this approach is based on the therapist's skill and the development of a strong therapeutic relationship. Bonding with clients and the sensitive utilization of self are essential to this therapy because the therapist must truly "know" the couple before embarking on a therapeutic direction and must be emotionally available in order to intervene on a process level.

The basic principles, described in this chapter, comprise the fundamental process elements of the Intersystem Approach. The process elements address the question of how. The structure established during the initial stage of therapy forms the foundation upon which the therapist and clients proceed to the working stage. The work of therapy involves simultaneous intervention on both the content and process levels of a couple's relationship. The ultimate goal is modification of the system so that problems can be overcome and the potential of the couple maximized for growth and change. The basic principles of the treatment process include the evolution of the agenda, sustaining balance, facilitating communication, modifying the system, and heightening affect.

The therapeutic agenda evolves over time as trust increases, more information emerges, presenting problems are reformulated, and attempts to intervene on one level reveal blocks to growth that exist on other levels. The therapist serves as a guide in the process of broadening and deepening the issues addressed in therapy. There needs to be a mind open to the emerging clinical material and a flexibility of approach that enables the therapist to shift focus and take advantage of alternate paths in the change process.

Engaging the couple in a working alliance requires balance in the therapeutic relationship. The basic principle of balance applies to two levels of therapy. On the level of the relationship, the therapist needs to sustain a position that is equally aligned and equidistant with each partner. In this way, the therapist conveys empathy and understanding to each partner, while sustaining a primary commitment to the marital relationship. The task of the therapist is to be available and involved, while separate from the system. From this position, the therapist can promote change while avoiding induction into the dynamics of the relationship.

On the level of case formulation, the therapist needs to sustain a balanced view of the interactional dynamics. Whatever content, issue, or problem is being addressed, the therapist needs to develop a conceptual framework that accounts for both intrapsychic and interactional dynamics. This involves an understanding of the individual contribution to the problems and the role each partner plays in maintaining the problems. Balance in the therapeutic relationship enables the therapist to have leverage when working with a relational system. A balanced conceptualization of the case enables the therapist to engage the couple in terms of their joint responsibility for change.

Communication is the primary focus of marital therapy and the task of the therapist is the facilitation of communication. The basic operating principle is to foster direct verbal and nonverbal interchanges between the partners. The goal is the enactment of the relationship dynamics in the session, not the impersonal reporting of dynamics. When a couple experience their relationship in the session, it becomes feasible to directly influence their interactional style. The therapist is then able to facilitate communication, modify behavior, heighten affect, and restructure cognition within the immediate experience of the couple's relationship. Saying what needs to be said, in an effective way on an emotional level that is congruent and real, can have a profound effect on a couple.

The three modes of functioning, emotion, behavior, and cognition, are all targets of therapeutic intervention. Change in one mode of functioning will impact on the other two, thus setting off a chain reaction. The choice of which mode to address will depend on the therapist's assessment of where the best leverage for change lies for a particular couple. Heightening affect is a powerful therapeutic technique. The emotional intensity created by this technique brings the couple to a heightened state of arousal that fosters experiential change on the emotional, behavioral, and cognitive levels of the relationship.

Modifying the relational system is the essential task of couple therapy. Change achieved in this way is enduring, as couples begin to relate in a new satisfying way that becomes self-reinforcing. The therapeutic task is finished when presenting problems have been resolved, when related problems have been overcome, and when the relational dynamics are no longer stuck in the old destructive patterns. The healthy, satisfying patterns that emerge allow for closeness, mutual accommodation, affective expression, and adaptation to changing circumstances. Positive outcome stems not from what a therapist does with a couple, but from the change processes that the therapist sets in motion.

REFERENCES

Fincham, F., & O'Leary, K. D. (1982, August). *Affect in the Eighties: A New Direction in Behavioral Marital Therapy.* Paper presented at the 90th Annual Convention of the American Psychological Association, Washington, D.C.

Gottman, J., Notarius, C., Gonso, J., & Markman, H. (1976). *A Couple's Guide to Communication.* Champaign, IL: Research Press.

Greenberg, L. S., & Johnson, S. M. (1986a). Affect in marital therapy. *Journal of Marital and Family Therapy, 12,* 1-10.

Greenberg, L. S., & Johnson, S. M. (1986b). Emotionally focused couples therapy: An integrated affective systemic approach. In N. S. Jacobson & A. S. Gurman (Eds.), *The Clinical Handbook of Marital Therapy.* New York: Guilford.

Greenberg, L. S., & Johnson, S. M. (1986c). When to evoke emotion and why: Process diagnosis in couples therapy. *The Journal of Marital and Family Therapy, 12,* 19-24.

Greenberg, L. S., & Safran, J. D. (1984a). Hot cognition: Emotion coming in from the cold. A reply to Tachman & Mahoney. *Cognitive Therapy and Research, 8,* 591-598.

Greenberg, L. S., & Safran, J. D. (1984b). Integrating affect and cognition: A perspective on therapeutic change. *Cognitive Therapy and Research, 8,* 559-578.

Haley, J. (1976). *Problem Solving Therapy.* San Francisco: Jossey-Bass.

Hansen, J. C., & L'Abate, L. (1982). *Approaches to Family Therapy.* New York: Macmillan.

Johnson, S. M., & Greenberg, L. S. (1987). Emotionally focused marital therapy: An overview. *Psychotherapy, 24,* 552-559.

Levant, R. F. (1984). *Family Therapy: A Comprehensive Overview.* Englewood Cliffs, NJ: Prentice-Hall.

Margolin, G., & Weinstein, C. D. (1983). The role of affect in behavioral therapy. In L. R. Wolberg & M. C. Aronson (Eds.), *Group and Family Therapy.* New York: Brunner/Mazel.

Nichols, M. P. (1984). *Family Therapy: Concepts and Methods.* New York: Gardner.

Watzlawick, P. (1978). *The Language of Change: Elements of Therapeutic Communication.* New York: Basic Books.

Watzlawick, P., Weakland, J., & Fisch, R. (1974). *Change: Principles of Problem Formation and Problem Resolution.* New York: Norton.

Weeks, G., & L'Abate, L. (1982). *Paradoxical Psychotherapy: Theory and Practice with Individuals, Couples and Families.* New York: Brunner/Mazel.

Chapter 6

Termination of Therapy

Richard N. Mack

Just as the beginning and middle phases of a course of therapy are appropriately governed by certain basic principles, so, too, is the end phase of the therapeutic process. Very little has been written concerning the termination phase of therapy. For the most part, that which has been written is directed toward the treatment of individuals. Since the thrust of this volume is directed toward treatment of the marital dyad from an integrated perspective, termination must also be explored in the same light.

The central focus in analytic and dynamic psychotherapy is the processing of the transferential relationship that develops between the client and the therapist. Successful treatment requires that constant attention be paid to this process. This transferential relationship continues to be the focus as each case develops into its termination phase. In the termination phase there still is much work to be done in order to appropriately end this intimate therapeutic relationship, particularly in the area of the client's feelings of rejection and abandonment.

The process of termination can be a lengthy one, including a period of regression in which the original symptomatology reappears, and painful associations are conjured up for both client and therapist. According to Kohut (1971), the client "recatheets once more his demands for the incestuous transference objects before he finally resigns himself to the fact that they are indeed unobtainable" (p. 94). The termination of the treatment becomes much like the weaning of a child (Strean, 1985) in which the client resists the requirements of independence and autonomy, and attempts to return to the care of the transitional object — in this case, the therapist. For the therapist there exist the same parental feelings evidenced in weaning — desire to complete the process, frustration at the difficulty that it entails, and pride in completion of the process.

When viewing the termination of a couple from therapy from a systemic perspective, the above issues are not clearly focused. The transference issues tend to be diffused through both partners, thus making them less a concern at the time of termination. Because of the more directive nature of marital therapy, reliance is placed on the couple earlier, and the couple is seen as the basic unit of ongoing work (Barnard, 1979). If the basic reliance in therapy has been on the strength of the marital dyad, termination becomes facilitated as this strength is mobilized at the conclusion of treatment. The couple carry within themselves a ready-made support network with which to deal more effectively with the feelings of rejection and/or abandonment which can still be a part of the end of therapy. The members of the dyad themselves have been the transitional objects needed for emotional health; they provide the basis for a smoother opportunity for termination.

APPROPRIATE TERMINATION

There are three criteria for appropriate termination from a systems perspective. They are: 1) when the chief complaint is taken care of; 2) when the clients have mobilized enough of their own resources to take care of the difficulty by themselves; and 3) when the concept of therapy as an "open door" has been understood (Gurman, 1981, p. 505).

One of the first tasks of therapy is to define clearly the goals of treatment. Termination appropriately occurs when the goals established for the therapy have been achieved. It is generally not the purpose of systemic treatment to shape individual personalities. Rather, the goal is to shift the system toward healthy, mutually satisfying interactions. When this goal has been accomplished, it is time for termination to take place.

Generalization of learnings gained during therapy is the key issue in successful termination for the couple in marital therapy (Barnard, 1979). Generalization is the ability of the couple to take learning from specific situations and raise it to a conceptual level which allows them to apply the concepts to other — different — situations which they may encounter in the course of their relationship.

In most cases the couple has come to the therapist as a result of a concern regarding a certain situation. It is not enough for the therapist to help the couple resolve the particular problem. In order for treatment to be complete, for termination to be appropriate, the couple must be able to use the methods, thoughts, feelings, and concepts explored in therapy in life, beyond the specific presenting difficulty. If the clients are able to own the tools, then termination can be appropriate. In effect, the couple will have moved from a position of dependence on the therapist to a reliance on the strengths of the relationship as they move further on the continuum of their lives together.

The first criterion for appropriate termination — when the chief complaint is taken care of — is a direct function of the goal-setting process at the beginning of the therapy. The couple, in conjunction with the therapist, sets goals to be pursued in therapy. When these goals have been achieved, it is appropriate to evaluate the process and either establish new goals or terminate therapy.

The second criterion is that the couple understand the strength of the couple in solving their problems. This strength of bonding is what has brought the couple to the office. This strength has been used to help them take care of the presenting problem. If the therapist has helped the clients to 1) attribute change to *themselves* and see the problem as *theirs*, not as "his" or "hers," 2) feel comfortable with their ability to take care of the problem, and 3) understand that if there comes a time when the strength of the couple receives a new, difficult challenge (the third criterion), the door of the therapist is open to them, then termination of therapy can be in order. The following case demonstrates the criteria of 1) taking care of the chief complaint, 2) couple understanding of the strength of the couple bond, and 3) the "open door" of therapy:

Case #1

Mr. & Mrs. A. first came into therapy before they were married. They had formed a relationship some two years before. Their relationship had been strong enough to assist each of them in getting out of highly conflicted marriages, of 19 and 17 years, respectively. They did not remarry immediately due to several legal and economic issues growing out of Mr. A.'s divorce action. They came to the office six months after they had begun living together, stymied by a problem which had arisen with the youngest of his two daughters.

The course of therapy focused on blended family issues. Initially, it was apparent that there had been much conflict between the couple in three areas: 1) relationships with "the children" (each had two); 2) relationships with ex-spouses; and c) money (a direct outgrowth of areas 1 & 2). A year later, they were more able to integrate difficulties with the children into their life together, difficulties with ex-spouses were nearly extinct, and money was clearly handled in a less provocative way. The couple announced their intention to wed at the same session at which they announced their desire to terminate therapy. It was decided that the therapy needed to be evaluated over a couple of sessions, but that they could proceed to termination.

The couple had clearly rediscovered their strength and had begun to use it effectively in meeting a broad range of situations. Armed with this strength and some knowledge about applying it to their life, they left treatment. One of their decisions was that they could return to therapy if they met something else that severely tested this strength.

They married three months after termination and returned to therapy three months after their wedding. They came for some help in dealing with two "crises" — one having to do with her son and the other having to do with his oldest daughter. In three sessions they became convinced that they did have the strength to handle their situations, as long as they respected themselves and their coupleness. They left therapy once again.

Mr. & Mrs. A. showed no anxiety concerning their initial termination. They showed little hesitancy about reentering therapy when a situation arose that they felt unprepared to handle. They easily terminated a second time after three sessions when it became apparent that their situation in no way threatened the solidity of their relationship. They may well return again if their situation warrants.

As noted in an earlier chapter, treatment goals specific to the client couple are developed within the beginning of the therapy. These goals provide the essential framework for treatment, including an appropriate time of termination. The goals of the case below determined the appropriateness of its termination.

Case #2

Mr. & Mrs. B. were referred to the Marriage Council of Philadelphia by Mr. B.'s employer. They arrived at the office complaining of an inability to spend enough intimate time together. Within the first four sessions it became clear that Mr. B. had another agenda, that of ending the marital relationship, moving to New York City, and completing work in his academic field. The goal for treatment shifted to exploring the question of whether or not this relationship should continue or be dissolved. Within 20 visits the dissolution of the marriage was accomplished, farewells were said between the members of the dyad, and arrangements for further therapeutic work were made. The "couple" therapy was terminated at the farewell session, and both Mr. & Mrs. B. were referred to therapists for further work on their individual issues. Termination of the couple's therapy was accomplished with little difficulty.

The treatment goals for therapy with Mr. & Mrs. B. were set by the end of the fourth session. Work then proceeded toward the goals that were established. Intermediate goals of the couple's therapy were finalized during the spousal farewell session. It then became appropriate to terminate the couple's therapy.

Sometimes, the course of therapy has a contract for a certain number of sessions of treatment as a part of its organizational and therapeutic structure. When this approach is chosen, termination is appropriate at the conclusion of the number of sessions contracted. An evaluation session, which looks at the progress that has been made, is held. Recontracting, referral, or termination are the options that emerge from this session. The couple and the therapist work together to make the evaluation and, as above, transference and countertransference issues are kept to a minimum. The case below is illustrative of this.

Case #3

Mr. & Mrs. C. came to the Marriage Council of Philadelphia presenting their difficulty in communication. They contracted for a course of therapy which would last four to six weeks. Both expressed a desire to limit their work in therapy to communication issues. They were coached in active listening and were asked to carry out homework assignments, including "caring days." At the conclusion of the fifth session, they agreed that their communication was much improved and expressed a desire to terminate therapy.

The therapist had taken note of some other underlying issues, which were shared in an evaluation session. He offered to renegotiate the original contract, and solicited feedback from them. It became clear during the evaluation session that the C.s were appreciative of the progress that they had made, were not in agreement with the therapist's perceptions regarding underlying concerns, and were prepared to terminate therapy in accordance with the original contractual agreement. The therapist accepted their decision, validated the progress that the couple had made, and terminated treatment.

Such a handling of the case allowed the door to remain open for further work, should the clients express need of it. It honored the original contract for therapy and effectively worked through the issues of termination.

PREMATURE TERMINATION

There are a number of conditions under which termination of therapy occurs outside our criteria. One such set of conditions comes into play when therapy is terminated before the goals of therapy have been reached. This is termed *Premature Termination*. There are times when such an ending occurs at the initiation of the client, while others take place at the initiation of the therapist. At times, the motivations of either or both are conscious, and at times the motivations are unconscious.

When the initiation of premature termination comes from the client, generally three underlying phenomena can be seen: 1) the amount of pain in the system is too great to confront; 2) "secrets" are present in the system; and 3) there is partner manipulation of termination.

Excessive Pain in the System

The primary concern is the amount of pain that the issues raise in therapy. If there is too much pain and not enough support and control, then the clients are prone to terminate therapy prematurely. This excess amount of pain may be seen by the couple as a whole, or by either partner as an individual. The following case will illustrate the effect of these three phenomena on the termination of therapy.

Case #4

Mr. & Mrs. D. entered therapy with a presenting problem of "endless conflict" over a number of issues. These included money, time spent together, each spouse's relationship with his/her family of origin, and responsibility for the care of their infant daughter. Both Mr. & Mrs. D. are mental health professionals who came into therapy assuming that they knew the "correct" approach to take to their problems. Their solutions were diametrically opposed to one another. As therapy began, both spouses became aware that understanding of the other's perspective was necessary if any movement was to be made.

In order for Mrs. D. to do this, it would have been necessary to repudiate a legacy message from her family of origin. The message was, "There are many people in the world who will try to break us apart. We have seen that in other generations and in other portions of this generation of our family. Our unity is the only key to our survival. Therefore, we must hold to our family's perspective against the onslaught of others in the world." The family had created dogma to deal with many areas of life, including, but not limited to, money, intimacy, child-rearing, and time spent with the family of significant others. For Mrs. D. to appreciate the opposing perspective of her husband was to cast doubt upon the veracity of the family myth and, indeed, to threaten the very fabric of the family itself. Mrs. D. suggested the early termination of therapy. Her husband concurred, as an attempt to create peace with his spouse.

The pain which Mrs. D. felt upon the recognition of the couple's need to understand one another's perspective was great enough to overshadow the attempts of the therapist, or of her husband, to provide support and the assurance that experiencing the pain would be well worth it in terms of health to the couple. Mrs. D. was made aware of both the need for understanding of her husband's perspective and of her family myth within the course of the therapy. It was at the time of this second awareness that she expressed her desire to terminate the therapy. The anticipation of the amount of pain to be gone through was too much for both her and her husband to bear. In this situation the therapist might have avoided premature termination by suggesting some individual work be done in a small, balanced number of individual sessions. This might have permitted Mrs. D. to approach her issues with more support and not threatened her position within the dyad, as well as making more difficult the collusion of Mr. D.

Secrets in the System

A second factor leading to premature termination is that of "secrets." When one partner has a secret which, they fear, will bring pain, turbulence, or the end to their primary relationship, the client may fear that this "secret" will be disclosed within the context of continued therapy. As long as this fear can be kept at bay, as long as it appears that revelation of the secret will not play an important part in the therapy, the therapeutic process can proceed. If, however, the client perceives that sharing of the secret will become, or is, necessary in the interest of the therapy, and the client is not willing to deal with the consequences of disclosure, then premature termination will be a possible outcome.

Case #5

Mr. & Mrs. E. came to therapy with a presenting problem of lack of sexual desire in the husband and a long history of failed therapies. This particular therapy had been requested by the husband's employer, since his job performance had begun to suffer noticeably. Both Mr. & Mrs. E. were open to the initial efforts of the therapist, which were centered in the area of behavioral sex therapy. It soon became apparent, however, that the couple was stuck at a relatively low level of Sensate Focus exercises. The therapist requested individual sessions with each partner. In the individual session with Mrs. E., it was discovered that Mrs. E. was involved in an ongoing affair with a mutual friend of the couple.

The therapist accepted this information in confidentiality, explaining to Mrs. E. that such behavior could have important consequences to the progress of the therapy and that it would be best if the affair were ended immediately. He further stated that, if that were not the case, it might become necessary for this information to be shared with Mr. E. at some time in the future if progress continued to be impeded. The therapist expressed to Mrs. E. that he would not share the information directly without her permission, but would, if the situation warranted, ask for some individual time with her and there make the request for disclosure. After a number of sessions in which progress continued to be blocked, Mrs. E. requested termination, a move supported by her husband since other therapies had ended in the same way.

Mrs. E.'s fear of disclosure of her "secret" prompted the premature termination of therapy. Her concern was for the pain and turbulence which such disclosure might cause, as well as for the pain of the possible ending of either her primary relationship or of the affair. Her choice was for the continuance of the status quo and/or for the avoidance of the pain which she felt such disclosure was sure to bring. The therapist might have avoided premature termination by maintaining the conjoint nature of the therapy, not calling for the individual sessions. Such an intervention might have eventually forced the "secret" material to emerge within the therapy in some form which could be dealt with conjointly.

Manipulation by One Partner

A third factor seen in conjunction with client-initiated premature termination occurs when a spouse who is reluctant to enter into therapy is able to manipulate the interested spouse into termination. In this situation, it is difficult to ascertain the etiology of the manipulation since, in most cases, the reluctant spouse does not present at all for treatment, leaving the therapist with the secondhand perspective of the presenting spouse. In some cases, both partners enter therapy, but the main focus of the reluctant partner's participation is often geared to convincing the partner to abandon the therapy. Probable causes for such a position may include: 1) the externalization of personal responsibility; 2) denial; 3) the anticipation of overwhelming pain; 4) the disclosure of "secrets"; 5) fear of intrusion by the therapist into the marital system; and 6) a personality disorder or other individual issues of the reluctant partner which may well include the first two items on this list.

Case #6

Mr. and Mrs. F. entered therapy with Mrs. F. presenting a complaint concerning Mr. F.'s possessiveness. They were both graduate students, having married at the conclusion of their undergraduate work. They had been married for a year. Mr. F. answered his wife's statement of the presenting problem with a remark about how difficult it was for a couple to remain together in the face of all the threats to a relationship that can come from life in the university.

The therapy lasted two sessions, with Mr. F. answering each statement of the therapist, or of his wife, with various resistant statements: explaining the nonsensical nature of the original statement or question, questioning the right of the person to make such a statement, attempting to show how various statements proved threatening to the ongoingness of the couple, and attempting to convince Mrs. F. to leave the office. In fact, Mr. F. did not attend the second session. Mrs. F. came in to explain that she had decided not to continue the therapy since it was so upsetting to her husband, and to express her sense that knowing services were available to her would help her to work things out with her husband.

It is difficult to completely understand Mr. F.'s motivation in one session. Clearly, he feared the intrusion of the therapist into the marital system. Quite possibly there was a personality disorder present in Mr. F. It is likely that closer examination would have revealed other reasons for his position. Suggesting individual sessions for the dissenting spouse may well have afforded the therapist the opportunity to join with him.

THE THERAPIST'S CONTRIBUTION
TO PREMATURE TERMINATION

Until now we have concentrated on the client side of the therapeutic triangle in discussing premature termination. The therapist is also a part of the therapeutic system and can, therefore, contribute to the possibility of premature termination. Of prime consideration in terms of the therapist's actions/responses is his/her ability to balance all of the segments of the system in the therapy.

Balance

When the client couple enters the therapist's office, their system has, in effect, undergone a significant change. They have incorporated another person into the system. By virtue of his/her presence, this new person will have the ability to shift the system or to become inducted into the existing system.

Since the couple comes recognizing some level of malaise, it is important that the therapist be able to avoid induction and remain a new force in the system. From this perspective the therapist will be able to shift the system from its presenting dysfunction. The therapist can, by being able to balance the perspectives of the partners, help the couple to move into a more harmonious set of dynamics. Should such balance not be kept, it is likely that premature termination will ensue. The therapist must be able to make necessary shifts within the various parts of the system without upsetting the balance of therapy. If this is not done successfully the level of anxiety within the clients will be increased, old issues for one or both of the partners will be raised, and the clients' perspective that undesirable pain will be the result of further therapeutic contact will also increase. The following case illustrates the effect that the therapist may have on premature termination.

Case #7

Mr. G. presented as an individual suffering from acute relational stress. He and Mrs. G. had been married for 10 years. At the time of their wedding, they had agreed to a marital contract which included "free nights out." Under the terms of their contract these nights out were allowed to include sexual activities with other partners. The mutually agreed-upon limitation within the contract was in the area of emotional attachment. This was expressly forbidden.

All appeared well until Mr. G. became emotionally involved with one of his "free night out" partners, Ms. Z. This emotional relationship had recently been discovered by Mrs. G. Two individual sessions were held in which the therapist joined with Mr. G. and gathered data about Mr. G.'s painful situation. It was then suggested that the most effective therapy might include both Mrs. G. and Ms. Z. Mr. G. was asked to consider inviting both women to a subsequent therapy session to be scheduled two weeks hence. The therapist agreed to see the G.'s as a couple first.

The focus of that session was very painful for both spouses. The therapist made two interventions. One was aimed at scrapping Mr. G.'s self-imposed, time-limited moratorium on *sexual* contact with Ms. Z., since its avowed purpose (not subjecting Mrs. G. to any hurt) could not be carried out (since Mrs. G. was already obviously in a great deal of pain). The second suggestion was that the couple consider inviting Ms. Z. to the next session also as she was an integral part of their therapeutic issues. Both Mr. & Mrs. G. expressed reservations about this second maneuver, but were told that they should not respond until they had examined the possibility thoroughly. A subsequent appointment time was agreed upon, and the couple left the office with each aware of uncovered feelings.

Less than 24 hours before the appointed time for the next session, Mr. G. called to cancel the session, thanking the therapist for giving him and his wife a lot to think about and reporting that there was nothing wrong, but that they had chosen to try to work things out by themselves. He further reassured the therapist that he would be in touch if there was any further need for therapy. Neither Mr. nor Mrs. G. has subsequently contacted the therapist.

It is clear that this case was one of premature termination in which the primary cause was the therapist's inability to shift back and forth between the fears and pain of each spouse while maintaining a focus on the resolution of the couple difficulty. While dealing with the dysfunctionality of the "free nights out" contract was an appropriate focus of the therapy, both individuals were heavily invested in that contract. Their individual investments had to be addressed before change could be accomplished. Mr. G. felt betrayed by the therapist and chose to cover up as quickly as possible to deal with the pain and to further resist making changes within the existing system. The therapist in this case had moved too rapidly and had upset the balance of the system. While the direction of the therapeutic intervention was in order, the pacing of the interventions disturbed the balance of the moment and led to the premature termination of the clients.

There are structural considerations regarding balance that are within the power of the therapist to control. Violation of balance can also lead to premature termination. Should the therapist allow an unbalanced number of individual sessions with one of the partners, therapy may end prematurely. It is best, if an individual session with one of the partners is necessary, to require an individual session with the other partner as well. This keeps both partners feeling "in" the therapy and makes it more difficult for one partner to take a one-down position vis-à-vis the therapist.

Interventions that are not systemically based are also in this same category. Interventions must be balanced to include both partners, otherwise the therapy may suffer. The omitted client may make a decision to terminate, based on his/her feelings of rejection and/or abandonment. The client focused upon may feel the weight of the marital problem and make the decision to terminate, based on the anticipation of pain or of not being fully understood by either the partner or the therapist. Such shifting back and forth within the dyad, in the interest of balance, is an important consideration in controlling the time of termination.

Gender

Another issue for the therapist which may have direct bearing on the appropriateness of termination is the sex of the therapist. It may well tap into issues that exist for the couple on either the conscious or the unconscious level. A couple whose presenting problem includes extramarital involvement on the part of one of the partners may find the sex of the therapist an extremely important issue. Particular family of origin issues which have affected the ability of either partner (or both partners) to relate straightforwardly with persons of a particular sex may affect the outcome of the therapy. The appropriate choice of therapist gender will depend on the specific dynamics of the couple, but will, in any case, be an important criterion for successful completion of the therapy.

Case #8

Mr. & Mrs. H. entered therapy with a desire to explore whether or not their marriage could withstand the stress created by extramarital involvement. They had chosen a male therapist, who was known to them because of community work that he had done. In the initial session, they shared that one of their concerns was Mrs. H.'s extramarital involvement in two affairs, both of which had ended by the beginning of this therapy. The most recent affair had been with a professional from whom she had sought counseling.

The therapist expressed his concern that therapy with him might not be effective because of the nature of Mrs. H.'s previous involvements and the concerns which might still be harbored by the couple about the possibility of a repetition of Mrs. H.'s having an affair with her therapist. The therapist stated that though this was to be couples' therapy, and that strict boundaries could be put in place and enforced, his feeling was that a female therapist or a cotherapy team would provide the most effective therapy. Mr. H. responded that he felt that such a referral would be in order since he was uncomfortable with his wife's choice of a male therapist, even though he had agreed in order to save the marriage.

Had the therapist in the above case attempted to work with this couple, even with the strict observance of the limitations stated, it appears likely that the anxieties shared by Mr. H. would have led to a decision to terminate therapy before it reached a successful conclusion. Mrs. H.'s previous involvement with her counselor was still very much an issue for the couple. Mr. H.'s inability to share its depth with his wife at the time of the original choice to pursue therapy indicates the likelihood of premature termination. The suggestion of a female therapist would provide some modicum of protection and balance for both partners. The suggestion of a cotherapy team would provide even more. Whenever similar sexual/gender-related problems are in evidence, the gender of the therapist takes on significance in working toward successful therapy and the avoidance of premature termination.

Induction

The fourth concern regarding premature termination that is within the control of the therapist is that of the therapist being inducted into the clients' dysfunctional system. The reasons for such systemic countertransference can be quite diverse. Some have to do with the personal issues of the therapist, while others have to do with the nature of the system that the clients present. The therapist must be aware of his/her own issues and the ways in which they fit into and can be used by the dysfunction inherent in the client system. If this self-awareness is not present, therapeutic progress will be stymied, with termination occurring before the goals of the therapy have been reached.

The marital dyad may be one in which one or both partners uses triangulation in order to sustain the homeostatic balance of the marriage. Should this be the case, and should the therapist wittingly, or unwittingly, make himself/herself available for such triangulation, a successful end to therapy is highly questionable. It matters little whether the therapist takes over any one of the general roles of triangulation — villain, victim, or rescuer. The acceptance of any of these roles will lead to the same end.

Case #9

Mr. & Mrs. I. were both recovering alcoholics, having met and married during the early days of their recovery from their respective pits of alcoholism. As the evaluation phase of therapy proceeded it became clear that each spouse had chosen the other as the one to be the rescuer. Yet the level of their individual needs made it extremely difficult for each to fulfill the other's need to be rescued. As their marriage of four years floundered, they came into therapy unaware of the situation in which they had placed themselves.

The therapist whom they had selected, though well intentioned, was not able to deal with the intensity of their need to be rescued. Her own need to caretake ran relatively deep, and she embarked upon the process of attempting to rescue both Mr. & Mrs. I. The first indication of the therapist's caretaking was her decision not to enforce a rule of couples' therapy—if the couple is scheduled to attend a session and only one partner is present, the session will not start until the other partner arrives, or the session will be treated as a broken appointment. Soon after, calls began to be received changing appointment times, cancelling appointments at the last minute, often with dubious excuses, or requesting spur-of-the-moment "emergency" sessions or telephone consultations. When this began to occur, the therapist became overinvolved in tracking the clients down, shaping her schedule to fit these clients, etc. At what was to be the final session of therapy (the fifth), Mr. I. announced that he would not be back, citing financial reasons.

The original marriage contract of the couple held that each would be the other's *rescuer* since they were both *victims* of the *villain* (alcohol). Initially, it was a closed, mutually dependent system. As time went on, it became clear that each individual's needs were more than the partner could handle. They needed some additional help from somewhere. Rather than be the facilitator of that process, the therapist made a decision to become the direct provider of the needed services. In doing so, she gave up the possibility of changing the system and became a part of it, subject to the rules of the system and responsible for it. With the therapist no longer in a position to create change in their couple dynamics, the couple terminated therapy. It had begun to feel like "more of the same."

AVOIDING PREMATURE TERMINATION

It would be useful if a therapist could be so aware of all of the above issues that premature termination would never occur in his/her office. Realistically, that is not going to happen. Every therapist will have, at one time or another, couples who decide to leave therapy before their work is complete. There are certain moves the therapist may make should this occur. This is especially the case if the therapist is concerned that there is a strong chance of serious deterioration in the couple at the time of termination. Tomm & Wright (1979) have outlined some steps which can be taken when the therapist is faced with this situation. Once again, the particular step chosen must arise out of the therapist's perceptions of the particular case at hand. The steps are:

1. *Explore with the couple their motives for termination.* This exploration helps the therapist establish whether or not the clients' motives are realistic. Perhaps the crisis which provided the impetus for entering therapy has ended, thereby decreasing their anxiety. Perhaps the symptoms that brought the couple into therapy have been brought under control. In some cases, these are valid reasons for termination; sometimes they are not. The reason could have to do with any one of the themes mentioned above. It could be the result of real change that has

taken place, but has not yet been reported to the therapist. There could be some real life issue "getting in the way," such as loss of employment, financial considerations, illness, etc. Because it is important for the therapist to have these data before dealing with the desire of the client couple to end treatment, this step is a necessary prerequisite for deciding whether or not termination should occur.

2. Review with the couple the present level of functioning of their relationship. As many different perspectives of the relationship as possible should be discussed, including strengths, positive changes that have occurred, weaknesses, and issues that may have deteriorated during the course of therapy. After this evaluation is carried out with input from all three persons present (both partners and the therapist), it may be appropriate to renegotiate the therapy contract, taking note of new goals and the benefits which therapy may have yet to offer the couple.

3. Decide if the situation is one in which serious deterioration of the relationship is likely if treatment were to stop. If this danger exists, the therapist should encourage the couple to continue treatment, either with the present therapist or by referral to another therapist. If the possible deterioration is likely to put the couple, either of the individuals, or members of their family in some danger, further action may be necessary. It might be helpful to actively seek out the support of persons who are likely to benefit from the continued therapy in order that they add their weight to the decision-making process.

4. Accept the couple's decision to end treatment. This acceptance is the decision of choice when it becomes clear that the therapist's desire for therapy to continue is clearly stronger than that of the client couple. Once these dynamics become clear, the probability of any therapeutic change within the context of the present therapy is minimal. It can be helpful, after the decision has been reached and confirmed by the therapist, to share with the couple an evaluation of the therapeutic process and progress to that point. Such an evaluation may serve as a positive springboard should the clients decide to reenter therapy at some time in the future.

Making use of the items outlined above may provide the therapist and client couple with a helpful transition to life after treatment.

RESISTANCE TO TERMINATION

At the other end of the continuum from those couples who choose to terminate therapy prematurely are those couples who are resistant to termination, who wish to avoid the end of the treatment process. Strean (1985) has pointed out a number of reasons why clients resist termination. While he writes from the perspective of individual psychotherapy, his points are also appropriate for those couple cases where resistance to termination is a concern. Sometimes there is a collusion on the part of the couple which brings these characteristics into consideration. Sometimes one partner's resistance in some way dominates the couple.

According to Strean (1985), a large number of clients resist ending therapy because termination carries with it an implication of success. He reasons that, while most people wish to strive for success on one or more levels, there are other levels on which success conjures up feelings of terror; one cannot achieve success without defeating the forces that hindered the striving. Since such forces not only hinder striving but include positive desirable elements, the client is faced with the paradox of having to defeat that which may be desirable from a different perspective. (A parent may offer the comfort of caretaking, which may stand in the way of the client's ability to be independent; in choosing one the client must deal with the loss of the other.) In order to avoid the hostile destructive wishes, many clients choose to regress and, in so doing, avoid success. Such a decision may reinforce the pretherapy homeostatic balance of the marital system that the clients sought to change.

Strean (1985) also commented that dependency conflicts provide an important basis for those clients who resist termination. Some clients resist the thought that they, upon ending treatment, will be responsible for their own lives. To succeed in therapy is to end a relationship in which the client has been taken care of. The responsibility for taking care of the client will then rest on his/her own shoulders. For such people, being independent and responsible has been associated with rejection/abandonment feelings (I/we have to take care of myself/ourselves since there is no one else who will do it).

The thrust of marital therapy is to place this responsibility on the marital bond in a balanced way. The partners are encouraged to take care of each other in appropriate ways. Each partner is encouraged to sort out which needs and wants are best met by the individual, by the partner, by the couple as a unit, and those which may never be able to be met completely. Until this is achieved and accepted by the clients, resistance to termination is a possibility.

Strean also points out the relationship between termination and the fantasies which exist for the client. He states, "Although clients spend much time in therapy trying to overcome childish wishes, omnipotent fantasies, grandiose desires, and other unrealistic aspirations, termination usually reactivates these old wishes" (p. 267). Termination brings about the reality that the fantasies have not been realized, that they have been punctured by reality. That is to say, the ideal marriage may never be achieved; the best relationship in the world may never be had, etc ... etc ... etc. ... If clients are unwilling, or unable, to achieve this level of appreciation, the termination of therapy will be resisted as they continue the struggle to find what is unfindable. When clients are involved in marital therapy, this resistance may manifest itself in the clients' unwillingness to recognize that the marriage is less than the perfect ideal, cannot spontaneously satisfy all individual needs, and requires a certain amount of give-to-get negotiation. Such an unwillingness may lend itself to a continuation in therapy in an ongoing search for the ideal while denying the reality.

Case #10

Mr. & Mrs. J. were not married at the point at which they entered therapy. They had, however, been married to one another previously. Their marriage had been fraught with some problems prior to Mr. J.'s decision to leave. They separated, were divorced, and in the course of time each entered into significant relationships with other people. Two children had been born to the J.'s, and regular contact with the children was maintained during this period. They entered therapy having rediscovered one another, the initial rediscovery centering around issues with the children. They had just begun living together once again, and were raising questions about the future security and stability of their relationship.

In therapy, the couple explored themselves, their relational pattern, their parenting styles, and their relationships to their respective families of origin. Nearly 18 months after the beginning of therapy, they were remarried to one another. The therapy progressed well, until the prospect of termination was raised. Sessions had become less frequent. Material discussed in the sessions had become repetitive. Their life together seemed to flow without major upset. A "termination" session was scheduled. At that session Mr. J. offered the therapist tickets to a trade show in which his business was participating, Mrs. J. noted that she had referred another couple to the therapist for treatment, and the J.'s forgot their checkbook and were unable to pay the therapist.

The signs of resistance to termination were clear. They were discussed, and a second "termination" session, this time with the inclusion of the children, was scheduled. The therapist's intent was to solicit further information about the anxieties concerning the whole family, to elicit, if appropriate, permission from the children for the parents to end treatment, and then to terminate. The information gathered seemed to indicate that the couple was adequately prepared to handle life without therapy, but the children were divided on what might happen without the support of the therapist. It was agreed that the family would "try it on its own for a while" and report back their progress to the therapist at a follow-up session six weeks later. At that session the J.'s raised issues concerning the youngest child that had been raised before in the therapy, and reopened the possibility of doing more extensive family of origin work. Seven months later, the couple called again with concerns around some potentially suicidal writing of their oldest child. This was evaluated and the family was seen in cotherapy for three sessions.

It is clear that the J.s were having difficulty accepting the termination of their therapy. In this case, it does not seem that the reason is that of punctured fantasies or of a fear of success, but rather a fear that the end of therapeutic dependence will make the J.s so vulnerable that, once again, they will fall apart in their attempt to achieve a satisfactory relationship. The thought of independence, viewed from the perspective of their past experience, is frightening to them; therefore, they resist making a complete break with therapy.

There are also issues for the therapist which may hinder the progression of a case to termination. These have to do with personal, countertransferential issues which need to be overcome. The hungry therapist may hold onto a case longer in the interest of more fees. The therapist unsure of his/her own abilities may hold on longer "just to be sure." The narcissistic therapist may be caught up in individual grandiosity and be convinced that without the therapist's help the couple will surely deteriorate. The therapist "caretaker" may wish to keep the clients in order to have "victims" to take care of. The therapist may be ensnared in the dynamics of the system, feeling unable to make any move which would create a change. These and similar issues can make it difficult for the therapist to see that the end has been reached and needs to be carried through.

TERMINATION STRATEGIES

Given all of the aforementioned issues and concerns, the question of appropriate methods of approaching termination must be addressed. A successful termination is not something that occurs within the context of one session of therapy. Termination is planned from the first day the client couple enters into therapy. The termination phase of the therapy with a couple at its best spans a number of sessions, with increased amounts of time between the sessions. This allows the gradual acceptance of the end of therapy, while the couple's health becomes a part of the reality of their relationship (Epstein & Bishop, 1981). The following concerns should be addressed in the termination phase.

1) The first concern raised is one of *orientation*. At the appropriate time, it is the therapist's responsibility to begin to talk about termination. The therapist should explain why the subject is being raised; e.g., the goals which were set in the beginning have been met, the number of sessions contracted for has been reached (or will be soon), or there has been little or no progress in the therapy.

2) The second concern to be addressed is *evaluation*. It is important that the therapist discuss the things that have happened during the course of therapy. A review is conducted, covering the entire course of therapy, including high points, low points, breakthroughs, stuck points, etc. The perspectives of both the couple and the therapist are of great importance in this evaluation. It is suggested that the therapist listen to the evaluation of the couple first, without commenting. This evaluation should reinforce the couple's sense of competence for the posttherapy period, and allow the couple to share their perspective relatively uncontaminated by therapist issues.

3) The next concern is that of *recognition*. The therapist takes time to carefully and deliberately recognize the initiative that the couple has taken in making the changes that are now seen as happening or having happened. It is important that the therapist reinforce that it is the couple that has worked hard to change, not the therapist. Credit belongs to the couple. This is a positive reinforcer for the couple, acknowledging the couple's own support network and recognizing their independence from the therapist and therapy.

4) The next issue is that of *anticipation*. The couple will not be going out of the therapist's office into a vacuum. It is therefore important that goals be set for posttherapy changes that will need to be made. The methods by which the couple will achieve these goals can be worked out prior to termination. Once again, it is suggested that comments from the couple come first during this portion of termination, with the therapist's comments to follow. The couple can feel themselves working together as they face the future of their relationship. It is here that the concept of the open door can be mentioned. It is important that the "open door" not sound to the client like, "You'd better save my number, because you're likely to fall apart again!" An appropriate statement might be, "I (the clinic) will always be here as you need me (us)" (Barker, 1981).

5) The final step in the process is that of *termination*. This step is the

one toward which the entire sequence of the therapy has led. The goal here is to allow the couple to end treatment without loyalties split between what they need and what they believe the therapist to need (Barnard, 1979). The couple is not left feeling they have let the therapist down because they no longer need him/her. The therapist has joined in the celebration and all are free to go.

6) There is one final part to the process of ending treatment. It comes after *termination*. The clients are asked to comment on the process of therapy. This step is a *recapitulation* of the entire therapeutic process. What interventions did not work? What things could have been done to make changes happen more efficiently? Were there times that things felt inappropriate to the couple?

These ideas provide a general outline for achieving a satisfactory and successful termination of therapy. There are a number of specific interventions that can be used within the context of this process to facilitate it. Below are some examples:

1). Weeks and L'Abate (1982) have suggested a paradoxical maneuver for use in the termination process. The goals of the intervention are to elicit thoughtfully provoked information from the client couple regarding their development within the therapeutic process, and to fix that information in the minds of the clients for their use in the posttherapy period. The following scenario is put before the couple: "Suppose that for some reason you set as a goal for yourselves the return to the place where your relationship was when you entered therapy. Further, suppose that you wished to accomplish that goal as quickly and efficiently as possible." The clients are then asked to "make a list of all of the things that you would have to do in order to achieve your goal as efficiently as possible." After the lists have been thoughtfully compiled, including some therapist input if necessary, the value of the lists is discussed with the clients. Certainly, if the goal were, in fact, to return to the previous level of functioning, the list could provide an effective blueprint for action. In addition, however, it provides an excellent map of those attitudes, actions, etc. that 1) can provide warning signs of impending regression, 2) should be avoided in order to ensure the present improved level of functioning, and 3) can give a sense of the foundation necessary for an increase in level of functioning in the future.

2) As cases are examined systemically, it becomes apparent that, while termination is appropriate in terms of the presenting issues, there is a likelihood of need for further work in the future. A positive relabeling of termination to that of "vacation" will permit the client to view the ending of therapy as positive, look forward to an interim

period of integration, and yet retain the idea that further work in the future is appropriate (at the conclusion of the vacation, of course). Generally, jobs are not lost while one is on vacation; therefore, the implication is also carried that the therapist will remain available at a later date. In other words, the door to more therapy, to further growth for the couple, will remain open.

3) Often, the process of therapy has centered predominantly on the negative, or problematic, parts of the relationship. Termination is an excellent time for the couple to share thoughts and feelings about the positive attributes of the relationship. This sharing can be done in terms of positive changes that they have seen, including positive things that they have done to bring about those changes. It can be done in terms of eliciting a discussion of the positive by-products of changes made during therapy. ("Our love-making seemed to improve as our ability to communicate with one another improved!") It can be done in terms of connecting growth in therapy with parts of the relationship that were good at the time of entry into therapy, thus integrating the growth with the whole. The purpose of these interventions is to reinforce the positive changes of the couple, to emphasize the solid foundation for the future, and to acknowledge the ability of the couple to continue on a positive track without dependence on therapy.

The role of the therapist throughout the process of termination, regardless of the specific interventions used, may best be described, in the words of Gerald Zuk, as the *celebrant* role (Barnard, 1979). Termination is a time for the therapist to join with the couple in a celebration of what they have accomplished. It is the responsibility of the therapist to orchestrate a celebration which allows for a healthy separation.

THE QUESTION OF FOLLOW-UP

One of the more intriguing questions in the area of termination of therapy surrounds the issue of follow-up to treatment. Certainly follow-up can be of great value to the therapist. He/she can know for certain whether or not the changes made in therapy have become integrated within the client system. Data can be gathered on outcome for research purposes. The validity of certain interventions and their applications for certain types of couples can be evaluated. Follow-up can provide a vital source of such information, but not without significant risks and costs.

Follow-up also has the potential of sabotaging that which has been diligently sought after — the feeling by the couple that they are OK, that they are able to generalize what they have learned from therapy, that they are independent and secure, and that they have not rejected their therapist by not needing him/her any longer (Barker, 1981). While it is positive for the couple to feel that help remains available to them if they are in need of it, a request for a follow-up session may well communicate the message that further difficulties are likely and, in fact, anticipated by the therapist. If the goals of termination are to be achieved it is vital that a request for follow-up not undermine them by communicating such a message.

In order to avoid such a happening and still obtain important follow-up information, it may be well to institutionalize the request for such a session in a policy. The therapist may then make a statement such as, "You don't need any more treatment, but it is my policy, with all the families I see, to contact them after six months (or whatever intervals the therapist adopts) because I am interested in knowing how they are getting along . . . (or for research purposes)" (Barker, 1981, p. 164). Such a statement will make clear that the intent is not a therapeutic one, and that it is equally applied to all clients, reducing the fear that there is something uniquely wrong with *this* couple.

If there is to be follow-up contact, it is important that its structure be different from that of therapy. This allows appropriate distance from therapy itself. Follow-up may be conducted by questionnaire, by letter, over the phone, or in a session that is not the normal length or at the usual time of the couple's regular therapy session. Any one of these maneuvers will provide the clients with the appropriate protection from the implication that further therapy is necessary.

RESPONSE OF THE CLIENT

There will be times when the client(s) will respond to the termination of therapy with more than words of "Thank you." Clients will on occasion give gifts, send immediate referrals of friends, neighbors, and extended family, offer invitations for ongoing socializing, or make requests for an ongoing relationship with the therapist as "friend." All of these offers must be carefully examined with an eye toward determining the underlying motive of the client.

At times, the underlying motives of the clients will indicate that there is further work to be done. Case #10 (pp. 135-136) provides an example of this concern. Mr. & Mrs. J., when faced with what was to be the final, "termination" session, responded with an outpouring to the therapist. Tickets to one of Mr. J.'s professional exhibitions were offered; a couple having marital difficulties were referred to the therapist by the J.s. The therapist decided that there were, in fact, some important issues underlying these offers, and chose to help Mr. & Mrs. J. to deal with them. After the couple were helped to confront their fear of being independent and their sense of vulnerability in life after therapy, they were able to feel more comfortable about ending treatment and about their ability to have a solid relationship.

Some clients simply want to be sure that the open door will be there for them if and when they do decide to reenter therapy. One client couple who had "terminated" a number of years ago after two years of therapy still send cards to the therapist on all religious holidays, even though they are of a different religious persuasion. Periodically over the years, one or the other of the couple has called the therapist — for a bit of information, for a bit of support, but mostly to know that the therapist is there should they ever decide to resume their work.

As in other phases of therapy, each response from clients is unique to their termination. The therapist must base his/her reaction on his/her perceptions of the clients and of where their response to termination fits into the stream of things. The therapist can then design an appropriate approach which takes into account the therapist-couple system.

REFERENCES

Barker, P. (1981). *Basic Family Therapy.* Baltimore, MD: University Park Press.

Barnard, C. P. (1979). *The Theory and Technique of Family Therapy.* Springfield, IL: Charles C Thomas.

Epstein, N. B., & Bishop, D. S. (1981). Problem centered systems therapy of the family. *Journal of Marital and Family Therapy, 7*(1), 23-31.

Framo, J. (1965). Rationale and techniques of intensive family therapy. In I. Boszormenyi-Nagy & D. N. Ulrich (Eds.), *Intensive Family Therapy.* New York: Harper & Row.

Gurman, A. (1981). *Questions and Answers in the Practice of Family Therapy, Vols. 1 & 2.* New York: Brunner/Mazel.

Kohut, H. (1971). *The Analysis of the Self.* New York: International University Press.

Lankton, S., & Lankton, C. (1983). *The Answer Within: A Clinical Framework of Ericksonian Hypnotherapy.* New York: Brunner/Mazel.

Strean, H. (1985). *Resolving Resistance in Psychotherapy.* New York: John Wiley & Sons.

Tomm, K. M., & Wright, L. M. (1979). Training in family therapy: Perceptual, conceptual and executive skills. *Family Process, 18*(3), 227-250.

Weeks, G., & L'Abate, L. (1982). *Paradoxical Psychotherapy.* New York: Brunner/Mazel.

Chapter 7

The Intersystem Approach at Work: An Analysis of Therapeutic Styles

James M. Bahr
and
Bea Hollander-Goldfein

It is fascinating to note the variety and seeming divergence of the therapeutic styles of therapists who work within the Intersystem Approach. To illustrate this variety and divergence, the styles of two therapists who operate within the framework of the Intersystem Approach will be compared. Differences in style will be illustrated through the use of excerpts from therapy sessions which focus on similar content, in this case each couple's sexual relationship. Comparison will focus on three areas. First, the therapists' different ways of operationalizing the basic principles of the Intersystem Approach (see Chapters 3 & 5) will be highlighted. (References to the basic principles will be capitalized.) In addition, the three-dimensional model of therapeutic focus (see Chapter 5) will be used to analyze the different levels of the system targeted by each therapist. Finally, more general elements of the therapists' styles will be discussed.

The sessions used herein were drawn from a larger study of therapeutic process in intersystemic therapy. At the time the sessions were recorded, both of the therapists were clinicians on the Senior Staff of the Marriage Council. Besides the choice of sessions from experienced therapists, the decision was made to analyze sessions from cases that each therapist reported to have been progressing well. These decisions were based on the desire to explore the Intersystem Approach "at its best."

While the transcripts have been edited for clarity and brevity, nothing has been added. Although much has had to be omitted, the authors refrained from changing what was actually said, or at least its meanings. The clients' names, and other identifying information in the transcripts have been changed to protect the identities of the individuals involved. In the transcripts, therapist statements are given the designation "T," statements made by the female in the couple are designated "F," and statements made by the male are designated "M."

"BRAVE NEW WORLD"

In this session, the fourth meeting of the therapist and clients, several issues were covered. Near the end, the therapist raised the issue of the couple's sexual relationship. This issue had been discussed in previous sessions. The problem was the partners' differing approaches to initiating sex. The wife tended toward provocative, spontaneous initiation. The husband preferred having a schedule or pattern of sexual initiation. The wife found her husband's approach too constraining, "like sex on demand," while he felt like she "pounces" on him.

The therapist acted as a mediator, actively engaging each partner to negotiate behavioral change, and as a coach, cheering the couple on to make the changes happen. The negotiation for change was based on reframing a "new reality" for the couple's sexual relationship. As a mediator, the therapist reframed the husband's approach to sexual contact as romantic; the wife's style of initiation was framed as fun, but "scary" for the husband. In order to help the partners understand each other's approaches and find a middle ground, the positive elements of their respective styles were highlighted. In coaching the couple, the therapist emphasized the benefits for the wife of the husband's less genitally focused approach, and encouraged the wife to find more gentle ways of initiating sex. By refraining from scaring the husband, the wife could have even more fun and release her husband's ability to be seductive. The focus of a majority of the therapist's interventions was on what could be changed in the couple's behavioral interactions in the future.

T: Okay. Well, while we are on the subject of schedules, what about sex?

Therapist initiates a shift in content.

F: *(Laughing)* This is very funny. I was plopped on the floor, listening to some music in a somewhat obscene position. So I said, "How 'bout it?" He looked down at me, puzzled and bewildered, and said, "How about what?" *(Laughing)* I said, "Robert, for God's sake, do I have to be stark naked to make some mark, and then you'll say, 'Oh'?"

T: I told you, you're too romantic. Being approached isn't your thing, but there is nothing wrong with that.

Reframe #1 — Husband is a "romantic."

M: No. I've always needed a lot of cues with women. I'm not very swift at nuances.

F: *(Laughing)* I didn't think that was too nuancey. I saw his face standing above me, he was truly and honestly bewildered and puzzled. He couldn't figure out what I was alluding to. Now I see what we were each doing was being so super careful. Robert doesn't want to impose early morning sex on me, and I'm trying to proposition him all over the place. So that hasn't worked. I would say that it isn't worked out yet. I guess, part of it is that I sometimes like to be the initiator, and I don't mind being turned down.

T: Is that okay?

Therapist laughs along with the couple. Choosing not to address the emotional meaning of the laughter, the therapist moves on to redefine and reframe the problem.

M: Yeah, except that I have got to get the schedule down a little better. *(Laughs)* Whether by the day, or the time of day, the cycle of the moon, or what.

F: No, it just happens suddenly. If it were up to me, there would be no schedule. It's just that all of a sudden, it will just pass into my head, "Hey, why don't we have a nice screw." And I don't think Robert's mind works that way.

T: You think about it a little bit, right?

M: Yeah. It's a different pattern, I guess.

T: Well, it's probably reasonable. What kind of pattern is it?

M: I'd rather get her up first thing in the morning and let it go.

Description of the problem by clients conveys a sense of having "irreconcilable differences."

F: We decide the night before that the next morning will be it. And I just bridle at that kind of thing. That seems like sex on demand, and it just makes me a little uneasy.

T: Well, let me ask you in a different way. Is there some way that Caroline can approach you that really does turn you on?

Interactional question focused on behavioral change.

M: Usually she just propositions me outright.

T: But that clearly is not working.

F: Yeah, that's not working.

Reaffirming that the old pattern does not work reinforces the necessity of exploring avenues for change.

M: Yeah, but part of the problem is that if I get too tired, it's a little difficult for me. That's why I'm more favorable to doing it in the morning.

T: I may have sounded like I was joking earlier, but I really wasn't. I really do think that Robert, besides being hooked on a schedule, is somewhat more of a romantic than you are. And, if you are going to approach him, you need to do it in a more romantic and less direct process.

Restatement of Reframe #1. Therapist actively mediates change between partners.

F: Yes. I'm playing it the man's way, "How 'bout it, kiddo?" *(Laughing)*

And that usually leaves the woman turned off. Yeah.

M: That sort of style appeals to her sometimes. *(Laughs)*

T: And that's super. But, I suspect that it would appeal to Robert if there were also some other ways that the two of you could do it. What do you think would happen if Caroline came to you, really very slowly, and said she loved you, and snuggled up and things like that, would that be fine?

Interactional question — Imbedded proposal for changes in the wife's behavior, addressed to the husband.

M: Yeah, that would be fine, but an alarm would go off the first time because it's a little bit out of character.

F: "What's she up to?"

M: Yeah.

F: That's interesting. I always thought that men, most of the time, prefer a straight, out front proposition.

T: Well, you have a very special husband who doesn't do it that way.

Reframe #2 — "Very special husband."

F: *(Laughing)* Yeah, who doesn't want a smack in the face! "Off with the clothes!"

M: I have to shift gears a little bit and prepare myself.

T: What about starting with something sensual, like having a bath, or a drink of wine together, or whatever you want to do?

Specific suggestions for changes in wife's behavior in the form of a question.

F: Yeah, I could pop in the shower with you, because that revives you. *(Laughing)* Oh, here we go again with my gangbuster approach! When you hop in the shower I'll just follow you! "Oh, I can't even take a shower on my own. Here's this creature . . . " *(Laughs)*

M: Yeah. *(Laughs)*

T: You have to offer very gently.

Directive to wife to be "gentle."

F: Oh, very gently. Okay. Tap, tap . . . Robert . . . ? *(All laugh)*

M: What you say is true, it's like being pounced on.

F: I'd say shocked. But I don't realize that. I really don't.

T: The other thing you forget is that, as men move into middle adulthood, they get more sensual and less genital. I think that can be a real advantage which you are not using.

Information about life cycle changes. Reframe #3— Husband's style is an "advantage" for wife.

F: Yup. I should make use of the handholds that I do have.

T: Really, I think you are kind of lucky because you are not an inhibited person yourself. That means that you don't have to fight past any old hangups. I think you really have a perfectly wide repertoire as to what you can imagine.

Reframe #4— Wife is lucky because she is not inhibited, offering a wide range of possibilities.

F: Yes. Yes, that's true.

T: And with this man, you really need to approach real slow. I think that's just fine.

Directive to approach slowly is framed as "just fine."

F: Yes. Yeah, okay. I mean, that could be kind of fun too.

M: Yeah.

T: I think you would have fun with it. For a while you could probably shift back and forth more easily with it, because I suspect that if you make a decision to approach Caroline at a time when you are tired, even if you are the initiator, it's easier for you if the two of you go kind of slowly, and think about it for a while. You mustn't feel as if, once you suggest it, you have to perform within the next five minutes.

Reframe #5— Using wife's language; changes can be "fun."

Observation about husband's behavior is used as basis of directive to couple to "go slow."

M: Yeah, that's true.

F: Oh, that's right. That's something I have to be a little bit more delicate with. I'm not really delicate enough, which I think is also a way of teasing Robert. I think there may be a malicious component to it.

Therapist ignores the emotional messages imbedded

M: I wouldn't say that. *(Laughs)*

F: It's a way I can get him going, tweaking him, because he is so easily shocked. Even the time when I wanted to catch his attention when he was reading, quite a while ago, I pranced out stark naked and said, "Now!" Robert went to the drapes and said, "I have to take this?" And I said, "No, maybe there's somebody out there." But, I would only take it so far.

T: You know, Caroline, that is fun, I understand that. But I think there is a piece that the two of you have lost. Most of the time, when the two of you work together, you have been able to figure out how to blend the fact that you are different. Now here's a place where you are different, where you have an enormous amount to give him, and he hasn't been able to take it, because it's gotten too scary. There's no reason why he can't be more uninhibited with you at the point where it becomes safe to do that. It's kind of like the issue with the money, in reverse. Correct?

F: Yes. *(Laughs)*

M: *(Laughs)*

T: He would have all of the information and you would say, "What the hell are you going to do next?" You've got it reversed for this one. I think if you share it instead of hoarding it, the two of you would have a hell of a lot more fun together.

F: Yeah, that's true.

M: It's a good point. Well put.

F: That will take time. I have to say to myself, "You don't have to use a hit in the head when a tap on the arm will do."

in this interchange. Acknowledging them would divert the process from the negotiation for behavioral change.

Reframe #6 — What may be "fun" for the wife is "scary" for the husband.

Reframe #7 — Wife can give and husband can take, but only if the approach is not too scary.

Parallel drawn to another aspect of the couple's dynamics that they already understand in order to facilitate their understanding of the sexual dynamic.

Reframe #8 — Behavioral change would allow "sharing" and would be "fun."

T: Sure. But it's also fun. You're missing the fun of the whole thing. This man could be very seductive if you let him. I have a very strong feeling about that.

Restatement of Reframe #4. Systemic interpretation — If wife can be gentle, husband can be "seductive."

F: Oh yes, he is.

T: And you've been missing that. So, what the hell? Why not?

F: Okay, yeah.

M: We'll give it a shot.

Comments on the Therapeutic Process

The therapist was active, and ENGAGED each partner in the process of negotiation. COMMUNICATION was directed through the therapist, as opposed to between the partners. This approach helped the therapist to mediate BEHAVIORAL CHANGE and reframe new ways of looking at the sexual relationship.

The wife was the leverage for change within the system, as evidenced by the therapist's interventions. The therapist proposed changes in the wife's behavior that, in turn, would enable the husband to react and behave differently. While focusing on the wife's behaviors, the therapist sustained BALANCE by engaging both partners through interactional questions and comments that addressed their interactional dynamics. The SYSTEMIC ELEMENTS were presented to the couple by the therapist's pointing out the role each partner played in the problem, and how each one had to change. The therapist predicted that the husband's sexual approach would change as a matter of course, in response to a change in the wife's approach to sex.

The couple's emotional material was not addressed, effectively limiting distractions from the THERAPEUTIC AGENDA of developing a change contract. In order to negotiate the change contract, the therapist reframed the partners' stylistic differences and offered suggestions for change in the form of direct questions, interactional questions, and directives. By shifting the COGNITIVE view of the problem, BEHAVIORAL change became a real possibility for the couple.

The therapeutic focus shifted along with the therapeutic interventions. The initial focus, reframing the "new reality," facilitated the focus on behavioral change and the belief that change was possible. With the three-dimensional model of therapeutic focus, reframing of the sexual relationship can be described as addressing the way the dynamics of the relationship currently operate (PRESENT) by talking about the sexual problem (CONTENT), and targeting change in the cognitive view of the problem (COGNITION). The negotiation of the behavioral contract can be described as addressing how the couple's sexual relationship could be (FUTURE) by talking about specific options (CONTENT), and targeting changes in approach (BEHAVIOR).

"THE ROAD LESS TRAVELED"

The couple in this session, the 36th meeting of the therapist and clients, reported a lack of sexual satisfaction due to the husband's inability to achieve an orgasm. His complaint was that when he was about to have an orgasm, he would back off if his wife did not seem to be near climax, thus losing his erection. Although he could regain erection with stimulation, the cycle would be repeated. Underlying this pattern were the partners' mutual, unspoken beliefs that the husband was not "masculine" enough, and the wife was not "feminine" enough. These beliefs were tied to the facts that the female was supporting the family while the male was working toward a degree.

The therapist guided the couple on a journey, instructing them about the road they had been traveling by questioning them about their experiences on that road. Acting almost as an ALTER EGO for the couple, the therapist let the couple talk to each other, and spoke briefly and directly to move them along. With the help of the therapist, the couple discovered a fork in the road. The therapist drew the couple toward an understanding of how they reinforced their perceptions of themselves and each other while ostensibly trying to protect each other from these negative attitudes. Their mutual lack of sexual satisfaction was demonstrated to be one manifestation of their "protection racket." The therapist mapped out the possible paths: The continuation of the path they were on would perpetuate the "protection racket;" if they were seeking a supportive relationship and the end of the tyranny of the past, then they needed to choose the road less traveled. The therapist warned them that this path would cause a "little anxiety," but it would be "wonderful." The therapeutic focus was generally on the couple's interaction in the session, although focus shifted occasionally to events outside of the session in order for the couple to find examples of their behavior.

T: What do you think those feelings might be that are burdening you?	*Therapist asks the couple to focus the content.*

What general area do they have something to do with?

F: You verbalized your anger and
depression about Christmas. We've
gone through it many times; you were
talking about all of the things that you
didn't want to do.

M: It was specifically when we were
talking about buying Christmas
presents. I thought about getting your
Christmas present, and I thought I
wouldn't have time. It was a very
difficult thing; it was all negative.
When I thought more about it, what
came to mind was the last time we
made love. That's what I need to talk
about; there has been a lack of
satisfaction the last several times.

T: For whom?

M: For me. I guess for Beth too.

T: Don't guess. I don't want you to
guess. Speak subjectively when you
talk.

M: I have a problem where I reach a
point where I think I'm going to have
an ejaculation early, so I back off. I've
done this for years, and we've had a
way of working that out. But, the last
three or four times we've made love
it's not possible for you to have an
orgasm. It's a problem for me; I lose
my erection. I think that makes it
harder for you to have stimulation for
orgasm. It seems to be a vicious cycle.
When I begin to have more stimulation,
I regain my erection, that gives you
more stimulation, then I think I'm
going to have an ejaculation and I
back off.

F: Yeah. It's only been a problem
since this fall. It's very unusual for me,
but I have not had an orgasm since we

*The expectation is stated that
the partners speak specifically
and personally, using "I"
statements.*

returned from our trip. Perhaps getting back home may have something to do with it. I put it all together one time; I thought, "He doesn't want to make a living for me. He doesn't want to be the head of the household." I tied those two things together — not reaching orgasm and your lack of direction and not having a job. I interpreted that as rejection, as a sign that you didn't love me.

T: And why wouldn't he love you?

F: You didn't think enough of me, because I wasn't enough of a woman; I wasn't exciting or demanding enough of you.

Interactional question — Deepens emotional issue for wife.

T: How do you interpret the fact that you have a temptation to shoot too quickly and then Beth has no orgasm?

Interactional question — Deepens emotional issue for husband.

M: That she's not seeing me or experiencing me as a virile male making love to her. Perhaps, if I was something different, if I had a big penis, or were a big masculine person.

T: Do those interpretations sound familiar?

Question makes connection to parallel issues in the relationship.

F: In the last session, I was able to pull out of you that you interpret me as not demanding enough. You said that you could have quit that job with no fear of anything that I would say or do. I don't want you to be afraid of me, but if I had a better opinion of myself, then you would rise to where you have a better opinion of yourself. It's difficult for me to see how that works, but there is an interplay there.

M: If I viewed myself as more of a male in terms of being the head of the family and being sure of myself, then I would come across that way to you.

F: Yeah.

T: Where did those tyrannical ideas come from, that so many interpretations feed from, that you're not man enough or the idea that you're not feminine enough?

M: It had to be way back when I was a kid — my life with my mother and father. But I don't know why I keep playing this over and over again. I've been doing it for a number of years. It's like I've never heard of it before.

Reframe — Subjective experiences of partners stem from tyrannical ideas. Interpretive summary of core issue — Husband is not "man" enough, wife is not "feminine" enough.

T: So, lately, what's been happening in terms of those tyrannical ideas?

Therapist guides the couple to stay focused on the present.

M: I think they've been diminished. Take the time we had the weekend in the mountains. We had the day together and did a lot of things. When we came back, after dinner, we knew we were going to make love. We were in bed and I thought that it was time to start making love. But you said, "Wait a minute. Let's have more closeness, more intimacy, more sharing." I thought we had already had that, it was time to make love. I misinterpreted it, evidently. I thought all of that had been part of the evening. Then I wondered, "What have I done wrong? Where did I miss the signals?"

T: Did you verbalize that?

M: No, I didn't.

T: How come?

Therapist shifts focus from the specific incident to communication patterns.

M: I don't know. I guess I was afraid that it would ruin the rest of the evening. In fact, it did, because I didn't verbalize it I didn't get much satisfaction.

T: You asked a very good question, Tucker, "Why does this get repeated so often?" Can you answer that?

Probing core issue — How partners understand repetition of old patterns.

M: It's almost like I don't want to let it go; like I feel safer with the old

pattern even though intellectually I
know it's no damn good.

T: How about you, Beth?   *Balancing with wife.*

F: I'm threatened and I thought it
was because you don't come across as
confident and I've had to be careful; I
protected you. I guess I try to turn you
off by not being my best self.

T: So, you've been protecting   *Reflection — Emphasizes wife's*
Tucker.   *statement.*

F: It's not just a circle, it's intertwined
in other ways.

T: Had you been protecting Beth?   *Balancing with husband.*

M: Yeah, I guess I have. Instead of
being direct about what I was thinking,
I guess I was protecting you. Maybe I
was protecting myself.

T: Do you know what I see? I think   *Reframe of core issue — Need*
you protect each other.   *to "protect each other."*

F: I did sense this, with this last
issue of your deep depression, because
of your professor. I sensed a greater
strength in me, like "I don't want any
part of that stuff."

T: You didn't protect him. And when
you didn't protect him, what happened?

M: It worked out well.

T: It worked out well. That was the   *Interactional question — How*
difference. That's what was terrific.   *do partners protect each other?*
Tucker, how do you protect Beth from
that feeling that she is not feminine
enough? Beth, how do you protect
Tucker from that feeling that he is not
man enough?

F: I try to turn you off sexually.

M: That sure keeps me from being
man enough. When you turn me off,
I'm not one to persist.

F: But, you see, that's what I want
you to do: persist.

T: How do you protect Beth?   *Balancing with husband.*

M: I don't pursue her. I don't come off as a big, sexy man. I don't tell her about some of the things she does that turn me off.

T: That's a good way of keeping interpretations alive. It seems to me that the interpretations have no meaning at all. What do you think it would be like if you stopped protecting each other?

Change question—What would happen if protection stopped?

F: I need to see more clearly. Perhaps it's so ingrained that I don't know when I'm doing it.

T: That's a very good question. Let's pursue that. Ask Tucker.

Pursuing wife's question about awareness of patterns.

F: Can you see how I protect you that I'm not aware of?

M: No. That's something I have to work on. I'm more aware of when I do it to you. But, then I'm fearful of changing it. Maybe we need to think of situations. What do you do that protects me?

F: Well, one little thing is, when the phone rings, I'll think that you don't want to be interrupted, so I'll go answer it.

M: So, you can say, "It's your turn" or something.

T: Do you hear what he's asking for? That will get you closer. What's the answer?

Interactional question—Asking wife to consider husband's proposal for behavior change.

F: He's asking to be expected to take a full part in whatever happens around the house. I was saying that we will have many opportunities from now until Christmas. When you were dumping all that you had yet to do in school between now and the 21st, I said "I can get the meals from now until then. You do, what, three meals a week. If that will give you more time,

I'll do it." Now, I was aware that I was letting you paint your sad story so I could come and protect you.

T: Did Tucker ask you to do the meals?

F: *(Laughs)* No, he didn't. Alright.

T: Let's talk about that. What is really behind you doing the extra meals?

M: I remember when you said that, I had just the slightest inkling of, "Now that she has offered, maybe I had better let her do it." But, instead, I said what I was feeling, "No. I need to do that because it gets me away from studying and all of that, and it gives me a feeling of contributing to the partnership."

T: It's quite a different thing if Tucker says, "Listen, I'm really busy, could you cook three meals?" You are saying, fine, that's a partnership; that's the kind of thing we do all the time. It's quite another thing to have somebody express a feeling and then walk into martyrdom. That perpetuates the interpretations just like when you go buy all of the gifts and write out all the cards. The question is, how do you define support? I've confronted both of you pretty strongly; did you ever feel like I haven't supported you?

M: No.

F: No.

T: Supportive doesn't mean soft and protected. That may be no support at all. Do you think the protection could stop?

F: I really protected you from the beginning, it's the way I interpreted your behavior early on, and I probably do it automatically now. I need to be more aware of what I'm doing.

Probing wife's contribution to old patterns.

Contrast between direct communication and mind reading.

Question confronting definition of support.

Redefinition/Cognitive restructuring— Support does not mean protection. Change question— Can protection be stopped?

M: If you had tried to be something different 10 years ago, I don't know whether I would have been better off for it or not. But now we know what's going on; when you say something that is different from what I've heard before, I'll know what you're trying to do. I hope I can be tuned into when you're asking me for the soft approach or protection and be able to offer support instead.

T: Then there would be no protection. Then you would have the opportunity to replace it with something different. It would be a wonderful thing to stop the protection racket. It will raise a little anxiety and it will be different, but it will be a wonderful thing.

Proposing how "wonderful" it would be to stop the "protection racket."
Reframe— Protection is a "racket" not an emotional need; therefore, the price of change is only a "little anxiety" as they explore new possibilities.

Comments on the Therapeutic Process

The therapist worked very closely with the couple, integrating their language into the definition of the problem, summarizing the content into core issues, and asking each partner to explore the meaning of the couple's interactions. As their understanding of the problem changed, the therapist explored the possibility of replacing the old pattern with something new.

At the beginning of the session, the therapist reminded the partners of the rule of COMMUNICATION that they needed to "own" what they said, using "I" statements. Based on the socialization to the therapeutic process that had already taken place, the clients easily complied to this request. The flow of COMMUNICATION occurred predominantly between the partners. The therapist's interventions were short, and focused the discussion between the partners. The therapist was able to address each partner and the couple without becoming part of their interactional system. The therapist maintained BALANCE with each partner by tracking the interactions statement by statement. The therapist utilized interactional and parallel questions to ensure that each partner responded to the issues raised and reacted to the statements made. The result was a symmetrical interactional process whereby each partner shared parallel information about self and perceptions of the other.

During the therapeutic segment, the therapist guided the couple toward a better understanding of their interactional dynamics. Originally, the couple saw themselves as wanting to protect each other. Building upon the work of prior sessions, the partners were able to articulate how they "protected" each other from *confronting* the "tyrannical ideas" of the past by being overly helpful, indulgently understanding, not communicating, and failing sexually. What they had thought was protection motivated by affection, they were able to see more clearly as protection motivated by the need to perpetuate the old ideas that he was not "man enough" and she was not "feminine enough." These beliefs, stemming from the husband's role as student and the wife's role as breadwinner, were paralleled sexually in their joint failure to be orgasmic. By sabotaging their sexual relationship, they successfully reenacted the old beliefs. To succeed sexually would have affirmed his masculinity and her femininity and thereby would have shattered the old belief system.

By means of this exploration, the therapist was able to foster a significant COGNITIVE SHIFT. This shift occurred when the therapist helped the couple acknowledge that what they wanted to provide for each other was support; that being supportive would be a more effective expression of their affection; and that being protective kept them stuck. "Protection" was reframed as a "racket," and the therapist presented a new challenge: Learn how to be supportive. The cognitive shift provided leverage for change, since it allowed the couple to experience their relationship differently.

It was apparent that the therapist and clients worked well together. The verbal interactions flowed and the deepening of clinical material was well paced to the clients' readiness. The therapist guided the couple to the point where they could reconsider the proposition for change. This task was accomplished through a sequence of interactional questions, change questions, summary statements, and reframes which facilitated a process in which the partners did most of the work under the vigilant guidance of the therapist.

The focus of the session was on how the couple understood the motivation for their behaviors. The target for change was the couple's COGNITIVE set, which was clarified by means of the exploratory process. In accordance with the three-dimensional model of therapeutic focus, the segment can be described as targeting the current functioning of the relationship (PRESENT) by exploring how the couple thought about their interactional patterns (COGNITION), which emerged from the direct verbal interchange between the partners (PROCESS).

SUMMARY

The operationalization of the basic principles of the Intersystem Approach in the preceding cases was clearly different. These differences were most evident in the flow of communication, the therapeutic agendas, balance, and the mode of functioning (affect, cognition, behavior) addressed. Aside from the differences between the couples in each case, which require a certain amount of adaptation from the therapist, the therapists acted very much in the style most typical of their work in general. Differences between the therapists in therapeutic focus were also representative of general differences in their styles.

In both case vignettes, the therapist provided direction for the session by targeting the dynamics of the marital system that provided the greatest leverage for change. The clinical summaries and transcript analyses highlight for the reader the diversity of approaches and styles that are encompassed by the Intersystem Approach to marital therapy. The primary focus, thematic content, and therapeutic process differed between the cases, but each therapist conceptualized the problem in systemic terms, engaged the couple in the effort to effect change, and incorporated the "meaning" of the problem into the therapeutic agenda. These commonalities form the foundation of the Intersystem Approach.

The differences between the therapists emphasize the flexibility provided by the Intersystem Approach. It is difficult to imagine a model of therapy that would have been more able to meet the couples in these cases where they were, as opposed to first getting the couple to fit the model. The same is true of the therapists themselves. While yet working within the framework of the Intersystem Approach, the therapists were able to adapt the therapy to their styles, however different, rather than molding themselves to the framework.

The three-dimensional model of therapeutic focus provided a useful tool for conceptualizing the movement of therapy. In the cases described, the therapeutic focus shifted in line with the therapist's progression from the "problem" to the "resolution." While it is doubtful that the therapists were thinking along the dimensions of the model, their work can be more easily understood in post-hoc analysis when guided by this framework. The analyses of the cases, based on the three-dimensional model, demonstrated that the divergence of approaches to the couples and their problems was not just a matter of working with different content and/or dynamics, but also represented differences in therapeutic domain.

In "Brave New World," the therapist reframed the interactional dynamics to facilitate a change contract. The focus was on the future, content, and behavior. In "The Road Less Traveled," the therapist explored the core issue that fueled the repeating patterns. The focus was on the present, process, and cognition. Both couples presented a problem in their sexual relationship, yet embarked on divergent therapeutic paths toward change.

PART II

Clinical Issues

Chapter 8

Extramarital Sex: The Treatment of the Couple

April Westfall

I came here this evening to tell you something. I've gone and fallen in love, you see. It's quite absurd and maybe it's all a goddamn mistake. It probably is a goddamn mistake. I met her during the convention in June. She was the interpreter and secretary. Actually she's studying for her degree. She's going to teach Slavic languages. She's nothing much to look at. In fact, you'd undoubtedly think she was ugly. I have no idea what this will lead to. I have no idea about anything. I'm completely bewildered. Of course I'm pleased in one way. Though I have a hell of a bad conscience about you and the children. We've always got along well, haven't we? I mean, things haven't been any better or worse for us than for the average family. Say something, for Christ's sake. (Bergman, 1973/1974, p.84)

So begins the confessional from Johan to Marianne in this sequence from Ingmar Bergman's tale of marital infidelity, *Scenes from A Marriage*. What is first felt by Marianne as only a dimly recognized rift in their well-ordered lives is now brutally brought out in the open with this sudden announcement. What follow for much of the play are embattled scenes of struggle interrupted by occasional moments of tenderness as we witness the couple's rather clumsy efforts to reconcile.

The therapist treating a couple in the midst of an extramarital crisis is likely to encounter the full gamut of conflicting emotions depicted in Bergman's play. The loss of innocence that can come so suddenly with the first disclosure of a spouse's extramarital involvement can have a shattering effect on the marital equilibrium. The therapist is asked to guide the married pair through and beyond this period of emotional upheaval, while keeping in check his/her own response to the events at hand.

This chapter offers a clinical guide to the marital/family therapist working with the problem of extramarital sexual relations. It begins with a brief consideration of definitional issues and values before moving on to more clinical material. The importance of careful assessment is emphasized, as well as the skillful management of the extramarital crisis. Special problems posed by the secret affair and the continuing affair are discussed. The process of recovery and its complications are traced. Finally, an outline of a multilevel explanatory model of extramarital sex is presented. The chapter concludes with a discussion of the common concerns of couples about the future of their marriages.

DEFINITIONAL ISSUES

According to Thompson (1983), there has been a confusing use of terminology pertaining to extramarital relations. Strictly speaking, extramarital sex (EMS) refers to the occurrence of sex outside the marital dyad; cohabitating couples — whether heterosexual or homosexual — are excluded by definition. Thompson has coined the term "extradyadic" to refer to the extra relations of both married and cohabitating couples. With few exceptions, research in the area of extradyadic relations has been limited to the marital dyad.

In their large survey of American couples, Blumstein and Schwartz (1983) interviewed cohabitating heterosexual and homosexual couples, as well as married couples. They then performed separate analyses on the three comparison groups. Among the heterosexual couples, the investigators did not find any significant difference in either the general desirability or actual incidence of non-monogamy between the married and cohabitating men and women. However, they did note differences in the level of secrecy surrounding extradyadic sex, with cohabitating couples dealing more openly with their partners about their outside sexual activities.

This finding is not surprising since marriage is an institution supported by legal and religious contracts that tend to favor conventional monogamous behavior. Having vowed to be sexually faithful, husbands and wives raise doubts about their basic trustworthiness when they go outside the marriage for sex. Only a small number of married couples ever revise the marital rules to permit a more open or swinging-type sexual relationship. Still, the lack of clear sanctions—for or against non-monogamous behavior—can sometimes work to the detriment of unmarried couples. Couples merely living together do not have available to them the same community supports (e.g., family, friends, and clergy) that their married counterparts have in facing the challenge of an outside sexual involvement (Humphrey, 1987).

Among homosexual couples, there is a notable disparity in the preference for and practice of non-monogamy between lesbians and gay males (Blumstein & Schwartz, 1983). While lesbians are often committed ideologically to sexual freedom from monogamy, it is more difficult to put this ideal into practice. Their outside sexual relationships tend to be less casual in nature, so that they threaten and compete with the relationship with the primary partner. Gay male couples differ from all other couple groups in their capacity to adopt a lifestyle that accepts non-monogamy as a normal and desirable part of everyday life. Gay men tend to seek more variety in sex, reporting a greater incidence of extradyadic sexual behavior with more partners than any other couple group. Moreover, their capacity to separate the emotional and physical components of sex allows them to engage in such outside activities in a way that does not usually disrupt the couple bond. The authors further noted that gay couples seeking to live monogamously may feel out of step with the rest of the gay world. They often receive the same kind of prejudicial treatment that heterosexual couples opting for non-monogamous relationships are likely to experience.

Since the interviews were conducted for this study in the mid-1970s, a devastating disease known as *acquired immunodeficiency syndrome* (AIDS)* has infiltrated the homosexual population in the United States

---

*Since the first documented occurrence of AIDS in this country in 1981, we have been faced with a viral epidemic here and elsewhere whose incidence continues to soar (Dwyer, 1987). To date, one to two million Americans are estimated to have been infected with the AIDS virus, many of whom are carriers capable of spreading the disease to others. No one really knows how many of those persons infected with the AIDS virus will go on to develop the disease, but experts estimate the incubation period for the disease to be at least five to seven years. Yet, much is now known about the disease—a sexually transmitted and blood-born infection—that can work toward its prevention. So far, the group hardest hit by the AIDS virus has been that of male homosexuals. In cities with a high concentration of homosexuals, public health officials have teamed up quite effectively with leaders from the gay community to curb the spread of the disease. In San Francisco alone, recent public health statistics have

in large numbers. In cities where information about the disease is widely disseminated, there has been a radical shift in sexual practices in an attempt to lower the risk of contracting or spreading the AIDS virus. Surveys of gay men indicate a significant decrease in the average number of sexual partners, as well as a modification of sexual behavior toward safe-sex practices. Whether these changes in sexual practice will continue and have a more lasting impact on gay attitudes toward sex is unknown at this time and will likely depend on the future course of the epidemic.

A QUESTION OF VALUES

Our long history of religious condemnation of and legal sanctions against EMS continues to constrain the way we think about the subject. This bias is built into the very structure of our language: "infidelity" referring to a religious-moral term for non-monogamy, "adultery" to a legal one. It is reflected in our Western literary heritage as well, with the great tragic heroines — e.g., Emma Bovary, Anna Karenina, Hester Prynne — acting as archetypal figures of the romantic, adulterous woman. More modern psychoanalytic theory (Strean, 1980) includes a continued negative valuation of non-monogamy. However, the verdict is now rendered in terms of clinical diagnosis and psychopathology rather than direct — and somewhat more honest — moral judgment. This is not to deny the clinical accuracy and therapeutic utility of psychoanalytic interpretation to individual case histories. But, to render all such behavior as ipso facto evidence of psychopathology or psychosexual immaturity is to betray a moralistic stance garbed in more modern, intellectually sophisticated attire.

Marital and family therapists are not free of such simplistic thinking in their assessment of EMS. There is a continued tendency to construe extramarital relations in pathological terms. The site of the disturbance has shifted, however, from the individual husband or wife to the couple relationship itself. Dysfunctional marriages rather than dysfunctional individuals produce EMS behavior.

---

shown a remarkable 75% decrease in certain kinds of venereal disease (McKusick, 1986). The impact of the AIDS virus within the heterosexual population is only beginning to be felt, with the disease until recently limited to a few high-risk groups, e.g., IV drug abusers, prostitutes, and hemophiliacs and others receiving blood transfusions prior to the development of effective screening procedures. The incidence is almost surely to rise in coming years. As AIDS now becomes a health hazard to the community at large, there needs to be the same kind of commitment to public education as shown by the gay community. Along these lines, recent appeals by the Surgeon General have called for radical measures to be taken toward prevention. Regardless of sexual preference, the practice of casual, indiscriminate sex with anonymous or little known persons is putting oneself and one's partner (when one exists) at a considerable health risk.

Other marital/family therapists have tried to rid themselves of the negative bias in the psychoanalytic viewpoint by adopting an uncritical and permissive attitude toward the subject (English & Heller, 1975). They minimize or overlook entirely the destructive aspects of EMS, arguing in favor of the personal growth of those so involved. In espousing the virtues of EMS, these therapists assume the role of rebellious adolescent within the larger therapeutic family. Such a stance only masks as a more enlightened perspective. In truth, it remains wedded to the same narrow, dichotomous thinking of its puritanical forebears.

Very little has been written that presents EMS in terms complex enough to help us with our clients' concerns. Yet, if properly dealt with, such an event "may play an important role in contributing to a couple's ability to understand the interrelationship of love, sex, and commitment" (Constantine, 1986, p. 421). In addition, there are some very important ethical questions raised by the presence of an EMS relationship that are addressed inadequately, if at all, in the usual debate. Issues concerning deception and secrecy, fairness and trust, are ever present in the therapeutic context of EMS relations and pose special challenges to the clinical management of the couple.

THE ASSESSMENT OF EMS

Cuber and Haroff (1965; Cuber, 1969) were among the first authors to point out the great heterogeneity concealed in the monolithic word "adultery."

> In such a category we would have the person who has had "one too many" at the office party, the one who "lives off the land" at every opportunity, the lecher in the literal sense of the word, as well as the one who feels mismatched and trapped and finds warmth and comfort where he can, and the one whose marriage is so seriously destructive that he desperately seeks and clings to another meaningful relationship which sustains him. (Cuber, 1969, p. 191)

The lumping together of such diverse and contradictory behaviors into an all-encompassing category obscures rather than clarifies our understanding. In an early paper on the subject, Ellis (1969) described a host of different motives for EMS and distinguished between healthy and unhealthy reasons for this behavior. Just as individual motives for EMS vary enormously, the impact on the marital and sexual relationship of the couple depends on a number of important considerations. We cannot assume the consequences for the couple are uniformly deleterious. Similarly, the effect of the EMS behavior on the mental health and emotional functioning of the individual participants should not be reduced to a few conventional stereotypes.

Building on the earlier work of Sprenkle and Weis (1978), some of the more important factors in differentiating EMS behavior include the following:

1) Type (heterosexual/homosexual) and level of sexual activity (flirting, petting, intercourse, etc.);
2) Frequency and duration, as well as location, of EMS activities;
3) Number of EMS partners (past and present);
4) Unilateral/bilateral nature of EMS;
5) Degree of secrecy surrounding EMS;
6) Degree of acceptance of and consent for EMS behavior in the marriage by both spouses;
7) Degree of emotional involvement with and commitment to the EMS partner;
8) Relationship of the nonparticipating spouse to the EMS partner;
9) Degree of emotional involvement and commitment between spouses; and
10) Tolerance of EMS behavior within the couple's ethnic community/ social group.

THERAPEUTIC HANDLING OF EMS: THE INITIAL STAGE OF TREATMENT

The clinician should attend to how the issue of EMS is introduced into therapy. Does the couple initiate treatment with EMS as the presenting problem or does it emerge as an issue only after several months of therapy for seemingly unrelated concerns? Is the subject raised in a conjoint session with the couple or during an individual session with one spouse? Has the relationship with the outside partner been terminated or is it still ongoing? These questions concerning the timing and circumstances surrounding the introduction of EMS into the therapeutic setting have important implications for the treatment of the couple.

Extramarital Sexual Crisis

The most likely time for couples to consult a therapist in regard to EMS is immediately following the revelation of a secret, nonconsensual, extrasexual involvement. This revelation may cause only mild perturbations in some marriages, in which it is easily accepted or somehow tolerated by the other spouse. This is rarely the case with the couples seeking therapeutic assistance in handling the EMS problem. Still, these couples are not so emotionally devastated by the news that they bypass therapy altogether and immediately turn to legal counsel. Instead, their reactions usually fall within the midrange of these extremes. At least one spouse believes the marriage has been seriously threatened by the presence of EMS, yet feels sufficiently committed to the partner to hope for possible recovery.

While most crisis situations are characterized by the experience of emotional turmoil and disequilibrium, the *extramarital sexual crisis* (Thompson, 1984) is accompanied by reactions that are unusually intense and persistent. Only in the case of separation and divorce can the marital therapist expect to witness such extreme affective responses and such rapid-fire oscillations in feeling states. According to Scharff (1978), couples sometimes experience a "honeymoon" in the midst of the crisis, covering a wide range of emotions, which include "sorrow, grief, anger, love, new closeness, panic, and finally, shared sexual feeling" (pp. 39-40). Grief reactions (Humphrey, 1987; Rhodes, 1984; Taibbi, 1983) are to be expected, as both spouses report often profound feelings of loss. For the nonparticipating spouse, there is a loss of self-esteem and personal confidence in his/her own attractiveness as a mate. For the participating spouse, the decision to give up the outside partner can be quite troubling when there has been a significant and/or prolonged attachment to that person. Both spouses must mourn the loss of an image of a more perfect marriage prior to the affair, and both long to return to this earlier, more innocent state.

Trust in the partner and the marriage is eroded by the presence of an unsanctioned EMS relationship, which strikes at the core of the spouse's sense of well-being. Fantasies of retaliation are quite common at this time, as are threats and actual incidents of physical violence (Whitehurst, 1971). In contrast to the spouse who reacts with anger, some blame themselves almost completely for their partners' EMS behavior. Beyond this, the nonparticipating spouse is often disturbed with recurrent thoughts and images of his/her partner's EMS activities, which may interfere with concentration and intellectual functioning at times.

At first, the participating spouse may feel relieved that the other spouse knows, no longer burdened by petty acts of deception or more elaborate schemes of concealment. This reaction is more common when the spouse responds to the discovery of his/her partner's behavior with initial calm and matter-of-factness, only gradually feeling the full hurtful impact of what has taken place. Consequently, it is only later that the offending spouse is likely to respond with feelings of guilt and shame.

Sometimes the spouse will attempt to reassure his/her partner that "it didn't mean anything," thereby hoping to minimize the breach of trust in the marriage. The partner is seldom convinced by such remarks and is sometimes infuriated by what seems like a belittling, dismissive attitude. On a few occasions, a spouse has reacted with so little affect and such apparent indifference on hearing of the partner's affair that the offending spouse feels and behaves like the injured party. The partner's lack of response is viewed as confirmation that he/she simply doesn't care enough to get upset.

The effective management of the extramarital crisis requires that the therapist be calmly, yet firmly, in control of the sessions. The therapist must resist being placed in the role of the one casting blame or passing judgment, yet not remain too aloof from the couple's struggle. While not taking sides with either partner, he/she must take seriously the emotional distress of both. Couples must be allowed to express their strong feelings in a safe setting—feelings that may have been actively suppressed at home or that surface only during embittered arguments. They need to know that the emotional and cognitive disequilibrium they experience is a normal response to the crisis and, what's more, is likely to continue to a lesser degree for several months. Far from alarming the couple, this knowledge usually allows them to relax somewhat their frantic and futile efforts to achieve a hasty return to pre-crisis normalcy.

At the same time, the therapist must carefully monitor the degree of emotional disturbance and impaired functioning of each spouse. He/she must be ready to take additional clinical measures when necessary. Sleep and appetite disturbances occur often and can be transitory. If, however, they persist or become severe, an evaluation by a psychiatrist for antidepressant medication should be considered. One study (Beach, Jouriles, & O'Leary, 1985) found that couples presenting with EMS reported higher rates of depression when compared to other couples entering marital therapy. Interestingly, it was the spouse engaged in EMS, rather than the nonengaged spouse, who showed higher levels of depression. The therapist should inquire directly about thoughts and acts of physical violence between spouses in those marriages in which the potential for violence seems high. Furthermore, the EMS partner can become the target of the jealous spouse's abusive rage. In addition, the therapist needs to be aware of other environmental stresses currently operating for either partner, leaving him/her psychologically depleted and less able to cope with the additional strain of the extramarital crisis.

The therapist should take steps to regulate the level of anxiety between spouses during this early stage of the crisis. More frequent sessions with the couple are often necessary during this period. Some couples need help in structuring time apart from each other. Emotions may run so high as to make continual contact with each other unbearable or even dangerous. Couples may need to plan different activities to be carried out in different areas of the house. They may want to limit the time they spend discussing the EMS issue at home or to confine these discussions to a more public setting or to the therapist's office. It is very important for the couple to reach some agreement on what will be told to whom about the EMS involvement, so as not to add to their feelings of shame and betrayal. Although a few couples seem so painfully sensitive to the mere presence of the other as to make continued living together impossible, a precipitous separation is to be avoided during the acute phase of the crisis. Although physical separation may provide some measure of relief to the embattled couple, it does so at the cost of increased insecurity over marital survival.

The therapist should begin to move beyond this narrow focus on the EMS issue to an enlarged assessment of the marital system, even during the first session. What is their observed style of interaction? What other problems in the marriage do they each identify? What are the particular satisfactions they associate with their married life together? How has the couple relationship evolved over time? Has it kept pace with the individual developmental changes of each spouse? How has the presence or absence of children altered their lives together? Somewhat more slowly, the therapist should follow his/her usual line of questioning with couples. He/she needs to understand the initial formation of the couple system and its various changes and adaptations over time. Moreover, this information is critically important to an eventual appreciation of the meaning of the EMS for the larger marital/family system.

In individual sessions with each spouse, the therapist can examine each partner's feelings about continuing the marriage, willingness to invest in the couple therapy, and personal goals for the therapy. While ambivalence in regard to the future of the marriage is common to both spouses at this stage of the crisis, an extremely low level of commitment to the marital partner can pose a serious obstacle to the couple therapy (Beach et al., 1985). In addition, the therapist should gather information concerning the family background of each spouse so as to be aware of important losses and discontinuities in each of their personal histories (through death, divorce, or geographic dislocation) that could aggravate the present trauma.

The therapist should inquire as to how the couple are handling the

EMS issue with their children. Are the children aware of the problem? If so, how did they come to know about it? How have the parents responded to their questions? A child's understanding of and reactions to a parent's EMS will vary depending on the age and the developmental stage of the child. Adolescents often have a more difficult time coping with their parents' extramarital activities. Their anxieties in regard to their parents' EMS behavior interact with their more personal sexual anxieties, intensifying both. Typically idealistic in their vision of love, adolescents feel particularly disappointed and even betrayed by their parents' example.

Regardless of age, a child will often side with one parent over the other during the early stage of the extramarital crisis. The therapist should carefully monitor the family situation to make sure that this early side-taking does not become fixed into a permanent arrangement. At certain times, the therapist should consider bringing the children in for a family session. This is recommended when their reactions to the crisis appear extreme. Sometimes the parents are unable to deal effectively with their children's concerns in the face of their own emotional turmoil. Feeling victimized by a spouse's EMS, a parent may solicit a child's sympathies in a way that overburdens the son/daughter with the parent's grief. Alternatively, the parent may seek revenge by fueling the child's anger toward the other parent.

A final word should be said about those situations in which one spouse presents for individual rather than couple therapy at the time of the extramarital crisis. A spouse may choose to come alone because of ambivalence in regard to the continuation of the marriage, the ending of the relationship with the EMS partner, or both. At other times, one spouse will refuse conjoint treatment because of angry feelings toward his/her partner. Conversely, the spouse may refuse because of fear of his/her partner's anger, not wanting to be publicly embarrassed. Others simply fail to appreciate the appropriateness of marital therapy for dealing with the extramarital crisis: "I'm the one with the problem, so why should my wife/husband have to come?" Whenever possible, the partner presenting alone for therapy should be encouraged to consider inviting the other spouse into the sessions. This is especially recommended in those instances in which there appears to be sufficient commitment to the marital relationship by both spouses. The possibility of a resolution of the extramarital crisis in favor of the marriage continuing is enhanced by their joint cooperation in therapy.

The Secret Affair

Therapists who operate from a model that integrates both intrapsychic and interpersonal approaches to the treatment of the dysfunctional couple (Beavers, 1985; Berman, Lief, & Williams, 1981; Feldman, 1982, 1985; Pinsof, 1983) routinely make use of individual as well as conjoint interviews. At the beginning stage of therapy, individual interviews help build rapport. They convey to both spouses a feeling that the therapist recognizes and values each of them as a separate individual. Additionally, these interviews permit the disclosure of certain information that the person might be reluctant to speak about in a conjoint session. For therapy to be successful, the therapist should have access to any information that is highly relevant to the presenting problem or to the couple/family system as a whole. This information should be taken into account in planning and conducting the therapy. As noted by Humphrey (1987), a secret EMS relationship can mask the source of a spouse's specific sexual dysfunction or lack of sexual desire. At other times, the sexual relationship of the couple continues undisturbed, but one partner's secret affair seems importantly implicated in the marital conflict or emotional distancing that brings them to therapy.

Nevertheless, the disclosure of secrets in individual interviews with each spouse can pose difficult ethical and strategic dilemmas for the therapist (Karpel, 1980). The therapist is given critical information, but is unable to use this information openly and freely. He/she can be drawn into a web of deception and distortion that makes it quite difficult to maneuver effectively. The therapist is likely to experience a variety of emotional discomforts and tensions: "S/he may feel guilty for deceiving the unaware, resentful of the secret-holder for having revealed the secret, anxious about the complications developing in the case, and powerless to do anything about them" (Karpel, 1980, p. 301). The therapist is inevitably drawn into a covert alliance with the secret-holder and estranged from the unaware spouse in the process. Finally, the secret-holder may expose the therapist's participation in the secrecy scheme in a sudden and disturbing disclosure, undermining the therapy entirely.

When the therapist is in a position to anticipate the possible disclosure of secrets, preventive approaches to avoid such entanglements can be undertaken. During the individual interviews with each spouse, they are told that the content of these discussions will remain confidential. Disclosure of certain information may be recommended, however, if the therapist believes that this is necessary for the conduct of therapy. In certain instances, the client may have to choose between disclosure or termination of the therapy. By outlining this position ahead of time, the therapist is better able to operate vis-à-vis any important disclosures and less likely to be taken off-guard.

When a secret EMS involvement is revealed, how is the therapist to determine the need for further disclosure to the other spouse? Certain therapists have attempted to eliminate the need for critical judgment by adopting fairly inflexible rules of procedure. On one end of this continuum, Scharff (1978)advocates full disclosure of secret extramarital liaisons, whether current and ongoing or over and done with. This view holds complete disclosure as basic to a recommitment to the marriage by a knowing, mutual choice of both partners. Furthermore, it can serve to clear the air of mistrust, equalize the conscious control of the marital partnership, and provide a "shot in the arm" to the marriage by alerting the spouses to critical dangers. Full disclosure is considered a prerequisite to offering sex and marital therapy to the couple. At the other extreme, Humphrey (1987) attempts to maintain confidentiality with both spouses in the face of a currently active, emotionally charged EMS relationship on the part of the husband or wife. In so doing, he aspires to a position of ethical neutrality in regard to the disclosure issue. This view holds that clients have a right to make their own decisions on such matters, and prohibits the therapist from imposing his/her values and standards on them.

Karpel (1980) recommends that the therapist adopt a stance of "accountability with discretion" in handling marital/family secrets. In practice, this stance amounts to a serious consideration of the relevance of the withheld information to the unaware spouse, while attempting to understand this from his/her point of view. When disclosure is recommended, it should be done with sensitivity to the timing of the event and the likely reactions of the unaware spouse. This approach does not eliminate all ambiguity nor substitute for sound clinical judgment. Yet, it offers the most useful guidelines for sorting out complex questions of ethics and clinical management in EMS cases.

A currently active, secret EMS relationship by one spouse is, with few exceptions, highly relevant to the other spouse. It points to a major violation of trust and reciprocity in the marriage. The spouse should consider the possibility of stopping the relationship with the outside partner at least for the limited period that the couple are engaged in therapy. Alternatively, the spouse can consider the possibility of dealing more honestly with his/her partner about the affair. He/she should not feel pressured to make an immediate decision and may require additional time and/or individual sessions with the therapist to consider the probable consequences of each option.

If the spouse refuses either to end the relationship with the EMS partner or to disclose the affair to the spouse, the therapist has little choice other than to refuse marital/sex therapy at this time. To attempt to treat the couple with the knowledge of certain withheld information that importantly affects the daily life of the unaware spouse is, in fact, to behave in an untrustworthy manner. Not knowing the facts as they are, the unaware spouse has not been granted a fair, informed choice to participate in the therapy. He/she is clearly operating at a power disadvantage. Furthermore, to work with the couple while unable to address the impact of the ongoing affair on the marriage could leave the therapist's hands impossibly tied. To deal with the EMS relationship in confidential, individual sessions concurrent with the conjoint sessions (Humphrey, 1987) seems like a misguided prospect from the outset. To conduct treatment under these conditions is to risk creating a confused and muddled therapeutic context, similar to that found in disturbed families.

Sometimes the refusal to give up the EMS relationship occurs because the marital tie is quite tenuous and the commitment to the spouse is so low. This refusal may be the first step toward marital separation. With other couples, one partner seems caught in a web of unresolvable ambivalence — what a colleague of mine, Terry Marek, has referred to as "the inability to choose between two loves." Yet, the husband/wife may remain in a devitalized marriage for still other reasons: security needs, status concerns, religious dictates, the sake of the children, respect for one's parents or grandparents, etc. For this situation to continue indefinitely seems to require, at the very least, the tacit cooperation and support of both the outside partner and the spouse. Sometimes the husband/wife seems genuinely distressed by this predicament; yet he/she is unable to extricate himself/herself from it or to deal more openly with the marital partner. In these cases, the therapist may recommend individual therapy.

The therapist has greater latitude in handling the disclosure issue when dealing with prior EMS behavior on the part of one or both spouses. Sometimes the relationship with the EMS partner(s) has ended some time ago and does not appear to have had a lasting impact on the marital relationship. In this case, the therapist can feel more comfortable in leaving the issue of disclosure to the client's discretion. This is also true in isolated instances of EMS activity involving little or no emotional attachment to the outside partner, when this behavior has not become fixed into a continuous, repetitive pattern over time. Still, the therapist cannot always accurately assess the impact of previous EMS behavior on the present marital relationship, especially during this early stage of treatment. Therefore, the client should be forewarned that at some point the therapist may insist on disclosure if he/she

believes that the prior EMS activity poses a sufficient obstacle to therapeutic progress.

At times, disclosure is necessary in order to break the couple's destructive cycle of deception and distrust. Some individuals experience
considerable guilt as a result of their previous EMS behavior. These
feelings can cause them to insulate themselves emotionally from their
spouses. At other times, it is the unaware spouse who seems somehow
to sense his/her partner's EMS behavior. This situation can give rise to
strange, ill-defined feelings of mistrust toward the partner. Sometimes
the spouse is almost apologetic for what seems like his/her paranoid
suspiciousness. What appears to be cognitive distortion and exagger-
ated emotional response on the part of the unaware spouse may, in fact,
be reality-based. Unless the couple is willing to deal directly with the
emotional repercussions of the spouse's earlier EMS activity, they may
not be able to put it behind them. Should it become necessary, the
therapist can request an individual session with the spouse to discuss
the disclosure issue. Sometimes the therapist will choose not to proceed
further with the couple without it.

Sometimes the spouse is not presently engaged in EMS activity, but
has had a history of such frequent occurrences that disclosure is made a
prerequisite to marital/sex therapy. When the EMS behavior has taken
place repetitively throughout the marriage, to choose not to address this
issue in the therapy is to collude with the spouse(s) in denying a
significant factor in their history together. Moreover, when the EMS
behavior has occurred with such persistence, the therapist has good
reason to believe that it will require the attention of both spouses to be
brought under control.

When an affair is revealed in the midst of ongoing treatment of the
couple, the therapist is faced with certain questions: Why is the spouse
electing to disclose at this time? How does this decision relate to what
has already transpired in the therapy? Does the disclosure occur in a
conjoint session or to the therapist alone? Sometimes the decision to
disclose is positively motivated, reflecting an increased commitment to
the marriage and/or a desire for greater intimacy with the spouse. A
husband/wife may be actively involved in an EMS relationship at the
outset of treatment. This fact is kept secret from both the other spouse
and the therapist. Disclosure comes later in the therapy when the
spouse begins to experience greater satisfaction in the marriage. The
spouse now feels ready to break off the relationship with the EMS
partner. At other times, a husband/wife senses that his/her earlier
secret affair acts as a barrier to more open communication in other
areas. With this recognition, he/she is more willing to risk disclosure.

On the negative side, the decision may be made at a time when there is greater harmony in the marriage, arising out of a spouse's need to sabotage the therapeutic progress. The disclosure returns the couple to their former conflicted or disinvolved state. As Framo (1982) has observed: "Some people cannot tolerate prosperity or good things in their lives" (p. 134). When disclosure happens rather abruptly and is made to the therapist alone, e.g., during a phone call, the therapist must question the client's motive for doing this. Can this act be construed as a power play by the client in an attempt to form a collusive, one-up relationship with the therapist?

Apart from the issue of motivation, the therapist should be concerned with the effect of a late disclosure on the ongoing treatment of the couple. Often the husband/wife is angered by the partner's holding out for so long and may question what other secrets have yet to be revealed. The spouse may want to reinterpret the events of therapy in light of the partner's affair. He/she dismisses all other marital difficulties as inconsequential in view of this one critical issue and disavows responsibility for most of the marital distress.

The Continuing Affair

The affair that continues with both spouses' open knowledge poses special challenges to the therapist. This type of affair usually has the effect of aggravating the emotional turmoil and uncertainty of the extramarital crisis, sometimes beyond limits that the therapist can comfortably work with. When there is greater allegiance to the marriage and/or sensitivity to the spouse's distress, the husband/wife will often agree to give up the EMS relationship. Other spouses hang onto the outside relationship quite tenaciously in the face of their spouses' often dramatic protests. This can occur out of hostility to their marital partners and/or indifference to their obvious suffering, or sometimes because of genuine caring for and attachment to their EMS partners. A few couples move to a position of real acceptance of this kind of arrangement and alter their marital contracts to permit a more open marital system.

More typically, the couple are caught in a deadlocked struggle on this one issue, which prevents them from attending to other important issues in the marriage. At other times, the spouse will reluctantly agree to allow the partner's outside involvement to continue, unwilling to take a stand on this issue and risk losing the partner altogether. This may leave him/her at such a power disadvantage that real growth in the marriage is made impossible. Here the spouse operates in a one-down position that limits his/her responses more generally in the marital relationship to ones of anxious or begrudging compliance. Moreover, the emotional fall-out from the partner's unwilling acceptance of the spouse's EMS relationship poisons the marital atmosphere with anger and hostility.

At times, the spouse's rather obvious victimization serves as a retaliatory protest and an indirect indictment of the offending partner. The spouse may suffer from very real depression, unable to live comfortably with the present predicament, yet too insecure emotionally or economically to leave. The therapist may have to take steps to break the marital stalemate by pointing out the futility of the couple's attempts to improve and enrich their marital life together as long as the affair continues. Under these conditions, there may not be enough flexibility in the marital system to encourage positive experimentation and growth. On occasion, the therapist may recommend bringing the outside partner into the session as a way of breaking the marital impasse. Although I have yet to have a couple or outside partner actually comply with this request, the idea does serve to shock and to confront them with the absurd task they have set for themselves.

THE PROCESS OF RECOVERY

As stated before, the emotional unrest and relationship disturbance that are part of the extramarital crisis are likely to persist for several months or even years. The process of rebuilding can be quite slow and unsettling for both spouses as they struggle to get on with their daily lives. When the couple continue in treatment beyond the immediate discovery period, the therapist can be instrumental in shaping this recovery process.

According to Whitehurst (1971), our culture tends to support emotion-laden and generally negative reactions to the EMS situation, which only deepen the marital rift and make more difficult the repair of the relationship.

> First, the righteous indignation, wrath poured on the wrongdoer, vindictiveness, hostility, punishment, heaped-on scorn and guilt are among the many responses culturally presumed to be justified. What the culture approves is often disruptive and destructive in that it is impossible to re-establish meaningful dialogue once the usual definitions of the situation are asserted. (p. 685)

Couples in treatment tend to reflect this normative pattern, most often polarized into victim/villain roles. Apart from the vast array of punishing responses outlined above, the guilty spouse is likely to be hit with an onslaught of questions concerning the details of the EMS. The partner's need for certain information — the identity of the EMS partner, the degree of emotional involvement, and the nature of their sexual sharing — seems reasonable enough. There can be, however, a repetitive questioning and concern with endless details that extend beyond reasonable bounds.

What sets the jealous response to the partner's EMS experience apart from other emotional reactions, e.g., anger and grief, is this quality of obsession. At times, especially when the husband is doing the questioning, there is an almost pornographic focus on the sexual practices with the outside lover(s). The husband/wife will appear to be sexually excited and titillated by the spouse's erotic depictions. These reactions are often short-lived, soon to be replaced by hurt and disgust. Women tend to seek out more generalized information about the EMS partner; they want to know details about the partner's physical appearance, style of dress, personal habits, etc.

According to Farber (1973), this seemingly endless request for details about the EMS partner is fueled by the spouse's rather desperate search for the "ideal rival": one that will reduce the intensity of his/her jealous rage. If the outside partner is portrayed in favorable terms, the spouse is assaulted with feelings of envy and self-doubt. On the other hand, if the rival is described as an inferior being — whether physically plain and unattractive or lacking in the social graces — the spouse is seldom reassured. The fact that the partner would desire such an inconsequential character seems all the more disturbing. In fact, there is no ideal rival; however one conceives of the person is sure to bring torment. The spouse should be encouraged to take control of his/her obsessive thoughts, which only serve to torment both partners and to pull them further apart. The jealous spouse must come to realize that no amount or kind of information about the EMS partner will prove really satisfying, except in the most limited way. Relief must be sought elsewhere!

Apart from this absorption in the details of the partner's EMS experience, the jealous husband/wife tends to be preoccupied with the daily comings and goings of the partner. He/she cannot be certain that the affair has really stopped. Consequently, he/she feels suspicious of any hesitation in response or change of schedule. To some degree, this heightened vigilance seems justified, and even necessary, so as not to return to the former complacent state. He/she may remember all the passed-over details and what now — with the benefit of hindsight — seem like rather obvious indications of trouble.

However infuriating, this suspicious attitude can represent a first step toward claiming more responsibility for his/her own collusion in the EMS process. More importantly, it is a move toward taking control of its prevention in the future. Still, the almost paranoid suspicion that comes with even a small deviation from schedule — as when the spouse returns home a half-hour late at night — can be quite annoying. The continued cross-examination about his/her every activity — requiring almost hour-by-hour accounts — can be tolerated for only a short period without protest. After a while, it is the guilty partner who begins to feel victimized by the badgering mate. Among healthier couples, the spouse's defensive cries can have a sobering effect on the jealous partner, serving to calm and restrain him/her. Other couples are less fortunate in that the spouse is too absorbed in his/her own feeling of self-injury to begin to recognize the injury to the other spouse.

When straightforward, commonsensical approaches to the partner's obsessive jealousy are not successful, some therapists (Constantine, 1976, 1986; Elbaum, 1981; Im, Wilner, & Breit, 1983; Teismann, 1979) advocate indirect, paradoxical techniques to deal with the problem. In selecting a strategy, the therapist should determine how the jealousy is perceived by the individual client (as ego-syntonic or dystonic) and by the couple (as system-syntonic or dystonic) (Constantine, 1986). When jealousy is experienced as both uncontrollable and undesirable, then certain paradoxical and rational-emotive strategies are likely to be effective.

There are numerous techniques of this kind for dealing with marital jealousy. Constantine has categorized them into those making use of: a) relabeling and reframing of the symptom in positive terms; b) role-playing and role-reversal; c) exaggerating and prescribing the symptom; d) imagery and spatial metaphors for clarifying individual and relationship boundaries; and e) cognitive theory and related concepts for modifying basic beliefs and assumptions underlying the emotional response. The first four categories make reference to the jealous system, as opposed to the jealous individual; both spouses are actively solicited in the change process.

Essential to this treatment approach is an attitude of "serious playfulness" which Teismann (1979) defines as "a dual appreciation and management of the tragedy and comedy in the drama of human problems" (p. 159). Couples caught in the grip of jealous fury tend to be grimly serious and unimaginative in their efforts to cope with the problem. The introduction of a sense of play into the therapeutic setting can foster more creative solutions to the EMS dilemma.

Couples sometimes turn to other outside sources to augment the work within the clinical setting. The husband/wife will consult a priest (or some other member of the clergy) as a way of easing a guilty conscience through the ritual act of confession. On more than one occasion, I have had clients on their own seek out a fortune-teller, hoping to get a more definite fix on their future together. (I might add that in my limited and rather loose association with fortune-tellers [*n*=4], the results thus far have been favorable, more so than with certain bonafide professionals I've come into contact with.) Other clients turn to literary sources (e.g., Irving's (1976) *The World According to Garp,* Jong's (1973) *Fear of Flying,* Kundera's (1969/1974) *Laughable Loves,* Malamud's (1977) *Dubin's Lives,* Updike's (1968) *Couples*) for help in coming to terms with the EMS experience. Immersed in these readings, the couple can begin to feel enough detachment from the deadly seriousness of their own situation to permit an element of novelty, surprise, and even humor to enter into their reactions.

FACTORS COMPLICATING THE RECOVERY PROCESS

The timing and circumstances surrounding the extramarital crisis can make the process of recovery more difficult. The therapist must work directly with these complicating factors so as to lessen or circumvent in some way their worsening influence. One such factor — and a fairly commonplace one — occurs when the participating spouse continues to operate in close proximity to the former EMS partner, who may be a colleague at work, neighbor, etc.

> Glen and Linda began marital therapy four years after the termination of Linda's brief affair with a colleague at work. Although their reasons for seeking therapy at that time were not directly tied to this earlier event, it soon became apparent that the affair continued to rankle both husband and wife. This relationship had begun when Linda, a corporate executive, was away on a business trip with her colleague. Since her disclosure of the affair, Linda had virtually stopped all business-related traveling, despite the inconvenience of doing so at times. At the office, she continued to associate occasionally with the former EMS partner when they would collaborate on business projects. However, she tried to keep such projects to a minimum.
>
> Neither husband nor wife had seriously questioned the emotional impact on the marital relationship of the wife's continued association with the ex-lover. Only when the husband, a lawyer by profession, was thinking of leaving his firm and applying for a position as legal counsel within his wife's company were they able to face the issue more directly.

In preparing for the job interview, Glen acknowledged his anger and discomfort at the prospect of coming into direct contact with his wife's former lover. Moreover, Glen began to suspect his own motivations for applying for the position within his wife's organization and decided to withdraw his application. Nevertheless, the interview process had served a useful purpose in helping the couple to face up to certain important issues: the husband's continued doubts as to whether his wife's affair had really ended; the wife's discomfort in having to be reminded continuously of her marital infidelity in the presence of her ex-lover.

A second obstacle to the couple's recovery occurs when there is an unfortunate coincidence of the extramarital crisis with other marital/family stresses, e.g., a difficult move, loss of job, etc.

Jack and Susan had been married 11 years before the wife's affair, lasting a period of four months, took place. When the affair became known to the husband, the couple entered counseling for a brief stint, which they both claimed had been helpful in working through the emotional issues surrounding Susan's EMS involvement. At the same time, they made a decision to start a family. Within the next three years, Susan had given birth to two children. Both spouses continued to function full-time in high-level professional positions.

The couple initiated treatment with me a year after the birth of their second child. The presenting complaint was their common concern with the infrequency of their sexual relations (usually not more than once or twice a month) and, in particular, with the wife's low level of sexual desire. Both spouses attributed the problem to Susan's earlier affair, since she had not felt or behaved romantically since that time. Moreover, Jack viewed her lack of initiative in sex as indicative of his loss of attractiveness to her as a lover.

Neither spouse was able to look beyond the wife's EMS experience to other factors that might be inhibiting the wife's romantic/sexual feelings. Both failed to take into account the physical and emotional exhaustion involved in her attempts to juggle a demanding job, daily child-care arrangements, household chores, and "quality parenting" in the evenings. Moreover, they did not take into consideration the radical adjustment required of them as a couple functioning as a tight twosome for 12 years before having their first child. Shortly after starting therapy, they began planning their first vacation since the birth of their first child almost four years before. Earlier in the marriage, traveling together had been a real source of pleasure and adventure. Still, this kind of reductionistic thinking —attributing any and all failures in the marriage to an earlier EMS experience—is not uncommon.

A third factor aggravating the extramarital crisis consists of a family history of EMS by either spouse. When a spouse's parent is known to have had such experience(s) — especially when the impact on the other parent and the family as a whole was perceived as harmful — the emotional trauma in relation to the current crisis is intensified and prolonged.

> Marie, a homemaker and mother of five children, was referred for individual therapy by the marital therapist who had attempted, rather unsuccessfully, to treat the couple in the face of the husband's disclosure of a single one-night stand. Marie continued to hover between feelings of intense rage and depression, even after several months of marital therapy.
>
> In the individual therapy, Marie came to understand better the source of her intense feelings through our exploration of certain important themes in her family of origin. Marie came from a family in which her father rather frequently gambled and engaged in brief sexual escapades with different women. Her mother would seldom deal openly with her husband about these matters, but tended to confide in her children, especially Marie, in his absence. Marie formed a strong coalition with her mother against the father. Her mother remained married to her father until the youngest of their six children had started school and she had found employment outside the home. Marie was 12 years old at the time of her parents' separation. She had only minimal contact with her father after their separation and remained fiercely loyal toward her mother.
>
> When Marie married her husband at 18, she had him promise that he would never be unfaithful to her. He supposedly kept that promise for 17 years until one weekend while away from home with his National Guard group. At first, he tried to keep the incident to himself, but he felt so guilty that he was eventually compelled to tell his wife. Marie had never really worked through her anger and feelings of abandonment by her father. At the time of her husband's revelation, these earlier feelings resurfaced in a torrent of rage commingled with the more immediate anger toward her husband.

A fourth factor complicating recovery occurs when other family members have acted as secret-holders before disclosure to the unaware spouse. Such an occurrence can cause divisiveness among family members and lead to loyalty conflicts throughout the entire system. When a parent confides in a son or daughter and swears this child to secrecy, all other family relationships are compromised. The formation of a cross-generational coalition between parent and child around the sexual secret marks a clear violation of normal family boundaries and hierarchy.

This pernicious alliance can cause serious internal conflict in the child, which may continue even into adulthood.

Rhona, a 17-year-old female, was referred for individual psychotherapy by her parents, Judy and Robert. Their main concern was with their daughter's sexually permissive and reckless behavior. At the time of referral, she had been pregnant twice already, each time followed by an abortion. In addition, Rhona's academic performance had sharply declined in the last year. In the initial family session, Rhona appeared openly defiant toward her parents, particularly toward her mother. She was more cooperative when seen by herself, so I proceeded to treat her alone.

After several sessions, Rhona revealed that her mother had been having an affair. She had discovered this by accident a year ago when she overheard a phone conversation between her mother and her mother's lover. When confronted, Judy readily admitted to the affair. She further cautioned Rhona to not so much as hint at this fact to her husband, lest he make a precipitous move to end the marriage.

At first Rhona felt quite grown-up and somewhat privileged to be sharing her mother's secret. These feelings soon turned to anger. She blamed her mother for her selfish disregard for her father's feelings and for the interests of the family as a whole. She also felt disloyal toward her father in conspiring with her mother to maintain the secret. She gradually withdrew more and more from both parents, unable to take a stand against her mother for fear of precipitating a family crisis.

In this case, the sexual secret threatened to undermine Rhona's personal comfort and ease with the parents. Her sexual acting-out seemed obviously connected to her mother's equally risky sexual behavior. With her repeated pregnancies and abortions, Rhona was able to draw attention, by comparison, to an ever-present danger at home.

In order to free Rhona from this untenable position, her mother's affair had to be brought out in the open. A session was first held with mother and daughter to confront mother with the need for disclosure. Judy was helped with her apprehension in facing-up to her husband. Following this meeting, a family session took place with Rhona and her parents in which Judy assumed responsibility for disclosing the secret. After one more family session, the couple requested marital therapy and were referred elsewhere. Rhona continued in individual therapy with me for the next few months, where she made excellent progress before terminating.

THE MEANING OF EMS:
THE SEARCH FOR UNDERSTANDING

Once the couple have moved past the immediate shock of the extra-marital crisis, they can begin to examine more carefully the question:

Why has the EMS taken place? While this question will most certainly be raised at the time of first revelation of the EMS, few couples are prepared to calmly and deliberately consider the problem during this period of heightened tension and vulnerability. Moreover, the initial replies to the question are apt to be somewhat simple-minded and to reflect whatever socially acceptable rationalizations for such behavior happen to be in vogue at the time.

At first the actively participating husband/wife is likely to present his/her spouse with a self-serving story that minimizes the importance of the marital transgression. In so doing, he/she hopes to put an end to the current crisis. Nor is this attempt to soothe motivated by selfish reasons alone, but may come from genuine concern for the partner's visible distress over the affair. In contrast, the nonparticipating spouse is likely to seize upon his/her worst fears as to the cause and plead, "You don't love me or find me desirable anymore," while hoping the partner will counter with more comforting notions.

The marital/family therapist is in a good position to assist the couple in their search for a more adequate understanding of the EMS incident(s). Just as an intersystem model of therapy calls for a multilevel assessment of both intrapsychic and relational dynamics, the therapist's approach to the more specific EMS issue makes use of both individually and interpersonally oriented concepts and techniques. At the *individual* level, the therapist studies how certain developmental, psychodynamic, and biological factors impinge on the marriage, increasing the likelihood of extramarital relations. Concepts relating to adult development, psychiatric disturbance, and major medical illness in either spouse are included in this category. At the *dyadic* level, the focus shifts to the spousal relationship with its special needs and tensions. Theories examining the contrasting nature of romantic and marital love, gender-role conflict and confusion, and the problem of couple infertility belong to this group. At the *family systems level*, the meaning of the EMS becomes embedded in an intricate and increasingly complex web of family relationships. Issues pertaining to sibling rivalry, family life-cycle transitions, and death and its emotional aftereffects are dealt with here.

At this point in the treatment of the couple, the line between crisis management in regard to the EMS issue and more intensive marital therapy begins to blur. The couple have moved further away from the earlier delineation of roles as victim and villain. Instead, they struggle to reach a better understanding of their individual and joint needs as played out through the EMS experience(s). Herein lies the real opportunity: to construe the EMS in more personally meaningful terms and to develop firmer control of this issue and their marital life in general with this new knowledge.

THE FUTURE OF THE MARRIAGE

Until recently, our society has fostered an attitude that regarded divorce as the natural and acceptable response to a spouse's extramarital behavior. Prior to the 1980s, adultery continued to be the primary legal ground for divorce in most states. The situation has changed radically with the recent popularization of no-fault divorce statutes. Still, the tendency remains for people to connect at some level of thinking the idea of extramarital sex with that of separation and/or divorce.

Couples in the midst of an extramarital crisis are invariably concerned with the future of the marriage. Consequently, they are most likely to raise the issue of separation/divorce in treatment and to enlist the help of the therapist in the decision-making process. Here, the therapist's task is simply to stand by as they struggle with their agonizing decision, but certainly not to decide for them. Moreover, the therapist should not be so presumptuous as to imagine that he/she can ever save the marriage when the couple have decided otherwise.

Nevertheless, the therapist can play an important role in seeing that the decision is made in a thoughtful and responsible manner, and only after a careful consideration of the more important reasons for the EMS in the first place. Divorce actions that are entered into hastily — or that follow soon after the turmoil at the time of the revelation of the affair — are to be discouraged. They forestall the possibility of eventual growth and reconciliation of the couple. Even though an affair can take the couple to the "edge of disaster, and often beyond," Napier and Whitaker (1978) have argued that it can act as an agent to break the marital impasse. As such, it can bring new energy into the marriage and force the couple to communicate on a more open and deeper level.

Couples who wish to continue their marriages are faced with decisions concerning the ongoing nature of their relationship in the future. One critical area of discussion concerns the issue of possible extramarital relations by either spouse at some later point. While most couples will continue to adhere to a traditional script — advocating a monogamous style of marriage — a few may choose to depart from this script, opting for some kind of sexually open marriage. More commonly, one partner will favor a nonexclusive arrangement, while the other hopes to continue a more conventional lifestyle. It would seem that for a small segment of the population of married couples (Macklin, 1980), mutually agreed upon non-monogamy can be a viable alternative to traditional marriage. Even with these more permissive arrangements, however, most couples have felt a need to place certain restrictions on the behavior of both partners in the form of mutually agreed upon ground rules (Buunk, 1980; Knapp & Whitehurst, 1977; Ramey, 1975). These restrictions are viewed as necessary in order to preserve the stability and integrity of the marital relationship.

The situation in which the couple are unable to agree on the exclusivity issue can be an especially trying one for the marital therapist. He/she is called upon to negotiate a fair agreement between spouses that in its final version is apt to be somewhat complicated, ambiguous, and not wholly satisfying to either party. At best, the therapist is searching for a solution that both spouses will be able to live with for a while, but is sure to need revision at some later time.

The effect of the therapist's values as they impinge on his/her approach to clients is particularly critical in the highly controversial area of sexually nontraditional marriage. The therapist who seeks to work fairly and effectively with these couples must be clear about his/her personal values and beliefs as pertains to non-monogamy. Constantine (1986) argues that the therapist's willingness to support workable solutions for clients that differ from his/her own lifestyle choices is the important factor in such cases, not the degree of similarity or compatibility of their values. Furthermore, when the therapist is unable to support a particular couple's lifestyle choice, he/she should make this fact known to them and offer to make an appropriate referral.

Still, it is difficult for therapists to separate their personal feelings from their professional interactions with clients. In a national survey of marriage counselors concerning their professional treatment of clients with sexually nontraditional marriages (Knapp, 1975), the counselors' personal attitudes and behavior with respect to outside sex were most influential in their attitudes and behavior toward these client couples. The author cautions that "personal objectivity is an ideal rarely achieved, if ever, and that 'detached' professionals are still judgmental human beings who must operate within a personal value framework" (p. 513). As therapists, we must remain mindful of our value choices, not only as pertains to sexually nontraditional marriage, but to extramarital relations more generally. Our values influence the way we think about and conduct the therapy from start to finish, including: our initial reactions to the couple on hearing of a spouse's extramarital involvement; our manner of handling the extramarital crisis; our tendency toward side-taking with one spouse over the other; and, finally, our notions as to what is an acceptable resolution of the crisis.

CONCLUSION

At the end of Bergman's play, the couple are simply left to continue in their muddled and compromised state. Yet, as "citizens of the world of reality," they appear somehow more truly real and more capable of loving. As Johan consoles Marianne in the final scene together:

Marianne: Sometimes it grieves me that I have never loved anyone. I don't think I've been loved either. It really distresses me.
Johan: I think you're too tense about this.
Marianne: (smiling) Do you?
Johan: I can only answer for myself. And I think I love you in my imperfect and rather selfish way. And at times I think you love me in your stormy, emotional way. In fact I think that you and I love one another. In an earthly and imperfect way. (Bergman, 1973/1974, p. 211)

Couples who are able to weather the extramarital crisis and struggle together to make some sense of these events may discover an earthly and imperfect bond of love. Others are left with only the recognition that all such feeling vanished some time ago and that their only real choice is to get on with their separate lives once more. Even so, some lack the capacity to release themselves, and so must settle for what remains of the outward trappings of the conjugal state. Regardless of outcome, the therapist who comes into contact with these couples is forced to learn about the difficult compromises we must all make with our partners and ourselves in love.

REFERENCES

Beach, S. R., Jouriles, E. N., & O'Leary, K. D. (1985). Extramarital sex: Impact on depression and commitment in couples seeking marital therapy. *Journal of Sex & Marital Therapy, 11,* 99-108.

Beavers, W. R. (1985). *Successful Marriage: A Family Systems Approach to Couples Therapy.* New York: Norton.

Bergman, I. (1974). *Scenes from a Marriage* (A. Blair, Trans.). New York: Bantam Books. (Original work published 1973)

Berman, E., Lief, H., & Williams, A. M. (1981). A model of marital interaction. In G. P. Sholevar (Ed.), *The Handbook of Marriage and Marital Therapy.* Jamaica, NY: Spectrum.

Blumstein, P., & Schwartz, P. (1983). *American Couples.* New York: Morrow.

Buunk, B. (1980). Sexually open marriages: Ground rules for countering potential threats to marriage. *Alternative Lifestyles, 3,* 312-328.

Constantine, L. L. (1976). Jealousy: From theory to intervention. In D. H. Olson (Ed.), *Treating Relationships.* Lake Mills, IA: Graphic Press.

Constantine, L. L. (1986). Jealousy and extramarital sexual relations. In N. Jacobson & A. Gurman (Eds.), *Clinical Handbook of Marital Therapy.* New York: Guilford Press.

Cuber, J. F. (1969). Adultery: Reality versus stereotype. In G. Neubeck (Ed.), *Extramarital Relations.* Englewood Cliffs, NJ: Prentice-Hall.

Cuber, J. F., & Haroff, P. B. (1965). *The Significant Americans: A Study of Sexual Behavior among the Affluent.* New York: Appleton-Century-Crofts.

Dwyer, B. J. (1987, January). Aids. *The Psychiatric Times, 4*(1), pp. 1; 8-10; 12-15.

Elbaum, P. L. (1981). The dynamics, implications, and treatment of extramarital relationships for the family therapist. *Journal of Marital and Family Therapy, 7,* 489-495.

Ellis, A. (1969). Healthy and disturbed reasons for having extramarital relations. In G. Neubeck (Ed.), *Extramarital Relations.* Englewood Cliffs, NJ: Prentice-Hall.

English, O. S., & Heller, M. S. (1975). Debate: Is marital infidelity justified? In L. Gross (Ed.), *Sexual Issues in Marriage.* New York: Spectrum.

Farber, L. H. (1973). On jealousy. *Commentary, 56,* 50-58.

Feldman, L. B. (1982). Dysfunctional marital conflict: An integrative interpersonal-intrapsychic model. *Journal of Marital and Family Therapy, 8,* 417-428.

Feldman, L. B. (1985). Integrative multi-level therapy: A comprehensive interpersonal and intrapsychic approach. *Journal of Marital and Family Therapy, 11,* 357-372.

Framo, J. L. (1982). *Explorations in Marital and Family Therapy.* New York: Springer.

Humphrey, F. G. (1987). Treating extramarital relationships in sex and couples therapy. In G. R. Weeks & L. Hof (Eds.), *Integrating Sex and Marital Therapy: A Clinical Guide.* New York: Brunner/Mazel.

Im, W., Wilner, R. S., & Breit, M. (1983). Jealousy: Interventions in couples therapy. *Family Process, 22,* 211-219.

Irving, J. (1976). *The World According to Garp.* New York: Robbins.

Jong, E. (1973). *Fear of Flying.* New York: Holt, Rinehart & Winston.

Karpel, M. A. (1980). Family secrets: I. Conceptual and ethical issues in the relational context II. Ethical and practical considerations in therapeutic management. *Family Process, 19,* 295-306.

Knapp, J. J. (1975). Some non-monogamous marriage styles and related attitudes and practices of marriage counselors. *Family Coordinator, 24,* 505-514.

Knapp, J. J., & Whitehurst, R. N. (1977). Sexually open marriage and relationships: Issues and prospects. In R. W. Libby and R. N. Whitehurst (Eds.), *Marriage and Alternatives: Exploring Intimate Relationships.* Glenview, IL: Scott, Foresman.

Kundera, M. (1974). *Laughable Loves* (S. Rappaport, Trans.). New York: Knopf. (Original work published 1969)

Macklin, E. D. (1980). Nontraditional family forms: A decade of research. *Journal of Marriage and the Family, 42*, 905-922.

Malamud, B. (1977). *Dubin's Lives.* New York: Farrar-Straus-Giroux.

McKusick, L. (Ed.) (1986). *What to Do about AIDS: Physicians and Mental Health Professionals Discuss the Issues.* Berkeley, CA: University of California Press.

Napier, A. Y., & Whitaker, C. A. (1978). *The Family Crucible.* New York: Harper & Row.

Pinsof, W. M. (1983). Integrative problem-centered therapy: Toward the synthesis of family and individual psychotherapies. *Journal of Marital and Family Therapy, 9,* 19-35.

Ramey, J. W. (1975). Intimate groups and networks: Frequent consequences of sexually open marriage. *The Family Coordinator, 24,* 515-530.

Rhodes, S. (1984). Extramarital affairs: Clinical issues in therapy. *Social Casework, 65,* 541-546.

Scharff, D. E. (1978). Truth and consequences in sex and marital therapy: The revelation of secrets in the therapeutic setting. *Journal of Sex & Marital Therapy, 4,* 35-49.

Sprenkle, D. H., & Weis, D. L. (1978). Extramarital sexuality: Implications for marital therapists. *Journal of Sex & Marital Therapy, 4,* 279-291.

Strean, H. S. (1980). *The Extramarital Affair.* New York: The Free Press.

Taibbi, R. (1983). Handling extramarital affairs in clinical treatment. *Social Casework, 64,* 200-204.

Teismann, M. W. (1979). Jealousy: Systematic problem-solving therapy with couples. *Family Process, 18,* 151-160.

Thompson, A. P. (1983). Extramarital sex: A review of the research literature. *Journal of Sex Research, 19,* 1-22.

Thompson, A. P. (1984). Extramarital sexual crisis: Common themes and therapy implications. *Journal of Sex & Marital Therapy, 10,* 239-254.

Updike, J. (1968). *Couples.* New York: Ballantine Books.

Whitehurst, R. N. (1971). Violence potential in extramarital sexual responses. *Journal of Marriage and the Family, 33,* 683-691.

Chapter 9

Spouse Abuse–
A Dyadic Approach

Richard N. Mack

INTRODUCTION

Spouse abuse has recently emerged as a major area of study within the field of marriage and family therapy. While social work and the community services fields have been aware of the problem for about 30 years, the literature in our field has emerged during the last 10 years. It is time that we recognize the extent of this most serious issue affecting relational systems.

The scope of the problem is truly frightening. It has been shown that most people have experienced a violent incident in the context of a male/female relationship (Bern, 1982). The incidence of reported occasions of violence in the dyad has increased dramatically in recent years. According to the National Institute of Mental Health, physical violence occurs between family members more often than it occurs between any other individuals or in any setting other than wars and riots. According to the Office on Domestic Violence, only one in 10 cases of spousal abuse is ever reported to the authorities (Women in Transition, 1985). Moreover, spouse abuse knows no social or economic bounds. While it is more likely to be reported in the lower economic levels of society, it exists to a significant degree at every economic level (Gelles & Cornell, 1985).

The data compiled by this research raise some interesting questions. Are there couples where abuse can be halted without destroying the couple? Would treatment of spouse abuse within a dyadic therapeutic context simply further mask the reality of the problem (a charge against marital and family therapists often issued by those more closely allied with the abuse field)? Is it possible that there have been some factors in spouse abuse, systemic in nature, that have been overlooked up to this point? The purpose of this chapter is twofold. The first is to address these questions. The second is to call attention to the serious challenge that spouse abuse presents to the practitioners of marriage and family therapy.

CONTRAINDICATIONS FOR A DYADIC APPROACH

Our perspective is that it is possible to treat spouse abuse within the couple context, provided that the level of abuse has not progressed to the instrumental level. It is the assessment of the level of abuse which is the key to determining the appropriate treatment of spouse abuse.

The conventional wisdom when dealing with couples where spouse abuse is an active concern has been to separate the partners physically and to then treat the separate individuals — victim and villain. Due to the real and present danger involved in abuse, there is much wisdom to this approach. Simply stated, the logic of this treatment is as follows: If the couple can be separated, there is less danger of further abuse; if the couple is kept together, danger remains at a significantly high level. Those involved in treatment based on this view do not discriminate between levels and function of abuse in the relationship. Separate treatment has been axiomatic in all abuse situations.

The chart opposite (Table 9.1) is reprinted from *Spouse Abuse—A Treatment Program for Couples* by Neidig and Friedman (1984). It illuminates the difference between "expressive" violence and "instrumental" violence, when applied to the couple. This difference is the key to effective treatment of spouse abuse. Couples who have experienced "expressive" violence, and for whom "instrumental" abuse is not present, may be effectively treated within the context of the couple.

Expressive violence is that which flows out of the emotional life of the couple. It is not the same in intention, intensity, or extent as instrumental violence. The expressive-violence couple cannot handle stress in a controlled way, unlike the couple in which one controls the other through vicious physical intimidation. With such expressive violence couples,

Table 9.1
The Violence Continuum

Expressive Violence	*Instrumental Violence*
Violence that is primarily an expression of emotion (anger, jealousy, etc.)	Violence that is used primarily as an instrument to achieve a goal
Absence of exposure to severe prior violence	History of exposure to severe violence
Mutual and reciprocal violence; victim and perpetrator roles not fixed	Unilateral violence: victim and perpetrator roles fixed
Violence in context of escalating conflict	Violence as deliberate effort to punish or control
Sequential, gradual, predictable progression to violence	Relatively sudden and rapid progression to violence
Mutual conflict, stress, frustration and anger precede violent incident	Low provocation for violence
Genuine remorse and sorrow; violence inconsistent with values, belief that violence will be controlled	Shallow manipulative remorse; violence consistent with values, resignation, and hopelessness
Unpredictable, high potential for escalation and "accidental" injury	Potential for violent retaliation, homicide, or suicide
Relatively benign psychological consequences	Serious psychological consequences; helplessness, depression, low self-esteem, external locus of control
Brief, skill-building therapy with couples	Long-term therapy with individuals, separation, legal sanctions
Termed mutual combat, spouse abuse, or domestic violence	Termed battering

Reprinted with permission from Neidig and Friedman (1984).

the issue of abuse is entwined with other marital issues. Once the abuse is stopped, the couple can be taught some skills in stress management and anger control, and helped with the other concerns of the marriage.

Instrumental violence is brutal and imminently dangerous. Because of the level to which the violence has escalated, the injuries that are inflicted in each go-round, the frequency of attacks, and the lack of emotional response to the act or the pain, it is too dangerous to treat the couple in conjoint marital therapy. Because the safety of the victim is immediately at stake, the couple must be physically separated and treatment should proceed as two concurrent individual therapies. In many cases of instrumental violence, the abused party returns to the abuser after flights to safety; these returns are not a sign of the stability or healing of the couple (Matthews, 1982). They are, rather, signs of an overwhelming bond of mutual dependence formed by two extremely insecure people with low self-esteem. In a situation where spouse abuse has become instrumental, it is unlikely that a healthy couple bond can be achieved. Therefore, separation and separate therapy constitute the appropriate treatment of choice.

There is another serious contraindication for the dyadic treatment of spouse abuse. Various studies on spouse abuse show that 36 percent to 52 percent of those who abuse their spouse also abuse alcohol. There appears to be a variety of perspectives on the connection between alcohol/drug abuse and violence in the family. Gelles and Cornell (1985) suggest, "Alcohol itself does not lead to violence, rather men drink (or say they drink) to have a socially acceptable excuse for violent behavior." Whatever the specific connection may be, one treatment axiom is clear: There will be no positive, lasting change in the cycle of spouse abuse until the substance abuse that fuels the pattern is under control. To enter into conjoint therapy with a goal for substantive change in the dyad without first having the substance abuse under control is fruitless.

DEVELOPING A SYSTEMS APPROACH

The first goal in treating spouse abuse must be to stop the abuse. The safety of the victim is the primary concern as the couple begin to work on their abuse issues. Throughout the therapy, the potential exists for another episode of abuse. If these clients regress, there is real danger. Therefore, stopping of the abuse is essential at the very beginning of the therapy.

Much of the early work in the field was aimed at delineating personality types for both the abuser and the abusee. Fleming (1979) notes the following characteristics of the abusee: (a) wide range of responses, (b) guilt, (c) emotional dependence, (d) economic dependence (ultimate determinant), (e) low self-esteem, (f) traditional value systems, (g) anger (depressed), (h) isolation, (i) fear, (j) ambivalence (corresponding to mixed realities), (k) embarrassment and shame, (l) fear of insanity, (m) physical illness, (n) learned helplessness, and (o) lack of prior knowledge about domestic violence.

Taken as a whole, this "profile of battered women" provides a conceptualization of one partner in the spouse abuse couple. Weitzman and Dreen (1982) found, in addition, that the abusee has usually been beaten as a child or witnessed some other beating (spouse abuse) within the family of origin, and is perceived as immature and dependent on his/her partner.

The abusers also tend to be of a predominant personality type.

Weitzman and Dreen (1982) describe the stereotypic abuser as one who feels inadequate and views his/her life as a failure, while feeling helpless to do much of anything to change this constellation. They add that these people have accepted a particular type of social conditioning in which they are led to repress feelings about distasteful or disturbing events or situations until they then explode in uncontrolled anger. Because of their conditioning, this cycle of repression and explosion is deemed appropriate and successful.

Taken together, these profiles show a couple woefully unprepared and inadequate to handle stress inside their relationship or in the external world. Stress, due to causes real or imagined, provides the trigger to explosive episodes of violence.

The stage is therefore set for the cycle of abuse to take place. Deschner (1984) outlined a seven-step cycle which each event of domestic violence follows. The steps are:

1. *Mutual dependence.* The beginning of the cycle is the involvement in relationship of two extremely needy people. The unexpressed contract of this relationship is that all needs of both partners will be met within the context of the relationship. It is a relationship with high intensity, one in which there are vows of devotion and passion, but which works to exclude the world outside the relationship. This serves to isolate the couple from the world outside, including potential sources of support and assistance in times of trouble.

2. *Noxious event.* At some point, the calm and peace of the relationship are broken. The potential victim does something that is perceived as undesirable by the potential abuser. The "unpleasant" something falls outside the contract for mutual dependence. A need of the potential abuser goes unmet by the partner.

3. *Coercions exchanged.* There is an attempt, on the part of the potential abuser, to stop the "unpleasantry," usually by a series of verbal threats. The potential victim participates in the escalation of exchanges, sharing in a positive feedback loop. The anxieties of the couple rise as the tension of the situation grows hotter, with neither side able to bring them down to a manageable level.

4. *"Last straw decision."* The potential abuser now senses that the situation is untenable. Things are perceived as totally unworkable and impossible. There seems to be no way out of the impasse.

5. *Primitive rage.* The potential abuser crosses over the line to become the abuser. Rage is called up as a response to the "last straw" impasse. The entire consciousness of the abuser becomes filled with rage, and the object of that rage becomes the object of violent attack. The rational mind appears turned off; even memory of actions done during the rage may be impaired.

6. *Reinforcement for battering.* In reaction to the explosion of uncontrolled rage, the victim submits, in a vain attempt to not spur even greater violence in the abuser. This is a self-protective measure which, though effective in the present, has some negative consequences for the future. By submitting, the victim sends a message to the abuser that says, "Violence works! I stopped doing the unpleasant thing." Thus, the practice of the same tactic is reinforced for the future.

7. *Repentance phase.* Both the victim and the abuser are clearly shocked by the actions that have taken place. The abuser denies responsibility and promises that this will never happen again. The victim senses genuineness in the abuser, responds by overcoming fear and angry rage, and makes the decision to once again trust the contrite abuser.

There are two extremely important points in this cycle of violence that clearly show the systemic nature of events of spouse abuse. The first of these is the "Last Straw" decision, the inevitable result of a conflict which has been acted through a symmetrical feedback loop. The level of conflict has escalated, with each partner doing more of the same with the other until the potential abuser feels his/her position to be untenable. The "Last Straw" decision is a key in this abuse process — without this decision there is no violence; with it, there is. If the couple can find some ways to terminate the conflict before this last-straw point has been reached, the abusive situation will not occur. If one or the other person can make a complementary move during the escalating steps of the conflict, the process can be halted here. A complementary move is defined as any behavior which will serve to curtail, lessen, or at least maintain the level of tension in the system at the time that the behavior takes place.

A second key point in this cycle of abuse is "Reinforcement for Battering." The reactions of the abused partner reinforce the continuation of the pattern. The victim takes a self-protective stance in an attempt to minimize the level of violence perpetrated by the abuser. It is necessary and desirable for the victim to do whatever is possible to be protected from further violence. However, this stance includes the stopping of the event/behavior that the abuser originally perceived as unpleasant, as well as breaking the pattern of exchanged coercions during the escalating verbal interchange prior to the explosion of abusive rage; the victim's side of the argument is silenced. In being silenced, the victim communicates to the abuser a reinforcing message: "If you abuse me, I will stop doing that which troubled you. It just happened. Your method, distasteful as it is, worked."

Logic would suggest that this is an undesirable message and should be changed. However, any attempt to change at this point in the cycle (i.e., "Go ahead, hit me again. Abuse doesn't work.") in the face of a person filled with exploding primitive rage is extremely dangerous, carrying a high risk of leading to a life-threatening reaction. This is not the place in the cycle for dyadic therapeutic intervention.

In addition to the key points of the cycle of abuse that Deschner (1984) describes, two other stages have emerged. The first is the affective reaction of the potential abuser to Deschner's "Noxious Event." Our experience has shown that this reaction is nearly always feelings of rejection and/or abandonment. It can be said that the definition of an event as "noxious" is dependent on feelings of rejection/abandonment. These feelings provide the emotional pool out of which comes the anger which develops into the primitive rage of abuse. The person feels rejected. The rejection turns to more intense feeling of hurt. When the hurt is not communicated directly, without anger, to the partner, or is not noticed and/or dealt with by the partner, it turns abruptly to anger. The cycle is then ready to continue to "Coercions Exchanged." If these feelings can be effectively communicated by the special efforts of either or both of the partners, the cycle can be interrupted. The following case will illustrate this dynamic.

Case #1

John and Mary entered therapy after a particularly explosive episode in which John struck Mary. The precipitating incident took place in the context of a discussion concerning the payment of a bill John had incurred for emergency automobile repairs. John conceived the basic contract of the relationship to be "One for all and all for one," a reactive response to the chaos of his family of origin. When Mary suggested that "Your car expense should be your expense, not ours," John viewed her position as a rejection of his lifetime efforts to protect against chaos and to provide unity and security. In processing the event in therapy, John volunteered "rejection" as the word which most clearly described his feeling at the time of Mary's suggestion. John was not able to communicate this feeling to Mary. Instead, he said nothing and allowed the intensity of the feeling to escalate. He reported that the feeling broadened until he was telling himself that Mary rejected his efforts not only in this one area (the car expense), but in *every* area of life. Shortly after Mary's suggestion, he became angry. Mary reported not seeing any feeling except anger. The anger escalated on both sides, until John exploded in rage and struck Mary with a hand-held sneaker.

A second addition to the cycle involves the instillation of fear in the abusee. This event occurs between the "Reinforcement for Battering" and the "Repentance Phase." Once one incident of violence has occurred within the relationship, fear becomes an active dynamic that emerges as the abusee assumes the self-protective stance. With each repetition of the cycle, the level of fear increases. With each increase, participation in the repentance phase becomes less secure for the abusee. The fear is then carried forward into the contract of mutual dependence on which the relationship is founded. The increased presence of fear raises the level of anxiety in the relationship, threatening the basic contractual tenet that the two partners would meet all of each other's needs, with nothing needed from the outside world. In fact, the anxiety that has been injected into the relationship has come from the only source of help given the marital dependence contract — from the partner. A logical paradox has been formed and the situation looms as untenable. Because of the fear of more violence, these feelings cannot be directly communicated to the partner, thereby creating distance, an undesirable flaw in the original contract.

With these two dynamics included, the cycle of violence appears as follows:

1) Mutual dependence
2) Noxious event
3) Feeling of rejection/abandonment (not communicated)
4) Coercions exchanged
5) "Last Straw" decision
6) Primitive rage
7) Reinforcement for battering
8) Feeling of fear/anxiety (not communicated)
9) Repentance Phase

A SYSTEMIC APPROACH TO TREATMENT

Dyadic treatment of spouse abuse begins, of course, with the intake interview. Few couples present themselves to the therapist with abuse as the presenting problem. Research suggests that only one in 10 cases of spouse abuse is reported (Women in Transition, 1985). Therefore, we know that for many couples entering therapy abuse is a silent, though important, presenting problem. Much criticism has been raised in our field for allowing other issues to mask the abuse in marital therapy. This criticism may be well founded. The denial of the abuser, the fear of the victim, the mutual dependence contract of the couple, and the uneasiness of the therapist can combine to facilitate masking. It is important that this potential for negative collusion be attacked as soon as possible in the treatment process. The potential for violence should be addressed during the intake process.

During the initial session, questions can be directed at the manner in which the clients handle conflict. The therapist can then compare the clients' style with his/her knowledge of the cycle of abuse noted above. This assessment will help the therapist to gain information about potential or real abuse in such a way that the couple are able to share it. It is useful to make a statement like, "You know, in every really close relationship there is bound to be some disagreement. No two people always think or act exactly alike. When disagreements occur, how do you handle them?" Such a statement normalizes the concept of couples disagreeing and provides opportunity for discovering how much the intensity of the symmetrical feedback loop increases as the particular couple attempt their style of conflict resolution. This line of questioning is not accusatory and does not immediately focus on abuse, but provides an opening for the therapist should the data gathered point in the direction of abuse. It is a line of questioning that can provide essential information about every couple, and should be included in everyone's intake process.

Stopping the Abusive Cycle

As has been mentioned before, the first goal in working with couples who have revealed spouse abuse as an ongoing behavior pattern is to stop the abuse. An effective way of achieving this goal is to have the couple enter into a *No-Violence Contract*. There are three criteria that such a contract must meet in order to be effective. First, the contract must be between the members of the dyad in treatment. Second, the contract must contain both a specific definition of the abusive behaviors to be stopped and carefully delineated, firm, unavoidable consequences should the abusive behavior occur. Third, the contract must be such that the victim is protected in any eventuality.

The first criterion for a no-violence contract is essential to its enforcement. Some therapists have attempted such contracts between the couple and the therapist. This has proven ineffective in most cases. The greatest power that the therapist can exercise is that of ending treatment. Such a move is contraindicated on two counts. It takes protection away from the victim of abuse and it plays into the terms of the underlying contract of mutual dependence of the couple. The abuser would welcome the opportunity to terminate treatment, since the therapist is, at best, an unwelcome intruder into the dyad. Discontinuance of dyadic treatment, when carried out in accordance with the basic guidelines of marital therapy, means that it would not be appropriate for the therapist to continue to see the individual victim separately. This would unbalance the therapy and make further work with the couple all but impossible. The abuse would not be stopped; it would be free to continue according to the rules established by the dyadic system prior to the entry into treatment. The no-violence contract can be effective when the contractual agreement is between the members of the dyad. The couple can then control the enforcement of the contract without affecting the ongoingness of treatment.

The second criterion is that of a balanced contract between the couple which delineates specific behaviors to be carried out. This makes it possible to make the abuse and its consequences explicit. In addition, it will become impossible to deny the reality and gravity of the situation. Both abuser and abusee share awareness of the undesirable behavior. An appropriate description of undesirable behavior would be, "when John strikes me, pushes me, touches me in an undesirable manner, or throws any object in anger." Such a delineation might also include threats of harm. These statements will serve to empower the abusee, since denial by the abuser is now more unlikely. They will also enable the abuser to directly recognize actions which must be brought immediately under control lest severe consequences result.

These severe consequences flow from the third criterion to be met by the no-violence contract, that of the protection of the victim. The consequence portion of the contract must be worded in such a way as to allow for the carrying out of the consequences in spite of intimidation or manipulation, conscious or unconscious, by the abuser. The consequences come into play when the no-violence contract has been violated. Having broken the contract, the abuser might attempt to avoid the consequences by threatening escalated violence. It is also possible that the repentance phase of the cycle of domestic violence would come into play, with the victim being tempted not to enforce the contract because of the expressed repentance of the abuser.

For these reasons, it is best if the enforcement of the consequences of the broken contract can be linked with some authoritative facilitator outside the context of the dyadic or therapeutic systems, thereby ensuring its effectiveness. It is a given in situations of abuse that the victim has been unable to ensure an atmosphere without violence by her/himself. To create a contract which depends solely on enforcement by the victim is to insure its ineffectiveness. To place responsibility for enforcement on the therapist is to endanger the continuity of treatment. If the relationship is to improve, treatment must continue. For both these reasons having a facilitator of enforcement outside both systems is essential. The case below will demonstrate how such a system works.

Case #2

The As entered therapy with a presenting problem of inhibited sexual desire in the female. They were not married, but were involved in a long-term, live-in relationship of significant duration. During the initial stages of therapy, it became clear that (a) Mr. A was a frequent abuser of alcohol, and (b) in recent months, as he became more frustrated with the state of the sexual relationship, Mr. A acted out in clearly more physical ways. There had been no direct abuse, but there were signs that abuse was a possibility should the acting out escalate. The As were made aware of the therapist's concern and chose to ignore it.

Several months into therapy, Ms. A called the therapist, explaining that there had been a violent episode in which she was shaken and made the target of a number of violently thrown objects. When the couple came in for an emergency consultation, they had separated, though by mutual agreement the separation was seen as short-term. The therapist recommended that the reconciliation be contingent on the development of a no-violence contract and on Mr. A's commitment to hasten his work to control his alcohol problem.

Both agreed to begin work immediately and a no-violence contract outline was worked out in the emergency session. The undesirable behaviors delineated in the contract were two: (a) any physical contact during a time of anger, and (b) the throwing of any objects at any targets during a time of anger. It was agreed that should either of these behaviors be carried out, a letter detailing the previous violent encounter and reporting the second episode would be mailed to Mr. A's sister, whose relationship he valued immensely. The mailing would be carried out by a close mutual friend, trusted by both partners. Further, Mr. A agreed to pay to Ms. A a substantial sum of money, pursuant to an agreement drawn up by an attorney and held by the same friend. Before the reconciliation took place, the working details of the contract were to be taken care of and Mr. A was to make arrangements to diligently work on his alcohol problem.

Within one week the details of the no-violence contract were in place. Mr. A had begun working in earnest on his alcohol consumption and the living arrangement resumed. Throughout the remainder of their therapy, the abuse issue was worked on and the situation closely monitored. At the time of follow-up, six months after therapy had been concluded and more than a year after the development of the no-violence contract, no episodes of abuse had occurred.

In this case the issue of abuse was dealt with straightforwardly, from the time it was initially presented. The properly prepared no-violence contract was able to achieve all of its goals. Most importantly, it stopped abuse and inhibited the continued escalation of an undesirable and dangerous pattern.

Working Toward Prevention of Further Cycles

The establishment of the no-violence contract is only one step of a successful dyadic treatment of spouse abuse. Further interventions need to be made in the cycle of violence. The earliest point of intervention in the cycle is in the area of feelings of rejection and abandonment. As has been mentioned above, the failure of these feelings to be communicated fuels the escalation of the cycle. Work can be done to facilitate (a) the abuser's awareness of these feelings, (b) recognition in the abuser that sharing of these feelings can be a productive option, (c) receptivity in the abusee to hearing these feelings, and (d) creation of some mutually acceptable responses to the expression of these feelings. Both partners can work together to avert continuity of the cycle in a dyad-supportive way.

Further on in the cycle of violence, more interventions can be made. Working in the "coercions exchanged" portion of the cycle, the therapist must help the couple to learn how to deescalate the rising tide of emotion in the symmetrical feedback loop. The most effective intervention is one which teaches the couple to provide distance between them during the time of rising emotions. Distance in this context can be defined as "time" as well as geographical space. The couple must learn to slow down the process of escalation as well as to put distance between them. Accomplishing both these goals will provide the couple with the opportunity to avoid approaching the "last straw" decision.

The specific intervention of choice in this situation is *Time Out*. After the couple become aware of the necessity of deescalating the rising tensions of a potentially explosive argument, the therapist explains the positive possibilities inherent in deescalating the process. The couple are told that each one of them has the right to call "time out" whenever they feel that the tension level in the relationship is reaching a dangerous level. The therapist may suggest the use of a special nonverbal signal (nonverbal in order to avoid confusion in the escalating emotional atmosphere that will be present), designed mutually by the couple and defined specifically as the "time out" signal. An effective signal can be anything, from a body gesture (pulling on one's own ear lobe) to the giving of a tangible thing to one's partner (a playing card — King of Hearts to the male, Queen of Hearts to the female — or a pleasing photograph of the partner). This sign should be mutually agreed upon by the couple.

The therapist further instructs the couple to designate a "safe place" for each one of them. Such a location should be truly safe (a private place, not in direct flow of other family members, with a door which may be closed). After the couple have settled on "safe places," the therapist discusses with them the setting of time limits on "time out." A major portion of the security of "time out" is the mutual recognition that if "time out" is used, it is not a threat to the relationship, as an angry separation might be, but rather a positive statement about the cooperative nature possible in the relationship. A time limit on "time out" is best agreed upon in advance. By doing so, several things are accomplished:

1) It allows the emotions of the moment to cool.
2) It protects each partner from the sense of panic at the thought of permanent loss of the other, a rejection which is often a precipitating factor in abuse situations.
3) It helps develop a sense of security and trust between the partners, knowing that they can be apart and come back together again. It is important that the therapist reiterate to the couple the importance of following this directive. Failure to follow it may well lead to panic, abuse, and the violation of the no-violence contract, with the resulting consequences.

The implementation of a successful "time out" is based on the following factors:

1) The cycle of an event of violence is noted.
2) One partner gives the other the previously agreed upon signal for "time out."
3) The partner giving the signal goes as quickly as possible to the place designated as her/his "safe place."
4) With the boundary of the safe place being respected, both members of the couple spend a prearranged amount of time cooling down the emotional buildup and attempting to find an appropriate solution to whatever situation was the precipitant of this go-round of the cycle.
5) The couple reconnects when a less volatile emotional environment is possible. The initial purpose of the reconnection is to evaluate whether such an environment is present. If not, the process reverts to step 2. If a safe environment exists, then the couple may go on with their pre-cycle activities.

If such a process can be introduced to a couple and successfully carried out by them, the physical distance and time necessary to interrupt the cycle of violence will have been provided. The couple will have learned to control the level of their own emotional expressions without approaching a breach in the no-violence contract. Once this level of control has been accomplished, the therapist can turn his/her attentions to work in the next area.

Maintaining a Positive Relationship

The third, crucial, underlying area to be dealt with is that of tools for use in the control and dissipation of anger, combined with information regarding areas of repeated conflict in the relationship (sex, money, in-laws, etc.). The therapist can, if s/he has been able to effect the first two levels of intervention, be the catalyst in the use of these tools and information.

Two types of training are useful for dyads in controlling or dissipating anger. They are assertiveness training and conflict resolution.

Salter (1949) provided the basic thinking out of which assertiveness training comes. Assertiveness training is a behavioral method which assists people in dealing with their issues of social withdrawal or control of aggressiveness (L'Abate & McHenry, 1983). With couples involved in abuse, its immediate appeal is the substitution of assertiveness for aggression by the abuser, coupled with the empowerment of the abusee, who has protectively withdrawn from many areas of interchange within the dyad. Alberti and Emmons (1974) suggested that assertiveness training could be a useful adjunct to marital therapy in certain situations. They "distinguish between aggressiveness, which is self-enhancing at the expense of another while attempting to achieve desired goals by hurting others; nonassertiveness, which is self-denying and allowing others to choose for them; and assertiveness, which is self-enhancing, choosing for self, and expressive" (p. 14). Their systematic method of facilitation of assertiveness has as its goal for the "partners to express themselves in a more clear, positive, calm manner, which will assist in their positive bonding as a couple." This is precisely the direction in which the dyad which has experienced spouse abuse must move. Fensterheim and Baer (1975) have delineated a five-step process of assertiveness training which moves couples toward this goal. Their five steps are:

1) Identification of behaviors to be changed in the marriage
2) Methods of changing those behaviors
3) Education regarding behavioral reinforcement
4) Communication skills—verbal as well as nonverbal
5) Short-term goal setting

Successful completion, internalization, and generalization of this process will enable the dyad to have a set of tools with which to deal with stressful situations that might otherwise produce the explosive rage of abuse.

The second skill, conflict resolution, also grows out of the work of Salter (1949). The underlying premise of conflict resolution strategies is that the couple can creatively use its energy to resolve issues which could otherwise end in abuse (L'Abate & McHenry, 1983). A number of methods of teaching these skills have been developed. Among the most successful are Fair Fight Training (FFT), developed by Bach and Goldberg (1974); Fair-Fight-For-Change (FFFC), created by Dayringer (1976); Rational Emotive Therapy (RET) by Ellis (1976); Sharing Hurt Feelings Approach, developed by L'Abate (1977); and the Conflict Resolution Model (CRM) by Strong (1975). All of these models have in common the development of skills which will assist the person in understanding him/herself as well as his/her partner, leading to the development of options in behavior which will help both the individuals and the relationship to grow. This skill provides positive alternatives to becoming stuck in repetitions of the domestic violence cycle.

Information, as well as skills, is important to the abusive dyad. It is clear that many of the precipitating events of abuse occur because the partners lack information in certain primary areas of conflict. The therapist can appropriately function as a trusted source of such information once the danger of abusive incidents is past. Such areas of concern as sex, money, and family loyalties may be the object of information given by the therapist, either in the course of the therapy sessions or via bibliotherapy. Care must be taken by the therapist not to overload the fragile system with information or allow the giving of information to mask other therapeutic issues or tasks. It is important that the information given to the couple be thoroughly processed, since some of it may well challenge the family mythologies of either or both partners. Within this framework, the couple will benefit by a broadening of their alternatives.

Once the process of dealing with the abusive aspect of the couple has been appropriately dealt with, the therapist will be able to broaden the base of the marital therapy, always careful to monitor that the preceding mutual agreements protecting against abuse are being honored. Other contributing issues can then be dealt with, either by referral or within the context of conjoint therapy, if appropriate. Dynamics which are not triggers for abuse, but which contribute to a feeling of dysfunction within the marital dyad, can be addressed. Only after the victim of abuse is protected and the abuse is stopped can marital therapy be broadened to focus on underlying or auxiliary issues.

ANGER CONTROL—THREE SPECIFIC INTERVENTIONS

Following are three interventions which can assist the couple in anger control and dissipation. They are not intended as substitutes for assertiveness training and/or conflict resolution, but are specific interventions that have proven effective in controlling anger in abusive couples.

Active Listening is a basic skill for helping each partner to fully hear what the other is saying, giving the speaker the assurance that s/he has been heard, and slowing down the interchange in order to allow thoughtful consideration of positions and the dissipation of angry emotions. Because the couple have shown their inabilities in this area by their involvement in violent outbursts, it is best to begin with a highly structured exercise in active listening. The process of active listening could be introduced in the following way, with the therapist stating: (a) the speaker says no more than a few sentences, while the listener only listens; (b) the listener is then to repeat to the speaker that which s/he has heard; (c) if the listener has repeated what the speaker has said, to the speaker's satisfaction, the speaker confirms the repetition; if not, steps (a) and (b) are repeated until a confirmation can be given; (d) the listener then becomes the speaker, with steps (a), (b), and (c) being used again. At each completion of the cycle, the speaker is encouraged to offer either a positive proposal for change or a statement of compromise on an earlier such proposal. The interchange continues with this process until some negotiated resolution of the issue at hand is achieved.

The above intervention can be taught and practiced within the therapy session. The goals of the intervention are: (a) to insure the communication of both partners' ideas; (b) to equalize the power between the partners; (c) to teach the couple to be goal/resolution oriented; (d) to eliminate dangerous emotions from the resolution process. In order to achieve these goals, care must be taken to insist that the participants use all parts of the process throughout each entire interchange.

A second intervention which has proven to be successful in this area is that of *Scheduling the Conflict* (Weeks & L'Abate, 1982). The couple is asked to refrain from discussing the particularly sensitive topic at any time except during the designated "special" times. The partners are instructed to pick a time each day when they can spend 15 minutes working on the issue without distraction. The 15-minute period is to be divided into three segments. In the first segment, seven minutes long, the first person shares his/her perspective on the issue, with the second person listening and refraining from comments or questions. Then a one-minute break is taken. The third segment, also seven minutes in length, is used by the second person to share his/her perspective on the issue, while the first person listens without comment or question.

Each day the sequence is repeated at the agreed-upon time, until there is resolution to the issue at hand. This intervention does not foster true communication, but allows the participants to speak about an issue of some importance from a safe distance, and work to insure hearing of both persons' perspectives on the issue while diffusing the anger and escalating tensions. In addition, power is equalized, leading toward the empowerment of the abusee and positively limiting the power of the abuser.

A third intervention in this area is one which involves the couple cooperating in the playing of a game. This technique was developed by Piercy (1983). The intervention begins with the identification of the behavior to be extinguished. In our application of the game, these behaviors would be related to the "coercions exchanged" portion of the cycle. It is important that the couple identify, as specifically as possible, the behavior in each partner that fuels the escalation of tensions. Such identification serves to make the implicit behaviors in the cycle of dysfunction become explicit. This will expand the couple's awareness of the dyadic nature of their difficulties.

Once this identification has been accomplished, the game can be played. Without appropriate identification, the game will fail. Each person is asked to mark seven pennies to be used as game pieces. The couple is then asked to agree to a prize for the winner of the game. They are told that the object of the game is for each person to get rid of his/her pennies first. The person who is able to do that is declared the winner of the game and is to receive the prize. A player is able to give a penny to his/her partner whenever the partner exhibits the behavior that has been identified as fueling the player's escalation of the tension that may precede an incident of violence. The couple is instructed that the person giving the penny is always right in the assessment of whether or not a penny should be given. It is important that the giving of the penny not be coupled with verbal exchanges which may fuel the old "coercions exchanged" patterns of dyadic behavior. The couple is warned about the indiscriminate use of his/her power, since the indiscriminate giving of a penny will probably result in the indiscriminate receipt of a penny.

The object of this intervention is to increase the couple's awareness of particular behaviors that increase tension and to extinguish those behaviors. In this case, the behaviors to be extinguished could lead to the escalation of an argument into an incident of violence or abuse. Each step in the escalation can be dealt with in this way provided there is ample time for doing so. Such an intervention facilitates the ability of the couple to handle anger by eliminating the negative methods that have been learned by the couple.

PITFALLS FOR THE THERAPIST

Cases in which spouse abuse is active at the time of intake bring some serious pitfalls. These must be avoided if the couple is to be helped and if treatment is to be successful.

Unbalancing the System

The most pervasive pitfall is that of failing to keep a systemic perspective, or, slipping into a victim/villain dichotomy. Without the balanced perspective, a dyadic approach to the problem will not be effective. Because of the potential for volatility within an abusive couple, the inducements for unbalancing the therapy can become extremely tempting. It may be the presence of the abuser which becomes the trigger to unbalance. His/her presence can be particularly intimidating if the therapist has experienced abuse, either directly or indirectly. Bograd (1986) described her work with a case in which spouse abuse was a presenting issue. She relates the atmosphere of intimidation which affected her work with the couple as follows:

> After the meeting, I felt uncomfortable and ill at ease. It is rare for me to hold back with clients, particularly when an important contract is broken. But Bruce's anger has scared me into colluding with the couple's denial of the violence. Feeling overwhelmed and inadequate, I sought help from my peer supervision group.... During the first half of my consultation, I could barely focus on treatment issues. I was furious with Bruce, who I now saw as an irrational and domineering man. I admitted that I was worried about his hurting or harassing me. In the midst of all this, I realized that I was feeling like Gayle. At the same time I was angry with her for not taking a stronger stand with Bruce. I also felt as if I should do more to protect her. Clearly this case had gotten to me. I needed help. (p. 44)

If the therapist succumbs to the intimidating presence of the abuser, the successful treatment of the couple will suffer, and the safety of the victim will be at risk. It is important that if the therapist feels intimidated, the client couple be referred to another therapist or the therapist be sure to use fully his/her supervisory network.

Inappropriate Caretaking

Another pitfall to successful dyadic treatment which grows out of the failure to keep a systemic perspective is that of inappropriately acting as caretaker for the victim of the abuse. It is important that developing safety for the victim not be confused with caretaking, which will serve to reinforce the "victim" status of the abusee. As attested to by Bograd (1986) above, this is a difficult distinction to make, since many abuse victims have been unempowered for so long that it almost seems impossible that they will be able to become empowered partners in the relationship. The therapist, sensing the imbalance within the marital dyad, may be tempted to act as caretaker rather than to empower. This is especially the case in situations where the roles of victim and villain are more extreme and more concretized within the relationship. It is also a function of the therapist's personal experience with abusive behaviors. The goal of treatment is to balance the power within the relationship, while providing for the safety of the abusee. This goal

will be sabotaged if caretaking is allowed to impinge on the therapeutic process.

The Therapist's Use of the Self

The therapeutic use of self is vitally important in the dyadic treatment of spouse abuse. One primary area of concern regarding this issue
is the therapist's ability to deal with issues of authority within the
context of the therapy. It is necessary that the therapist be in control of
the therapy, without controlling it. Further, the therapist must see to it
that the couple is not following his/her directives out of a sense of
forced compliance, but rather out of a sense of mutual commitment to
the couple's own healing process. Until commitment is achieved, the
denial present in the mutual dependence of the dyad will make it
virtually impossible for positive change to take place. A therapist who
has difficulty using him/herself in this way will have difficulty dealing
successfully with dyadic treatment of spouse abuse. The following case
illustrates the successful dealing with this pitfall.

Case #3

Scott and Lisa C came into therapy upon the referral of their next-door
neighbor, a former client of the therapist. At the initial session, they
related that they had talked about the referral for about six months
before making the decision to enter therapy. The decision was made after
a particularly stormy argument in which Lisa told Scott that he was
beginning to act just like his father. Scott had experienced his father as an
alcoholic, sometimes physically abusive man, who had deserted his wife
and six children shortly after the birth of the youngest. Scott's mother had
become alcoholic shortly thereafter. Lisa, raised in a rather rigid environment where Father ruled without objection from anyone, married Scott
expecting him to make all important decisions himself, and make them
in such a way as to satisfy her needs and wants. Both Scott and Lisa had
very distorted images of authority with which to operate in the world. In
fact, the pressure of being the responsible authority figure was too much
for Scott, and he responded by feeling pressured/rejected and angry, and
then lashing out, sometimes at inanimate things, sometimes at Lisa.

If the therapist in this case were simply to authoritatively make some
prescriptions (no-violence contract, etc.) to break the cycle of the Cs'
violent confrontations, Lisa would have responded compliantly. However,
Scott, with some negative images of male authority figures, would likely
have resisted. Lisa brought him to therapy to get him fixed, and when
Scott's father had fixed him as a child, it usually meant pain. The

therapist chose to accept authority from Lisa and use it to spend some time being sensitive and yet firm with Scott.

The therapy began with some history of the presenting problem—a series of angry confrontations between Scott and Lisa, including some in which Scott damaged property (his own), threatened physical harm to Lisa, or pushed/shoved Lisa in dangerous situations (near the stairs, etc.). Then, some history of the families of origin was briefly gathered. Near the end of the session, the therapist assured the couple that their pattern, though a difficult one, was one they could change if they worked together diligently, but that it would take some time.

The therapist then began to talk in some detail about how difficult it had been for him to overcome the deficit of having an alcoholic father and a chronically ill mother. He finished with the sentence, "I certainly know how difficult it is to fill in these gaps with solid stuff, but I also know the warm, secure feeling of satisfaction from a job well done." A second appointment was scheduled two days later, with the expressed purpose of the couple putting in place a no-violence contract to protect themselves (Lisa from Scott, and Scott from reacting like his father) while they began to work on their relational issues.

By the use of some self-disclosure, the therapist was able to bridge the chasm of opposing concepts of authority held by Scott and Lisa and use the bridge as leverage for getting the couple to work together. This successful use of self provided the springboard for a successful treatment of this couple, who were now in a position to work together without the therapist's authority being a stumbling block.

THE FUTURE OF DYADIC TREATMENT

Members of the 1985-86 training class at the Marriage Council of Philadelphia were asked to note the areas of application of marital therapy in which they would like further and most immediate information and assistance. Spouse abuse was near the top of their list. Further discussion elicited the perspective that, when intake procedures included questions designed to measure the methods with which couples dealt with conflict, a high percentage of the couples mentioned behaviors which were either clearly abusive or possibly preabusive in nature. Those in the field of marital therapy know that the vast majority of clients entering couples' therapy do not do so with the specific intention of separation. With those couples, the common practice of treating spouse abuse by separation and separate treatment would likely not be possible. With abuse being highlighted as an issue of the 80s, it is essential that the marital therapy field develop prescriptions for the effective treatment of such couples.

There is much work to be done, both in terms of focused research and in the development of more prescriptions for the effective dyadic treatment of spouse abuse. Marital and family therapists are beginning to recognize the systemic nature of abuse. We are beginning to realize that spouse abuse can be seen as an issue of the dyad, make some attempts to treat spouse abuse within the marital therapy setting, and learn how to be effective agents of change in this process. It is no longer acceptable to simply hear the criticism of other fields to the effect that marital and family therapists only serve to allow the masking of abuse. We have the capability to respond to the criticism with effective work and treatment.

Our answer to such criticism, our ability to become mobilized, springs from the strength of bonding within the dyad. That strength, which can serve to reinforce abuse within a couple, can also be used to create change and health within the couple. The power of the bond which exists within an abusive couple is intensely strong. It certainly has the power to resist any intrusion from the outside. However, that power exists just as intensely to internalize personal changes and incorporate them into the dynamics of the relationship. Building on the mutual dependence of the couple can enable the therapist to create shifts within the system toward the elimination of abuse and the development of positive and growthful patterns of interaction.

There have been other attempts at finding successful approaches to dealing with this issue. Group approaches to spouse abuse have proven successful in some cases, but with one significant limit of their effectiveness. Those groups which have had some success (Neidig & Friedman, 1984) have worked within the context of the U.S. military, where attendance at the groups was made a mandatory requirement of satisfactory military performance. Such use of authority is not available within the broad spectrum of society as a whole. If abuse is to be stopped before it reaches the public eye, then treatment must be provided on a voluntary basis. Experience has shown that couple groups with an "abuse" label attached to them have not been successful in recruiting participants. This fact has to do with the unwillingness of the abuser to make his behavior public knowledge. Attendance at such a group directly challenges such unwillingness.

The feminist movement has done vital work in raising the consciousness of society about the severity of the problem of spouse abuse. Thanks to that movement, efforts to bring effective treatment to the abusive relationship have continued. In terms of dyadic treatment, however, there would appear to be a paradox. To call abuse a systemic issue is to contradict the basic tenet of the movement that the female is singularly victimized by an oppressive male-dominated set of social and economic values. To view abuse as systemic is to imply that the female plays a role in the episode of abuse that is somewhat more than the purist role of victim. This has been a difficult piece of reasoning for the feminist movement to integrate. In order to work with members of the feminist movement in confronting the issue of abuse, one must try to broaden understanding of the abuse process. Such a broadening may prove difficult because of the political nature of the position of the movement, but the movement can provide, as it has in the past, invaluable assistance in the task of eliminating spouse abuse.

BIBLIOGRAPHY

Alberti, P. E., & Emmons, M. L. (1974).*Your Perfect Right: A Guide to Assertive Living.* San Luis Obispo, CA: Impact Publishers.

Bach, G., & Goldberg, H. (1974).*Creative Aggression.* Garden City, NY: Doubleday.

Bograd, M. (1986). Holding the line — confronting the abusive partner. *Family Networker,* May/June, *44.*

Bern, E. H. (1982). From violent incident to spouse abuse syndrome. *Social Casework, 63,* 41-45.

Chapman, J. R., & Gates, M. J. (1978). *The Victimization of Women.* Beverly Hills: Sage Publications.

Dayringer, R. (1976). Fair fight for change: A therapeutic use of aggressiveness in couple counseling. *Journal of Marriage and Family Counseling, 2,* 115-130.

Deschner, J. P. (1984). *The Hitting Habit: Anger Control for Battering Couples.* New York: Free Press.

Ellis, A. (1962). *Reason and Emotion for Psychotherapy.* New York: Lyle Stuart.

Ellis, A. (1976). Techniques of handling anger in marriage.*Journal of Marriage and Family Counseling, 2,* 305-315.

Fensterheim, H., & Baer, J. (1975). *Don't Say Yes When You Want to Say No: How Assertiveness Training Can Change Your Life.* New York: David McKay.

Fleming, J. (1979). *Stopping Wife Abuse.* Garden City: Anchor Press/Doubleday.

Gelles, R. J. (1972). *The Violent Home.* Beverly Hills: Sage Publications.

Gelles, R. J. (1979). *Family Violence.* Beverly Hills: Sage Publications.

Gelles, R. J., & Cornell, C. P. (1985). *Intimate Violence for Families.* Beverly Hills: Sage Publications.

Langley, R., & Levy, R. C. (1977). *Wife Beating: The Silent Crisis.* New York: Dutton.

L'Abate, L. (1977). Intimacy is sharing hurt feelings: A reply to David Mace. *Journal of Marriage and Family Counseling, 3,* 13-16.

L'Abate, L., & L'Abate, B. S. (1979). The paradoxes of intimacy. *Family Therapy, 6,* 175-186.

L'Abate, L., & McHenry, S. (1983). *Handbook of Marital Interventions.* New York: Grune & Stratton.

Martin, D. (1977). *Battered Wives.* New York: Simon & Schuster.

Matthews, M. H. (1982). The battered woman: Is she ready for help? *Social Casework, 63*, 131-137.

Moore, D. M. (Ed.). (1979). *Battered Women.* Beverly Hills: Sage Publications.

Neidig, P., & Friedman, D. (1984). *Spouse Abuse: A Treatment Program for Couples.* Champaign, IL: Research Press.

Piercy, F. (1983). A game for interrupting coercive marital interaction. *Journal of Marriage & Family Therapy, 9*(4), 435.

Pizzey, E. (1978). *Scream Quietly or the Neighbors Will Hear.* New Jersey: Ridley Enslow Publishers.

Roy, M. (1977). *Battered Women: A Psychological Study of Domestic Violence.* New York: Van Nostrand Reinhold Co.

Salter, A. (1949). *Conditioned Reflex Therapy.* New York: Capricorn.

Steinmetz, S. K., & Straus, M. A. (1974). *Violence in the Family.* New York: Harper & Row.

Strong, J. (1975). A marital conflict resolution model. Redefining conflict to achieve intimacy. *Journal of Marriage and Family Counseling, 1*, 269-276.

Walker, L. E. (1979). *The Battered Woman.* New York: Harper & Row.

Weeks, G., & L'Abate, L. (1982). *Paradoxical Psychotherapy: Theory and Practice with Individuals, Couples, and Families.* New York: Brunner/Mazel.

Weitzman, J., & Dreen, K. (1982). Wife beating: A view of the marital dyad. *Social Casework, 63*, 259-265.

Women in Transition (1975). *Women in Transition: A Feminist Handbook on Separation and Divorce.* New York: Charles Scribners & Sons.

Women in Transition (1985 unpublished). *Fact Sheet.* Philadelphia, PA.

Chapter 10

Separation and Divorce Therapy— A Struggle to Grow for Clients and Therapists

Terry Marek

When a couple begins to talk about divorce, at least one and often both individuals are experiencing searing pain. As they review their life stories, they are fighting for their love and for their dreams. They are at their most frightened, their most urgent, their most sad.

Couple and family therapists who sit in the vortex of this pain undergo a parallel crisis; we also have had dreams which have gone awry. As we experience the intensity of feeling in our clients, our more profound anxieties are stirred—about our competency as therapists; about the extremes of behavior we are witnessing; about our own divorces or marriages. At an even deeper level, the clients' separation may bring up our feelings about our roles in our parents' marriages. As family therapists, we have often chosen this profession after a baptism of pain involving watching and believing we must mediate our parents' marriages.

In this chapter, a model for separation and divorce therapy is presented which speaks to the intense feelings evoked both in clients and in therapists. Given the perilous emotional waters in a separation and divorce, therapists need self-awareness, maturity, heart, and courage; we also need a clear treatment model with which to proceed. Specific guidelines can keep the therapy from becoming muddled or chaotic and can help to lower the anxiety level of clients and therapists. In presenting this model, the following issues are highlighted: 1) assumptions about separation and divorce; 2) criteria of a constructive separation-divorce; 3) the structure and stages of separation-divorce therapy, including composition of sessions and the tasks and role of the therapist; 4) the kinds of cases a therapist is most likely to see; and 5) the complex feelings evoked in the therapist.

While there is a glut of articles on separation and divorce, they are often dry and devoid of feeling. It is as if the pain is so great that clinicians and researchers rely on intellectualization, isolation of affect, sociological jargon, and psychobabble to make the pain tolerable. Most of the articles focus on the divorce process for the client or on sociological trends. Very few articles clarify the role of the therapist in separation-divorce work as distinct from marital therapy. The work of Martin Goldberg (1957, 1982, 1985), Nate Turner (1980, 1985), Don Bloch (1980), Florence Kaslow (1981, 1982, 1984), and Kressel (1980) and Kressel and Deutsch (1977) are exceptions in describing the divorce therapy process in some emotional depth.

Although the impact of divorce on children will be dealt with in a separate chapter, it is impossible to talk about separation and divorce without considering parents' guilt and despair about their children. The writings that most vividly and passionately describe the fallout on parents and children are the fictional works of Judy Blume (1982), Henry James (1985), and Sue Miller (1986). In the field of clinical writings on disentangling children and helping parents become emotionally divorced, the work of Marla Isaacs (1982) and Isaacs, Montalvo and Abelsohn (1986) are standouts. Henry Friedman's incisive articles (1980, 1982) are unique in emphasizing the growth and mastery in fathering that can occur in a divorce. We need parallel inquiries into the development of mothers in a divorce.

The works of Carol Gilligan (1982) and Lillian Rubin (1983) may help explain some gender differences in separation-divorce. If women's sense of self is defined through attachment and men's through separation, it makes sense that women may mourn longer, and that their sense of themselves may be more fractured by marital separation.

ASSUMPTIONS ABOUT SEPARATION AND DIVORCE

Separation and divorce involve loss and mourning of every aspect of a couple's life — from the most mundane habits and rituals to the most idealistic hopes and aspirations about marriage, children, and their sense of family and generativity.

The most significant loss in divorce is the relinquishing of the dreams of the perfect family. These dreams emerge first out of the pains and joys of living with our parents and then are created and recreated at each life stage. As children, we watch our mothers and fathers: what works about their marriage; what mistakes are devastating; what is good in their relationships with their children; what hurts like hell. We promise that our lives and our children's lives will be different. We make resolutions about what kind of parents we will be when as young children we feel we have been unfairly punished; we make decisions about our ideal mates as teenagers fantasizing with our best friends late at night; we are full of emotional intensity as we create our own vows as newlyweds; and we have ecstatic visions of our offspring when life first stirs in pregnancy and we take part in the miracle birth of our children. The more acute the pain our parents and we as children have suffered, the more devoted we are to our dreams, and the more devastating the letting-go. The universal wish to make life more perfect for our children than it was for us is especially wrenching to give up. A client put it this way:

> I grew up in a poor coal miner's family. We had little heat, money, or food. I did not get much. I suffered a lot, including being molested over many years by my father. But I had high hopes for myself when I left home and had my own family. I had this dream of a beautiful house with a white picket fence. My husband and I would be so happy, and I'd have beautiful, smart, loving children. Well, I worked as hard as I could and I believed my dream was within reach. I thought I was safe. Now, my husband and I are separated and everything that kept me going is shattered . . . it kills me that my children are in pain.

Separation-divorce involves a crisis exposing individuals to acute and extreme life stress at or near the limits of their coping resources. However, the crisis may become an opportunity for mastery and change. If separation-divorce is about loss and mourning, it is also about growth and development. For many individuals, marriage brings premature closure on questions of identity and self-growth. Dreams can be truncated or put on hold. Divorce can present a chance to reopen self-exploration and to rework questions of identity in a more realistic manner. Divorce provides the opportunity:

1) To understand the reasons for the marriage and for the divorce in the extended family/multigenerational context;

2) To become more differentiated from one's family of origin;

3) To become more comfortable with one's sexuality;

4) To form a new, more gratifying intimate relationship.

These issues will be explored in this chapter.

CRITERIA OF A CONSTRUCTIVE SEPARATION-DIVORCE

In trying to describe an ideal separation-divorce, I have amplified on the criteria described by Kressel and Deutsch (1977) in their interviews with 21 prominent family therapists (see Table 10.1). The criteria are guidelines which place a premium on equity, fairness, self-knowledge and responsibility. The criteria set the parameters for separation-divorce therapy, guiding the therapist and client in setting treatment goals. Once a decision to separate has been made, I actually share the following outline with my clients. Few clients quarrel with the norms and expectations set forth in this list. I share my outline with individuals early on and then suggest that it be read over and reflected on "in tranquility." It seems to serve not only in setting goals, but also in checking destructive acting out behavior.

The most crucial achievement in an emotional divorce is a more realistic self-appraisal which acknowledges the problems to be worked on as well as the lovable qualities one brings to an intimate relationship. The corollary is a set of realistic expectations for an intimate relationship and family. Before a client can form realistic expectations for the self and for intimate relationships, the dream of a perfect self and perfect family which would compensate for all past hurts must be renounced. Mourning, demythologizing and a realistic acceptance of one's self as a real person with strengths and vulnerabilities become the organizing themes of separation-divorce therapy.

STAGES AND STRUCTURE OF SEPARATION-DIVORCE THERAPY

Composition of Sessions

In describing the structure and composition of therapy sessions, it is helpful to break down the therapy into distinct stages. Storm and

Table 10.1
Criteria for a "Best Case"
of Separation and Divorce

1. An increased self-understanding:
   a. At the least – an acknowledgment of one's contribution to the problems in the marriage
   b. For clients who wish to explore further – insights into unconscious difficulties and distortions and their historical origins
   c. A working-through of excessive feelings of self-blame, failure and guilt
   d. A more realistic acceptance of one's self as a real person with strengths and vulnerabilities

2. A mourning of the old intact family; a balanced view of the marriage and of the partner, along with a sense of closure:
   a. "Here are the good things which are part of me; here are the things that went wrong" (Kressel & Deutsch, 1977, pp. 419-420).
   b. Both are disabused of any magical thinking: "It could have worked if only . . . " (Kressel & Deutsch, 1977, p. 419).
   c. Both accept separation, although one partner may be sadder

3. The ability of former partners to work together cooperatively as parents:
   a. Permission to the children to visit with and love both parents without feeling disloyal
   b. Reassurance to the children that they did not cause the marital separations nor should they feel responsible for reconciling the parents

4. Active negotiation of both partners over the terms of a legal settlement:
   a. A healthy self-protective sense of one's own needs – no masochistic sacrifices of money, visitation, property
   b. A spirit of fairness – an absence of revenge-seeking

5. An increased sense of competence; an ability to move on to develop a gratifying intimate relationship

6. More mourning and demythologizing; a giving up of the dream of the perfect family that would make up for all earlier injuries, losses and deprivation

Sprenkle's (1982) division of divorce therapy into three stages – decision-making; restructuring (legal, financial and parental arrangements); and recovery – is a useful and clear conceptual framework.

The therapist must consider questions of ethics as well as timing in making decisions about couple versus family versus individual sessions. During the first stage of decision-making, conjoint therapy and family therapy (*not* individual therapy) are ethical imperatives.

The nature of the membership of the sessions is so crucial in the decision-making stage that even if a client requests individual therapy, a therapist needs to inform clients of the statistical probability of individual therapy increasing the likelihood of divorce. A therapist needs to point out the danger of "the road not taken" — the danger of excluding the exploration of the possibility of growth within the marriage.

Balance is of the essence in every stage of separation-divorce therapy, but particularly in the decision-making stage. There should be no individual sessions for one spouse without the other. Any change in composition should be contracted for by all three parties — the two partners and the therapist.

In the second stage of divorce therapy — the restructuring stage — a flexible approach is helpful. This is a combination of some conjoint, some family, some individual sessions. The conjoint sessions should precede family sessions to help the couple deal with some of the unresolved anger and sadness without triangling the children into their conflicts or acting out their anger through custody or visitation disputes. The family sessions are multipurpose: 1) to help the children mourn the old family system; 2) to help the children begin to come to terms with massive changes in their lives; 3) to deal with the children's fears about one or both parents falling apart and being unable to care for them; 4) to help the children understand that they did not cause their parents' marital problems, nor can they engineer a reconciliation; and 5) to relieve them of the burden of mediating and monitoring their parents' conflicts.

Throughout the first two stages of divorce therapy, clients are highly ambivalent about the dissolution of the marriage. Because of the clients' paralyzing vacillation and self-doubts, the therapist must be careful that the use of conjoint and family sessions does not feed into nostalgia, ambivalence and regressive longings. Sitting in the same room together as a couple or family can sometimes foster unrealistic reconciliation fantasies, particularly for the partner who is more reluctant to separate.

In the recovery stage, the therapist must recontract with the clients for individual treatment. Separate therapists for each partner are needed to encourage an emotional divorce, psychological closure, and autonomy. The therapist must gently but firmly let the couple know that he/she can continue to work with one but not both partners. When the contract is renegotiated and termination effected with one partner, a mourning process is heightened and recapitulated. The couple's separating is formalized with one more marker. In most cases, the therapist continues with the more depressed client. Often, the individual who initiated the separation chooses to terminate therapy at this point and is relieved that the spouse is in good hands. The therapist can help make a referral for one partner if she/he wants more therapy. If custody or visitation problems emerge in the recovery stage, a few conjoint sessions to get over the impasse may be helpful. Separate family sessions with each parent help consolidate the new single-parent systems.

Role and Task of the Therapist

When a couple comes to therapy to discuss divorce, the stakes are so high and the scope of issues so broad that it is crucial for therapists to be specific about the limits of our role and clear about biases. A couple teetering on the edge of a separation is unbelievably sensitive to any biases or value judgments on the part of the therapist. An individual who desperately wants to salvage the marriage will be terrified that a single, divorced or remarried therapist might facilitate or help the partner push for separation. An individual in an extramarital relationship who may want to separate will be exquisitely sensitive to anything that smacks of a judgmental attitude about infidelity or divorce.

A therapist should deal with values about marriage and divorce up front — explicitly and openly. A therapist should disclose his/her own marital status in such a way that it has minimal impact on the clients' decision. In the first interview with a couple, I will say:

> I am divorced. I had to work hard to make this a good divorce for myself, my child, and my ex-husband. I hope that I will be neither pro-divorce nor pro-marriage for you, but only pro-person. If you feel at any time that I seem to be biased or grinding an axe, I want you to let me know, to bring it up. Let's talk about it together. My one bias is for the growth of each of you as individuals.

A therapist needs to clarify that the decision-making responsibility is the clients', not the therapist's. The therapist can state explicitly:

> My job is to help you recognize *your* needs and to form *your* goals. This will be your decision, not mine.

Because of the monumental importance of the decisions in separation-divorce therapy, a couple comes to treatment ambivalent about whether they want therapy; they are tempted to deny and obfuscate rather than to acknowledge and process what is happening. The most important task of the divorce therapist is to build a sense of trust about the impartiality and fairness of the therapy process. When this does not occur, either the therapy is aborted by one or both partners dropping out, or the therapist may be blamed for the outcome of the decision-making. The task of building a sense of trust about the fairness of the therapy process is the anchor in every stage of divorce therapy. The other crucial therapeutic tasks evolve and change in the three stages of divorce therapy — decision-making, restructuring, and recovery. The tasks will be described in some detail.

Tasks of the Decision-making Phase

In the decision-making stage, the therapist helps the couple try to understand what has happened in the marriage. The therapist asks the couple to review their original attraction and their strengths. The therapist enables the couple to formulate a systemic description of the marriage, encouraging both partners to accept their part in the marriage. The therapist removes the distinction of the person more ready to leave being the "abandoner" and confronts the abandonment of each spouse at an earlier stage in the marriage. The therapist helps the couple suspend a judgment of irreversibility if it is clear both partners are ambivalent. When the therapist helps move a couple from assuming a blaming stance and externalizing to assuming individual responsibility and developing an observing ego, a couple may feel released to change the contract and work on the marriage (to not proceed toward separating). The therapist also labels the unresolved problems from the family of origin, or as Framo (1976, p. 203) puts it, "find out whom they are getting divorced from." The anger and disappointment focused on the marital partner may be rediagnosed as originating with a parent, and then worked through in the therapy.

The therapist tries to decipher with the couple whether for at least one partner the marriage "has passed the point of no return" (Bloch, 1980, p. 95). In this exploration, it is useful to pinpoint whether too much cumulative pain has already occurred and whether there was a marker event, a "last straw" in the marital history (Pino, 1980, p. 34). If a decision of irreversibility has, in fact, been made by one partner, the therapist encourages the partner to tell the spouse clearly and to help the spouse arrive at equal readiness. Although one partner may bolt from the therapy, the therapist encourages a dialogue. If one partner terminates abruptly, a door can be left open for him/her to return to bring closure. A therapist may need an individual session with each partner to reiterate that the therapist is not judging nor vilifying the client who may be projecting his/her own critical self-appraisal and guilt on to the therapist.

If the couple are moving toward separating, the therapist accompanies them through the stages of denial, depression, anger and acceptance to "proceedance" (Martin Goldberg, personal communication, September, 1985). When clients get paralyzed in one stage or another too long, the therapist helps them move. The therapist encourages this progression by relabeling and rebalancing lopsided feelings. For example, a therapist may relabel anger when it masks grief or anxiety. A therapist may encourage anger to cut through the idealization of a partner and excessive self-criticism. A therapist may move a client from pleading, "I can't survive without you; I need you so," to asking, "Why shouldn't I be genuinely loved?"

The therapist also helps clients work through shame and guilt and bring closure on the decision-making stage by arriving at a forgiveness of self and other.

> If one cannot in sadness and understanding bestow forgiveness on an ex-mate, my belief is that one cannot bestow it on oneself and that one is therefore endlessly committed to a residue of guilt and blame. To be married, in the best sense of that word, requires that one forgive one's mate for having married one. In the same spirit, a similar act must be performed when people part. (Bloch, 1980, p. 107)

The Tasks of the Restructuring Phase

In the restructuring phase, the therapist helps to set a favorable climate for negotiation of a separation agreement. The therapist encourages reasonableness and fair play and discourages revenge and retaliation. When it comes to issues involving the children, it is impossible and inadvisable for the therapist to adopt a neutral or value-free position. The therapist becomes an advocate, an ombudsman for the children's free access to both parents (unless there is gross neglect or dangerous behavior). The therapist strengthens the parental alliance and ensures that parents protect their children from their battles.

In the settlement phase of a separation, the therapist takes an active role to make sure both partners are equally mobilized. Referral to a legal mediator with training in marital therapy is often helpful. The therapist may need to be a gadfly for the passive, more reluctant spouse. The client who does not want to accept the end of the marriage is prodded to stop dragging her/his heels and choose a lawyer, or to break an impasse and compromise on one piece of the separation agreement. The therapist intervenes if a client, out of excessive guilt and self-recrimination, is masochistically agreeing to an unfair or inequitable settlement (with a huge alimony as penance, or taking no possession whatsoever from the home). Conversely, the therapist challenges the client who is being punitive or small-minded, and discourages continued reactivity to the ex-spouse. In general, the therapist helps the couple keep a perspective on their continued relationship in the future and the need for a legal détente.

The Tasks of the Recovery Phase

In the recovery phase, the treatment shifts from the couple to individual work. The therapist is the midwife in the client's rebirth. The therapist encourages the development of parts of the self which had been stillborn or atrophied. For many women, therapy focuses on development of a career — sometimes for the first time or more seriously because of financial need. For many men, therapy may work on development as a parent — especially for fathers who were more peripheral during the marriage. Relationships with friends also become a focus in the recovery phase. The therapist asks, "Who are your friends?" The therapist actively pushes clients out into the world. Some clients discover for the first time that they are really liked — not just as one half of a couple.

The therapist can encourage a better resolution of problems with the family of origin. In working through the anticipation of and the family's actual reactions to divorce, a client can become less dependent on their approval. For some individuals who have been parentified children, divorce is the first time they have disappointed their parents. In no longer being "super stars" now that they are becoming divorced, clients can begin to free themselves from the constricting role of parentified child. This change reverberates to relationships with siblings. Clients can change their relationships and roles with siblings who have resented their "goodness" or competence.

Kaslow (1982) has indicated that a family may demonstrate unexpected strengths during a divorce. An enmeshed family may provide more space. A cut off or distant family may move closer. A parent or stepparent who went through a divorce may feel closer to his/her child or stepchild for the first time.

The therapist can help the client reexamine unquestioned loyalty to parents' assumptions about intimacy and sexuality. The messages from the same-sexed parent may be particularly compelling and inhibiting. A daughter can face her mother's legacy of "Men are not to be trusted, will leave you, run around, be weak, get depressed, be unfeeling, be stingy, gamble all your money away, be oversexed." A son can face his father's legacy of "Women are not to be trusted, will leave you, run around, be dependent, be weak, get depressed, be hysterical, use you for your money, be profligate, withholding, frigid. . . . " An individual can choose whether to repeat and perpetuate parents' loneliness, barren sex life, battles over money, or whether to change the model of intimacy.

The therapist can work on development of a greater comfort with sexuality. Distortions about body image can be corrected or improved. Primitive (ninth grade) fears of being too short, tall, skinny, long-nosed, flat-chested, top-heavy, too small emerge with the prospect of dating, and can be modified as they emerge in the therapy.

The therapist can facilitate a new learning and exploration about sexuality. Some women can be empowered to feel free to masturbate for the first time. Some women are determined to become orgasmic. Some men can overcome problems around erectile difficulties or premature ejaculation with a new supportive partner. A therapist may be able to capitalize on a healthy element of competition: "I'll show her/him that I'm not a lousy lover." Some individuals feel they can explore homosexual relationships or bisexuality for the first time or with greater comfort.

Lastly, a therapist can help a client work on the development of a new level of object relations. As clients begin new relationships, they can learn how to experience greater trust, a sense of mutuality, a greater recognition of the needs of others (Singer, 1985). Once clients become involved in new relationships, they often bump up against problems in handling anger. They may find themselves expressing anger in the same destructive ways they did in their marriages. The therapist can help the client learn how to handle anger more appropriately.

The client can face and begin to change underlying fantasies about relationships. A client can work through fantasies of grandiosity.

"I am desirable, lovable, an ideal person." (Rice, 1977, p. 124)

A client can modify fantasies of masochism.

"I will do anything, sacrifice anything to feel loved."

A client can work on other relationship fears — of closeness, loss of identity, fear of merging. More importantly, a client can arrive at a more realistic self-appraisal.

"I have some good qualities. I have some troublesome qualities. If I work hard enough on myself and on developing a relationship with another individual, I can learn to be loving and receive love."

KINDS OF CASES A THERAPIST IS MOST LIKELY TO SEE

There are various kinds of separation-divorce scenarios. Although divorce is "many things to many people" (Bloch, 1980, p. 91), there are some common presentations which require specific interventions and a different use of the therapist. Each kind of case can stir up a unique set of feelings and can present different dilemmas for the therapist. In order to highlight special treatment issues, I have developed a typology of separating couples. I have arrived at these ideas after 15 years of practice in family therapy in which I have worked with over 100 couples or individuals who were in the process of separation and divorce. I have also been influenced by the weekly case presentations of my colleagues at the Marriage Council of Philadelphia. Although there is a myriad of articles on typologies of couples in family therapy literature, very little has been written on kinds of separating or divorcing couples.

I will delineate a typology with the most straightforward cases first and then proceed to what to me are the most problematic cases.

1. *The Parallel Couple*

This is a couple who comes for permission to separate, in a marriage of short duration, often with no children. Couples with little emotional investment and little passion who can break up without *sturm und drang* are relatively rare.

> A couple in their 20s came to therapy after four years of marriage. They had met and married in college, but once out, they realized they shared few common interests. The wife, now 24, had decided she was interested in having a baby; the husband, who often traveled in his job as a set designer for the theater, did not want a child. The couple was able to amicably discuss their differences, and separate after five interviews.

2. *The Reemerging Self*

This client is already separated and is working on mourning and moving on to his/her own self-growth. When one works with only one member of a couple, the therapist and client often have some questions and regrets about what might have been different if they had been able to work earlier with both partners. The therapist also loses a valuable source of information about the marriage by not hearing from both spouses.

> A 29-year-old female client, Jane, came to therapy after 10 years of marriage. When Jane initiated therapy, her husband had told her he no

longer loved her, nor did he want any joint counseling. She had been depressed for some time, sensing her husband's dwindling interest in her. He had told her making love was a "chore" and she had a "lousy" self-image. She felt fat, stupid, inadequate. She had little energy to invest in work or with friends. Her main social tie was with her mother.

In the course of three years of therapy, Jane has worked on developing a stronger sense of self. She has developed a greater comfort with sexuality after experiencing success in overcoming vaginismus. She has risked getting involved in intimate relationships and continues to work on trusting again. She has a new job where she is more physically active and is less socially isolated. She has pushed herself to reach out to peers and rely less on her parents who after 30 years of living in the same home moved down to the shore.

Jane is now in the most gratifying relationship she has had with a man and is trying to take some final steps in becoming emotionally divorced. One step has been to write a letter affirming what was good in the marriage, but negotiating one last concrete act signifying closure: "You will always be a special part of my life. This does not mean that I want you actively back in my life.... You don't need to leave your things in my garage to maintain a tie with me. I would really appreciate your coming to get the stuff. I really need for you to do this.... I have put our marriage behind me and gone on with my life.... I wish you the best that life has to offer, my friend. Take care of yourself. Jane."

3. The Ambivalent Couple

This is a couple who comes for therapy truly undecided about whether to separate or to work on their marriage. This is a high-functioning, reflective couple who want to clarify their needs and differences and work out a comfortable decision in either direction. Both outcomes — toward separation or toward marital therapy — can be positive.

A couple came to therapy after 25 years of marriage. They had met and married as teenagers. They had been effective co-parents and run a business together. Each individual had many strengths and would be able to survive alone. The therapy focused on clarifying and separating out life-stage and family of origin issues which were stressing the marriage: the sudden death of the husband's father; some recent business losses; the launching of the couple's last child who was a senior in high school. Although the husband lived apart for a brief time, the couple did some grief work together around the losses and were able to reinvest in their marriage.

4. *The Suddenly Abandoned Client*

This client is one whose spouse precipitously and with little forewarning leaves the home. The client presents in acute crisis. Crisis intervention is needed, with more frequent interviews, phone contacts, networking. The therapist can feel drained by the more frequent contacts and by the emotional turmoil of a client in crisis. Often a consultation with a psychiatrist is an early first step if a client is severely depressed or suicidal.

> A client came as a walk-in. She was crying profusely, so overwhelmed that she feared she could not cope with her two-year-old child. Her mother was chronically absorbed in the care of her schizophrenic sister, so she did not feel she could use her as a resource. The first month of treatment was tumultuous, with phone calls to the clinic at night and weekends, and an angry suicide gesture when she discovered her husband at his lover's house. I was in touch with the client's daughter's school, with her friends in her apartment building, and with her ex-husband, and I helped set up an emergency support system.
> Limit setting was crucial. An appointment was set up with a psychiatrist. The client was told she might have to be hospitalized if there was another suicide gesture. She calmed down, restabilized, and began working on losing weight, resuming her career, consolidating friendships, and becoming emotionally divorced.

5. *The One-Foot-Out-the-Door Client*

This is a client who has secretly made the decision to leave and who wants the therapist to break the news or rescue the to-be-abandoned spouse. A therapist should avoid being the bearer of the news and should insist on the client who plans to leave telling the partner face to face.

> A male client made the initial phone call. He was concerned about how devastated his wife would be by his wanting a separation. After the couple had a few interviews with the therapist, the husband announced he no longer needed any counseling but would continue to pay for his wife's ongoing therapy. Months later, he became depressed when a new relationship was not going well and did call for a referral for his own therapy.

6. *The Rage-to-the-Grave Client*

This is the client who desperately fights a separation. There is an unrecognized expectation in one or both partners that the marriage would heal a deep childhood wound. The "abandoned" spouse feels he/she is once again being done in by an ungiving parent. This kind of client, in the course of therapy, often turns some rage on to the therapist when the therapy does not work the miracle of bringing the spouse back.

> A client came for counseling after her husband had left the home and become involved in another relationship. She deluged him with phone calls from 4 A.M. to several times at work, to late at night to check on his whereabouts. She insisted on long marathon talks during which she asked repeatedly why he did not love her any longer, with her rebutting and pleading her case. She had a cold and critical mother and had lost her father at age 16 when he died of a heart attack. She had few friends, but had fused with her husband, depending on him in every area of her life—driving, child care, all emotional supplies.

7. The Pseudo-Separated Couple

There are two kinds of pseudo-separated couples. The first consists of conflict-habituated couples who separate briefly and then reconnect in the same dysfunctional way. These individuals become intimate through intense conflict à la Edward Albee's *Who's Afraid of Virginia Woolf.* The therapy is exhausting and frustrating for the therapist who does not catch on to their underlying bond, but takes their statements about separation literally.

Another group of pseudo-separated couples are couples who separate but have more contact after separating than during marriage. They continue to sleep together, talk on the phone every day, review all important decisions, and even take vacations together. The therapist who is consulted may need to suspend his/her judgment and conventional ideas about separations to understand how the unorthodox arrangement might work well for the couple. A strategic approach may be helpful with pseudo-separated couples:

> A couple came to me after seeing several different therapists. They had been married, divorced, and reconciled, and now were on the verge of separating again. A consulting team behind a one-way mirror composed a paradoxical message, part of which addressed the marital limbo.
>
> "The team believes Terry Marek is totally wrong in trying to pigeonhole these two creative individuals into a conventional mold. By neither fully separating nor marrying, Annabelle and Frank have sustained romance, intrigue, and mystery in their lives. The team feels Terry Marek should stop tampering with originality and stop pushing this couple toward a more humdrum relationship..."

8. The Severely Pathological Couple

These are couples who have severe psychopathology such as a major depression or a borderline or narcissistic disturbance. What is difficult in separation-divorce work is distinguishing between psychopathology and behavior that looks"crazy" but is part and parcel of the separation process. If a client appears or sounds suicidal, the therapist can become anxious that the client will successfully act and the therapist will bear the legal responsibility. The therapist may need to consider setting up an evaluation with a psychiatrist to assess the need for medication, hospitalization and ongoing psychiatric follow-up. Because the client's self-esteem is already precarious and the sense of humiliation acute, the therapist must try to set up a consultation without infantilizing the client or eroding his/her confidence even more.

> A couple came for counseling, with the husband desperate to salvage the marriage, the wife desperate to separate, but fearful that her husband would kill himself. The husband dramatically left the first session when the word "separate" was mentioned. He was out of work, cut off from any family members, and enraged toward any friends who were at all supportive of his wife's separation.
>
> Two years previously, the husband had become psychotically depressed when his wife had a baby. As a child he had suffered severe and early object losses – a depressed father who was hospitalized; his parents' acrimonious divorce when he was 10 after his father was discharged from the state hospital; a narcissistic mother who was alternately rejecting and seductive toward her son; a close friend's death.
>
> The wife also had a long history of depression. When her son was born and her husband decompensated, she sought individual therapy which unbalanced the marriage and exacerbated the husband's distrust.
>
> After the initial couple session, the wife refused any conjoint therapy. The husband continued for a brief time, but decompensated and became rageful toward the therapist when his wife continued to refuse to participate in counseling.

This typology can be useful if the categories are viewed as fluid and not static, self-fulfilling prophecies. The last three categories are the most complex and emotionally demanding for the therapist. Cases which fall into these categories, however, should not be viewed with pessimism, nor dreaded as terminal cases. Many clients who initially present as "rage-to-the-grave" clients have in the course of therapy moved to the issues of "the reemerging self." These are challenging cases which often involve in-depth family of origin work, but these cases can in the long run be the most satisfying ones. In the end, client and therapist can rejoice in the work they have accomplished together. Similarly, some pseudo-separated couples who break up and come together do eventually disengage. These pseudo-separated couples can frustrate the therapist's need for order and closure, but they can also stretch the therapist to be creative and transcend the limits of her/his own value and personality structure.

The typology can be helpful if used to normalize the feelings evoked in the therapist by separation and divorce cases. A familiar framework can serve as a map with recognizable landmarks for the therapist who may feel isolated, confused — a weary traveler in dark and lonely woods.

THE INTENSE FEELINGS EVOKED IN THE THERAPIST

Separation and divorce may stir up intense feelings and anxieties for the therapist. In considering the range of reactions, one must evaluate in both the therapist and clients such factors as personality style, marital status, religious value systems, comfort with sexuality, and where one is in the family life cycle. The permutations are infinite when one thinks about the various matches possible between therapist and clients: an older therapist, married for 30 years, with a younger couple where one partner is involved in an affair; a therapist whose daughter has separated from a beloved son-in-law with a separating couple the same age as the daughter; a nun or priest with a couple contemplating divorce; a divorced therapist with a female client who is desperate to salvage the marriage with a husband who wants to separate, etc.

The anxieties that get tapped in therapists focus most around our feelings about our marriage(s) or about not being married; feelings about our parents' marriage(s) or divorce(s); feelings about competency; feelings about extremes of emotion and regressed behavior; and feelings about the unpredictability of the therapeutic contract.

The divorced therapist may have particular vulnerabilities — unresolved issues around "being left," affairs, money, sexuality. The therapist who moved quickly into a divorce may have difficulty tolerating a couple's ambivalence and perseveration about a decision. Conversely, the therapist who moved slowly into a divorce may have difficulty tolerating a couple's moving quickly to divorce.

If the therapist is not divorced, there may be a different set of unresolved issues. A therapist who has a conflictual marriage and uses repression or suppression, denial or reaction formation may feel threatened by a couple's decision to separate. At the other extreme, a therapist may derive vicarious satisfaction by encouraging separation.

The client's divorce may stir up therapists' feelings about the role played in our parents' marriages. Therapists may reexperience feelings of anger at the energy invested in trying to "save" our parents' marriages. We may find ourselves feeling guilt or depression about having "failed" as rescuers if our parents got divorced.

The therapist may have a déjà vu experience around being triangled, which manifests itself as fatigue or a feeling of depletion. When feeling so drained, the therapist needs to self-monitor, talk to his/her own therapist, get supervision, or talk to other colleagues.

A therapist may have trouble tolerating the depths of depression of a client. It may feel hard to stay outside of it, not to overidentify, to stay hopeful. Therapists may need to bring in other "players" — clients' children, siblings, friends, or parents, so we do not feel we are carrying the emotional burden in the therapy.

A therapist may feel anxious or upset at the extremes of emotion and regressed behavior. Suicide gestures or suicide threats from clients and threats of or actual physical violence are not uncommon. A therapist may have a strong reaction if parents involve their children in their rage toward one another. Therapists may get depressed, furious, or frightened or more rigid when we witness regressed behavior of every variety: temper tantrums, mean tricks, tit-for-tat behavior, rubbing the other's nose in one's sexual activities, competition vis-à-vis the kids, or punishing or retaliatory acts.

Therapists may feel anxious about competency. If the couple split, we may feel incompetent. The therapist may fear that a better clinician might have "saved" the marriage.

A therapist can get anxious about lawyers, and may fear being asked to testify, or fear being used in a legal battle. The therapist may have concerns that lawyers may reignite conflict which the therapy has diffused.

The unpredictability of the contract in separation-divorce therapy can threaten the therapist's sense of order. The contract to work on the marriage can suddenly become a divorce contract. After a long, exhausting therapy to help a couple separate, the therapist may feel "betrayed" if the couple reconcile. The therapy can imitate the course of the marriage — always teetering on the edge of terminating. Often, sessions are stormy with threats of one spouse to terminate, with sometimes abrupt, unplanned departures. A client may drop out in a flight into health — an initial euphoria — only to return deeply depressed.

Having catalogued a range of emotionally charged issues for the therapist, we ask what the therapist can do to get in touch with his/her feelings and to handle feelings without becoming depleted. First, what goes on mentally within the therapist to help him/her stay out of pitfalls? Asking a series of questions can be an important first step in marking potential trouble spots.

1) Do I like these two individuals?
2) Do I like one partner more?
3) Do I feel guilty that I wish one partner would leave the other?
4) Do these individuals remind me of myself, my spouse, my ex-spouse, my parents, anyone significant?
5) Do these individuals have marital problems I had or I have?
6) Is this couple more motivated or less motivated than I was, or my spouse or ex-spouse was, or my parents were to work on the marriage?
7) Am I feeling overly responsible for the outcome of the decision regarding separation and not keeping the decision-making responsibility with the couple?
8) Am I identifying with this couple's children or parents?

The therapist can benefit immensely from talking over questions and sharing angst with trusted colleagues, a supervisor, or a therapist. If the therapist has never been divorced, it might be important to talk with a colleague who has been divorced. With especially draining cases, one might consider bringing in a co-therapist. Given how vitriolic couples can triangulate therapists, it would be crucial to select a co-therapist with whom one has a good, trusting relationship, from whom one cannot be split. To offset the isolation and burden of responsibility in divorce cases, it often helps to bring more people into the therapy, even for brief periods — couples' children, siblings, parents, important friends, ministers, rabbis, school counselors, etc. Reflecting on other divorce cases with equally difficult beginnings that one has treated with successful outcomes can also put things in perspective. Therapists treating separation-divorce cases should make certain they are not seeing too many depressed or needy clients at the same time. It helps to develop a balanced caseload, with some clients in the upbeat recovery phase or close to terminating where you and your client are looking back on the pain and basking in the progress!

CONCLUDING REMARKS

Separation-divorce is a clinical problem that unleashes profound feelings for clients and therapist. The intensity of the grief and rage of a couple in treatment can trigger the therapist's own sadness and conflict about separation and loss in his/her life. Although the recovery stage — with the rebirth of a greater sense of self — is exhilarating and tremendously gratifying, the initial stages of the work can be lonely and overwhelming. Given the emotional overload of divorce therapy, the clinician needs access to peer support, supervision, and consultations with colleagues in related fields.

Because of the range and scope of issues in separation-divorce work, there are important implications for the training of therapists. The ideal preparation would include courses on economic and legal aspects of divorce; ethics; life cycle development; child development; psychopathology; and family and marital therapy. A course on common coping responses to stress and trauma (bereavement-death of a spouse or child; loss of a body part; natural disasters) would emphasize and put in context the normal adaptive stages of mourning. In addition, there should be a separate course on separation-divorce, with role playing, videotapes of therapy sessions with separating couples, genograms, family sculpting of the therapists' multigenerational marriages and divorces and much affective discussion of the feelings, questions, and self-doubts evoked by this work. Readings would include Sue Miller's *The Good Mother* (1986) and John Updike's *Too Far To Go* (1979); movies like *Shoot the Moon* and *Scenes From a Marriage* would be included in the course work. Above all, the most important concept to convey would be a functional and humanistic definition of what constitutes "success" in separation-divorce therapy.

REFERENCES

Abelsohn, D. (1983). Dealing with the abdication dynamic in the post divorce family: A context for adolescent crisis. *Family Process, 22,* 359-383.

Bergman, I. (1974). *Scenes From a Marriage.* New York: Pantheon Books.

Bloch, D. (1980). Divorcing, clinical notes. In M. Andolfi & I. Zwerling (Eds.), *Dimensions of Family Therapy.* New York: The Guilford Press, pp. 91-107.

Blume, J. (1982). *It's Not the End of the World.* New York: Bantam Books.

Framo, J. (1976). Family of origin as a therapeutic resource for adults in marital and family therapy: You can and should go home again. *Family Process, 15,* 193-210.

Framo, J. (1985). Breaking the ties that bind. *Networker, Sept.-Oct.,* 51-56.

Friedman, H. (1980). The father's parenting experience in divorce. *American Journal of Psychiatry, 137,* 1177-1182.

Friedman, H. (1982). The challenge of divorce to adequate fathering: The peripheral father in marriage and divorce. *Psychiatric Clinics of North America, 5,* 565-580.

Gilligan, C. (1982). *In a Different Voice.* Cambridge, MA: Harvard University Press.

Goldberg, M. (1957). Divorce problems as seen by the clinician. *Man and Wife.* New York: W.W. Norton, pp. 112-122.

Goldberg, M. (1982). The dynamics of marital interaction and marital conflict. *Psychiatric Clinics of North America, 5,* 449-467.

Goldberg, M. (1985). Remarriage: Repetition vs. new beginnings. In D. Goldberg (Ed.), *Contemporary Marriage: Special Issues in Couples Therapy.* Homewood, IL: The Dorsey Press, pp. 524-544.

Isaacs, M. (1982). Helping Mom fail: A case of a stalemated divorce. *Family Process, 21,* 225-234.

Isaacs, M., Montalvo, B., & Abelsohn, D. (1986). *The Difficult Divorce.* New York: Basic Books.

James, H. (1985). *What Maisie Knew.* Middlesex, England: Penquin Books.

Kaslow, F. (1981). Divorce and divorce therapy. In A. Gurman (Ed.), *Handbook of Family Therapy.* New York: Brunner/Mazel, pp. 662-694.

Kaslow, F. (1982). Divorce: A potential growth experience for the extended family. *Journal of Divorce, II,* 115-126.

Kaslow, F. (1984). Divorce: An evolutionary process of change in the family system. *Journal of Divorce, 7*(3), 21-39.

Kressel, K., & Deutsch, M. (1977). Divorce therapy: An in-depth survey of therapists' views. *Family Process, 16,* 413-443.

Kressel, K. (1980). Patterns of coping in divorce and some implications for clinical practice. *Family Relations, 29,* 234-240.

Miller, S. (1986). *The Good Mother.* New York: Harper & Row.

Pino, C. (1980). Research and clinical application of marital autopsy in divorce counseling. *Journal of Divorce, 4*(1), 31-47.

Rice, D. (1977). Psychotherapeutic treatment of narcissistic injury in marital separation and divorce. *Journal of Divorce, I*(a), 119-128.

Rubin, L. (1983). *Intimate Strangers.* New York: Harper & Row.

Singer, L. (1985). Divorce and the single life: Divorce as development. *Journal of Sex and Marital Therapy, I*(3), 254-262.

Storm, C., & Sprenkle, D. (1982). Individual treatment in divorce therapy: A critique of an assumption. *Journal of Divorce,* 87-97.

Turner, N. (1980). Divorce in mid-life: Clinical implications and applications. In W. Norman & T. Scaramella (Eds.), *Mid-Life, Developmental and Clinical Issues.* New York: Brunner/Mazel, 149-177.

Turner, N. (1985). Divorce: Dynamics of decision therapy. *Journal of Psychotherapy and the Family, 3,* 27-38.

Turner, N., & Strine, S. (1985). Separation and divorce: Clinical implications for parents and children. In D. Goldberg (Ed.), *Contemporary Marriage: Special Issues in Couples Therapy.* Homewood, IL: The Dorsey Press, 484-500.

Updike, J. (1979). *Too Far to Go.* New York: Fawcett Crest.

Chapter 11

Relational Therapy with Lesbian Couples

Virginia J. Swartz

INTRODUCTION

All loving couples encounter problems in their relationships. Most of these couples will go about working difficulties out through their own coping strategies or through their natural support networks. These natural support networks include extended family, church, and close friends. If a relationship problem is serious enough to be threatening the stability of the relationship, if the couple is motivated, and if the individual and support network efforts have not proved successful in resolving the problem, many couples will turn to professional social service agencies for help. These couples may be heterosexual and married, heterosexual and cohabitating, or heterosexual and premarital. They may also be homosexual.

Since the "marriage" of homosexual men and women is not permitted in this country (as it is in Denmark), homosexual couples will be self-identified as couples, whether living together or separately. They may come to the professional for relational counseling at any stage in their relationship and may present with the same types of issues as heterosexual couples. Relational therapists must be aware of both the commonalities and differences in treating heterosexual and homosexual couples. They should also be aware of their own bias regarding sexual preference and be comfortable with their own sexual identity if they are to be effective therapists to homosexual couples.

In this chapter, I will focus on the issue of lesbianism and the lesbian couple in therapy. The chapter is divided roughly into four sections: psychological theories; lesbianism and lesbian women; lesbian relationships; and relational therapy with lesbian couples.

The purpose of this chapter is to bring together a historical overview of the research on lesbianism with the current theories on sexual orientation, and then to discuss implications for practice with lesbian couples.

LESBIANISM – PSYCHOLOGICAL THEORIES

As Freud pointed out (1905), the subject of homosexuality in women had "been neglected by psychoanalytic research." Although the number of research studies concerning homosexuality has been increasing in recent years, the majority of these studies focus on male homosexuality and attempt to generalize findings to lesbian women. The actual reasons for this oversight cannot be articulated, but, as Horney (1926) and Jones (1927) suggested, inattention to lesbianism is derived from the phallocentric culture we live in and does not appear to have changed over the past 50 years.

This view is shared by many current feminist scholars and clinicians (Lyon & Martin, 1972; Oberstone & Sukoneck, 1976; Sang, 1978; Vida, 1978). These feminist authors suggest that research on lesbianism has been scarce because women are not seen as important in our society, the majority of researchers are men, editorial boards of respected journals are male dominated, research money is controlled primarily by men, and these men have difficulty imagining that women might prefer other women as mates.

Another theory concerning the lack of research on lesbianism was articulated by Romm (1965) and others. Romm pointed out that lesbians are less disturbed than their male counterparts and seek psychiatric help less frequently, and, since most early studies on homosexual people were done on a clinical sample, they were less available for study. This theory has many flaws. Lesbian women have been able to "pass" as heterosexual much more easily than gay men. They can have successful heterosexual intercourse regardless of the amount of emotional discomfort they may feel. They can remain single with less question of their sexual orientation since traditionally they had to be chosen by a man in order to marry. Women can live with each other with less suspicion of homosexuality. They can be more openly affectionate with each other. Women, in general, are more free to express a wider range of emotions, behavior, dressing styles, and, recently, occupational choice.

Because of the ability of lesbian women to pass for heterosexual (straight), they are under less overt societal pressure to conform. Gay men, because they are men, are under much more overt societal pressure to conform to the norms of our society. Men are expected to emote, dress, work, play, and relate to others in more circumscribed ways than women. The ranges of acceptable behavior are much narrower for men. Therefore, men who love men face tremendous pressure to hide their sexual orientation, which creates an enormous psychological burden for them. This pressure may generate more psychological disturbance, as Romm (1965) has suggested, or it may be that lesbianism goes undiscovered more frequently in the clinical setting due to lesbians' ability to "pass" and therapists' insensitivity to the possibility of lesbianism.

Even though the literature contains more research on male than on female homosexuality, theories of lesbianism have been articulated since 1882 with the publication of *Psychopathia Sexualis* by Krafft-Ebing (1906) in Germany. Using clinical case studies of 17 lesbians, Krafft-Ebing concluded that lesbianism was a condition caused by a cerebral anomaly which was the result of an inherited diseased condition of the central nervous system. He considered that lesbians developed their tendency spontaneously from an inbuilt predisposition.

Freud believed that lesbianism was not necessarily a neurotic illness. He did not try to determine whether lesbianism was congenital or acquired. Freud considered lesbianism to be a sexual practice that "deviates from the usual one." He felt there were degrees of nonaverage behavior and that all people were born bisexual. Freud developed several theories about the psychological development of lesbianism around his concept of penis envy, fixation, regression, etc. He said (1905) the determining factor might turn out to be constitutional, that the strength of the homosexual element in the original bisexual makeup would turn out to have been greater than the heterosexual element, thus tipping the balance. Therefore, a girl could transfer her erotic wishes from her mother to her father, transfer her penis envy to wanting a child, resolve her Oedipal situation, follow the path to adult heterosexual behavior, and still "regress" to homosexuality in adult life through a strong predisposition and/or a revival of the Oedipal situation.

Freud did not hold much hope for a "cure" of lesbianism, but felt that a female therapist might be more effective in fostering a transference with the client. One of Freud's disciples, Helene Deutsch (1948), wrote of a case where a strong positive transference was developed with a lesbian client. Following therapy, the client was no longer depressed, anxious, or suicidal, but was instead happily involved in a very rewarding love relationship with another woman. Deutsch believed this to be a successful outcome (Klaich, 1974).

Since Krafft-Ebing, Freud, Deutsch, and others began to address homosexuality as an inborn condition or, at least, predisposition, homosexual activity moved in the public mind from a vice to an illness. Once it was identified as an illness, the medical profession began to spend energy trying to find a cure.

When homosexuality was considered solely a crime or vice, homosexual men and women were punished by legal or church authorities; some were jailed, killed, or banished. The advent of the disease model brought incarceration in mental hospitals, years of psychotherapy, electroconvulsive therapy (ECT), and surgical interventions such as clitorectomies, lobotomies, and castration.

The search for causes continued. Rosen (1974) listed several "theories" of lesbianism that were found in the literature of the 30s, 40s, and 50s. These theories included fear of pregnancy; castration complex and subsequent repulsion from heterosexuality; an attraction for females through an early fixation on the mother; and aggressive hatred for the dominating mother, warded off by libidinous feelings.

Many other lesbian causation theories have been noted by Lyon and Martin (1972). Some of these are: fear of growing up; fear of dominance and destruction; fear of the opposite sex; fear of the penis; desire to possess the mother; neurotic dependency; heterosexual trauma; tomboy behavior in childhood; seduction by someone of the same sex in adolescence; prolonged absence of the mother; masturbation with resulting clitoral fixation; and various physical factors such as genetic, constitutional, or endocrine abnormalities.

Current Thought on Lesbianism

Until the Kinsey, et al. study (1953), no scientific study had been done on "normal" women's sexuality. This work provided the first glimpse into homosexuality as a natural sexual behavior. The Kinsey study suggested that every person has the physiologic capacity to respond to any sufficient stimulus, that it is an accident which leads to a person's first sexual experience, that the person's first sexual experience is a conditioning experience, and that other persons' opinions and social codes strongly affect an individual's decision to accept or reject any type of sexual contact (Kinsey, et al., 1953, p. 447).

Rosen (1974) reviewed a number of studies in nonclinical populations reported in the literature in the 1960s. Some of the results are as follows: The failure to find many clear-cut differences between heterosexual and homosexual women would suggest that homosexuality is not a clinical entity; lesbians were somewhat more hostile towards and afraid of their fathers than were married women; English lesbians scored higher in neuroticism than a comparison group of heterosexuals; lesbians were not necessarily neurotic and were more independent, more resilient, more reserved, more dominant, more bohemian, more self-sufficient, and more composed; in a global measure of psychological adjustment there was no difference between the lesbian and the control group.

Rosen (1974) found that the vast majority of rigorous studies done in the 1970s failed to show any significant difference in the psychological adjustment of lesbians and heterosexual women. In his own study (1974), Rosen found that lesbians have the same or lower incidences of psychiatric disturbance when compared with matched heterosexual controls; no significant difference in the prevalence of neurotic disorders, depression, suicide attempts; and a higher level of self-confidence. Oberstone and Sukoneck (1976), using the MMPI and 60-item structured interview questionnaire, found the only difference between 25 white, single lesbians and 25 white, single heterosexual women was that of sexual orientation.

Research has failed to uncover a cause for homosexuality. The research done on nonclinical subjects with control groups of heterosexual women shows that lesbians and heterosexual women are equally psychologically adjusted and show no significant difference in pathology.

The research in the literature of the 1980s tends to compare sex-role identity, sex-role behavior, and issues related to life satisfaction and relationships. It appears, at least in the literature, that professional caregivers are becoming more concerned with helping homosexual men and women who request it with their concerns rather than trying to find etiology and "cure" for a disease. At least on the surface, it appears that most enlightened researchers have accepted homosexuality as a normal variant of sexual behavior. It is not known if practitioners have come to the same level of acceptance.

LESBIANISM AND LESBIAN WOMEN

No one knows the number of lesbians who live in the United States today. Estimates range from 5 million to 10 million, and from 4% of all adult women to 10%. Because lesbianism has been considered a sin, a crime, and an illness, women throughout history have had to hide their lesbianism from society and even from themselves.

Lesbians come in all shapes and sizes. They come from all ethnic and racial groups and every socioeconomic stratum. Lesbians come from farms, small towns, and large cities. They are first born, last born, middle kids, and only kids. They are Baptists, Buddhists, and nonbelievers. Lesbians work in any occupation in which women work. They are single, married, divorced, or widowed. Lesbians wear jeans and dresses, boots and heels. Lesbians can be sexually active or celibate, single or coupled. Lesbians can be teenagers or senior citizens, or any age in between. In short, lesbians are women who are different from other women only in their orientation toward loving women. They are an invisible but sizable minority that permeates society and all of its institutions.

LESBIAN RELATIONSHIPS

In examining the ways that gays and lesbians relate to each other, Bell and Weinberg of the Institute of Sex Research (1978) conducted an extensive study involving face-to-face interviews with approximately 1,500 persons. This study was commissioned by the National Institute of Mental Health and sought to examine the sexual circumstances, the social lives, and the psychological adjustment of homosexual men and women. They found that lesbians fell into five categories: closed-coupleds, open-coupleds, functionals, dysfunctions, and asexuals. They also found that one-third of their sample of lesbians had been married at least once and that one-half of these women had children. These marriages tended to be unhappy and short-lived, lasting, on average, three years. For the purpose of this chapter, I will concentrate on the relationship of women with women.

Closed-Coupleds

The closed-coupled relationship is described as the closest thing to a heterosexual marriage. In this relationship, the women tend to look only to each other for sexual fulfillment and frequently live together, share resources, and plan together for the future. In the Bell and Weinberg (1978) study, they demonstrated the smallest amount of sexual problems and had little, if any, regret about being homosexual. They were unlikely to frequent bars, were well adjusted socially and occupationally, and were unlikely to seek professional help for personal problems. Of the sample, 38% fell into this category.

Open-Coupleds

The open-coupleds tend to live with a special sexual partner, but often seek satisfaction outside their relationship. These women are not fully committed to their relationship and place more reliance on a large circle of friends. They are less happy, self-accepting, and relaxed than closed-coupleds but were found to be basically as well adjusted as the closed-coupleds in social and occupational measures. Bell and Weinberg (1978) suggested that the lesbian women may have more difficulty with this type of relationship than their male counterparts and it appeared that lesbians tend to be happier in the exclusive closed-coupled relationship. Of Bell and Weinberg's sample, 24% fell into the open-coupled category.

There is considerable pressure in the lesbian feminist community for women to reject monogamy as a patriarchal form of oppression. The theory is that monogamy is man's creation and that it has been used throughout history to force women to submit to men for support and protection. This rejection of monogamy runs counter to the value of fidelity so prevalent in our society. It could be that this value conflict may be, in part, responsible for the diminished happiness in the open-coupled relationship. The open-coupled lesbian may intellectually reject monogamy but emotionally feel betrayed and threatened by infidelity.

Functionals

The functionals are described as "swinging singles." They are involved in gay activities, engage in more sexual activity than other groups, have little regret about their homosexuality, and are not particularly interested in finding a primary relationship. They tend to be involved with many friends and are described as energetic, self-reliant, cheerful, and optimistic. Of the lesbian sample, 12% fell into this category.

Dysfunctionals

The dysfunctionals are described as the stereotypical tormented homosexual. These women regretted their homosexuality, had more sexual problems, were poorly adjusted in other areas of their lives, and were most likely to require long-term professional help for an emotional problem. Of the sample, 8% fell into this category.

Asexuals

The asexual women are described as having a very low level of sexual activity and involvement with others. They are the least likely to consider themselves exclusively homosexual. They tend to live alone and spend the majority of their leisure time alone. They were the most apt of all lesbians in the study to seek professional help concerning their sexual orientation, but drop out of treatment quickly. Of the sample, 16% fell into this category.

Summary of Relationship Types

Bell and Weinberg (1978) found that 62% of their sample of lesbians were involved in a primary relationship and that another 22% of their sample related sexually with other women. Jay and Young (1979) reported that 80% of their lesbian respondents had a lover and that the average length of these love relationships was three years. The most frequent type of lesbian relationship was the closed-coupled, followed by the open-coupled, and then the functional (casual) relationship.

Relationship Style

One of the most common myths about lesbian relationships is that each woman in the couple assumes a role as either masculine (butch) or feminine (femme). Jay and Young (1979) found that fewer than 10% of their respondents believed they played butch/femme roles in their relationship. It has been this author's experience with lesbian couples that lesbian relationships differ in style as much as heterosexual couples. The primary difference between lesbian and heterosexual relational styles is that the lesbian or gay couple, being a same-gender relationship, is free from sex-role stereotyped behavior patterns common to the heterosexual couple. Cardell et al. (1981) examined sex-role identity, sex-role behavior, and satisfaction in heterosexual, homosexual, and lesbian couples. They found that members of heterosexual couples were more sex-typed and more sex-role differentiated in their behavior than were members of lesbian couples. The Bem Sex-Role Inventory scores predicted sex-role differentiation in heterosexual couples, but not in lesbian couples. In this study there was no significant difference in satisfaction by couple type.

A study on sex roles and intimacy (Fischer, 1981) compared same-sex and other-sex relationships. It was found that the highest level of intimacy was possible in lesbian relationships, that intimacy is linked most strongly to femininity and that androgynous women had significantly higher intimacy scores than the sex-typed and undifferentiated women. The authors concluded that the higher intimacy of the female-female relationship may be the result of both femininity and behavioral flexibility and freedom from rigid sex roles.

Relational styles, in addition to sex-role behavior, are affected by each partner's personal relating style. Sager and Hunt (1979) outline seven personal styles of relating and the various combinations of styles found in couples. Examples of the latter are: the equal partner, the childlike partner, and the romantic partner. Like heterosexual couples, lesbian relationships are made up of two individuals with individual relating styles. Lesbian couples will exhibit the same types of combinations, i.e., parental-childlike, equal-equal, and romantic-rational.

In addition to the concepts of sex-role behavior and relational style, the lesbian couple may be made up of women from different racial, cultural, ethnic, and/or socioeconomic backgrounds. It has been shown that these variables influence a couple's ability to relate, communicate, and understand each other (McGoldrick, Pearce, & Giordano, 1982).

Common Problems in Lesbian Relationships

As has been noted above, recent research has shown that lesbians are as well adjusted psychologically as heterosexual women. Lesbian couples have dynamics similar to gay males and heterosexual couples. Lesbian couples have similar strengths and weaknesses as other types of couples and will present for relational therapy with similar issues. Lesbian couples do, however, present frequently with problems surrounding issues of boundaries and differentiation. A review of the literature reveals four articles on fusion or psychological merger in lesbian couples (Burch, 1982; Gartrell, 1984; Kaufman et al., 1984; Krestan & Bepko, 1980). Some factors thought to contribute to this phenomenon are:

1) The lack of legitimacy, cultural and legal, afforded lesbian couples forces them to band together, i.e., us against them;
2) No traditional healthy role models;
3) High level of intimacy potential of women, more permeable boundaries, less differentiation from mother;
4) No gender difference (creates less distance);
5) Social isolation caused by secrecy;
6) Individual's fear of abandonment.

One article suggested that disapproval of the lesbian relationship by a partner's parents created special problems in the lesbian couple (Murphy, 1983). One article examined the problem of jealousy in lesbian relationships (Morris, 1982), and another article described alcoholism and the gay subculture as a special problem for lesbian couples (Nardi, 1982). Several other articles dealt with problems common in heterosexual relationships, such as communication problems, battering, sexual dysfunction, and parenting. No research on life-cycle issues in lesbian couples or on lesbian identity development and its effect on relationships is available.

RELATIONAL THERAPY WITH LESBIAN COUPLES

Therapist Qualifications

In order to do relational therapy with couples, a therapist should be trained and certified in couples work. Lesbian couples, like any couple, deserve fully trained and competent marital and family therapists. In addition, lesbian clients require a therapist who is sensitive to and knowledgeable about lesbians, their issues, and their life-style. The therapist must accept homosexuality as a normal variation of sexual/affectional orientation and must be comfortable with his/her own sexuality (Gartrell, 1984).

Studies have evaluated the effectiveness of therapist-client similarity on the therapeutic outcome. Such attitudes as race, ethnicity, and cultural backgrounds have been studied and have been found to influence the outcomes of therapeutic interventions. Commonality of experience — and not simply a theoretical understanding of it — can produce a more favorable outcome (Jones & Seagull, 1977; Roll, Millen, & Martinez, 1980). Liljestrend et al. (1978) examined the relationship between sexual orientation of therapist and client and found the client similarity in sexual orientation was correlated with a more successful treatment outcome than therapist-client difference. Gartrell (1984) stresses that a lesbian therapist should be "out of the closet" to her colleagues and her clients where appropriate to the situation as she has found that "closeted" lesbian therapists allow their own fears of homophobia to dictate a life of secrecy and, therefore, may be unable to help lesbian clients who are struggling with the risks of coming out. Gartrell believes that a lesbian's self-esteem and mental health improve in direct proportion to her ability to be honest about her lesbianism to the outside world.

Assessment of Lesbian Couples

Although no research on assessment of lesbian couples is available, the relational therapist would need to gather additional information from the women on such areas as lesbian identity development, internalized homophobia, stages of "coming out" of each partner, involvement in the lesbian community, social pressure for nonmonogamy, and family of origin's acceptance-rejection of each member's homosexuality or partner. It would also be important for the therapist to assess the nature and quality of the support systems used by the couple and the amount of stress placed on the relationship by fear of discovery of either partner. If either or both partners have children, it is important to know if the children are aware of their parents' homosexuality and if there is any fear of a custody battle.

Since the lesbian couple is free of gender-based roles, the therapist will also need to evaluate how decisions are made regarding division of labor, financial arrangements, employment or career priorities, and recreation. Because lesbians cannot marry, in the legal sense, the therapist will also need to assess the level of commitment of the couple. Have they had a commitment ceremony? Do they wear "wedding" bands? Have they made major purchases together? Are they in each other's will? Does one support the other? How do they divide expenses? Do they have joint investments? Do they consider themselves married, living together, or friends?

In addition to the above information, the therapist needs to assess the relationship as he/she would assess any other couple: establishing the relationship, defining the problem, tracing the development of the problem, examining solutions attempted, looking for changes in the environment, examining communication patterns, and assessing the level of enjoyment, forgiveness, responsibility, protectiveness, caring, sharing, and positive regard each member has for the other. What is the level of motivation for change? What are the family of origin issues, scripts, loyalties, etc.?

As mentioned earlier, the therapist should be honest with his/her homosexual clients about his/her sexual orientation and be up front about any feelings about homosexuality. It is our belief that any therapist who is uncomfortable dealing with lesbians should find a qualified therapist who is comfortable with these clients and refer. The literature is replete with horror stories told by lesbians of psychic harm done to them by therapists who attempted to convince these clients that their lesbianism was sick and who spent all their "therapeutic" effort trying to help these clients become heterosexual. Also, many lesbian clients report spending half of their sessions educating their therapists about lesbianism.

INTERVENTION FOR SPECIAL PROBLEMS

Fusion or Psychological Merging

Clinicians have recognized a problem common in lesbian couples that has been labeled fusion or psychological merging (Burch, 1982; Gartrell, 1984; Kaufman et al., 1984; Krestan & Bepko, 1980). Symptoms of fusion include: inhibited sexual desire, irritability, battering, depression, a feeling of suffocating, outside sexual relationships, intense jealousy, and social isolation. A couple who are fused often share all friends, social activities, recreational activities, vacations, professional services, clothing, space, and sometimes places of employment. They minimize all differences and attempt to agree on everything, from politics to food preferences.

This couple usually present for treatment at the point where one member of the couple begins to contemplate leaving the relationship (Burch, 1982).

Treatment recommendations for the problem of fusion involve helping the couple to establish distance in six areas: territorial space, such as separate drawers, closet space, side of bed, study space; temporal space, such as time spent with separate friends, involvement in different activities, separate vacations or weekend trips; financial space, such as separate money, checking and savings accounts; cognitive space, such as separate interests, reading, ideas, unshared fantasies; emotional space, such as recognition of one's own feelings, drives, separate therapists; and environmental space, such as own social networks, separate hobbies and activities (Kaufman et al., 1984).

While supporting each member of the couple, the therapist attempts to bring out differences and negative emotions in a way that is nonthreatening to the partner. Assertiveness and conflict resolution skills are taught in session, while homework assignments, such as instructing each partner to take an evening out alone, are given in incremental steps. At times, the therapist may want to act as side-taker with one member of the couple to unbalance the system, to get past the stuckness. Side-taking, of course, is risky and must be used with caution at appropriate times and with sufficient rapport with both partners. In extreme cases, temporary separation may be required to allow each member of the couple enough space for differentiation. Separation may also lead to dissolution of the relationship, which may be the best therapeutic outcome for some lesbian pairs (Burch, 1982).

Jealousy

Jealousy in the lesbian couple can be a special problem for several reasons. Since there is no legal marriage, it is easier to leave a relationship. The boundaries around the relationship are invisible or may be disrespected by others, and the relationship is not supported by society. A partner may fear that her lover may reject the life-style and "go straight" in order to gain acceptance by society. The lesbian feminist community promotes nonmonogamy and pressures lesbian couples to have "open relationships."

Treatment should help to recognize and declare feelings of jealousy; clarify misinformation and possible payoffs provided by jealousy within the relationship; encourage lesbian-feminist consciousness raising; negotiate needs and rights; and provide individual therapy if needed to explore early antecedents of jealousy (Morris, 1982).

Parental Disapproval of Lesbianism and/or Partner

Rejection by family of origin of a lesbian's life-style or lover can have profound negative impact on the lesbian couple. Parental rejection often creates a situation where a lesbian must choose between spending holidays with her family of origin or with her lover. If she chooses one, she is rejecting the other. This tension can affect the everyday interaction of the couple, as well as interfere with the establishment of trust (Murphy, 1983).

Treatment involves extensive work on separation-individuation of the lesbian from her parents. As long as she needs their approval, their attitude will affect her ability to relate to her lover. In addition to the individual work, the couple will need support, validation, and consciousness raising regarding homophobia and oppression.

Alcoholism

Nardi (1982) stresses that there is no evidence that alcoholism is more prevalent in gays or lesbians, but treatment must consider the significant others in a gay person's life somewhat differently from a straight person. Nardi identifies three different "families" that most gay people are engaged in: the family of origin; the extended family of a few, very close gay friends; and the primary relationship, which may include children. Nardi stresses that effective treatment of alcoholism in gay people involves consideration of all of these family systems and participation in treatment of the "significant others" via ALANON, ALATEEN, etc. Nardi also points out that a therapist must understand the gay subculture and its bars as well as the oppression faced by gay people in order to help the alcoholic and his/her "family" to build and/or strengthen a non-drinking environment. Most large cities have gay AA and ALANON chapters.

CLINICAL CASE EXAMPLES

Case 1—Julie and Jen, a Fused Couple

Julie initiated contact for couples therapy following the discovery that her lover, Jen, had engaged in a "one-night stand." The discovery was made when a postcard arrived addressed to Jen from a woman whom Julie did not know. The card was a thank you note "for a wonderful time and many fond memories."

An angry fight followed a tearful confession, and both women agreed to see a therapist. They contacted friends in their lesbian support network for a referral and came to their initial evaluation within a week of the precipitating event.

Julie and Jen arrived for their first session in nearly identical dress. Both wore Hawaiian printed blouses, chino pants, and high-top sneakers. Julie was taller and had darker skin tones and hair color than Jen. They had similar haircuts and carried similar handbags.

After exploring the presenting problem of the affair and all of the feelings surrounding it, the therapist began to explore the couple's pre-crisis relationship. It was revealed that Julie (age 29) had met Jen (age 28) while in college. They had shared a dorm room during Julie's sophomore and Jen's freshman year. They became each other's first homosexual lover toward the end of that first year of living together and have been together monogamously for over 10 years.

Their relationship was described by both women as close and compatible. They both enjoyed cooking, collecting and playing jazz records, going to movies, and socializing with friends. Neither woman had individual interests or friendships enjoyed without the company of the other. In the initial conjoint session, both women said they were satisfied with their sex life in quality, if not in quantity. They reported having very satisfying sexual experiences once every three or four months; when they did have sex, Jen was usually the initiator.

An individual session with Julie revealed that she worked as a nurse supervisor at a local teaching hospital and was working toward a master's degree in nursing in the evenings. She was the oldest child of an Italian working-class couple and had two younger brothers and one younger sister. She described her childhood as "happy" and her family life as loud and emotional. She said that her father yelled when he got mad and that her mother would cry. Julie remembered trying to cheer up her mother and remembered being afraid of her father when he yelled. She said that she and her siblings would stick together when her father was angry. She denied any physical or sexual abuse.

Julie reported being happy with her lesbian life-style and with her relationship with Jen. She reported that she has had a problem with jealousy since the beginning of the relationship and said that, although she knew that Jen loved her, she knew Jen would eventually cheat on her. Julie had never talked about this fear with Jen and often kept her feelings to herself.

The individual session with Jen revealed that she worked as an art therapist in an inpatient psychiatric treatment facility. She was the only child of a W.A.S.P. family from the Midwest. Jen described her childhood as happy and had many memories of trips taken with her "devoted" parents. Jen described both of her parents as warm and loving, but noted that her mother tended to use guilt to control Jen's behavior. Jen said she was always a "good kid" growing up and that she still has a hard time not pleasing people. Jen described herself as a "soft touch" and an "easy mark."

Jen stated in the couples session that she was somewhat satisfied with the couple's sex life. In the individual session she had complained that Julie was not interested in sex and had to be seduced and plied with wine in order for her to respond sexually to Jen. Jen became tearful and said that she needed more sex than Julie was interested in having. She then admitted that she had never told Julie how she felt. When pressed further, Jen admitted that she feared rejection if she asked Julie for more sexual contact.

This couple represents the fused lesbian dyad. They minimize all differences, tend to agree on everything, and avoid confrontation at all cost. They are experiencing inhibited sexual desire within the couple. The one-night affair was a successful, if not maladaptive, attempt to establish distance and to unbalance the closed system.

Treatment involved supporting each partner while bringing out negative feelings and differences. Julie was able to express her jealous feelings and anger. Jen was able to express her desire for more physical closeness and sexual expression. Julie was able to ask for one night out a week with her friends from work, and Jen was able to take a class in glassblowing without Julie also taking the class. Both partners were instructed in assertive behavior, conflict resolution, and communication skills. Therapy included exploration of both women's families of origin and their relational patterns. It was discovered that Julie tended to avoid conflict in her relationship with Jen as she equated conflict with her father's verbal outbursts that frightened her as a child. As a result of this fear, Julie avoided sharing any feelings with Jen that might evoke strong emotions in Jen. Her withdrawal would then be interpreted by Jen as rejection, which is how Jen was punished by her guilt-inducing mother. Recognition of these early patterns of conflict avoidance helped both women develop more direct communication of negative feelings.

Within a month after beginning treatment, the couple reported increased frequency and intensity in their sexual relationship. Both women reported a new sense of closeness even though they were both spending more time away from each other. The remainder of therapy dealt with issues surrounding negotiation of each woman's transition issues at age 30. The couple attended conjoint "marital" sessions once a week for 16 weeks. At one year follow-up, they reported that they were doing well.

Case 2 — Laura and Mary, Substance Abuse

Laura contacted the clinic, requesting individual therapy for herself. In the initial telephone call with her therapist, it was learned that she was involved with a woman who suffered from drug and alcohol addiction. Mary, Laura's lover, had refused to come with her for the intake appointment. However, she changed her mind as Laura was leaving for the clinic.

Laura and Mary were both in their early 40s and worked as park rangers at a nearby state park. Laura was an education programs specialist. Mary was a supervisor and park administrator. They lived together on the park property in what they both described as a "fishbowl." They had very little privacy, worked varying shifts, and were constantly trying to pretend they were heterosexual. The stress this couple lived under was remarkable.

Mary and Laura had become involved with each other slightly less than a year before entering couples therapy and had lived together less than three months. Both had been involved in previous lesbian relationships. Mary had shared 15 years with her previous lover. That relationship ended four years ago when Mary's lover, at age 36, suddenly announced that she was leaving to marry a divorced man who had custody of his two children. Mary, who had abused alcohol periodically since her teen years, began to drink regularly while taking anti-anxiety medicine prescribed by her family physician in the aftermath of her separation. Since that time, Mary continued to drink alcoholically, while simultaneously abusing Valium. Although Mary continued to work satisfactorily in her position, she admitted increased absenteeism and a lack of motivation.

Laura reported having left her previous lesbian relationship because of her former lover's severe, chronic depression. She stated that she had functioned more as a mother than as a lover in that relationship and was determined not to make the same mistake in this relationship. Laura claimed that she did not realize the extent of Mary's substance abuse until they moved in together. Her complaints about Mary's behavior included Mary's lying about her substance use, her lethargy around the house, and the lack of communication between them when Mary was "high." Laura also feared that Mary might overdose herself or become involved in an accident while driving.

Mary's only complaint about the relationship was that Laura often treated her like a child and would nag her about her drinking. Mary said that she realized her drinking had gotten out of hand, but that she didn't want Laura to be her mother.

After the initial evaluation, it was recommended that Laura attend the gay ALANON meetings in the city and that Mary admit herself to a detox and 28-day inpatient alcoholism treatment program. Upon completion of the inpatient program, Mary was supervised by a gay alcohol treatment counselor and attended gay alcohol anonymous groups. In addition to the alcoholism treatment and ALANON, the couple attended 20 weeks of couples therapy.

Couples therapy involved examining patterns of interaction in the relationship that were destructive. One such pattern was Laura's parental behavior which had been present in her previous failed relationship and which probably resulted from her role as a parentified child as oldest of seven siblings. Another part of the pattern was Mary's rebellious and irresponsible behavior which took the form of self-destructive acting out as shown by her drinking, drug abuse, and lack of responsibility in household chores and work attendance. Mary was the youngest child of three and came from a home that was emotionally distant.

Another focus of couples therapy was internalized homophobia and the stress of trying to hide their sexual orientation from their employer while at the same time living together in the park's residential complex. After the 10th week of therapy, Laura and Mary decided that they had to either "come out" to their boss or move off the complex. After assessing their financial assets and career opportunities, the couple decided to tell the park supervisor about their relationship. To their surprise and relief, the supervisor told them that he had suspected that they were lovers, that it would not affect their jobs, and that he knew that there were several other gay rangers working for the park service. He later told them that his sister-in-law was a "very fine lesbian."

Through their contacts with the AA and ALANON groups, this couple developed a supportive non-drinking network of "extended family." During therapy, both women made trips home to their families of origin. Mary's mother, who had been aware of Mary's life-style for 20 years, was pleased with her daughter's sobriety and hoped that they could become closer as friends. Mary's siblings were also supportive; her father is now deceased.

Laura's parents would not discuss her relationship with Mary, but were able to talk with her about regretting putting so much responsibility on

Laura as a child. They told her that she never really had the chance to be a kid. Although they have never discussed Laura's lesbianism, Laura reports that they have always welcomed her lovers in their home and that they had stopped asking her about boyfriends when she was 25. It appears that Laura's parents know on some level of their daughter's lesbianism. She regrets not being able to share more intimately with her parents and hopes that as she becomes more comfortable with being open about her sexual orientation she will be able to do so.

This couple worked very hard on their issues in therapy. Both women were in their early 40s and appeared to be ready to make some changes in their lives. Mary was ready to give up her reliance on pills and alcohol and to take responsibility for her life. Laura was willing to give up always being in control and to take the risk of being rejected by others by "coming out of the closet."

Follow-up two years later revealed that the couple have bought a house together and are looking forward to "growing old together." Laura is now teaching environmental science courses at a state college, and Mary is the park supervisor at another state park in the same geographical area.

Case 3—Carmen and Sue, Parental Disapproval

Carmen and Sue came to the clinic, requesting help in dealing with Carmen's mother. The couple reported that they got along great until the holidays and then "all hell breaks loose."

Carmen is a 24-year-old Puerto Rican woman involved in her first and only lesbian relationship. She comes from a highly religious Catholic family of eight. She is a middle child, has a graduate degree in business, and holds an excellent position in fashion marketing at a large firm.

Sue is a 26-year-old Irish Catholic businesswoman. She is the oldest of five siblings and the mother of a five-year-old son (from a short-lived marriage). The couple has been together for two years. Carmen shares in parenting responsibilities, and both women get along well with the boy's father who shares custody mostly on weekends and holidays.

Carmen initially explained the problem as Sue's inability to deal with Carmen's mother. Carmen reported that Sue gets mad whenever her mother calls and gets "really irrational" whenever Carmen makes plans to fly to Puerto Rico for the holidays.

Sue expressed the problem as Carmen's change in behavior whenever her mother calls or when Carmen comes back from trips to Puerto Rico. Sue claimed that Carmen would become distant and irritable, avoid sex, and start talking about men and marriage after every conversation with her mother. Carmen's behavior would spark insecure feelings in Sue who would then become angry and demand that Carmen not see her mother. Carmen would, in turn, label Sue's behavior as irrational and possessive.

Therapy with this couple involved dealing with issues of separation, individuation, differences in culture, establishment of trust, internalized homophobia, and improved communication and conflict resolution.

Carmen had not done much work in separating from her parents. As a middle child and as a female in the Puerto Rican culture, she did not receive much attention from her hardworking father and her overburdened mother. Although she was educated and had lived on the mainland for most of her life, her family maintained strong cultural ties to Puerto Rico and relocated to the island when Carmen began college. Carmen's mother is a traditional woman who had remained married to an abusive, extremely macho husband for 36 years. She had six children and three miscarriages.

According to Carmen, her mother believes it is better to live with a husband who beats you than to live with a woman who loves you. Carmen stated that her mother called her up, telling her about bad dreams that she has about Carmen. Dreams are often given much credence in Puerto Rican culture. Her mother's worry caused Carmen much sorrow. On a recent visit to the mainland, Carmen's mother spent time at their house but did not speak to or look at Sue during the visit. Carmen's father had recently become a born-again Christian. He now spent most of his free time at church or in prayer. The two youngest siblings are still in the parental home and are in their early 20s.

Carmen's work in therapy revolved around understanding her family's developmental life cycle and her family scripts and loyalties. This work was done conjointly with Sue to give Sue better understanding of Carmen's family and her struggle with them.

Sue also had to work on her family of origin. She was cut off from the family since getting divorced three years ago and had very little contact with them. Sue realized that she would get angry at Carmen when she talked to her mother because Sue rarely spoke to her own family and felt rejected by them.

Both of these women had been raised in large Catholic families. They had developed a large "extended family" of gay men and women and were heavily involved in the gay community. They attended Dignity, a gay Catholic organization for their religious needs.

In addition to the work on family of origin, cultural difference, and establishment of trust, Sue and Carmen had to learn to communicate and resolve conflicts more effectively. Each week they were given homework assignments designed to give them practice in discussing their own needs, concerns, hurts, wants, and joys. They were also referred to an organization of lesbian mothers.

Carmen and Sue spent five months in weekly couples therapy. At Christmas, Carmen stayed home, but invited her parents to visit with the stipulation that they recognize and respect Sue. Her parents did not visit.

The couple completed therapy one month ago at this writing. They both have much work to do with their families, most of which will take the passage of time, mutual support, and open communication.

CONCLUSIONS

This chapter has noted that the etiology of lesbianism is unknown; lesbians are as psychologically well adjusted as heterosexual women; lesbians tend toward coupled relationships; lesbian couples have relational problems similar to those of heterosexual couples; lesbian couples have some special problems caused by same genderness and oppression; and therapist characteristics affect the outcome of treatment.

The need for research on lesbians and lesbian relationships is vast. Until recently, the subject of lesbianism was largely ignored by researchers. The past decade, however, has seen an increase in the quantity and quality of nonclinical studies. More research is needed on treatment outcomes for lesbian clients who come for treatment for their relationships.

Effective therapy with lesbian couples requires that therapists have both a theoretical understanding of lesbianism and knowledge of the special problems faced by lesbians in our society. Therapists need an understanding of the psychology of women and the effects of sexism, racism, and heterosexism on the lesbian couples. Therapists need to know the gay community, its problems, and its resources. They must evaluate and be comfortable with their own sexual orientation and be honest with their clients about their own biases. Therapists must also be trained in couples and family work. Additionally, since so much of the difficulty experienced by ethnic, racial, and sexual minority couples is caused by institutional prejudice, therapists need to work toward the elimination of oppression for the betterment of all of their clients' experiences.

REFERENCES

Axinn, J., & Levin, H. (1982). *Social Welfare: A History of the American Response to Need*. New York: Longman.

Bell, A. P., & Weinberg, M. S. (1978). *Homosexualities: A Study of Diversity Among Men & Women*. New York: Simon & Schuster.

Burch, B. (1982). Psychological merger in lesbian couples: A joint ego psychological and systems approach. *Family Therapy, 9*(3), 201-208.

Cardell, M., Finn, S., & Marecek, J. (1981). Sex-role identity, sex role behavior, and satisfaction. In: Heterosexual, lesbian, and gay male couples. *Psychology of Women Quarterly, 5*(3), 488-494.

Clark, D. (1978). *Loving Someone Gay*. New York: Signet.

Deutsch, H. (1948). On female homosexuality. In: *The Psychoanalytic Reader*, Vol. 1. New York: International Universities Press.

Fischer, J. (1981). Sex roles and intimacy in same sex and other sex relationships. *Psychology of Women Quarterly*, 5(3).

Freud, S. (1905). *Three Essays on the Theory of Sexuality*. In J. Strachey (Ed.) *Standard Edition of the Complete Psychological Works of Sigmund Freud*, Vol. VII (1953). London: Hogarth Press.

Gartrell, N. (1984). Combating homophobia in the psychotherapy of lesbians. *Women & Therapy*, 3(1), 13-29.

Gartrell, N. (May 3-4, 1986). Sexuality/sexual dysfunction/sexual ethics. Unpublished paper presented at The Second National Lesbian Physicians' Conference. Provincetown, MA.

Gearhart, S. (1978). The spiritual dimension: Death and resurrection of a hallelujah dyke. In G. Vida (Ed.), *Our Right to Love*. Englewood Cliffs, NJ: Prentice-Hall.

Hall, M. (1978). Lesbian families: Cultural and clinical issues. *Social Work*, 23(5), 380-385.

Harrison, E. (May 3-4, 1985). Relationship merging. Unpublished paper presented at The Second National Lesbian Physicians' Conference. Provincetown, MA.

Horney, K. (1926). The flight from womanhood: The masculinity complex in women, as viewed by men and women. *International Journal of Psychoanalysis*, 7, 324-339.

Jay, K., & Young, A. (1979). *The Gay Report*. New York: Summit.

Jones, A., & Seagull, A. (1977). Dimensions of the relationship between the black client and the white therapist. *American Psychologist*, 32, 850-855.

Jones, E. (1927). The early development of female sexuality. *International Journal of Psychoanalysis*, 8, 459-472.

Kaufman, P., Harrison, E., & Hyde, M. L. (1984). Distancing for intimacy in lesbian relationships. *American Journal of Psychiatry*, 141(4), 530-533.

Kinsey, A., et al. (1953). *Sexual Behavior in the Human Female*. Philadelphia: Saunders.

Klaich, D. (1974). *Women & Women: Attitudes Toward Lesbians*. New York: Simon & Schuster.

Krafft-Ebing, R. von (1906). *Psychopathia Sexualis*. Trans. F. J. Rebman. New York: Rebman.

Krestan, J., & Bepko, C. (1980). The problem of fusion in the lesbian relationship. *Family Process*, 19, 277-289.

Kurdeck, L., & Schmitt, P. (1986). Early development of relationship quality in heterosexual married, heterosexual cohabitating, gay and lesbian couples. *Developmental Psychology*, 22(3), 305-309.

Liljestrend, P., Gerling, E., & Saliba, P. (1978). The effects of sex-role stereotypes and sexual orientation in psychotherapeutic outcomes. *Journal of Homosexuality*, 3, 361-372.

Lyon, P., & Martin, D. (1972). *Lesbian/Woman*. New York: Bantam.

Marecek, J., Finn, S., & Cardell, M. (1982). Gender roles in the relationships of lesbians and gay men. *Journal of Homosexuality*, 8(2), 45-49.

McGoldrick, M., Pearce, J., & Giordano, J. (1982). *Ethnicity & Family Therapy*. New York: Guilford Press.

Morris, V. (1982). Helping lesbians cope with jealousy. *Women & Therapy*, 1(4), 27-34.

Murphy, B. (1983). Intergenerational contact and the impact of parental attitudes on lesbian and married couples. *Dissertation Abstracts International*, 43(12-B), 4156-4157.

Nardi, P. (1982). Alcohol treatment and the non-traditional "family" structures of gays and lesbians. *Journal of Alcohol & Drug Education, 27*(2), 83-89.

Nicholas, M. (1982). The treatment of inhibited sexual desire (ISD) in lesbian couples. *Women & Therapy, 1*(4), 49-66.

Oberstone, A., & Sukoneck, H. (1976). Psychological adjustment and life style of single lesbians and single heterosexual women. *Psychology of Women Quarterly, 1*(2), 172-188.

Pendergrass, V. (1975). Marriage counseling with lesbian couples. *Psychotherapy: Theory, Research & Practice, 12*(1), 93-96.

Roll, S., Millen, L., & Martinez, R. (1980). Common errors in psychotherapy with Chicanos: Extrapolations from research and clinical experience. *Psychotherapy: Theory, Research and Practice, 17*, 158-168.

Romm, M. E. (1965). Sexuality and homosexuality in women. In J. Marmor (Ed.), *Sexual Inversion: The Multiple Roots of Homosexuality.* New York: Basic Books.

Rosen, D. (1974). *A Study of Female Homosexuality.* Springfield, IL: Charles C Thomas.

Roth, S. (1985). Psychotherapy with lesbian couples: Individual issues, socialization, and the social context. *Journal of Marital and Family Therapy, 11*(3), 273-286.

Rothberg, B., & Ubell, V. (1985). The co-existence of system theory and feminism in working with heterosexual and lesbian couples. *Women & Therapy, 4*(1), 19-36.

Sager, C., & Hunt, B. (1979). *Intimate Partners.* New York: McGraw-Hill.

Sang, B. (1978). Lesbian research: A critical evaluation. In G. Vida (Ed.), *Our Right to Love.* Englewood Cliffs, NJ: Prentice-Hall.

Steckel, A. (1985). Separation-individuation in children of lesbian and heterosexual couples. *Dissertation Abstracts International, 46*(3-B), 982-983.

Swartz, S. (1980). Counseling lesbian couples: Significant factors involved in maintaining a lesbian dyad. *Dissertation Abstracts International, 41*(5-B).

Vida, G. (Ed.) (1978). *Our Right to Love.* Englewood Cliffs, NJ: Prentice-Hall, pp. 15-19.

Chapter 12

Effects of Parental Separation and Divorce on Children

Sherry Farmer

It is not possible to give accurate emotional weight to the factors which determine the effects of parental separation/divorce on a child. The relatively few longitudinal studies (Hodges & Bloom, 1984; Wallerstein & Kelly, 1980) which have attempted to do so have focused on the child's age at the time of the separation/divorce. However, regardless of the child's age at that time, the child will spend a significant part of his or her life in a deteriorating pre-separation/divorce situation, experiencing emotionally draining legal proceedings and major changes in his family life. He or she will live with parents with varying abilities to weather the storm, provide adequate parenting and communication with an ex-spouse, and regain equilibrium in personal and family life.

It is the combination of the situations to which the child is exposed before, during, and after all of the separation/divorce related events, as well as the child's developmentally-linked and idiosyncratic reactions, which will determine the overall effect that parental separation/divorce will have (Gardner, 1978; Hodges & Bloom, 1984; Kelley & Berg, 1978; Koch & Lowery, 1984; Rosen, 1977; Wallerstein, 1984; Wallerstein & Kelly, 1980).

Events acquire significance as the individual assigns cognitive and emotional meaning to them. Thus, the effect of separation/divorce related events on the child is shaped to a large extent by the meanings attributed to them by the child. The meanings are, in turn, clearly related to the particular cognitive, emotional, physical, and social skills the child is acquiring or has acquired at the time separation/divorce related events occur. It is important to remember that these events can span a number of years and several developmental stages of childhood and can result in significant changes in the perceptions and meanings the child ascribes to past and present separation/divorce related experiences.

In this chapter, important overall issues of the various stages of normal childhood development will be briefly reviewed. Ways in which the child's response to parental separation/divorce related events may be influenced by his developmental level in cognitive, emotional, and social skills at the time the events occur will be discussed. Examples of how to use a developmental perspective to decide what can, should, and should not be said to the child about these events will be presented. How individual and family counseling can be useful in this regard will also be discussed. Various types of developmental skill-related support which can be offered to the child will be described.

EFFECTS OF PARENTAL SEPARATION/DIVORCE ON THE OVERALL DEVELOPMENTAL NEEDS OF THE CHILD

The child's primary objective in the first 18 years of life is to proceed adequately through a known sequence of physical, intellectual, emotional, and social skills acquisition. If these skills are sufficiently mastered, the child will be able to conceptualize accurately and act realistically in coping with both internal needs and the demands of the world. Specifically, the child will: 1) be able to use his physical and intellectual energy efficiently; 2) possess and be able to use attention sufficiently for good cognitive and emotional comprehension; 3) acknowledge, express, communicate, and take responsibility for his thoughts, feelings, and actions; 4) make and follow through on decisions based on simultaneous consideration of his needs, the needs of others, the demands of the situation.

Child rearing is a complex task for parents, even those who have a satisfactory relationship. In the event of severe marital discord, separation, divorce, or single parenting, the opportunity to acquire and use knowledge and the opportunity for contemplative, developmentally geared, and sensitive child rearing may be limited.

Separation/divorce usually leads to a period of decreased quantity and quality of parenting. A crucial factor in determining the effect of divorce on the child is the severity and duration of this period of disruption. Frequently, the child is given too little, too much, or age-inappropriate parental attention. This attention will be perceived as being of limited help, and may significantly impede the developmental progress of the child. For example, there will be difficulty if: 1) the 7-year-old is refused *any* parental assistance with homework; 2) the 12-year-old is never permitted to do homework *without* parental assistance; 3) the 4-year-old who sees monsters in his bedroom is allowed to sleep with his parent(s) until he "grows out of it."

The post-separation/divorce period of emotional upheaval lasts for at least two years for the parents. The period of upheaval for the child exceeds that by a wide margin. Some observers think that there is no complete recuperation from parental divorce, that it permanently alters the child.

The child tends to go on "emotional hold" during a crisis such as separation/divorce. He only begins to digest the impact of what has happened after the crisis period has passed and he perceives that his parents have regained emotional stability. The child is accurately aware of his dependency on his parents. He understands that without them he would not survive, and that diminution of their capacity and willingness to care for themselves also diminishes their capacity to care for him.

It is known that the child will put pursuit of essential developmental skills in the background if he perceives that such pursuit would cause significant emotional distress to his parent(s). For example, an important task of toddler development is his ability to comfortably move away from his parent to explore the physical surroundings. If he perceives that his upset parent has a strong need for physical contact with him, the child may continue to cling to his parent(s). An older child may forego essential peer activities which contribute to his emotional and social skills and general knowledge if he perceives that he is needed at home for company, to care for siblings, or to "parent" the parent(s).

Parents are frequently unaware that their child has put his own essential developmental tasks aside. For example, rather than expressing concern that the teenager does not have any interest in after-school activities or weekend socializing, parents report with pride that the child is "unusually mature" for his age. The parent is pleased that the child is able to shoulder substantial personal and household management tasks; that he is a "wonderful friend" to the parent; and that he rarely (if ever) expresses disappointment or protests the lack of parental help and attention to his (the child's) interests since he "understands" the reasons for the parental omissions. Parents must take care that they are not fooled by the child's apparent maturity (Rosen, 1977). After the separation/divorce, the child may refrain from reasonable requests for parental attention out of a desire to protect the parent from feeling guilty for the decreased time the parent has available to spend with the child. The fact that the extraordinary empathy displayed by the child towards his parent is not extended to others lends credibility to the idea that the child's empathy capability is probably not beyond expectations for his age (Rosen, 1977; Wallerstein & Kelly, 1980).

SPECIFIC DEVELOPMENTAL ISSUES FACING SEPARATION/DIVORCE CHILDREN

The developmental tasks and needs of the child at different ages affect the child's response to parental separation/divorce. Some practical suggestions concerning developmentally appropriate help are available.

First 18 Months of Life

The primary developmental tasks for the child during the first 18 months of life are: 1) gradual perception and acceptance that he is an entity separate from other people and objects in the world; 2) establishment of a mutually responsible and responsive system of communication between himself and the world which ensures that the child's physical and emotional needs are met; 3) formation of a lifelong overall perception of himself and of the world as more or less trustworthy entities.

When separation/divorce affects the child in this age range, the couple should consider which living situation will most benefit the well-being of the spouse who will be the child's primary caretaker. The child only gradually learns to distinguish between physical and psychological events, between what is inside and what is outside his "self." Therefore, he includes in this core overall self-perception the physical and psychological qualities of this outside world, i.e., of his primary caretaker. If the primary caretaker is emotionally overwhelmed, anxious or depressed for long periods of time, the child may come to perceive himself as "anxious" or "depressed" or as one who cannot give or who is not worthy of being given to. This may in turn become a self-fulfilling prophecy.

The importance of this phenomenon cannot be overstressed. Whereas adults usually recover from the prolonged period of stress resulting from separation/divorce related events, there is no comparable recovery from such stress for a child of this age. Disruption in this child's relationship with the primary caretaker(s) during these first months is perceived by the child as disruption in the continuity of contact between essential, related parts of the child's own self.

It is also important to note that although parents may be able to shield the child from verbal fights, they are unable to shield the child from the tension experienced by each spouse as a result of the marital situation. This results from the fact that the child's primary form of perception is through sensory experience. The child "reads" the emotional state of his caretakers through the nonverbal interaction with them. The parent may say, "Everything will be all right." The child will believe it only if the tension in the parent's body confirms this.

Two to Four Years of Age

The primary developmental task of the child at this age is to acquire the ability and desire to make realistic (rather than fantasized) assessments of himself, others, and the environment. The child is engaged in discovering the extent and limits of his power and importance in the world (i.e., his family). Once again, it is important to keep in mind that the child's learning takes place primarily physically, through sensory experience (Ginsberg & Opper, 1969). The child's learning is greatly affected if it takes place in three households (original family, mother's and father's).

If a child is told, "It is wrong to hit your mother," the child understands that there is an interdiction against both the act of hitting and (more damaging) his angry feelings. By contrast, the child understands that he has a sufficiently secure place in life to realistically expect adequate, reliable care despite his age-appropriate drastic fluctuations in intense feelings if the following sequence regularly occurs: 1) the parent sets a limit, e.g., denies the child a cookie because it is too close to dinner time; 2) the child cries out, "I hate you. Go away for ever and ever," and throws his stuffed bear on the ground and jumps on him; 3) the parent comments that he/she can tell how angry the child is at him/her by the strength with which the child threw the bear and jumped on him; 4) the child is given the opportunity to cool down and the parent ensures that he/she has the space to do so as well; 5) the parent doesn't relent and give the child a cookie, doesn't attack the child for being angry at him/her or for throwing his toy around, and does insist that the child vent his anger on inanimate objects.

Verbal explanations about the divorce and why it is happening are neither emotionally nor cognitively understood; the child believes what he experiences with his senses. The child *sees* that one parent has left the family. He wonders: "Will my other parent leave? Am I supposed to be the other grown-up now because Daddy isn't here, and we need a Daddy? I don't know how I made my Daddy go away. Will I do it again? Did he leave because I got really angry? If I get really angry again, can I make him come back? If I do things like that, I am frightened because I need my parents with me in order to survive."

The child's capacity for verbal expression is limited. Verbalization isn't reliable communication until the child is five years old; verbalization by the child about his fears, concerns, and feelings doesn't provide adequate dissipation of their emotional intensity. Thus it can be helpful to give the child a "hitting pillow" to use when he feels upset about changes in family life.

Maintaining a generational boundary between parent and child helps the child maintain a realistic and, therefore, comforting view of his power and responsibility. The child needs to know that the parent will still stay and cook supper, even if he does say, "I hate you, go away," and he needs to know that the parent will not let the child interfere beyond a predictable point with the parent's pleasure, e.g., if the child is having a fit or is making too much noise in the room in which the parent is reading, the child is removed so that the parent can continue his/her adult activity.

Maintaining this generational boundary may be particularly difficult if only one parent remains involved with the child on a daily basis, and if that parent is particularly stressed, depressed, or lacking in adult support. In such cases the parent may be strongly drawn to the child for warmth and companionship and/or for venting the adult's emotions. This elevation to adult status, as the child will perceive it, increases the difficulty the parent will have at other times when he/she attempts to assert "parental" authority over the child.

Frequent contact with the noncustodial parent is very important. The child's sense of time and ability to carry warm memories in his mind and to benefit from telephone contact are limited. As we have said, his capacity to learn is limited to sensory experience. The child cannot be expected to believe a parent loves him if there is little sensory contact with that parent.

Three to Five Years of Age

There are several developmental tasks for the child during this time which can be affected by parental separation/divorce.

First, during this period the child solidifies sexual identification with one parent, and, following that parent's lead, becomes interested in attracting the attention of the parent of the opposite sex. In an intact family, the child's same-sexed parent is present to limit the quantity and quality of contact between the child and the child's opposite-sexed parent. In a single-parent home, care must be taken that too much and/or too emotionally intense contact does not develop between the child and the child's opposite-sexed parent and that good contact is maintained between the child and the child's same-sexed parent. Insufficient attention to this can lead the child to an unrealistic assessment of his/her attractiveness to his/her opposite-sexed parent, and his/her responsibility for meeting that parent's needs.

Second, the child starts to see that he has a vested interest in adhering to external rules of behavior and he develops an internalized sense of right and wrong. This inner parental/policing voice, or conscience, allows him to refrain, on occasion, from taking the forbidden extra cookie, even though his parent is not present to see whether he takes it or not. It also allows him to cooperate with others on the basis of empathy, rather than on the perception of the relative power of those involved in particular situations.

Third, during this period he grows to experience satisfaction by expressing intense feelings in more sophisticated verbal expression and in indirect actions. Making pictures for, or dictating letters to, an absent parent helps the child cope with feelings of sadness. In play/creative activities, the child can alter "the facts"; he can, without consequence, experiment with being the one who makes important decisions about what is to be saved or demolished and rebuilt, who is the one who leaves and who is left, and who arranges reunion. In his play, the child does and undoes, "proving" to himself that events and time are sometimes both under his control and are reversible.

The child spins endless fantasies of family restoration in verbal monologues, art work, and play activities. The fantasies include amazing causes of the family upheaval (Hodges & Bloom, 1984). This activity may reflect another attempt to deny personal responsibility for the family's situation. There is no way to speed up the child's cognitive development. When the parent tells the child, "The divorce isn't your fault," the child *knows* he is being lied to. In fact, the child may go about proving to the parents through regressive or disruptive behavior that he has, indeed, the power to cause big problems.

The parents can help the child with this by acknowledging repeatedly that there is a difference between the parents' and the child's version of the causes of the divorce. A parent may offer the child the following thought: "I understand that *you* think that you made this happen and that it is your job to fix things again. I have different ideas than you do about who causes divorce. I think that only grown-ups can cause unhappy marriages and decide to divorce or to get back together again." This type of statement will not convert the child to the adult's perception of causality, but it will validate the child's right to continue to receive parental support even though their respective perceptions and feelings differ. It may also give the child, who wishes to grow up to be like the parent, hope that in the future he may see events differently and more comfortably.

Fourth, the child begins to understand that time is linear and events are nonreversible. The child is only beginning to understand the linearity and nonreversibility of events. This lack of understanding combines with the child's perception of himself as primary causal agent in all that happens to him so that divorce can, in the child's mind, be followed by family restoration. A parent's upset state is thus at varying times inconsequential, incomprehensible, and very disturbing to the child, who will pat the weeping parent's hand saying, "Don't cry, Mommy. Daddy will come back soon," in order to remind his mother of a "fact" she seems to have forgotten.

Fifth, as part of his learning about time, the child acquires increasing ability to sequence and organize materials and activities, and to work within time limits. Letting the child know what the rules and behavioral expectations of the respective parental households are and requiring that the child take some responsibility for personal care are helpful for the development of self-esteem. The fact that the rules are different is not particularly troubling, as long as they are reasonable, are made clear to the child, and are consistently enforced.

The child's interest in organization, rules, sequencing, and causality is evident in the frequent unending stream of "why" questions. If the parent asks, "Why do *you* think?" in response to the child's "why" question, important information about the child's ideas and thought processes can be gained.

Frequent contact with the noncustodial parent is important to provide proof that the parent cares about the child. It is helpful for the child to spend time at that parent's home. The child is starting to venture out into the world, and is very interested in discovering what, why, where, and how things are to be found; through the repeated experience of leaving and returning to each parent, the child will come to believe that both parents continue to care about him, desire to be with him, and will be there to welcome him when he returns from his explorations. It should be kept in mind that transitions between homes are very difficult for children of this age, and having the child return to the same parent's home as many nights as possible will probably be easiest on the child.

Six to 11 Years of Age

The child's attention at this age is primarily directed toward increasing his personal competence in academic and social skills outside the home.

Separation/divorce can redirect the child's energy back to the home with negative consequences. For example, if the custodial parent is severely upset over a long period of time, the child may forego needed association with peers and inappropriately curtail attention to his school work and social life in order to care for the parent.

Peer relations, group activities, and membership teams are all very important to the child at this stage. They encourage the child to believe that there are others in the world besides his parents who can help him. This allows him to focus on acquiring skills which will enable him to increasingly leave his parents' care. The child is often very self-conscious about the divorce. In general, he uses peer relationships to escape emotional preoccupation with family difficulties. However, if one or two friends have experienced divorce in their own families, and/or if the child is given a structured group opportunity, he is usually quite willing to talk about his situation and feelings with peers, and readily gives and receives important emotional support.

Parents must actively support the child's increasing need for independent nonstructured free time and peer interaction. They must guard against the temptation to use the child as an ally against the ex-spouse, as a primary emotional support person, or as co-household manager and co-parent of younger siblings, even though the child may be willing and able to "help" the parent in these ways.

Children of both sexes frequently refuse to express anger toward the noncustodial parent, regardless of that parent's behavior toward the child or other members of the family, and regardless of the amount of contact between the parent and the child. To the dismay of the custodial parent, this anger gets directed towards siblings, peers, classmates, teachers, and, most frequently, the custodial parent, e.g., the parent who did not abandon him. The child seems to imagine that he may cause the noncustodial parent to abandon him entirely if he causes that parent further aggravation.

The following example is common, although it sounds extreme: six-year-old Susan's mother complained that Susan often had temper tantrums at the mother's custodial home, but that she was always the "perfect" child at her father's house. The mother stated that Susan often told her about things her father did which made Susan mad, but she steadfastly refused to speak directly with her father about any of the incidents which upset her. When asked when she thought she would be able to tell her father she was angry with him, she answered without hesitation, "Not for a long time, like when I grow up and don't need him anymore."

The child needs to be encouraged to express his anger directly at the noncustodial parent as situations arise. Ideally, the noncustodial parent will help the child do this when the parent notices the child is not expressing any sad and/or angry feelings, by telling the child about his feelings concerning events in *his* everyday life and what *he* does with them, e.g., "It makes me so mad when my boss puts extra work on my desk and says, 'You'll have time to get this done today, won't you, Bob?' When I bowl, I imagine that he is one of the pins and I mow him down!"

The child can also be helped if the parents maintain good communication concerning the child. This enables the parent who is aware of the child's concern to let the other parent know that something needs to be done. It is best if the child is strongly encouraged to take his concern *only* to the parent involved. For example, the custodial parent might say, "You seem really angry about being picked up late on Saturday. That problem is between you and your father. You need to talk about it with him. If you don't choose to talk with him, that is all right with me, but stay out of my space until you have calmed down. I won't sit here and let you take out your anger at your father on me." The crucial event here is the uninvolved parent's steadfast adherence to his/her uninvolvement. Having an "angry book" at the custodial parent's home can be helpful if direct communication is not possible or is not being exercised between the child and the noncustodial parent. The child can be directed to make entries in it with impunity, since the noncustodial parent will not be reading it without the child's permission.

Frequently there is difficulty when the child leaves or arrives at each parent's home. The transition can often be eased if the child is permitted to spend some time by himself, perhaps in his room, when he first arrives. During this period, no attempt should be made to involve him in the ongoing household events until the child indicates that he is ready and able emotionally to be present.

It is clear that the child continues to experience pain and sadness over the loss of the family years after the separation/divorce occurs. Therefore, each parent needs to give the child continuing opportunities to express his feelings about past events and situations in the family life (Wallerstein & Kelly, 1980). The child has important memories and strong feelings and thoughts about the pre-separation time in particular. It helps him maintain a sense of continuity in his life if he is encouraged to go over the "old times" in conversation or perhaps by looking at family photographs with the parent(s). Providing ample opportunities to review the past encourages the child to participate positively in the current family life (Wallerstein & Kelly, 1980).

During these review sessions it is important to give the child opportunities to express his thoughts about the causes of events. As the child grows, his understanding of events changes. Toward the end of this period and continuing into early adolescence, the child begins to develop the ability to use abstract thinking, including the ability to believe that he is not necessarily a causal agent in all that happens to him. With support, he can come to have a more realistic perception of the causes of the separation/divorce, custody arrangements, and other changes he has experienced in his family life, or which may be necessitated in the future.

Twelve to 18 Years of Age

The developmental task of the parents of adolescents is gradual relinquishment of responsibility for and authority over the life management of the adolescent. The child's task is to assume increasing responsibility for his personal life management, including relationships with people both in and outside the home. The transition is rarely smooth. In the normal course of adolescence, the child swings through extremes of independence-dependence in emotions and actions, and idealization-rejection of the parents as role and value models. The parents also experience swings through extremes of giving the child too little or too much responsibility for making decisions and paying too little or too much attention to the child's activities and lifestyle relative to the attention paid to their own lives.

The adolescent has developed the capacity to know his parents as people and to perceive them realistically. This makes the parents both more and less attractive to the adolescent as people to be with, to emulate. In order to separate from the parents and move out on his own the adolescent needs to develop an increasing capacity to emotionally disengage from them as figures of power, as policy setters, and as individuals, and, instead, pursue emotionally-invested relationships with others outside the home.

When parental divorce occurs, it is just one of a host of factors with which the adolescent must cope. The effect of the divorce on the adolescent depends on the extent to which he has acquired strengths in past years; the meaning the divorce has for all family members; the way that the divorce is handled; and the emotional, financial, and situational effect of the divorce on family members. The blend of factors is idiosyncratic to each family, to each child. For instance, divorce is upsetting to a child at any age and the upset is bound to be reflected in his behavior in some way. Hopefully, by adolescence, the child has good impulse control; he has the capacity to discharge his upset feelings safely. However, if impulse control has not been firmly established at a younger age there can be serious consequences.

For example, a 16-year-old experiences rage over his parents' intention to divorce. It is one thing to throw a building block in the kindergarten room when angry, but quite another to wreck a car as a result of a similar burst of anger. The adolescent clearly has increased opportunity and ability to express distress in harmful ways. Frequently, the child is in his 20s before he can accept the reality that each parent had valid positions on the issues between them and equal responsibility for the divorce. Meanwhile, his allegiance fluctuates from one parent to the other — one parent being the "good" parent, the other being the "villain" (Kelley & Berg, 1978).

On a practical level the divorce may result in: 1) a significant drop in the financial resources of the adolescent; 2) a geographical relocation; 3) a situation in which he has to co-parent his younger siblings or his own parent(s); 4) loss of needed attention from his parents due to their all-consuming upset over the marital breakup. These circumstances may cause the adolescent to feel he does not have the right to devote attention to his own concerns; it may prevent him from pursuing age-appropriate activities which enable him to establish his own independent life or believe that it is worthwhile to engage in family relationships of his own.

On the other hand, the adolescent's intense concern with peer relations and interests outside the home often causes conflict with parents over custody and visitation arrangements. Often the adolescent expresses a preference to live with the parent of the same sex, or with the parent he perceives will be most lenient with respect to behavioral expectations.

His need for consistency in parental limit-setting frequently becomes obscured by separation/divorce related parental bickering. It is extremely helpful if the parents can stand together on behavioral expectations and consequences for the adolescent's behavioral failures. Parents can do this in several ways: 1) agree to enforce the same requirements; 2) agree that the rules of the parent who has custody in general, or at a particular time, will apply to the adolescent's behavior; 3) each parent has the final say about the adolescent's behavior in specified areas of life.

Any system allows the adolescent to separate from the parents, since the parents are in agreement concerning rules which apply to his behavior. Without the parents' divergent policies and bickering, there is no room in any of these systems for the adolescent to gain adult policy-setting authority for himself. It is important that the parents recognize that significant steps can be taken to prevent the scenario described by one 17-year-old: "After high school graduation, I thought I would move away from home. Instead, home disintegrated and moved away from me. There was no parental wall to bounce my rebellion off of; my parents just used whatever I said I wanted to do as ammunition in their own divorce warfare."

Sometimes, divorce means the end of a situation in which, as the adolescent is well aware, one or both parents have been experiencing substantial disrespectful or injurious behavior from the spouse. The fact that his parents have been unable to enjoy a mutually satisfying relationship is likely to cause the adolescent anxiety about his own ability to form and maintain a lasting, satisfactory intimate relationship in his own adult life. This may be particularly true if the parents' marriage was acutely unhappy for both, the separation and custody arrangements acrimonious, and the divorce resulted in intense and lasting unhappiness for one or both parents.

Divorce can force the adolescent to see his parents as individual, sexual adults. This perception may impede the adolescent's job of separating from his parents. For example, separation is aided by the perception of difference. Thus, the adolescent may find it easier to move away from parents he sees as two people merged together in a nonsexual relationship which obscures their individual personalities. Trying to stand out in the "in" crowd as a sexual individual when his father is also trying out his postseparation rusty, single, sexual, male wings can be a disturbing sign of similarity between father and son.

On the other hand, it is possible that the adolescent may make more satisfactory choices in partners for himself if he experiences his parents in their new and more satisfactory lives and adult relationships. This may lessen the adolescent's negative reaction to parental separation/ divorce. This is probably more likely to occur if: 1) the adolescent is older; 2) he has spent some time living away from home; 3) he has been exposed to other successful marriages/committed relationships. These experiences tend to increase the scope of the adolescent's perspective on his own parents' marriage.

Summary

From the above it can be seen that the effects of separation/divorce on a child vary depending on the developmental stage of the child. Because the developmental tasks vary from age to age, the child's response to the changes caused by the breakup will vary accordingly. In like manner, it is necessary that the parent(s) response to the child vary according to the developmental stages of the child.

TALKING TO THE CHILD ABOUT PARENTAL SEPARATION/DIVORCE

In this section, guidelines for talking with the child about separation/ divorce related events are presented. These issues are: 1) when to talk to the child; 2) the role of counseling; 3) what should/should not be said to the child; 4) the child's reaction to being talked to; 5) timing of talking to the child; 6) life after separation; 7) visitation logistics; 8) new parent partners; 9) the child's relationship with the noncustodial parent.

When to Talk with the Child

The parents' first task is to let the child know that there is marital unhappiness and that both parents are sad about it and are trying to find a way to make life happier for everyone in the family.

The child cannot absorb and digest this emotionally laden information all at once. Therefore, parents need to speak with the child honestly and repeatedly about upcoming changes and attendant feelings and thoughts of both adults and child. Unfortunately, parents tend to think that the child is unaware or unable to understand what is happening. Sometimes parents are so "drained" that they have no energy with which to adequately address the child's concerns.

The parents' second task is to ascertain the extent of the child's awareness of the marital/family difficulties. They are then able to provide opportunities to listen to and respond to any questions, observations, or suggestions the child wishes to make. This reassures the child. He knows his parents will be available to talk with him about what will be happening, and about his thoughts and emotional concerns.

It is essential to keep discussions with the child on a level commensurate with the child's ability to conceptualize the changes being discussed.

In general, the child, regardless of his age, will have concerns in two areas. The first is: Who will meet the nurturance and protection needs of family members? In cases where there has been extreme verbal and/or physical abuse, the child may have intense fear and anxiety, i.e., "What will happen to me when Daddy gets mad and Mommy isn't there to keep Daddy from hitting me?" If the mother has been the primary caretaker, the child may wonder, "Who will take care of me and the baby if Mommy has to be at work?" The second concern of the child is the extent of his imagined causal involvement in the marital troubles, i.e., "What did I do to make this happen? If I stop arguing with my sister, will/can I make my parents stop fighting and not have to get divorced? Why not?" (Kelley & Berg, 1978).

Failure to talk to the child at all or failure to talk to the child on his developmental level about his fears and what will happen keeps the child in a passive role. This leaves the child, like the non-divorce-initiating spouse, more prone to depression as a reaction to the marital separation/divorce process (Waldron, Ching, & Fair, 1986).

Research indicates that the child with the most severe responses to divorce comes from a closely knit family in which the parents provided little verbal confirmation of the extent of marital unhappiness prior to the separation/divorce (Waldron, Ching, & Fair, 1986). By contrast, the child seems to do better if he is told, prior to the separation, that there is marital difficulty; that a family crisis is approaching or occurring; that although the parents expect life will be very difficult for everyone for a while, they do have hope that it will eventually get better for everyone.

Unfortunately, couples are often at or beyond the point of actual separation before they inform the child verbally about the situation (Waldron, Ching, & Fair, 1986). Couples who seek counseling in an attempt to save the marriage or to ease the separation/divorce process often do not tell the child that they are seeking such help. Parents tend to assume that the child would worry more if he were told that the parents are deeply concerned about their relationship and that they are not able to improve the situation on their own. Most likely, the child already knows that there is marital trouble.

What the child does not know, until the parents speak about it, is that the parents themselves think that there is serious trouble. The child usually experiences relief when the parents finally acknowledge that something should be done and that the parents are the ones who are going to do it. This information provides excellent modeling that adults can accept themselves as fallible, that they can and do seek help of one kind or another at certain times. The young child has to seek help frequently each day and he cannot imagine not needing to seek help. It is reassuring to know that adults seek help on occasion. Anxiety sets in when the child thinks that attaining adult status and power is beyond his grasp, or that the cost of attaining it (wanting help and not being able to ask for it), is too high.

Role of Counseling

Counseling is not necessarily the essential ingredient in good separation/divorce since each family situation is unique. However, the magnitude of the emotional and lifestyle upheavals involved makes it likely that one or more family members may benefit from professional help at some point in the process. In all cases in which separation/divorce is being contemplated, the children should be informed of its possibility. If the parents are already getting counseling, a family session might help establish good communication between the parents and their child concerning possible or impending family changes. Holding family counseling sessions prior to actual parental separation lets the child observe the parents as they try to manage the changing family situation and their emotional reactions to it. This encourages the child to ask questions, validates the appropriateness of the upset feelings aroused by the situation, and provides concrete confirmation that the parents are interested in helping him cope with the situation (Rosenthal, 1979). Counseling should focus on the entire family structure and organization since the child's adjustment to the separation/divorce is directly dependent on the adjustment of his parents (Nichols, 1984).

In the presence of the parents, the therapist can ask the child what he thinks might happen to his parents' marriage if the situation were to stay unchanged, or if it were to get worse. Once asked, the child almost always expresses some concern that the parents may not stay together, even if the child has never given the parents any indication of having this concern. This can open the door for a discussion of the situation, the practical options being considered by the parents, and the feelings which all family members have about the situation.

In some cases, it is helpful to have the therapist continue the discussion with the child, while, with the child's knowledge, the parents observe the conversation from behind a one-way mirror. For example:

> Paul and Pat were unable to discuss the possibility of a separation with their children. They thought that their children were unaware of the

possibility of divorce since "all parents fight sometimes." The couple had been in marital counseling for some time and agreed to a family session when the therapist suggested a connection between the unhappy marital situation and recent behavior of two of their children. Eleven-year-old Mike had taken to urinating in paper cups and leaving them around the house; eight-year-old Mary had become tantrum-prone. The parents reported that four-year-old Becky was fine, believing that "since she is a baby, she doesn't know anything."

The therapist began a game of catch with the children. As they tossed the ball, the therapist asked each child to say what he/she thought was likely to happen to the parents' marriage. Four-year-old Becky volunteered, "They will get a divorce because they 'fighted' all of the time." Mary said she thought that someone might get hurt because she once saw her mother throw a pitcher at her father. Mike agreed that a divorce was likely because the parents frequently fought and did not sleep together anymore.

The therapist then asked what each child did when the parents were fighting. Mary reported telling them to stop or asking questions about other things in order to distract them. She said that these approaches didn't work since they went on fighting, and she would then go to her room to cry. Becky reported trying to make her parents laugh by being silly. Both older children corroborated this statement, stating that Becky was sometimes successful. All agreed that Mike was successful by getting directly involved in the argument.

The parents were then invited to reenter the room. It was clear to them that the children were well aware of the magnitude of the marital problems. The therapist was able to facilitate a discussion between parents and children about what could be done to lessen the children's involvement in parental discord, and to accept/acknowledge/adjust to the possibility of separation.

Adults frequently pursue individual psychotherapy in order to help themselves with the emotional turmoil resulting from separation/divorce. The author's experience indicates that children benefit from having their own professional support person during the period between actual separation and the post-divorce family reconstitution if the parental relationship is strongly acrimonious. Usually, few people besides parents, siblings, and other relatives (who may be emotionally overloaded themselves) are available to help the child. The child is bound to be caught in loyalty conflicts. Contact with a neutral adult provides the child with loyalty/conflict-free support.

Clearly, counseling for the child as an individual or in a family context should be considered if he develops somatic complaints, sleep disturbances, fear of abandonment and/or impending disaster, hyperactivity, emotional constriction, poor peer relations, disinterest or underachievement in school, or signs of clinical depression.

If the child is going to receive counseling there are usually one or two initial meetings with the whole family. Thereafter, a number of meetings take place with the child alone and then with the parents and other family members as the situation requires. The frequency of the sessions decreases as the child adjusts to the new living situation. The door is kept open for intermittent future meetings in order to provide continuity of support for the child. In this way new concerns can be addressed as they arise (when a parent remarries, for example) and before they become entrenched difficulties. Intermittent meetings with parents can be valuable opportunities to alert them to subjects each needs to take up with the child. Care must be taken to respect the confidentiality of each person involved.

What Should Be Said to the Child

When parents talk to the child about an impending divorce, they should take into consideration the difference in the way that adults and children conceptualize. The parent may consider the following explanation a sufficient opening announcement: "Your mom and I have irreconcilable differences and so we are going to get a divorce. We both love you and we always will. Neither of us will ever leave you." This is an abstract statement, referring to ideas such as "love," "irreconcilable differences," and "leaving."

Until the age of 11, the child conceptualizes concretely. He only understands direct sensory knowledge — that which literally "makes sense" to him. It would be more helpful, therefore, if the parent said something like this: "Your mother and I fight with each other too much of the time, and so we have decided to live in different houses and stop being married. This is called getting divorced. Your mother and I will decide when you will live with her and when you will live with me. Parents can decide not to live with each other and they can live alone. But parents never decide to let their child live alone, even if the child is afraid that might happen. One of us will always be living with you and you will have your own room and belongings both at your mother's house and at my house."

Because of the child's loyalty to both parents, it is best if the couple can present the decision to separate as a mutual one. It is usually true that one partner is less ready, at least overtly, for the change than the other. However, the reluctant wife, for example, may be able to state with honesty that although her husband had the idea first, it is now a mutual decision, since she "doesn't wish to live with a husband who isn't happy living with her."

Adjustment to the divorce is also aided if: 1) the child is not used as a pawn in parental conflict; 2) the parents always take into consideration the child's developmental age; and 3) the parents actively initiate and encourage non-blaming communication with the child on separation/ divorce related subjects.

It is important for the parents to speak to the child together initially. Feelings run high and trust runs low between the parents at this time. When both parents decide in advance what will be said and both are present to hear what is actually said by the other, the chance that the announcement will be blame-laden is lessened. It is also important to have the parents speak to the child separately at other times, since the feelings, thoughts, perspectives, and relationship of each spouse to the child are apt to be quite different. As long as the parents can make and honor an agreement to speak solely from their own viewpoint and not blame the other spouse, having each parent talk with the child alone at times will strengthen the child's relationship with each parent. It will also lessen the pain of the split loyalty which the child feels as a result of the parents' separation.

When the therapist suggests that parents tell the child in specific terms some of their dissatisfactions with their spouse, most recoil. Many parents tend to feel strongly that it is harmful for the child to hear one parent "blame" the other. They are correct. The child has difficulty hearing his parents' or his own actions criticized. Statements such as "Your father always was an insensitive jerk" are offensive. However, parents frequently do not distinguish between blaming statements and descriptions of unacceptable behavior: "I could never get your father to listen often enough about how I felt" is a descriptive statement which is safe for the child to hear. Description by the parents of what each likes and dislikes about the other spouse merely confirms what the child has seen and heard and helps him make sense out of the reasons being given by the parents for the divorce.

The one area of marital difficulties about which it is not helpful for the child to hear is explicit sexual dissatisfactions. Those dissatisfactions can be accurately described as difficulty the couple had showing that they loved each other in ways that their partner liked, or difficulty the couple had giving each other enough hugs and kisses at the right times.

It is important to find a way to encourage parents to let their child know things about the ex-spouse that they like or respect, that they found attractive in the past. The child identifies with both parents and is, unfortunately, routinely exposed to each spouse's blaming the other. It is essential for the child's development of adequate self-esteem that he be reminded of each parent's positive qualities as well.

Child's Reaction to Talking About the Divorce

When parents do speak to their child about marital difficulties or divorce, they often report that the child does not say much; he asks few, silly, or no questions. The parents report frustration because the child's response leaves them without any sign of how he is taking the news.

For instance, 10-year-old Susan's first question following announcement of the parents' upcoming separation was: "Will Daddy still take me to get new sneakers for school?" Her six-year-old brother then asked: "What will happen to my fish?" The parents brushed these questions aside, saying, "Don't worry about that" and "We're not talking about silly things like fish right now." The parents were not being cruel. To them, the children's concerns seemed insignificant compared to the extensive changes which were about to occur. They wanted to move the children on to grapple with the "really important" questions. The children, trying to grasp what was happening, were responding on their conceptually concrete level of understanding. They *were* asking about important events in *their* daily lives which they thought might be affected by the separation.

The more seriously the parents consider the child's questions, the deeper and more completely the child will reveal his concerns. Silence on the part of the child should not be presumed to indicate dissipation or absence of intensely held feelings or thoughts (Kalter, Pickar & Lesowitz, 1984). The parents' acknowledgement of what is important to the child is proof of their intention to continue to be there to help the child. Parents need to both initiate such discussions and be willing to join in them following their initiation by the child.

Talking and Actual Separation Timing

Another way for parents to help the child cope with divorce is to have both parents remain in the home for a time following the announcement of separation so that they can share the job of responding to the child's concerns. It is also the only way that the child has time to digest one fact (the announcement that family life is going to change) before he has to cope with the second (the actual change).

The length of the interim period is significant since parents must consider the child's developmental ability to understand time. A week is forever to a four-year-old. Waiting three months for this child to adjust to the news is far too long. Furthermore, a child of this age considers time and events to be reversible: "Daddy will move out and be gone for a long time, maybe forever (more than a week), and then he will be back after forever because families have daddies in them." He cannot imagine a relationship changing in a way that he has not experienced.

A child of this age cannot imagine a different family structure. Therefore, he is unable to understand his parents' intense emotional reaction to the upcoming separation. Three or four weeks is about as much preparation as a four-year-old needs; two months would be helpful for the six- to nine-year-old; three months for the child older than nine, if the living situation is not intensely acrimonious.

Children learn by repetition and this period provides numerous opportunities to hear the "news" and to tell others the "news." It gives the child ample opportunity to think of his questions and concerns, to express them to the parents, and to have them repeatedly addressed. Keep in mind that if both parents are employed full-time, or have unusual schedules which otherwise limit their contact with the child, there may actually be very few child-contact hours during the course of even a four-week period.

It is helpful if both parents make an increased effort to spend time with the child during these weeks to increase the opportunity for thoughtful exchange about mutual concerns. The interim period can also be used to good emotional advantage if the child is given the opportunity to see where the noncustodial parent will be living. Information can also be given about how that location will affect the child's ability to see that parent, get to and from school, and visit with friends when he stays with that parent.

The parents can make a book for a young child with drawings or photographs of family members. In it something can be said about each spouse's disagreements with the other which caused the divorce, what is going to be different in the child's daily life after the separation, and custody and visitation arrangements. The book should contain reassurance that the people who care for the child will continue to do so and will continue to be an important part of his life. It needs to include the stated expectation that: 1) there will be difficult and good feelings, unhappy and fun days for all family members in the future; 2) the parents and the child will continue to talk about what happens and how they feel; 3) there will be enough loving feelings and good days for everyone in the future.

Life After the Separation

Life following the separation is difficult for everyone. There is generally a marked decrease in the quality of parenting as the parents seek to stabilize financial and other practical details of their lives. The parents are also digesting feelings about the loss of their former life. The pain of not having family members close by with whom to share feelings may be intense for the noncustodial parent. By contrast, the custodial parent may have no time or place to be alone with his/her upset feelings. In addition, when the child is upset he looks to the custodial parent to demonstrate how to handle emotional turmoil. The result of this pressure is almost always a substantial increase in intense and angry exchanges between the parent and child.

Moreover, the custodial parent frequently becomes aware that there is a familiar quality to his/her exchanges with the child. The parent might say, "I know that Jeff is just a 10-year-old child. However, there is something purposeful and attacking about his interactions with me that causes me to 'lose it' and we fight just the way I used to fight with my ex-husband. Jeff knows that I can't stand it when newspapers are left on the floor. He heard me yell at his father for years about it. He knows that I'm trying to do things my way now. He's acting as though he hates me and doesn't want me to have anything my way at all. He is just like his father."

Far from being hate-filled behavior, Jeff's behavior may be loving action based on what he had learned about the way his mother liked to be treated. It may also be an attempt to alleviate sadness he feels at the loss of his familiar life. Parents frequently assume that the child's primary way of learning is by listening to what the parent says. On the contrary, the child learns by observing what the parent does, and assigning his own developmentally-linked meaning to the behavior.

Jeff saw the following sequence repeated in his family life: Father left newspapers all over the floor; mother yelled at father about it; father yelled back, but did not pick up the papers; later, mother picked up the papers; parents did not talk to each other for a while; mother and father were nice to each other again and had fun; father left papers on the floor again; etc. The child imagines that whatever happens in the parents' lives happens because the parents wish it to happen. Parents are seen as all-powerful. Thus, father wanted mother to yell at him, mother wanted father to continue to leave papers on the floor so that she could yell at him, etc., etc., etc.

After separation there is disruption of many old patterns that the child believes the parents found appealing. These patterns, even if unpleasant, provided security because they were predictable. In his upset at the divorce, Jeff may long for the old family patterns, which were the only ones he knew and from which he received some nurturing. He perceived them as loving patterns. He may assume that his mother longs for them also, and he may move to reinstate one family ritual by replacing his father with himself in the known "loving" newspaper cycle.

Also, Jeff's mother may need to participate in an overly intense pattern of interaction with one of her children to make up for the loss of the intense relationship she previously experienced with her now absent ex-spouse (Wallerstein & Kelly, 1980).

Visitation Logistics

Frequency and timing of visitation depend on the child's age; younger children need more frequent and consistent contact with the noncustodial parent than older children do. The child should be increasingly involved in negotiating visitation arrangements as he moves through the adolescent years. Activities and alliances outside the family are important for the development of skills he will need as an adult. Rigid adherence to custody and visitation arrangements is perceived by the adolescent as parental attempts to control him. However, letting the adolescent have the primary or sole decision-making authority gives him too much power within the family structure. It may also be perceived as parental desertion by the adolescent. Negotiation between parent(s) and adolescent in order to balance their mutual need for time together and time apart can be a significant step toward establishment of a mutually responsive adult-adult relationship between the two generations.

Parents' Relationships with New Partners

As single parents begin to date and become seriously involved with new partners, they should keep in mind that the child will always experience a loyalty conflict between the new partner and the biological parent. The child should be allowed to dislike or to ignore the new partner, although parents should insist upon minimal standards for the child's behavior toward the new partner and acceptance of the parent's right to enjoy the relationship. In these circumstances, the chances that the child will develop a satisfactory relationship with the new adult partner will be improved. If a casual partner of the parent takes care of the child on occasion, the biological parent should assign disciplinary rights to the new partner as he or she would assign them to a babysitter; in both cases standards for behavior should be established by the biological parent.

The child, as we have said, reads the nonverbal behavior of his parents, which conveys the way they truly feel about what they are saying. If the parent is in a committed relationship with a new partner, and feels comfortable with the new partner's assuming parental responsibility, then the child will have an easier time accepting the new partner's status. In this situation the standards for behavior and consequences for misbehavior should be discussed and agreed upon by both adults involved.

The parent should continue to spend time alone with the child, without the new partner, to reassure the child that he or she is not going to lose the relationship with the parent.

Sometimes the child has assumed quasi-adult status in the post-divorce household, and the arrival of a new adult partner as the child's "parent" means a demotion for the child back to lower status and power. The integration of a new person in a family takes time and careful planning on the part of everyone in the household. For example, a family meeting might be held to decide which parent (biological or "new") will have responsibility for parenting during weekday mornings and which parent will be in charge of weekday bedtime parenting. This might be a gentler way of introducing the child to the new adult as "parent" than just announcing one day that from time to time the new adult will have full parenting authority over the child.

Relationship with the Noncustodial Parent

The child's feelings about the divorce and about the noncustodial parent remain intense even when there has been an unhappy relationship with that parent prior to the separation/divorce and even when there is little or unrewarding contact with that parent following the separation/divorce (Wallerstein & Kelly, 1980).

It is as though the child recognizes that his loyalty to each of his parents is biologically equal. Thus, the child gives equal emotional weight to his relationship with each parent although the quantity and quality of his contact with the two parents may differ dramatically.

The child who is encouraged to maintain a relationship with both parents may survive the family breakup better (Koch & Lowery, 1984; Rosen, 1977). This decreases the pressure on the child to split his loyalty to his parents. Pressure is also decreased if both parents cooperate in significant decisions involving the child (Isaacs & Levin, 1984; Wallerstein & Kelly, 1980).

Stuart and Abt (1981) point out that the noncustodial father's role with the child is strongly affected by the quality of the father's relationship with his former spouse. They found that if there has been an intensely unpleasant relationship, contact with the child tends to be less frequent and less satisfactory. They also believe that the relationship is affected by the father's pre-divorce experience in parenting and as household caretaker. In general, the more experienced, comfortable, and content the father is with household management activities and with being involved in general (nurturing and disciplining) interaction with the child, the more supportive the father/child relationship after the separation/divorce.

CONCLUSIONS

A number of conclusions can be drawn from the preceding information concerning how to help the child cope with parental separation/divorce related events.

First, it is important to keep the child's cognitive, emotional, and social skill level in mind when deciding what help will be most useful since to a significant extent his developmental situation shapes his perception of and reaction to these events and there are developmentally-related common concerns affecting all children experiencing such changes in family life.

Second, it is clear that the course of the child's development can be substantially affected by the degree and length of time that the parents' ability to effectively respond to the child's need for support, nurturing, and limit setting is diminished. While two years may be a manageable period of disruption for the adult, it may be a critical period for the child, with far less chance of recovery. Ensuring that the adults are making the best and quickest possible recovery is essential, since the child does not begin to adjust to the changes or turn his full attention to his own developmental concerns until he perceives that his parents are on the road to their own recovery.

Third, it is important that adults in the child's life be neither misled by a child's pseudo-mature behavior nor lulled by the absence of overt signs of distress in the child into thinking that the child is coping well enough with the changes. The parent needs to take continuing responsibility to initiate and facilitate discussions with the child on pre-, post-, and future separation/divorce related subjects. The adults must be alert to indications that the child is not participating fully in age-appropriate activities and is having difficulty taking age-appropriate responsibility for the expression and communication of his thoughts and feelings, and for his actions. Ongoing conversations between parents and the child should be held concerning ways in which home life can be made more comfortable for everyone.

Fourth, parents should realize that there is a wide range and depth of separation/divorce related subjects they can pursue with the child as long as what the adult says in terms of thoughts, feelings, and perceptions is not critical of those of the other parent and is geared to the cognitive and emotional developmental situation of the child.

Fifth, there are ways for adults to help the child cope with the consequences of separation/divorce outside the home, including family and individual counseling. It has been found that such outside-the-home supports can facilitate the child's adjustment to changes by increasing the child's understanding and acceptance of the events and by increasing the quantity and quality of discussion and interaction between the child and family members, and between the child and those with whom he interacts outside the home.

It is apparent, therefore, that the effects of parental separation/divorce on the child depend on the quality of life the child and the parents eventually establish in the post-separation/divorce years.

REFERENCES

Erikson, E. (1950). *Childhood and Society*. New York: W. W. Norton.

Gardner, R. A. (1978). Psychotherapy with children of divorce. *J. of Am. Acad. of Psychoanalysis, 6*(2), 231-247.

Ginsberg, H., & Opper, S. (1969). *Piaget's Theory of Intellectual Development: An Introduction*. Englewood Cliffs, NJ: Prentice Hall.

Hodges, W. F., & Bloom, B. L. (1984). Parents report of children's adjustment to marital separation: A longitudinal study. *J. of Divorce, 9*(1), 33-56.

Isaacs, M. B., & Levin, I. R. (1984). Who's in my family? A longitudinal study of drawings of children of divorce. *J. of Divorce, 7*(4), 1-21.

Kalter, N., Pickar, J., & Lesowitz, M. (1984). School-based developmental facilitation group for children of divorce: A preventive intervention. *Am. J. of Orthopsychiatry, 54*(4), 613-624.

Kelley, R., & Berg, B. (1978). Measuring children's reaction to divorce. *J. of Clin. Psychology, 34*, 215-221.

Koch, M. A. P., & Lowery, C. R. (1984). Visitation and the noncustodial father. *J. of Divorce, 8*(2), 47-65.

Nichols, W. C. (1984). Therapeutic needs of children in family system reorganization. *J. of Divorce, 7*(4), 23-44.

Rosen, R. (1977). Children of divorce: What they feel about access and other aspects of the divorce experience. *J. of Clin. Child Psychology, 6*(2), 24.

Rosenthal, P. A. (1979). Sudden disappearance of one parent with separation and divorce: The grief and treatment of pre-school children. *J. of Divorce, 3*(1), 43-54.

Stuart, R., & Abt, L. E. (1981). *Children of Separation and Divorce: Management and Treatment.* New York: Van Nostrand Reinhold.

Waldron, J. A., Ching, J. W. J., & Fair, P. H. (1986). A children's divorce clinic: Analysis of 200 cases in Hawaii. *J. of Divorce, 9*(3), 111-121.

Wallerstein, J. S. (1984). *Children of divorce: Preliminary report of a ten-year follow-up of young children. J. of Orthopsychiatry, 54*(3), 444-458.

Wallerstein, J. S., & Kelly, J. B. (1980). *Surviving the Breakup: How Children and Parents Cope with Divorce.* New York: Basic Books.

PART III

Theory

Chapter 13

The Relationship Life-Cycle

Edward P. Monte

The goal of this chapter is to explore the developmental life-cycle of the committed relationship. This task can be viewed from two separate perspectives: theoretical and clinical. This chapter will focus on life-cycle issues from a theoretical perspective. Although not a primary focus, appropriate clinical interventions will be highlighted for each life-cycle stage. Additionally, a life-cycle schema for clinical interventions will be presented at the end of the chapter.

Our task as clinicians, regardless of orientation, is to provide a cohesive, meaningful framework for the client who, more often than not, is unable to see beyond his or her pain. We strive to understand the meanings, layers, motivations, connections, patterns, stages and consequences of our client's experience. It is a considerable challenge. In addition, we are asked to facilitate change wherever necessary. If we are courageous or foolish enough to attempt to fulfill these requests, we can easily be overwhelmed with the complex nature of experience.

Conceptualizing therapy integratively involves balancing two considerations. First, we must keep in mind a multitude of factors from a multitude of perspectives. A view too narrow will miss the richness of experience and overlook important information we need. Second, we must maintain a concentrated focus because a view too broad will lack clarity and structure and contribute to the sense of confusion. Not an easy balance to maintain.

Specifically, it is essential to view what is presented in therapy from the integration of three perspectives: individual, interactional and intergenerational. This integration is the basis for the Intersystem Model proposed in this book.

Historically, these three therapeutic perspectives have often been taught and used independent of one another. Without their integration we will view the individual in isolation, the system without the individual and one's legacies and loyalties without present-day influences and personal interpretations.

Certainly, a total integration remains an ideal rather than a day-to-day reality. It is clinically difficult to maintain a broad perspective, with a clarity of structure and direction, as three distinct perspectives are perfectly integrated. Each of us tends to emphasize one perspective more than the other. Realistically, therefore, we must keep the ideal of integration in mind and balance as best we can.

Accordingly, as we seek to intervene clinically, any one therapeutic perspective can be effective, but the ability to systematically integrate approaches allows us to fit the therapy to the system rather than the system to the therapy. As such, an integrated approach of various perspectives and interventions is needed to capture the intricacies, ambiguities and contradictions presented. Whatever clarity is possible will hopefully emerge from a woven understanding of many factors and perspectives.

GENERAL ASSUMPTIONS

In this chapter, the developmental life-cycle of the committed relationship is viewed from such an integrative approach. As with any approach, certain assumptions serve as a general foundation from which specific statements and directions are formed. For relationship life-cycle development, general assumptions concerning both human experience and development will be briefly presented.

Experience

Assumptions concerning experience underpin our assumptions concerning development. We assume that experience is immediate, innately primitive and simultaneously colored by reflection. Its meaning is intensely individual, unique and, by definition, interactional. We exist in a social world where personal meanings are shared and converge to create an agreed-upon common reality. A dialectical union exists. That is, there cannot be individual experience without an interactional context and there cannot be an interactional context without individual experience.

Experience also exists within a temporal context. Though we experience in the present, our perceptions are shaped by our personal history as well as by our understandings and expectations of the future. Additionally, experience is purposive. Each person is always in the process of fulfilling individual needs. It can therefore be said that relationships are purposive. They, too, exist for a reason. Relationships are systems constructed to meet the individual and collective needs of their members. The complexity of any relationship has everything to do with the multitude of individual needs of each of its members combined with the struggle to integrate those needs in a way that is mutually satisfying.

Experience is also never static. Its most reliable characteristic is change. We are always in the process of becoming—whether biologically, emotionally and/or socially. For most, an inner core of self-identity acts as an anchor for this perpetually evolving process. Change is a natural, innate phenomenon. It often takes place despite our efforts to stop it. Biologically, we continue to age. Social and familial systems evolve. When there is resistance to this change, emotional difficulty can occur on all levels.

Developmental life-cycle issues are issues of change. As much as there seems to be a need in all of us for progress, change and, sometimes, even upheaval, there is simultaneously a need for security and familiarity. Consequently, a tension often exists between wanting change and wanting things to remain the same. This tension is an ongoing aspect of living. A given moment can be filled with nostalgia, contentment, hope, fear, excitement—in short, a multitude of conflicting emotions.

Development

Development is experience that is predictable. It is experience with assumed stages that everyone, in some variation, passes through. Yet, as with experience, life-cycle development is intensely individual. Developmental stages are not rigidly set. We progress uniquely. We pass through life-cycle stages, deal with issues, complete portions of developmental tasks at our own pace, in our own way. Yet, if experience is interactional, then development must be interactional. We do not develop in a vacuum. We develop in the context of the social world, with others.

This process can be described in two parts. First, a convergence of shared realities emerges. Inasmuch as we each develop uniquely, there are parallels and similarities of development between people. General patterns of development can be described in which each of us recognizes bits of our own experience.

Secondly, it is not that we develop individually in a parallel fashion and then, after the fact, share the experience of that development with others. Rather, we often develop simultaneously in direct relation to others. There is an overlapping or intersection of individual developmental processes. It can be said that individual life-cycle development occurs in sync with the interactional nature of experience.

In developmental literature, specific terms used to describe individual life-cycle issues, such as Erikson's (1959) trust vs. mistrust, initiative vs. guilt, and intimacy vs. isolation, are all interactional terms. Certainly, there are biological determinants to development. Yet, without the social, interactive component of experience, individual development would be impossible. A dialectical union again exists. That is, we cannot describe individual development and change without describing interactional development (Bopp & Weeks, 1984; Weeks, 1977; Weeks & Wright, 1979). This description parallels that of Riegel (1976) who discusses this union as "the interface between intra and interpsychic development."

If we follow the assumption that life-cycle development, like experience, is simultaneously individual and interactional, then we must assume life-cycle development is also intergenerational. Development therefore exists within a temporal context. It is, in part, a progression based on our personal history and guided by our expectations of the future.

In light of the interactional dimension, development is also based on the experience and evolution of past generations. Again, the legacies of former generations, as well as the expectations of the future generation, influence our development in the present. For example, issues of individuation can form a pattern between generational lines. Often an adult child will be as individuated in a present relationship as he/she is in relation to his/her parents and even possibly as his/her parents are in relation to their parents. It needs to be noted that the directness of this correlation is not universally agreed upon within the field of system thought. The general systemic process, however, is often quite visible clinically when one is faced with three generations of one family where the level of individuation is quite similar.

Life-cycle development is also purposive. It happens for a reason. Again, there are individual, interactional and intergenerational needs to be met which influence the process of change. On all three levels, there are specific emotional issues and agendas we need to resolve.

Terkelsen (1980) stated that "need-attainment is the mainspring of development." The structure and quality of a relationship is dictated by the developmental needs of each of the participants. Development, conversely, can therefore be described as the dialogue between what is needed by the individual and what the person perceives a relationship can provide.

Relationships not only serve as the interactional context for experience, but also become entities with which we find ourselves interacting. Within that interaction, certain of our abilities and issues are able to expand or evolve, while others are avoided or repressed. We are repeatedly asked to face hidden aspects of ourselves in a relationship. We then have to decide whether or not to finally begin to deal with those hidden aspects. We must not only deal with the other person, we must deal with the "relationship."

RELATIONSHIP DEVELOPMENTAL LIFE-CYCLE

As entities in themselves, relationships have a developmental life-cycle of their own. As with the individual, relationships are always involved in the process of change. As they evolve, they present new developmental issues and tasks at different stages. Following the assumption that relationships are separate entities, it is important to understand that the life-cycle development of the relationship is "not just the neat summation of two individual developments" (Carter & McGoldrick, 1980) but is its own process, with its own meaning.

It has already been proposed that individual and interactional development are dialectically related. Each is needed for the other to exist. True to the definition of a system, change in one guarantees change in the other. And, usually, individual development and interactional development exist in a parallel fashion. One's individual mid-life reassessments usually occur simultaneously with the joint reassessment of the relationship. Yet it is not necessarily true that a specific relationship life-cycle stage will always directly parallel an individual life-cycle stage of an individual involved. For example, a woman in her 70s with developmental issues centering on her mortality may still experience the initial bliss and future expectations of early love.

Development occurs via distinct life-cycle stages. Biologically, those life stages are obviously marked by the passing of chronological years as we age. Emotional, cognitive and social life-cycle stages are marked by specific life-cycle events such as leaving home, first job, marriage, first child, children leaving home, and retirement. These can be distinctly seen. But, what needs to be further described is how the developmental issues corresponding to these life-stages are experienced and dealt with as one progresses through life.

Even though many life-cycle stages are clearly visible, their corresponding issues are often more elusive. Definitely, our expected goal is that we immediately understand issues as they present themselves and move in appropriately responsive ways. However, in daily living, we often miss this mark. We find ourselves in the midst of an experience without fully understanding the issues involved or the possible resolutions to our conflict. Resolutions are typically attained via trial and error. And, successful patterns of resolution are typically established as a result of working with our mistakes over time.

If there is a "natural sequence to a life-cycle" as Neugarten (1979) stated, that sequence will be more convoluted than straightforward. Alapack (1984) stated that "We face certain life issues repeatedly; rarely do we deal with them once and for all. We return to certain meanings again and again in a spiral fashion." As an example, each of us continually learns about intimacy from the day we are born until the day we die. It is a developmental issue dealt with again and again, in different contexts, at different times and for different motivations. Relationships also develop in this spiral fashion. Whatever the particular life-cycle issue or developmental task, it is dealt with repeatedly throughout the lifetime of the relationship. It would be safe to say that even some distinct life-cycle stages, both individual and interactional, are relived in this same repetitive way.

The normative model used here will be the committed monogamous relationship with some specific characteristics: that the couple is middle class and heterosexual, that the partners are relatively the same chronological age, that they entered the relationship in their mid to late 20s, that the committed relationship is acknowledged publicly, that if they have children they do so within the first few years of their relationship, that the births of the children are spaced a few years apart, and that the relationship endures over the lifetime of each partner.

Normative events of the relationship life-cycle will be the central focus. Exceptions to these normative events, what Terkelsen (1980) describes as "paranormal" events — such as separation/divorce, illness, death, relocation, and loss of financial security — will be referred to at different points but will not be fully discussed in this chapter.

RELATIONSHIP LIFE-CYCLE STAGES

From a traditional psychoanalytic perspective, much has been written on the historic childhood development of the individual. Without question, Jung, Buhler and others enriched this earlier work with their focus on individual adult development. Since the 1950s, the work in the adult development area has been expanded by a growing number of theorists and researchers such as Benedek (1959), Erikson (1959), Gould (1972), Levinson, et al. (1978), Lowenthal, Thumher and Chiraboga (1975), and Vaillant (1977).

In the last decade, researchers have explored more actively the developmental life-cycle of the system. Although much of this work has focused on the broader based societal and family system, work done by such researchers as Berman and Lief (1975), Carter and McGoldrick (1980), Golan (1981), Goldberg and Deutsch (1977) and Terkelsen (1980) has addressed the life-cycle development of the dyadic relationship.

Conceptually, there is a distinction which can be made between the primary issues of individual life-cycle development and those of the life-cycle development of the relationship.

Differentiation is a primary issue for individual life-cycle development. Becoming an adult has to do with the establishment of an evolving awareness of autonomy. We must ideally, as adults, possess a solid sense of self with appropriate boundaries from which intimacy, productivity, initiation, and the like are possible.

In contrast, the primary issue for the relationship life-cycle is the balancing of two opposing phenomena: interdependence and differentiation. The systemic task is not for further autonomy, but for an interaction of two distinct identities. Frequently, what a couple might describe as fear of intimacy may primarily be a struggle with boundaries. The question for them might be: How can we be in a relationship (be interdependent) and retain a strong sense of self (differentiation)? Mistrust of one's ability to set boundaries and one's partner's ability to respect those boundaries may be great. In this atmosphere, any wish to be more intimate is undoubtedly lessened.

If a balance between interdependence and differentiation is attained, the inherent purposiveness of the relationship can be experienced in a positive way. If boundaries are in place two things can happen. First, individual needs have a much better chance of being fostered and, second, emergent systemic needs have a better chance of being successfully integrated. Developmentally, life-cycle issues, needs, tasks and transitions will also be more successfully acknowledged and integrated.

Clinically, there are a few general points to keep in mind. When faced with a couple or individual in therapy, we must always keep part of our focus on the life-cycle stages, tasks and issues at hand. Any assumption of dynamics and behavior must be conceptually bracketed by a developmental life-cycle framework. We must have an idea of what is developmentally appropriate for the individual partners and for the relationship.

Reframing has repeatedly been described as a powerful therapeutic tool when used in a genuine way. This is particularly true in the area of life-cycle development. A powerful reframe is to translate a confusing set of experiences for clients as, in part, appropriate for a particular individual and/or relationship life-stage. This is not a magical solution, but it can be helpful in returning to the clients some sense of normalcy and dignity. A difficult time is often made considerably worse by the fear that what one is experiencing is outside the norm. Once the appropriateness of an experience is established, work can usually proceed from a more positive vantage point.

It is also essential to keep in mind the spiral process of development and to present this process to clients. We assume that most life-cycle issues reemerge at different points of development, with various shades of meaning. Again we can use the issue of intimacy as an example.

People tend to struggle with their fear of intimacy at different points in life. Perhaps, in the midst of the excitement of a new relationship and in the security of a newly created family, this fear has felt more manageable. At that point, the clients may experience intimacy as no longer the difficult issue it once was. Around mid-life, considerable transition occurs and questions of personal identity often emerge. The struggle for balance between interdependence and differentiation might be disturbed. Intimacy, during this time, may again be experienced as a problem. The clinician needs to assure the clients that it makes developmental sense that this difficult issue has reemerged. Variations of meaning need to be pointed out. It is essential that the clients see that they are not back at square one with the issue, but are having to look once more at those aspects of intimacy that are being challenged in the new situation.

A RELATIONSHIP LIFE-CYCLE
SCHEMA AND PRIMARY ISSUES

The dilemma at this juncture is how to present a schema of the developmental life-cycle of the relationship which is simultaneously simple and yet does some justice to the work of these aforementioned researchers. Scarf (1987) presents a partial schema which is very

Table 13.1

Relationship Life-Cycle Stage	Approximate Time Frame	Focal Issues
Starting Up	(0-2 years)	Differentiation, Identity, Intimacy and Trust
Settling In	(2-4 years)	Identity, Inclusion/Exclusion, Power
Decision Time	(3-7 years)	Commitment
Moving On/ Latency Age	(7-15 years)	Identity, Production, Competence, Commitment
Mid-Life/ Adolescence	(15-24 years)	Identity, Self-Esteem Competence, Power, Intimacy
Launching	(25-35 years)	New Beginnings and Resolutions versus Stagnation and Despair
Older Age and Death	(35 years +)	Endings, Intimacy, Continuity

helpful. With some adjustments and additions, the following model will be used (see Table 13.1).

With each of these stages, countless issues come to the fore. Again, they emerge from both individual developmental processes and the relationship life-cycle itself. As would be expected, each issue is interconnected. For example, we cannot talk about identity without talking about individuation. These concepts need to be described as they exist separately from one another and as they are woven in context with one another.

What will follow is a brief description of some primary developmental issues for each life-cycle stage of the relationship. Individual life-cycle issues will be described only to highlight dyadic issues.

Issues described at different stages are primarily taken from the works of Berman and Lief (1975) and Carter and McGoldrick (1980).

Starting Up: (0-2 years)

Focal Issues: Differentiation, Identity, Intimacy and Trust

Theorists typically present intimacy as the central issue for the beginning relationship. If we define being intimate as experiencing an essential closeness and connectedness between two individuals, then it is essential to have two separate, hopefully well differentiated individuals coming together at the beginning of any relationship. In contrast, if each person lacks a basic awareness of self and a basic sense of personal boundaries, there is a greater likelihood of fusion than of intimacy.

Again, the ideal is that we have an interaction between two separate people. For example, if John and Mary come together in order to form one complete person, chances are the relationship is in trouble from the start. Differentiation and identity must be present before intimacy can be truly attained.

If we assume the couple of our normative model is in their mid-20s at this stage in the relationship, each partner is in the process of young adulthood. The adolescent struggle for an identity separate from family of origin moves towards a greater sense of responsibility and commitment. Choices are hopefully made more independently, apart from parents, and founded on a clearer awareness of personal needs, self-awareness and direction. Choices begin to have more profound and long-term consequences. Commitments to relationships, work, values, and goals are seen as having more weight personally and in the social world.

Identity undergoes further transitions in forming a committed relationship. One's identity as a single person is ended, his/her primary identity as a member of one's family of origin is ended, and the identity of the new couple is begun. No longer is Joan described as Joan, single woman, daughter of Henry and Marge. She is now Joan, partner of John, and daughter of Henry and Marge.

This shift in personal identity is often accompanied by feelings of loss, anxiety and fear. It is hoped that at this beginning stage of the relationship there is a sense that more is to be gained than lost by committing to another. Generally, the hope is that the creation of a new relationship and personal identity will be viewed as a personally enriching experience. However, any transition in identity can feel risky and frightening since the ultimate outcome cannot be guaranteed no matter how initially promising it might seem.

The creation of the new intimate relationship brings with it exclusivity from other relationships. A realignment of personal priorities and interpersonal commitments is made. Also, many personal and interactional skills are tested, such as one's ability to be aware of his/her needs, communicate them, negotiate for them, and reach a resolution of differences and conflicts with a sense of personal and mutual fulfillment.

The process of integrating individual needs, values and goals demands a great deal of mutual trust. At the start of any relationship, each person is asked to begin sharing needs without total assurance that those vulnerabilities will be accorded the appropriate respect. Trust requires time and experience with the other person. As this incrementally occurs, confidence in the other is established. However, new relationships are routinely begun on the promise that the other is trustworthy. When that promise is fulfilled, the relationship thrives. However, this assumption of trustworthiness may not be fulfilled and the relationship may be placed in jeopardy or dissolved.

As an additional note, with an older couple beginning a relationship, the same issue cluster will most likely present itself. However, depending on how much work each person has done toward his or her own individuation, the focus might be more on issues of intimacy and trust than on identity and differentiation.

Settling In: (2–4 years)

Focal Issues: Identity, Inclusion/Exclusion, Power

This stage follows the later part of the honeymoon period and precedes a stage of intense involvement with having children and/or with one's life work. The couple in the normative model is now in their late 20s and very early 30s. A primary developmental task in the "settling in" stage is to further establish identity, interactional patterns and boundaries in the relationship. The couple's identity, apart from families of origin and other outside relationships, is cemented. Inclusion and exclusion issues are central. Everyone knows which two people have committed to one another. A couple once described this stage as one where they received their collective name "Joan-n-John," a time when family and friends find it hard to refer to one partner without referring to the other. The relationship now has a clear, separate identity.

The evolving experience of this separate identity of the relationship is paralleled by the ongoing assessment of individual autonomy and boundaries within the relationship. Questions such as "Who am I apart from this relationship?" and "Who am I within this relationship?" exist. Given the newness of the relationship and the absence of old stored resentments and hurts, answers to these questions appear to be more available and less troublesome than in later stages.

A process of grieving is visible in this stage and primarily centers on three areas: one's loss of identity as a single person, the fading of intense feelings of connectedness during the honeymoon stage, and a burgeoning awareness that expectations for the relationship were, in part, naive.

The establishment of joint traditions, values, goals, and belief systems also begins to take shape. As with the handling of identity issues during this time, the ability to establish a separate system with all its necessary components is indicative of the ever-present process of differentiation. For example, a young couple recently came into therapy with the presenting problem that he was angry she would not spend more time with him and she was angry he wanted to spend so much time together. Both referred to their parents' relationships as the model for the quantity of time "healthy" couples should normally spend together. This was a good indication that a new, joint belief system—how much time we spend together—could not be established between them as long as they individually defined what was proper in the world based on family of origin models.

The ongoing process of blending needs brings with it a more obvious awareness of the distribution of power in a relationship. At this stage, with some relationship history, each partner begins to feel his/her power or lack thereof. A hierarchy is perceived as beginning to take shape. Roles, such as that of parent and child, become more and more visibly established. For example, a woman recently described the second year of her marriage as the time she became convinced she was now her husband's mother. With some urging, she also became aware that by the second year she had firmly recreated her role as surrogate parent from her own family of origin.

Decision Time: (3–7 years)

Focal Issue: Commitment

Without a doubt, other issues exist during this relationship life-cycle stage. However, most of the primary concerns at this time can be viewed as commitment issues. The couple in our normative model, now facing or just past age 30, are faced with many decisions which will require a continuation and/or increase in their commitment to each other and to their own development. There are three main areas of commitment which demand a decision: the marriage, children and life's work. Each of these areas represents fundamental personal and interactional meanings which make this a very significant life-cycle stage.

By this time, the marriage is an institution. Its existence is taken for granted even though its continuation, for some, may be in question. Basically, each partner has become family for the other. There is a kinship which exists and carries with it all the positive and negative components of such a relationship. Some couples describe their relationship, at this time, as similar to a sibling relationship with all that that image can unfortunately imply. For the most part, relationships at this stage are usually described as a positive, integral part of each individual and whose absence couldn't be imagined.

Parallel to the experience of being settled into the relationship, a reevaluation of the quality, structure and direction of that relationship frequently occurs during this stage. The outcome of this reevaluation process is usually the making of decisions concerning one's continuing commitment to his/her partner. Obviously, this and any reevaluation process can be difficult and filled with anxiety and upheaval. There are couples who move into and successfully complete this process with a manageable amount of anxiety and with a sense of excitement and confidence for a positive outcome. However, it is doubtful that any couple moves through this stage with no difficulty. The degree of stress in this stage is directly connected to many basic developmental factors of the couple and of the individuals involved. Once again, the primary factors involved are: the level of individual and interactional differentiation, identity and self-esteem development, and communication and resolution skills.

One other distinction needs to be made. One must be aware that in this process of commitment and decision making there are differing demands, shades of experience, implications, and consequences for each gender. The specifics of these cannot be reviewed in the scope of this chapter.

Before describing the primary decisions and commitments of this stage, it is important to reestablish where the partners might be in their individual development. We are, again, assuming that the partners in the committed relationship are young adults, usually in their late 20s or early 30s. This can generally be an exciting time of continued personal growth as a young adult. Individual identity should include an evolving awareness of increased competency and power. There are certain developmental tasks which have been, to some degree, mastered by this time, such as: maintaining a committed relationship, finishing one's training or education, establishing oneself in one's life's work, and/or feeling more confident to stand next to one's parents as an individuated adult.

Transitions therefore present themselves as the natural outcome of having developmentally reached a certain level of growth. One then needs to move on to the next task.

What the individuals and couple are usually now faced with is the decision whether or not to have children. Certainly, this is a decision with profound individual and joint ramifications. Ours is a pro-natalistic society. This means that it is assumed that couples who are biologically able to have a child will choose to do so. It is the "natural" next step once the relationship is firmly in place. And yet, whether or not the couple decide to have a child, they are, in this stage, making a public and private statement about their commitment to each other. If the relationship is to survive, they need to reaffirm their commitment to one another with or without children. It can also be said that their commitment changes in conjunction with their decision — hopefully to a deeper level.

If the couple decide to have a child and their motivation is not purely to save a failing relationship, they are stating that they believe their commitment to each other is strong enough to form the core of a larger family unit. If they decide not to have a child, they are making a statement that their commitment to each other is strong enough to both provide a fulfilling personal life and withstand the judgement of a society confused by their decision. In both instances, the sense of commitment has a very good chance of being strengthened by their decisions.

There is also the decision to commit to one's life's work. Certainly, there are individuals and couples who decide not to have a child based on the decision to devote their energy, and possibly their generativity needs, to their work. There are also individuals, primarily women, who decide that having and raising children is, at least at this phase, their life's work. Overall, in this stage, the level of commitment to one's work is increased. One's personal identity becomes more closely tied to what one does and what one produces.

Generally, the commitment and decision-making processes in this phase are prime indicators of adulthood. The fact of having children and/or holding down a responsible job has always been a rite of passage to adulthood in this culture.

How the couple handle the process and consequences of the commitment and decision-making depends on many factors such as: levels of differentiation, dyadic distribution of power, established roles and position within the relationship, gender, overall quality of their interaction, demands from extended family, friends and community to conform to rules other than those valued by the individual and couple, and economic status.

Moving On: (7-15 years)

   Focal Issues: Identity, Production, Commitment, Competency

These are the latency-age years of the relationship. As with the latency-age years of childhood, what looks like a relatively inactive time in regard to development is actually a period marked by considerable covert change and growth. At this stage, issues heretofore encountered are hopefully refined, further resolved, and woven into one's identity. The couple in our normative model are now in their 30s.

An evolving sense of identity, both individual and interactional, is the barometer by which development is measured. Up to this point in the life-cycle, identity has been described primarily in terms of the process of differentiation from family of origin. At this stage, identity is viewed more in terms of such issues as productivity, commitment to the maintenance of the relationship, child rearing, commitment to life's work and connection to the broader community. Identity is, therefore, assessed and enriched by issues of competency in daily living. How well one maintains a committed relationship, parents children and/or does one's work is a prime reflection of who one is and his or her general value. It is at this stage that Freud's two basic life issues of "love and work" (DiCaprio, 1974) seem to be best exemplified.

This stage is less historically focused. A focus on the present and the future overshadows the focus on the past as the relationship matures, children develop, work becomes established, and life plans are set in motion. Intergenerational issues are centered more on the interactions between the present and future generations. They are less centered on the interactions between the present and past generations. The obvious illustration of this is the focus on the parent-child relationship. A parallel on the job would be the hope and vision that one's work will influence the future and its generation of workers.

Definitely, connections to one's family of origin are present as one becomes a parent and/or becomes competent on the job. These connections are generally indicative of the individual's continued movement into full adulthood – similar to one's parents. The evolution of one's present relationship into a mature, adult union further indicates that certain rites of passage have taken place.

Conflicts arise as each person experiences a level of competency and influence and moves to assume more control. Patterns of individual decision making, conflict resolution, and accomplishing tasks are well established. If these patterns have not developed in a parallel fashion within the relationship, that relationship experiences difficulty. It is clear which couples have found a way to work together and which couples spend the time allotted for a joint task arguing over who is in charge. Distance can also emerge in the relationship if the partners have not developed along similar paths. Shared perceptions, interests, communication styles, and belief systems may not be similar enough to permit the relationship to possess a solid identity.

Relationship boundaries are tested as children and work commitments intrude. A good deal of this intrusion normally happens. If the relationship is clearly delineated by this stage, the result will be added stress but no permanent damage to the relationship.

Individuation from family of origin should have evolved to the point where the individual and the relationship have developed a strong sense of identity and can tolerate some level of intrusion. If this has not happened, two things can occur. First, either boundaries get set too rigidly in an attempt to ward off the perceived threat to one's identity or, second, boundaries are not set strongly enough and the relationship begins to fragment. In the first example, one might see a relationship where one partner is highly noncommunicative and accuses the other partner of wanting to take control and not respecting his/her privacy. In the second example, it is common to see families where a child has been co-opted into his/her parent's relationship as an equal third partner.

Basically, it is at this stage that much of the structure and quality of the relationship is set for the long haul. By now, it should be clear whether the relationship is primarily a positive, nurturing union or a destructive one. Further change is assuredly on the horizon. And, depending on that quality and structure, future development will be either aided or hindered by this well-established system.

Mid-Life/Adolescence: (15-24 years)

Focal Issues: Identity, Self-Esteem, Competence, Power, Intimacy, Developmental Life-Cycle Parallels

This is the central developmental stage of any long-term relationship. It is a stage of self examination, upheaval, major life transitions, crisis, reorganization and increased tension on most fronts. It is perhaps the most perilous stage for any relationship in that so many fundamental issues are at question at one time with so few clear answers immediately available.

The title of this stage, mid-life/adolescence, refers solely to the adult relationship and does not assume that a couple has children. The word "mid-life" refers to the individual life-cycle stage where one strongly becomes aware that an unlimited future is no longer the reality. Life is literally half over. Not a difficult estimation if we assume the couple in our normative model are now in their early 40s. One's mortality becomes the issue and we begin to prepare for the rest of our lives. We do so by evaluating our lives as individuals and as a couple. There is a sense of pride in accomplishments and futility in failures, resolutions for the future, and attempts to place the past in some perspective.

The word "adolescence" refers to the stage where one experiences increased differentiation, need for autonomy, rebellion, contrasting feelings of personal competence and incompetence and of security and insecurity, restlessness, and the like. This experience is shared both by teenagers and by 40-year-olds alike. Certainly, there are many qualitative differences between the two stages which are primarily based in the levels of differentiation and general life experience. However, as the couple reach approximately their 13th to 20th year together, a spiraling back to some adolescent issues is common and defines this stage. This collision of mid-life and adolescence is strikingly difficult for most couples.

The intensity of this stage varies from one couple to the next, one partner to another. This stage is similar to the previous decision stage of the relationship life-cycle in that both are marked by self and joint examination and decision-making. There is an awareness in both stages that a pivotal moment in development has arrived whether one is ready for it or not. Also, there is a sense in each that the pull for change is often ambiguous. This is different from the clear basis for change as a response to concrete life-cycle events such as job opportunities, birth of child, and death of parent. Without a precipitating event, what one experiences is a strong sense that one needs something more than one has and yet can cite only the more obvious reasons why it is necessary. The result is that in both stages there is a piece of experience which feels beyond one's understanding and, therefore, a bit out of one's control.

For example, the 30-year-olds can talk about the biological clock in regards to having a child, but find it more difficult to clearly define why they want a child at all. The 40-year-olds can certainly talk about their mortality, but have a more difficult time clearly defining why so much is being questioned.

In the mid-life stage, identity comes to the fore once again. Who one is as a person and who we are as a couple are the focus. Having passed through the last life-cycle stage, the couple now see competency as an indicator of self-worth. Unfortunately, during this time competency is often in question. On all fronts — the relationship, child-rearing and work— change leaves the individual and couple feeling less able both to predict what is coming next and to count on historically reliable coping skills to alleviate problems. The outcome is often a lowering of self-esteem and a lessening of feelings of competence. This can be additionally anxiety-producing and frustrating. This is particularly true when these feelings are accompanied by the expectation that one should be more able to deal with life given a general experience level.

By this stage, power presents itself as a focal issue, frequently in terms of contrasts. Each partner is usually established in his/her life's work and has a sense of power within that prescribed area. This is often in marked contrast to what is happening in the relationship. Couples repeatedly complain at this stage that their partners do not listen to them or afford them the same respect they get from co-workers, employees and friends.

We have defined the ability to be intimate as indicative of the level of one's differentiation. More specifically, in order to be truly intimate one must have a solid identity apart from the other and a solid sense of self-worth. In light of this definition, intimacy is typically a struggle in this stage. If we assume that development is a spiral process, each partner is once again working hard, amidst the transitions, to establish a solid sense of self and attempting to maintain appropriate boundaries and connections with the other.

This is a stage in which each partner is reassessing his/her needs, discovering them for the first time or continuing with the struggle to have old needs met. Depending on the trust and communication patterns available within the relationship, the expression or lack of expression of needs is an essential element in the intimacy level of the relationship. Relationships often falter at this stage.

Definitely, affairs, separation and the dissolution of the relationship can happen at any stage for countless reasons (see Chapters 8 and 10). As with general experience, it is often helpful to understand these occurrences from a relationship life-cycle perspective. We again assume that with some understanding will come more of a sense of being in control. Usually, affairs, separation, and the dissolution of a relationship foster an intense feeling of being out of control.

Basically, these occurrences are viewed as attempts to have needs met. Whether or not we judge them as appropriate ways of fulfilling needs is secondary here to their meaning as indicators of the developmental process. In light of the stages we have already discussed, some of the reasons they occur might be linked to the following.

In a new relationship, the lack of differentiation and maturity can contribute to a failure to appropriately integrate issues and needs. In the settling-down period, perhaps the disappointment over the decrease in blissful feelings and the emerging realization that a relationship exists in the practical world can increase the distance between partners. Clearly, the struggle whether or not to commit to having a child, or the commitment to pursuing one's life work, has divided many couples.

And certainly, in the pressures of everyday living, with energy demanded by one's work and/or children, the primary focus on any intimate relationship can be lost.

Another factor might be that, as the relationship progresses over time, the partners will begin to categorize each other and the relationship. They experience each as able to supply satisfaction for personal needs in a prescribed way. They will split their needs between the partner, the relationship as a whole, and, oftentimes, a significant other. For example, a woman recently said that she felt her husband was good only for one thing, a basic sense of security. No matter what else was going on in her life, her partner was consistently there. This does not mean he was particularly proficient at direct emotional care-giving. Rather, his mere presence held some meaning for her. Her relationship provided her with status in the community and a connection to her family of origin who greatly valued long-term marriages. She also made it very clear that her lover provided her with the passion, intrigue and excitement in her life.

Yet another factor, specifically in regards to the ending of a relationship, might be the feeling that one must escape an intolerable situation for one's perceived sanity. This is the reason individuals commonly give for leaving their partners. Unfortunately, too often the intolerable situation is one of emotional or physical abuse. Also, if the relationship is perceived as being unable to meet present needs, it is often felt necessary to leave that relationship. This is particularly true when it is perceived that, developmentally, one partner has outgrown the other. Of course, there are individuals who remain in a relationship long after the awareness that individual needs are not being met and long after they have outgrown their partners. The result is most likely devastating.

The general interface between the individual developmental life-cycle of the child and that of the parent is well documented. In our normative model, it is assumed that the 40-plus-year-old couple would, by this stage, have children in their teens. What becomes apparent is the parallel between the developmental tasks involved at both stages.

For both the adolescent and the parent in mid-life the struggle for identity is profound. The need to individuate from one's "intimate others," whether that refers to one's family of origin or to one's partner, is strong. The awakening of heretofore unfelt needs is powerful. And, often the differentiation and exploration of those needs may bear a tone of rebellion and anger which can serve to push others away.

Since one's sense of intimacy generally parallels one's sense of identity, both evolve in an ebb and flow fashion throughout the life-cycle. As already discussed, the ability to be intimate is a prime indicator of a separate identity and, therefore, is also an indicator of one's level of differentiation.

For the adolescent, the ability to be intimate is very much in process. For the parent at mid-life, the ability to be intimate has hopefully been achieved, on some level, for many years. However, with the struggle for new aspects of one's identity in mid-life, the parent and the adolescent often find themselves struggling with intimacy in a parallel fashion. Given this parallel, it is not surprising that parents and children at this stage often find it difficult to be intimate with each other.

What is also particularly striking is the interface of the adolescent's sexuality with that of the parent. The teenager's increased sexuality, with all its fresh excitement and passion, often throws the sexuality of the mid-life parent into marked contrast. Physically and emotionally, many 40-year-olds are not as sexually focused as they were in their teens and 20s. Possibly, too many distractions to spontaneous sexuality exist: the real burdens of adult responsibilities; stored frustrations and anger; lessened physical stamina and fitness; diversion of time, tension and passion into work; fighting with one's partner; raising a teenager. In addition, sexuality in the adult's relationship possesses, by mid-life, a long history. It is often more difficult to reach the heights of passion once fostered by the mystery, newness and feelings of trust at the start of the relationship.

It has already been noted that relationships survive when each partner develops and changes at relatively the same pace, and along relatively the same path. This isn't to say that these couples fuse in their development or that they do not experience distance, uncertainty and tension as other couples do. Rather, the degree of incongruence between them is kept within tolerable limits as defined by the couple. As also stated earlier, the degree of contrast between individual and joint development should be a central concern from the start of any relationship.

Launching: (25–35 years)

Focal Issues: New Beginnings and Resolution
Versus Stagnation and Despair

Life-cycle development is a cumulative process. Each stage builds on the one before it and forms the foundation for those to follow. Past completion of developmental tasks forms the basis for completing those of the next stage. The quality of the present stage relies on the successful passage through preceding stages. This stage of launching is a good example of the cumulative process of development. The mid-life/adolescent stage was marked by change. A primary task was to evaluate and reorder one's life and relationship in better accord with evolving needs and to prepare for the second half of life.

The process of change in mid-life can often be dramatic and far-reaching. Stories abound of striking transitions: career and life-style changes; political, religious and philosophical shifts; role changes within the structure of the relationship; new interests, friends, and connections within the broader community. The process can also be more specific in focus. In that case, the transitions are less dramatic and the original structure, world-view, value systems, and interactional patterns in one's life and relationship are retained.

Whatever the changes in this stage for the couple and the individual, the purpose of mid-life is, again, to prepare for the second half of their lives — a future hopefully experienced as more fulfilling and settled.

We now assume that the couple in our normative model are in their 50s and very early 60s. This launching stage represents the evolution of that second half of their lives. And, the degree to which change had been a primary goal in the preceding stage, stability emerges as a primary goal in this stage. Mid-life evaluations often result in reordering facets of the relationship and of the individual's life. As a result, time is needed, and taken here, to refine the new order and to settle into the changes. Although this sounds very sedate, the label "launching" refers to an active process of growth which takes place in this stage. This label and process will be described in a moment.

This life-cycle stage is not stagnant. As in other stages, the process of change can occur in two ways. First, integrating previous transitions into one's present life-style is an active process which generates its own changes. For example, in the mid-life stage, a woman who had stayed home to raise her children, primarily because of tradition, begins to question and redefine her role in her relationship and family. In response to this process, she enters the work force in her late 40s. This transition may result in an increased sense of competency in the outside world, which may in turn upset the balance of perceived power within her relationship. If her partner does not accommodate the changes occurring for her, he will interact with her as he always did before. Conflicts will inevitably arise.

Second, change occurs as a response to developmental life-cycle events. At this stage, for example, the leaving home of a child as a young adult is characteristic. It is a profound transition for everyone. It is also a predictable normative life-cycle event. One's response, no matter what it might be, is seen in relation to that concrete, visible event.

It is interesting to note that during this life-cycle stage two central normative life-cycle events usually occur which are intergenerational in nature. One has already been mentioned – the adult child leaving home. The second event is the death of the last surviving parent.

Typically, by the mid-50s, many people have already lost one or both parents. Or, as is the case for many couples, they are responsible for elderly parents who are incapacitated. This latter example is a very difficult situation and is commonly a topic in therapy. However, when the last child leaves home and one's parents have died, the middle generation becomes the oldest generation. This shift in identity is frequently sobering. One client recently said that he thought the realization that his life was half over in his 40s was tough, but it was easy to handle in comparison to the realization that he was now part of the next generation to die.

A person's response to this realization is dependent on many factors. One such factor is how well he or she has passed through mid-life and how effectively one's priorities help fulfill needs. It is basically a question of the quality of one's life at this stage.

In regards to the more general quality of the relationship at this stage, it is also highly dependent on the manner in which the relationship had passed through the mid-life/adolescent stage. If the relationship had successfully survived that stage by incorporating change, then the current stage will be one of new beginnings and resolutions. If the relationship did not successfully survive because it rigidly resisted change or growth, then either it was dissolved or this stage will be one of stagnation and despair.

The foundation for new priorities and directions was laid in mid-life based on needs and values brought into one's awareness. This foundation was laid for both the individual and the relationship. If we also assume that a successful transition from the previous stage to this stage has been made, the primary task here will then be to set into motion formulated plans and goals based on those mid-life foundations. The task in this stage is to launch the future.

Typically, the term "launching" is reserved, at this time in the life-cycle, to refer to the launching of children. Much has been written on the "empty-nest syndrome." However, it is used here in a broader sense. It is the launching of the future for the relationship, for the individual partners, and for the children, if there are any.

The ability to move forward, to launch what has been planned, is aided by the lessening of one's load. It is hoped that during the mid-life stage the excess baggage of unresolved issues has been somewhat lessened. As we have discussed, these unresolved issues often center on the continued process of differentiation from family of origin. During mid-life, and also in this stage, attempts are made to resolve these issues as the individuals and couple struggle with such issues as: individual identity and self-esteem; the need for fusion; stored emotional debts; boundary placement.

An outcome of a successful transition through mid-life is an enriched sense of self-worth and competency. One has climbed a mountain — for some a very high mountain — and lived to tell the story. This is obviously true for the couple. Having watched several of their friends dissolve their relationships, couples at this stage often feel a real sense of accomplishment for having survived.

Central to their survival is the ability to integrate change. This ability may be newly achieved or well developed from the first stage. The flexibility of any system is a hallmark of the health of that system. If the relationship is too rigidly structured or defined, change will be met with resistance and often sabotaged. Countless relationships have been dissolved because of an inability to accommodate individual growth, changing roles, needed individuation, and the like.

At any life-cycle stage, when the relationship refuses to meet change with change, the resulting experience is usually one of hopelessness. The feeling of being helpless is pervasive. Here, there is no launching of a hopeful future because each person is stuck in his or her own unresolved issues. Their rigidity is usually symptomatic of their level of pain. Coping skills, which were not previously acquired, are not available to deal with the anxiety, disappointment, frustration and anger generally felt. The result is an internalized sense of despair for the individual and a joint sense of stagnation for the couple.

Older Age and Death: (35 years +)

Focal Issues: Endings, Intimacy, Continuity

Primary individual life-cycle issues for this stage are generally accepted as "integrity vs. despair with wisdom emergent" (Erikson, 1959). By the time one reaches the 60s, 70s and 80s, the hope is for contentment, with an identity which is whole and individuated. The expectation is that experience has been a good teacher and that much of the internal and interactional struggles of our youth have been replaced with wisdom and acceptance.

The relationship, after 35-plus years, will hopefully also possess integrity and be perceived as having been a consistent source of intimacy, nurturance, and security, and a context for personal growth. Whatever the persistent, major conflicts have been, the expectation is that we have now replaced them with viable resolutions which have stood the test of time.

The experience of despair stands in sharp contrast to this idyllic picture. Our worst fear is that we will reach the end of our life with a sense of desperation for what has gone before; that we will have learned nothing from our history; that we will still be struggling with the same unresolved issues we struggled with in our youth.

The relationship, in our desperation, will be blamed as the consistent block to our personal growth and happiness. Anger and resentment will be primary feelings as we rage, silently or directly, at our partners for having failed to provide support, respect and, most fundamentally, a sense of intimacy. Rather than feeling that our committed relationship has been the most private, essential and familiar one of our lives, we perceive it as empty and distant. What is often striking is the amount of differentiation that some couples never achieve. To have a separate identity is an unknown both individually and for the relationship as a whole. Responsibility for one's life and one's interactions is a concept and reality not within their grasp.

Whatever scenario this life-cycle stage presents, it is a time of endings. This does not mean it is only a time for retrospection, goodbyes and facing death. However prominent those experiences are as time passes, these years can be vital ones of relative freedom from responsibilities and restraints. For the relationship, these can be years unencumbered by the intense distractions of children and work. The focus can be more easily redirected to each other. Even if one decides never to retire, and if one's children and grandchildren are in constant touch, the focus and intensity of these outside distractions do not have to be what they once were.

In addition, since the luxury of an extended future is gone, daily living becomes more focal. Again, if contentment and integrity are present, day-to-day life together is savored. If despair is present, it can be unbearable. For most couples, life is experienced somewhere in the middle.

For most couples, the assumption here is that life and the committed relationship are realistically perceived as having been, and continuing to be, a mix of good and bad. Our strengths and growth are in evidence. Where the relationship works, it solidly works. Where issues have been resolved, the old conflicts rarely occur. And, simultaneously, the unresolved issues of our youth are still in evidence. With enough experience, work and luck, they have decreased in intensity and no longer render us helpless every time they are encountered. Hopefully, the general projections, fears, defenses, and need for fusion are not as powerful as they once were. But, they persist.

Those unresolved issues that persist seem to take a purer form in this life-stage. Many of the more secondary issues and responses fade as the more fundamental issues take hold. Countless times, older people complain that their partner has gotten more rigid or frightened or angry with age. This seems to be true for the relationship as well. If those issues that have been fundamental throughout the life-cycle, such as trust, power, and boundaries, persist, they do so in a clearer way. It is as though the partners and the relationship are stripped of some of the pretentions and excuses of youth.

The task of this stage seems to be to attend to endings. The relationship, however intimate it may be, is in its last years. For those couples in the middle ground, these are years spent with attention paid to resolution. Between the partners, some care is taken to not continue the old conflicts at the same intensity. In response to the added vulnerability that comes with the realization of one's mortality, partners generally tend to be a bit more careful with one another.

Where attention to ending is clearly visible is in the area of legacies. How one is remembered becomes an important focus. The issue of continuity between the generations is felt strongly by most couples. They want their children, their grandchildren, their younger co-workers and friends to remember them and to benefit from having known them. There is oftentimes an attempt made to rectify past misjudgments and to salvage one's reputation.In therapy, couples in this life-stage frequently will be quite concerned with the disengagement of their children or of a surviving sibling. The need for reconciliation is often great. Even if reconciliation is not sought and the individuals or couple hold on to their hurt or resentments, there is often a heightened desire that the person who wronged them understand what they are feeling. There is a need to put in order relationships in much the same light as people put their financial estate in order.

Generally, the issue of loss is pervasive in this life-cycle stage. The couple have been witness to years of sickness and death which will eventually intrude on their relationship. Preparing for the loss of a partner is a difficult task. Even for those couples who are embroiled in unresolved resentments, the death of one's adversary can be as devastating as the death of a friend.

If communication is open and honesty is sought, obviously feelings concerning death will be discussed. The opposite is more likely true. The topic of death is usually avoided unless one is discussing a will or a partner's health. One man in his late 70s once said in therapy that he had gotten as old as he had by refusing to think about death. The not so surprising thing was that his wife could not stop thinking about it.

CLINICAL FOCI AND SEXUALITY

As was stated earlier, a lengthy detailed description of possible clinical interventions, sensitive to the relationship life-cycle, will not be described in this chapter. However, it should be briefly noted that, as with any other psychological condition, several clinical approaches would be effective. In regards to life-cycle issues, certain clinical foci would be appropriate at differing stages of development. These foci may be similar from stage to stage, but the balance of focus changes over time. Following is a schema (see Table 13.2) which suggests possible clinical foci at differing relationship life-cycle stages. It is meant only as a guide.

In regards to sexuality and the relationship life-cycle, there is a great deal to be said which cannot be detailed in this chapter. A few points must be kept in mind. As a clinical observation, it appears that sexuality changes during the life-cycle in accordance with three primary parameters: first, the emotional quality of the relationship; second, the individuals' sense of personal well-being; third, the physical condition of the body. Interest and energy for sexuality may vary during different life-cycle stages. However, given the countless examples of couples in their 30s who are no longer sexual with one another and couples in their 60s who remain sexual with one another, it is difficult to make a strong case for a direct correlation between sexuality and the relationship life-cycle.

It also appears that, despite a decrease in sexual interest and performance with aging, those couples who integrate feelings of intimacy with sexuality early in their relationship have a better chance of maintaining this mode of expression later in life.

FINAL STATEMENT

A tension exists when describing the relationship life-cycle. On one hand, there is a desire to propose a model which is normative, universal and simply understood. On the other hand, there is a desire to detail the richness and complexity of the experience and to further describe, at every turn, the countless variations for each relationship, each stage, each issue, each task.

Table 13.2

Relationship Life-Cycle Stage	Focal Issues	Possible Clinical Foci
Starting Up: (0-2 years)	Differentiation, Identity, Intimacy, Trust	Communication and Conflict Resolution, Skills Training, Family of Origin Work
Settling In: (2-4 years)	Identity, Inclusion/ Exclusion, Power	Continuation of Communication and Conflict Resolution, Skills Training, Family of Origin Work
Decision Time: (3-7 years)	Commitment	Didactic Focus on Specific Life-Cycle Stage and Issues, Individual and Joint Values Clarification, Crisis and Conflict Resolution Skills Training
Moving On: (7-15 years)	Identity, Production, Commitment, Competency	Parenting and General Coping Skills, Stress Management, Communication and Conflict Resolution, Skills Training
Mid-Life/ Adolescence: (15-24 years)	Identity, Self-Esteem, Competence, Power, Intimacy, Developmental Life-Cycle Parallels	Didactic and Insight Approach to Individual Family of Origin Issues and Life-Cycle Stage and Issues, Coping Skills for Crisis, Anxiety and Anger Management, Support for Individual and Relationship Strengths
Launching: (25-35 years)	New Beginnings and Resolution versus Stagnation and Despair	Assessment of Mid-Life Survival, Addressing Issues of Change and Loss
Older Age and Death: (35 years +)	Endings, Intimacy, Continuity	Present-focused Coping Skills Training, Communication Skills Training, Life Review, Multigenerational Family of Origin and Family of Creation Work, Facilitation of Discussions Concerning Death

This theoretical dilemma is parallel to a clinical dilemma. We perceive experience as multifaceted and endlessly complex. Yet we need, for our own clarification and that of the clients, to conceptualize and present experience in the simplest, most understandable way we can. The clinician is always aware of what is not being presented.

The normative model presented in this chapter is needed. As any model, it provides the structural framework for our discussion and, by definition, provides it in as broad a manner as possible. As earlier stated, it is a starting point of which the reader must be consistently reminded.

From the normative model presented, the clinician must continually watch for where it is applicable and where it is not applicable to his/her clients. For example, basic assumptions, such as the chronological age of our couple throughout the model and the matched chronological age of the couple at the beginning of the relationship, do not describe a good percentage of our clients. We must continually question whether what was described would fit the 41-year-old married to the 28-year-old who have just walked into our office. If what is described doesn't match our experience, the contrast will hopefully spark critical thinking. Further formulations can then be explored by everyone in the therapeutic setting. Variations can instruct us about the uniqueness of our clients. One of the best questions to ask a couple is, "How do you imagine your experience is similar to and different from that of the norm?" A great deal is to be learned from comparative thinking.

If we view experience as unique, we must view development as unique. One's interaction with the social world and the resulting internalized sense of self constitute the meaning of one's experience and development. My place in the social world, the world's response to me, my response to the world, how I end up feeling about myself must all influence my development individually and interactionally.

In addition to being aware of where our clients vary from the norm, the clinician must be aware as to why this might be so. There are infinite variations and influences possible in relationship life-cycle development. A comprehensive listing of the primary influences may include the following: age, gender, race, cultural ethnicity, social and economic status, and sexual orientation. In this context, it is possible only to give an idea of the influences of the variations due to these factors.

If we take the issue of power as it is dealt with in the relationship life-cycle, it becomes apparent that its appearance as a primary issue seems to vary for different couples, based, in part, on these variations. The following examples will use distinctive relationship models for purposes of clarity.

For a conservative, white, rural, middle-class, heterosexual couple where the definition of roles is well cemented, it is doubtful that power will be a passionately debated issue at the beginning stages of the relationship life-cycle. It is more likely that one will see such a debate during the mid-life/adolescent stage and more likely still that it will be initiated by the female who, traditionally, has not been readily handed a mantle of respect and power by society.

For a black, urban, lower-class, heterosexual couple where the pervasive life experience has been one of being socially powerless and historically disenfranchised, the relationship becomes a microcosm for issues of power in the larger society. The distribution of power is typically a primary focus at the beginning of the committed relationship. If it isn't negotiated, one may end up without any.

Finally, for a middle-class, urban, male homosexual or lesbian couple, who have been denied appropriate role models and who have both been raised to generally expect the power afforded to their gender, power as a conflictful issue arises seemingly within moments of the initial relationship commitment.

What is hoped is that this chapter will be used as the beginning of a creative process of evaluation and treatment of couples from a relationship life-cycle perspective. It should not be used too literally as a blueprint of what issues must be present and what clinical approaches must be assumed at each life-cycle stage. It was written from the author's phenomenological/systemic approach and clinical experience; given the uniqueness of that experience, it should be only partially applicable to the reader's work.

REFERENCES

Alapack, R. J. (Spring, 1984). The hinge of the door to authentic adulthood: A Kierkegaardian inspired synthesis of the meaning of leaving home. *Journal of Phenomenological Psychology.*

Benedek, T. (1959). Parenthood as a developmental phase: A contribution to the libido theory. *Journal of the American Psychoanalytic Association, 7,* 389-417.

Berman, E., & Lief, H. (1975). Marital therapy from a psychiatric perspective: An overview. *American Journal of Psychiatry, 132*(6), 586.

Bopp, M. J., & Weeks, G. (1984). Dialectics metatheory in family therapy. *Family Process, 23,* 49-61.

Carter, E. A., & McGoldrick, M. (1980). *The Family Life Cycle: A Framework for Family Therapy.* New York: Gardner Press.

DiCaprio, N. S. (1974). *Personality Theories: Guides to Living.* Philadelphia, PA: W. B. Saunders, Co.

Erikson, E. (1959). *Identity and the Life Cycle.* New York: International Universities Press.

Golan, N. (1981). *Passing through Transitions: A Guide for Practitioners.* New York: Macmillan Publishing Co.

Goldberg, S. R., & Deutsch, F. (1977). *Life Span Individual and Family Development.* Monterey, CA: Brooks/Cole Books.

Gould, R. (1972). The phases of adult life: A study in developmental psychology. *American Journal of Psychiatry, 129,* 521-31.

Levinson, D. L., et al. (1978). *Seasons of a Man's Life.* New York: Knopf.

Lowenthal, M., Thurnher, M., & Chiraboga, D. (1975). *Four Stages of Life.* San Francisco: Jossey-Bass.

Neugarten, B. L. (1979). Time, age, and the life-cycle. *American Journal of Psychiatry, 136,* 887-94.

Riegel, K. (1976). The dialectics of human development. *American Psychologist, 31,* 689-700.

Scarf, M. (1987). *Intimate Partners: Patterns in Love and Marriage.* New York: Random House.

Terkelsen, K. (1980). Toward a theory of the family life cycle. In E. A. Carter and M. McGoldrick (Eds.), *The Family Life Cycle: A Framework for Family Therapy.* New York: Gardner Press.

Vaillant, G. (1977). *Adaptation to Life.* Boston: Little, Brown.

Weeks, G. (1977). Toward a dialectical approach to intervention. *Human Development, 20,* 277-292.

Weeks, G., & Wright, L. (1979). Dialectics of the family life-cycle. *American Journal of Family Therapy, 7,* 85-91.

Chapter 14

An Intersystem
Approach to Treatment

Gerald R. Weeks

The purpose of this chapter is to present an integrated approach to psychotherapy, particularly marital therapy. The Intersystem Approach described in this chapter integrates elements from the three major approaches to therapy. These approaches are the individual, interactional, and intergenerational (see Figure 14.1).

These approaches have usually been considered mutually exclusive. Each approach represents some facet of a whole which we have to comprehend in order to develop a unified theory. The task is to discover the commonality across these major modalities, especially whether there is a common theory of change.

The task of integrating therapeutic modalities, schools, methods, and techniques has become popular in the past several years (Berman, Lief, & Williams, 1981; Feldman, 1982; Kaslow 1981; Lebow, 1984, 1987; Pinsof, 1983). Articles have pointed out how combinations may occur, but generally lack originality because most of these articles are eclectic, not integrative.

Inner Dialectics
Individual-Biological/Psychological

INDIVIDUAL

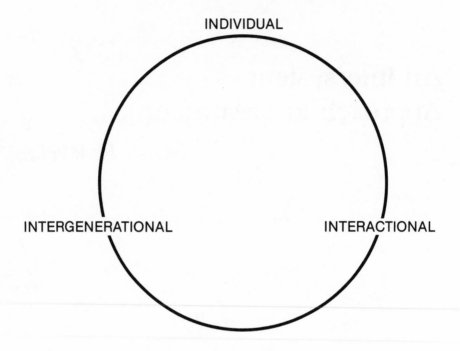

INTERGENERATIONAL   INTERACTIONAL

Outer Dialectics
System-Sociological/Cultural/Historical

Figure 14.1. Components of the intersystem model.

Eclecticism refers to the principle of drawing upon various doctrines in order to create greater unity. Integration refers to the act of making a whole out of parts. The word *integration* is derived from the Latin *integratus* which means whole, entire, fresh.

The principles for developing an integrated or comprehensive psychology were developed in a seminal book called *Existential Foundations of Psychology* (van Kaam, 1969). In order to create a comprehensive theory of therapy, two constructs are needed — the foundational and the integrational. The foundational construct provides the frame of reference for the integration of the phenomena from the various theories. The foundational construct requires a close examination of the philosophical assumptions on which the theory is built. Dialectic metatheory serves as the foundational construct for the Intersystem Approach and has been described elsewhere (Bopp & Weeks, 1984; Weeks, 1986).

The integrational construct allows us to bring together a variety of phenomena which have been revealed in different theories. In this chapter there are three basic integrational constructs. Two of these constructs — the affirmation and negation paradoxes — are used to integrate prescriptions from all the psychotherapies. These two constructs support the development of a comprehensive theory of psychotherapy. The third construct is a model of interaction which unifies different marital therapies.

PARADOX AS A UNIVERSAL ASPECT OF THERAPY

Weeks (1977) suggested that the common element of all psychotherapies was paradox. In their 1982 book, Weeks and L'Abate compared and analyzed the Adlerian, behavioral, gestalt, logotherapeutic, direct analysis, provocative, and hypnotherapeutic schools in order to demonstrate the common element of paradox.

Seltzer (1986) has significantly extended Weeks and L'Abate's (1982) work in this area. He presented a thoroughgoing analysis of paradox in both Eastern and Western approaches to therapy. In order to give the reader an idea of just how prevalent paradoxical thinking is in other schools of therapy, he considers the labels used to describe paradoxical techniques within a few.

> From the psychoanalytic perspective, which includes the work of paradigmatic psychotherapists, we have inherited the descriptors "antisuggestion," "going with the resistance," "joining the resistance," "reflecting" (or "mirroring") the resistance, "siding with the resistance," "paradigmatic exaggeration," "supporting the defenses," "reduction ad absurdum," "reenacting an aspect of the psychosis," "mirroring the patient's distortions," "participating in the patient's fantasies," "outcrazying the patient," and "the use of the patient as consultant." From the vantage point of behavior therapy, we may appreciate paradoxical elements in such procedures as "blowup," "implosion," "flooding," "instructed helplessness," "massed practice," "negative practice," "paradoxical intention," "stimulus satiation," and "symptom scheduling." In gestalt therapy, an approach where the term paradox is rarely employed, the attempt to foster the term paradox is rarely employed, the attempt to foster change paradoxically may be recognized in the therapist's cruel-to-be-kind suggestions to "stay

with the (negative) experience," or to "exaggerate the feeling" (sensation, experience, speech, movement, etc.). (p. 20)

Seltzer's (1986) theoretical analysis led him to develop a metatheory of paradox in psychotherapy. He argued that paradoxical strategies are present in all systems of therapy. These strategies all share the common element of defying the clients' expectations and involve some form of reframing and/or symptom prescription.

A metatheory or metaexplanation of change is required to bind together the various therapeutic approaches. This analysis will show how all psychotherapies share a paradoxical foundation. Omer (1981) was among the first theorists to proffer a unified concept of paradox. In an effort to arrive at the single common denominator (p. 332) of therapeutic efficacy, he proposed the concept of symptom decontextualization. This idea consists of the therapist modifying both the form and context of the symptom. Modification of form, in his definition, refers to the request to continue the symptom under different conditions (e.g., scheduling, exaggeration, different time or place). Modification of context refers to allowing expression of what one had been trying to stop.

In this writer's view, these changes create new meaning. The client must alter his or her attitude toward a behavior if it is allowed expression. Omer's (1981) term, decontextualization, however, is not as descriptive as Deissler's (1985) term, recontextualization. The meanings of these two terms are similar. Deissler stated that in symptom decontextualization the symptom is changed by altering the "recursive context" (i.e., the number of people involved in the problem) and/or the temporal and spatial contexts. It seems more descriptive to say that the symptom is recontextualized. When a client is able to change the context of the symptom, the meaning inevitably changes if only because the client is able to demonstrate some control over the uncontrollable, some volition over the nonvolitional, and some mindfulness over the spontaneous (mindless or automatic behavior).

Common Elements in All Therapies

What is it that all therapies have in common which is inherent in the paradoxical view of therapy?

Seltzer (1986) stated that *all* therapies can be perceived as endeavoring to assist clients in comprehending the voluntariness — and controllability — of behaviors which have come to appear nonvolitional (p. 164). He concluded that all paradoxical strategies change the meaning of the symptom from that which is uncontrollable to that which is controllable.

This view is consistent with the core of Weeks and L'Abate's (1982) approach, which offered five principles for paradoxical intervention. These principles dealt with both form and context. The third principle required that therapist change the direction of control of a symptom. In an individual, the symptom is placed under voluntary control; for systems, the symptom is placed under the control of those the symptom had heretofore controlled.

This metatheory of paradox can now be used to examine the universal aspects of therapy. Seltzer (1986) discussed this problem from several different perspectives. First, the nature of the therapeutic relationship is such that the therapist must be in control. Establishing a therapeutic relationship is synonymous with taking control. However, the control the therapist takes is not to eliminate the problem, but to help the client eliminate the problem.

Secondly, Seltzer argued that the therapist maintain a positive view of symptoms. In other words, in all systems of therapy, the symptom is never directly attacked. The symptom is seen as serving some need of the client. It is important to understand, not attack, the symptom. This attitude is translated into action via a permissiveness toward symptoms. Even behaviorists give clients permission to have their symptoms during the baseline period. Weeks and L'Abate (1982) found that symptoms always presented something positive. Symptoms have previously been defined as allies, communications, existential statements, and vehicles of change. In fact, Weeks and L'Abate found that the newer schools of therapy had started to define "symptom" in more explicitly positive ways, especially the strategic school. They and countless other therapists have proposed that symptoms be viewed as "friends" and not the enemy as many clients believe.

The third universal factor is how the therapist views not only the symptom, but the person. The client enters therapy expecting to be changed and fearing the therapist may disapprove of his or her symptomatic behavior. The client discovers the therapist to be attentive, supportive, empathetic, friendly, and receptive. The therapist maintains his/her attitude of acceptance, including acceptance of resistance, and the client's effort to resist not only fails but is somehow redefined in a way that indirectly brings control back to the therapist.

The therapeutic relationship is marked by a number of characteristics which run counter to the client's expectations. It is a unique social relationship in several paradoxical ways. The therapist shows an attitude of detached concern or uninvolved involvement. She/he takes control by giving it away. This process is accomplished by being indirectly direct (Seltzer, 1986). The goal is to help the client change spontaneously (Haley, 1973; Strong & Claiborn, 1982; Weeks & L'Abate, 1982). Change is not directly attributed to something the therapist did. Change is defined through the interaction of the therapist and client, with the client attributing change to self.

The fourth unifying theme is the paradoxical nature of the therapeutic process. Seltzer (1986) summarizes this idea in terms of the client(s) working *through*, rather than *around* (p. 41). In every system of therapy, the client is encouraged to move toward the symptom rather than flee from it. Otherwise, the therapy would simply support the avoidant behavior of the client. In the psychodynamic literature, the term for this process is literally *working through* (Singer, 1970). The behaviorist has the client focus attention on the symptom in order to reduce the anxiety associated with it through some type of conditioning procedure. Gestalt therapists encourage the client to stay with the feeling. Beisser (1970) stated the heart of Gestalt therapy was a paradoxical theory of change. He asserted that change occurs when one becomes what he is, not when he tries to become what he is not. In long-term analytic therapy, the therapist assumes that change will occur *very* slowly and only after a therapeutic relationship involving transference has occurred, precipitating greater insight. The underlying message to the client is 1) don't change quickly, and 2) be who you are.

Seltzer's (1986) two final points deal with the paradox of how the therapist takes responsibility for the client taking responsibility for her/his problems. In short, the common denominator for different therapies is that the client learns to exercise self-control. The therapist must convince the client that she/he can learn to help her/himself. This task may be accomplished directly or indirectly. The responsibility for change is always put back on the client. The therapist provides a framework for this task, without offering ready-made solutions.

When clients accept that they can do something to alleviate the symptomatic behavior, they are also forced to accept the fact that it must be under their control. By definition, a symptom is defined by the client as a behavior which is uncontrollable, involuntary, and spontaneous. Every system of therapy seeks to teach the client that symptoms are behaviors which are controllable, voluntary, and volitional. Every system of therapy recognizes and has techniques to deal with clients' denying, disqualifying, and externalizing their responsibility for symptomatic behavior. Contrariwise, every system has a system of rules which allows the therapist to deny, disqualify, and externalize any responsibility for having forced change to occur. This set of contradictory conditions sets up a context in which the attribution for change must be in the client.

Seltzer (1986) and Weeks and L'Abate (1982) have shown how paradoxical strategies are deeply embedded in many systems of psychotherapy. Seltzer (1986) has now extended this work through his theoretical analysis to show that paradox is a unifying concept which is universal in the various systems of therapy. In spite of the fact that content differs, the therapeutic process at the metatheoretical level remains constant. This metatheoretical understanding provides a new framework for integrating differential theories of therapy.

The bridge between the metatheoretical work of the authors reviewed thus far and the integration of different therapies has been developed by Strong and Claiborn (1982). These authors proposed a theory of change based on the principles and research of social psychology and psychotherapy.

The Paradox of Spontaneous Compliance

Strong and Claiborn (1982) identified two types of change processes. The first type is forced change or compliance. The second type is spontaneous compliance. Forced compliance refers to a change in oneself which is attributed to another person. This experience of the change is that of *doing* something different, rather than *being* different. Every parent, spouse, or therapist who has ever tried to force another person to be (act) different knows this effort is futile. If compliance does occur, it is only under duress, and will persist only as long as is needed to placate the other person. This understanding prevents therapists from telling clients what to do or giving advice.

Therapeutic change is best defined as the therapist's ability to create the context for spontaneous compliance. The term itself is contradictory. The task of the therapist is to get the client to comply without appearing to force the client. The therapist must take control without appearing to take control. Therapy is a paradox.

The idea of spontaneous compliance may strike the reader as unusual. In fact, it is a universal human experience. When we want someone to go to lunch with us, we do not say, "You will go to lunch with me at 12:00." You might say, "Would you like to go . . . ?" In marriage, spouses do not give each other orders. If they do, they find themselves in an untenable situation. Spouses attempt to influence each other indirectly by making statements such as, "I want to be with you," or "Would you like to talk?" When spouses attempt to control through forced compliance, dysfunctionality results. The therapist working with couples must help each member of the couple learn how to take control indirectly by taking control without appearing to take control.

The "affirmation" and "negation" paradoxes are used to create spontaneous compliance (Strong & Claiborn, 1982). The affirmation paradox is made up of three elements:

1) The therapist presents the desired behavior and insists that the behavior be adopted as part of the definition of the relationship.
2) The therapist communicates that change is a result of processes internal to the client and is not in compliance with the therapist.
3) The therapist identifies an agent responsible for change that acts beyond the client's volitional control. (p. 145)

The therapist wants to create a context in which the client spontaneously complies and attributes change to self. The communications therapist may teach the couple new ways of talking. Such techniques are useless unless the client wants to learn to use them. Thus, the client-couple can attribute success to *their* wanting to work together in communicating more effectively.

The therapist using the negation paradox (explicitly paradoxical strategies) encourages the client to change by encouraging the client not to change. In fact, that behavior which is not to be changed has been defined as involuntary by the client. By encouraging the involuntary behavior, the therapist is bringing it under control, which changes its meaning. In couples and families, the direction of control is changed by placing the person being controlled in charge. This task is done by reframing the behavior in such a way that it is good for the other person or it is perceived in such a way that the other has control over the symptom (Weeks & L'Abate, 1982). In both cases, what the client must change is his or her behavior vis-à-vis the therapist in order to gain control.

THEORY OF INTERACTION

Strong and Claiborn (1982) have developed a model of interaction based on social psychology which helps to achieve the goal of integrating different theories of therapy. Their model is based on three familiar assumptions — that people are open systems, are social beings, and behave in order to seek control. Control should not be exercised through force (forced compliance), but by creating circumstances which make certain responses more attractive and others less attractive. They use the metaphor of "inviting" the other person to respond in certain ways.

This invitational process is, in fact, circular. Each party is trying to control the other and trying to control the other to control himself/ herself in the way she/he wishes to be controlled. For example, in a marital relationship, each partner wants to be seen as giving. This means partner X wants to be seen as giving and wants to be controlled by Y in such a way that what X gives is what Y wanted to receive and what partner X wanted to give.

This model of interaction has both an intrapsychic and an interactional component (see Figure 14.2). The intrapsychic component has three elements. The first is *interpretation*. People interpret the communications they receive from others (feedback) within an interpretative framework. This framework serves as a mental template. The feedback received is both selected and molded by the receiver's psychological structure. The second element is *definition*. Definition refers to the way each partner wishes to define self and other in the context of the relationship. Every relationship is defined in some way. Most of our relationship definitions are based on past experiences with our family of origin. The third element is the ability to *predict* what will stimulate desired feedback from others. This element is also based on past experience with people, especially family of origin.

The second component in this model is interactional dynamics. The first element is *congruence*. In a congruent relationship, the feedback from the other matches each partner's desired definition. However, when the feedback shows the definitions are different, then the relationship is incongruent. When this discrepancy exists, the effect is to create tension. If the discrepancy is too great and persists, the relationship will

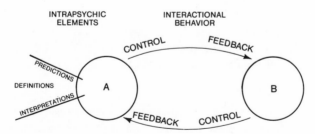

Figure 14.2. Intrapsychic/interactional model of relationships. (From *Change through Interaction* (p. 34), by S. Strong and C. Claiborn, 1982, New York, John Wiley. Copyright 1982 by John Wiley Publishers. Reprint by permission.)

probably terminate. In most cases, discrepancy leads to a change in the relationship.

The tolerance for discrepancy and the degree to which each party will change is a function of the second interactional element — *interdependence*. In a relationship, both parties depend on each other to fulfill specific needs. The other person may be perceived to fulfill these needs in actuality or in potentiality. The greater the level of interdependency, the greater the tolerance for discrepancy. The parties believe the relationship can provide them with what they want. When one party is more dependent (has less social power), then that person is more likely to accommodate to change in order to establish relationship congruency.

The change which occurs may be defined in a number of different ways: (a) complying to the other because the other is more powerful; (b) complying to the other and attributing the change to one's own desire; (c) defying the other and attributing the change to something temporary; and (d) defying the other because of one's desires. The direction of change — compliance or defiance — is a function of *attribution and impression management*. Impression management refers to how we create the impression others have of us. If the other person creates the impression that he/she has the resource we want (social power) and that he/she is acting in a way that is intended to benefit us, rather than to harm us or to fulfill his/her own self interest, then we are more likely to want to comply. The way others manage their impressions of themselves sets the stage for our attributions. We attribute motives to others' behavior. We think of behavior as good, bad, empathetic, insensitive, caring, selfish, etc. When a positive motive is attributed to another's behavior, we are more inclined to spontaneously comply.

The meaning of the term definition in Strong and Claiborn's (1982) model is operationally defined by each person's attempt to take some form of control in the relationship. The way partners define a relationship or attempt to define their relationship is an essential part of couple therapy. When marital therapists consider this aspect of the relationship, they normally talk about what each party wants to give and get, or the expectations (L'Abate & McHenry, 1983).

Relationship Control via Symptoms

The model of interaction formulated by Strong and Claiborn (1982) leads to several principles of control. A relationship is guided by a definition of its participants. The definition which develops is the guiding principle. In order to control another, a person must have an accurate understanding of the other person's definitions, interpretations, and predictions. This principle means it is necessary to understand the internal or intrapsychic components of the other. This understanding grows from a willingness to be understood by and to understand the other. Once these factors are understood, it is possible to predict how behavior will affect the other.

Finally, the person must possess the communication skill to get across intended meaning. Behavior is subject to multiple meaning. Behavior must be defined in relationships. This manipulation of meaning is part and parcel of impression management and attribution. The meaning the other person attributes to the behavior must be managed through the impressions conveyed.

It follows from this discussion that symptoms are behaviors used to gain control in a stable and incongruent relationship. The symptom is designed to help resist the other's effort to bring about change and to stimulate that person to change. The symptom claims power through the attributional strategy that it is not under one's control. The symptom-bearer attributes his or her uncontrollable behavior to some force beyond control while denying that the symptom is being used to resist control by others or to gain control of others. At the same time, other people attribute the symptom to some malevolent intent on the part of the symptom-bearer. They do not see that the symptom is a result of some *relationship* incongruency of which they are a part. This fact in turn leads to denial that they have control over the symptom.

INTERSYSTEM THERAPY

The first part of this chapter shows that all psychotherapy is paradoxical in nature. It has been demonstrated that paradoxical strategies and techniques are embedded in many systems of therapy—a fact which has not been recognized or admitted because of practitioners' adherence to their own theoretical biases. The metatheoretical analysis of psychotherapy has shown how change is essentially facilitated in the same way across therapies. The therapist adopts a number of paradoxical stances vis-à-vis the client. This metatheoretical description has been reduced to an even more parsimonious description by showing that therapy is some combination of affirmation and negation paradoxes (Strong & Claiborn, 1982).

The task is now to show how these metatheoretical and theoretical analyses can be applied in marital therapy. Although marital therapy will become the focus, the processes of therapy to be described in the following pages could apply to psychotherapy in general. This chapter is, in fact, a general theory of psychotherapy which focuses on working with a particular treatment unit—the marital dyad.

The goal of therapy is to enhance the fact that it is paradoxical—to work toward creating conditions of spontaneous compliance. There are two basic therapeutic processes which help achieve this end. These processes are reframing and prescriptions. Before discussing these concepts, the focus will shift to what needs to happen during the assessment phase of therapy with a couple.

Assessment Phase Tasks

The therapist needs to join with a couple in the same way a couple voluntarily join with each other. The couple have been able to join with each other because they have been able to work out a relatively congruent definition of their relationship and because they believe an interdependent relationship will meet their needs. The therapist must also form a congruent relationship. When couples present for therapy, they are in a state of relationship incongruency. Each partner is trying to stimulate the other to change, with one or both defined as symptomatic. Each partner attempts to induce the therapist to help stimulate the other partner to change by getting the therapist to accept his or her definition of the relationship. Joining in such a context refers to the therapist appearing to accept, understand, or empathize with each partner's definition. This apparent congruency with each fosters a state of interdependence. The client believes the therapist will assist in gaining control. Thus, each partner believes it is the other who will be stimulated to change. The therapist's apparent acceptance of each one's position (and symptom) is part of the paradoxical nature of change—change us without changing me.

Therapist-client congruence and interdependence are formed as the therapist explores the presenting problem(s). These problems have been defined as symptoms which represent interpersonal control tactics. In this chapter, problem and symptom are considered synonymous. As already stated, the control tactics are further defined as involuntary, uncontrollable, spontaneous, and denied as efforts to control the other partner. The symptom needs to be carefully examined in order to use it to effect change. Understanding the symptom means understanding what the symptom means to each party and what the symptom is designed to accomplish.

The therapist needs to gain an understanding of the intrapsychic, interactional, and intergenerational components of the relationship through the problem. In assessing the intrapsychic component, the therapist is interested in the meaning of the problem. The clients can be asked to give their interpretation of the problem behavior within the context of how each defines the relationship. The responses provide information about each spouse's interpretive framework, relationship definition, and predictions of the other's behavior.

The interactional component is examined concurrently with the intrapsychic component. The discrepancy or incongruence in the relationship must be evaluated. The therapist must determine how much compromise is needed. Are the partners at great odds with each other or are the differences small? The degree of incongruence can be subjectively evaluated by the therapist, but must also be validated by each partner. It is quite common for one partner to feel the situation is "very bad," while the other says if one or two small changes occurred, everything would be fine. This evaluation leads to a prioritization of problems from least to most severe. Secondly, the interdependence of the couple should also be assessed. A typical question used to begin this inquiry is, "What attracted you to each other, and what attracts you to each other now?" Questions like this allow partners the opportunity to reassess why they are still together. These questions also address the issue of commitment.

The therapist also wants to discover how each partner attempts to create the impression of care, concern, and love for the other. When the problem occurs, does the spouse respond with anger or with concern and empathy? Do the partners ever appear to care how they impress the other or are they so indifferent as to continue without accommodation? The attribution of responsibility for the problem is of critical importance. As stated earlier, the problem has been defined as being out of control. The responsibility for the problem is externalized, i.e., placed outside of self. This externalization is part of the linear attributional process. One spouse is okay, the other is not. In couples, the spouse bearing the symptom (e.g., depression) may simply blame the partner for his or her mood.

Reframing and Prescribing

Reframing is the most generically used strategy in the systems therapies as well as in psychotherapy in general. It is fundamental for psychotherapy because it helps the client change perspective in such a way that change is easier to make. Systems therapists have referred to this concept as: relabeling (Haley, 1973; Minuchin, 1974); reframing (Watzlawick et al., 1974); content reframing (Bandler & Grinder, 1982); redefinition (Andolfi, 1979); seeing the good (L'Abate, 1976); positive connotation (Palazzoli, Cecchin, Prata, & Boscolo, 1978); ascribing noble intentions (Stanton, Todd, & Associates, 1981); nonblaming (Alexander & Parsons, 1982); and context markers (Bateson, 1979; L'Abate, Ganahl, & Hansen, 1986; Viaro, 1980).

Watzlawick et al. (1974) were among the first to discuss the central role of reframing in therapy. They defined reframing as changing the conceptual and/or emotional meaning attributed to a situation. The behavior which is reframed is the behavior which has been defined or framed as being symptomatic by the client.

A reframing statement is quite different from an interpretation. An interpretation carries some truth value. The therapist actually believes the statement represents some aspect of reality. Reframing statements are not intended to have the same validity. The theory of truth which is used by the therapist is pragmatic. In the pragmatic theory of truth, that which works is considered true (James, 1907). The therapist is attempting to construct a view of reality which is more conducive to change, rather than replace the client's faulty world view with one that is correct (Kelly, 1955). In order to effectively reframe the symptom, the therapist must first join with the client system and understand the symptom.

Every system of therapy attempts to change the meaning of the problem or symptom in some fashion. The use of reframing in the literature usually has two meanings (Weeks & L'Abate, 1982). One is to change the way in which a symptom is defined in terms of some polarization such as good vs. bad, crazy vs. sane. This use of reframing stems from the various models of psychotherapy, including medical, moral, psychological, statistical, and personal discomfort. A symptom defined in terms of the moral model is wrong, sinful, or bad. Individuals frequently attribute bad intent to behavior. This attribution leads one to the moral perspective that he or she is good and the other is bad. Reframing can be used to change the value attributed to the problem. For example, couples usually believe their fights are exclusively negative behaviors. The fights have been framed as destructive, negative, and so on, and seen as representing negative intent. In reframing the fighting behavior, the therapist wants to change the attributed meaning from bad to good. For example, the therapist might say:

> The two of you must care a great deal about each other and yourself, because you invest so much of your energy in fighting. Couples who don't care or are indifferent don't fight. Your fighting shows there is something

worth fighting for in spite of the fact that you may end up appearing to fight against each other.

The second use of reframing is to move the focus from the individual to the system. When couples or families present with problems, there is usually a symptom-bearer who is carrying the problem for the rest of the family. The other member(s) do not see the connection between what they do and the behavior of the "sick" one. In couples, the "healthy" spouse externalizes and/or denies any responsibility for the problem. The attributional strategy in the couple is linear, not circular. One of the therapeutic tasks is to get them to see how the problem stems from their interaction. Reframing is the method whereby the therapist can move the couple from a linear attributional strategy to an interactional, or circular, attributional strategy.

The two uses of reframing described above are usually combined in a statement given to the client system. Palazzoli et al. (1978) call this technique positive connotation. The symptom is given a positive meaning and all the members of the system are linked together. Reframing as thus defined addresses all the factors comprising Strong and Claiborn's (1982) model. Reframing changes the definition of the relationship, changes the meaning of the behavior by altering or disrupting the interpretative framework, and disrupts one's ability to predict another's behavior. It also puts the participants on the same level so that one cannot take advantage of the other, thereby creating greater congruence.

One goal of the reframe is to prescribe a shared meaning in the relationship (e.g., fighting means you care). In other words, the reframe helps create a shared definition of the relationship that produces congruency. It also increases interdependence by suggesting that both desire the same goal for the relationship. Finally, one of the most significant effects is to change the attributions from linear to circular and negative to positive. If the reframe is successful and the couple believe they both deserve the same thing, then they must ask themselves if there aren't better ways to achieve it than by engaging in the same endless game. The result should be new efforts to change the other's impressions of oneself by changing his or her behavior.

The use of reframing in psychotherapy and marital therapy deserves considerable attention. This discussion has centered mostly on the theoretical aspects of reframing. The reader who wishes to gain a greater understanding can consult several recent reviews (Jones, 1986; L'Abate, Ganahl, & Hansen, 1986; Weeks & L'Abate, 1979, 1982).

In summary, reframing the symptom(s) has multiple effects. The most important effects in Intersystem therapy are to change the linear attributional strategy of the couple to a circular attributional strategy and to change the attribution of meaning given the symptom to one which is positive. Positive actually refers to relationship congruency. The positive dynamic (e.g., protection) helps to create greater congruence by defining something both desire. Once both partners see how each participates in the symptom, they are ready to work cooperatively rather than competitively. Additionally, by attributing positive intention(s), each partner is invited to try different strategies to manage the other, which means each partner must change.

Although reframing is an essential part of the therapy, it is usually not sufficient to bring about change by itself. Weeks and L'Abate (1982) have presented cases where reframing was enough to effect change, but these are the exceptions. Reframing sets the stage for the second phase of therapy. The second phase of therapy is prescriptive in nature.

Prescriptions

The second major task of the therapist is to provide prescriptions for change. Reframing was used to create a context for change by altering the meaning of the problem. Reframing operates at the cognitive/perceptual level. The client is not being asked to change behavior, except by implication. The therapist must now proceed with a strategy designed to bring about change in the behavioral/affective areas. This task is accomplished through the use of what are called *directives* (Haley, 1976) or *prescriptions* (L'Abate et al., 1986; Weeks & L'Abate, 1982). These two terms may be used interchangeably. The author has chosen to use the term prescription. A prescription is a set of instructions or injunctions the client is requested to follow. Unlike reframing, a prescription possesses some demand characteristics for change. The prescription may take a variety of forms and may be performed in session or extra-session (homework).

It may seem too simplistic to reduce all the various techniques of therapy to reframing and prescriptions. However, by viewing psychotherapy as a coherent or systematic set of prescriptions, it is easier to break the bond of adherence to a particular theoretical system.

Prescriptions fall within the two categories of affirmation or negation paradoxes. In either case, all prescriptions are essentially paradoxical within the context of therapy because the therapeutic encounter is essentially paradoxical. Whatever prescriptions are used must be congruent with the paradoxical context of therapy (Seltzer, 1986). The reader will recall that he discussed: 1) taking control by giving it away; 2) maintaining a positive view of the symptom and the person; 3) not attempting to force change; 4) allowing the client to have the symptom; 5) helping the client attribute change to self rather than outside forces; and 6) placing the client in charge of the symptom so that it is seen as controllable, voluntary, and volitional. The prescription should be made in such a way that the client wants to spontaneously comply.

Strong and Claiborn (1982) discussed three principles which are useful in increasing spontaneous compliance. The first principle is choice. It is important to give the prescription in such a way that the client perceives choice in how to respond. Common techniques include asking the client to think of alternatives, asking focused questions which lead the client in certain directions, and providing latitude for what the client does. The use of language is important in creating a sense of choice. The therapist needs to avoid terms which have a polarizing and pejorative effect. Concepts such as right vs. wrong, good vs. bad, sane vs. crazy, and absolute vs. relative need to be avoided. These terms suggest that the client and therapist know the "facts" of a situation; facts which represent an immutable reality; facts which demand that certain actions be taken.

Language creates choice by creating a sense that reality is created interactionally. The therapist communicates this concept through language by talking about perceptions, opinions, beliefs, and appearances. The therapist can talk about what will work, be useful, be productive, fit, rather than about the right/perfect solution which leaves no choice. When extra-session prescriptions are given, language is even more important. For example, in systems therapy, homework or tasks are frequently given. Consider what happens when "homework" is given to a school dropout or someone who felt homework was a forced behavior in school. This term stimulates reactance immediately and thus represents an attempt at forced compliance by the therapist. On the other hand, consider the person who believes homework is the only sensible way to learn. Many teachers and professionals, for example, find the idea of homework immediately practical. *They want* to comply with the task.

Extra-session prescriptions must be congruent with the client's framework of how change occurs. These extra-session prescriptions may be called prescriptions, homework, tasks, assignments, chores, experiences, exercises, experiments, and so on. The prescriptions may be given with more or less structure, more or less input from the client, and more or fewer parts which can be altered by the client.

The second factor which can be used to increase compliance and attribution of change to self is called personalism. Personalism refers to the idea that the compliance stems less from the communicator's personal desire for change and more from the requirements of the situation. If the client equates the request to the person-of-the-therapist, then a greater sense of forced compliance may result. The therapist can avoid this problem by softening statements such as, "I know" to "I think," "You're wrong about that," to "Let's take a look at what was just said," and "You should do . . . " to "It seems one choice is . . . . "

When giving a prescription, the therapist can emphasize the need to do certain things as a function of the situation. A good example of how this works can be drawn from the behavioral approach. It is easy to think that in behavioral approaches such as marital contracting (Sager, 1976), the partners are being forced to act in certain ways. Each party in a couple may be trying to force the other to act in particular ways. In actuality, the contract diffuses this power struggle by placing control in the contract which was developed. By giving control over to a mutually agreed upon contract, the partners are able to exercise more control. An "external" system is now in control. Many systems of therapy rely on this principle. The therapist is seen as implementing a program, system, technique, etc. — not his/her own will.

The degree of implicitness vs. explicitness is the third variable in attaining compliance. The more implicit prescription produces greater compliance and self-attribution. The Rogerian technique of reflective listening is an implicit form of prescription. Although it may appear that the therapist is exercising little control, the content of the material reflected and the way in which the material is reflected have a tremendous impact on the client.

INTEGRATION OF PRESCRIPTIONS

It is now time to focus more specifically on integrating the prescriptions from different marital therapists. In order to form a relationship, two individuals must experience relationship congruence. This principle applies to marital partners, friends, therapists, and clients. As noted earlier, joining is the term usually used to denote this process. Congruence does not stop with simply joining in the assessment phase of therapy. The prescriptions the therapist chooses must be congruent with the client's (a) expectations, (b) needs, and (c) explanatory system of change. As therapy proceeds and the clients become more dependent, greater incongruence can be introduced without disrupting the therapeutic relationship.

Clients enter therapy bringing a set of expectations. Some believe therapy will focus on the past, others on the present. Some believe insight is essential, others simply want the problem solved in a behavioral way. These expectations can be assessed by noting how the clients present themselves and their problem(s). For example, if a couple present by stating they have a communications problem, the therapist may begin to speak their language and use communication prescriptions. These prescriptions could be framed as teaching the clients to use I language, reflective listening, and so on. The mere use of the term teaching implies a voluntary relationship between teacher (therapist) and pupil (client). The therapist can gradually shift the focus of therapy by shifting the expectations of the clients.

The major dimensions on which shifts are made in prescriptions are space and time (L'Abate, 1976). In this case, space refers to the depth of treatment ranging from surface-conscious material to deep-unconscious material. Time pertains to the temporal range of treatment from past history to current behavior. Prescriptions may be integrated from schools of therapy which have different spatial and temporal foci in order to be congruent with clients' expectations. Prescriptions from the analytic and Bowenian schools emphasize the past and the intrapsychic; prescriptions from the contextual and experiential schools emphasize both the past and present and the intrapsychic and interpersonal; and prescriptions from the strategic, structural, communications, and behavioral schools emphasize the present and the interpersonal (Kaslow, 1981).

The second concern is about being congruent with the needs of the clients as they are experienced by the client and with the needs of the clients as assessed by the therapist's model of interaction. In the model of couple interaction employed here, there are six key concepts: definition, interpretation, prediction, congruence, interdependence, and attribution of change and impression management. The therapist should assess which areas of this model are most problematic for the couple. A simple example would be the problem of mind reading which is so common in couples. Mind reading refers us back to the prediction component in the model. The therapist could point this problem out. Once the problem is assessed, prescriptions would be offered to establish control.

A more complex example might be conflict resulting from the partner's interpretive framework based on unresolved experience in the family of origin. In this kind of case, one partner might be wanting the other to compensate for the lack of love provided by the parents. This partner might feel unloved, rejected, and in constant need of attention.

What needs to be addressed is the faulty interpretive framework. As Bowen (1978) has shown, this interpretive framework cannot function effectively because of the fusion between feeling and thinking. Talking about the unresolved family of origin issues in therapy reduces the emotionality. Assigning tasks involving going back to the family, rather than using the partner as a substitute, enables the problem to be confronted directly.

A couple presenting with the complaint of incompatibility which has resulted in loss of interest in each other and the perception that the other has changed for some selfish reason is even more complex. Yet, prescriptions drawn from the straightforward contracting approach may still prove to be effective. Prescriptions requesting that each look inside to see what she/he wants to give and take help to change the perception of selfishness. Just realizing that the other wants to give alters the impressions and the attributions of selfish interest. A successfully developed contract enhances the couple's feeling of interdependence and sense of congruence.

The process of choosing prescriptions involves identifying which components in the interactional model need changing and matching affirmation or negation prescriptions from the various approaches to marital therapy. The chart (see Figure 14.3) gives the relative emphasis of several major approaches to the key components in this model.

Model of Interaction

	Intrapsychic Inner Dialectics			Interactional Outer Dialectics		
	Relationship Definition	Interpretations	Predictions	Congruence	Interdependence	Attribution Impression Management
ANALYTIC	+	+	+			
BOWEN	+	+	+			
CONTEXTUAL	+	+	+	+	+	+
EXPERIENTIAL	+	+	+	+	+	+
STRATEGIC				+	+	+
STRUCTURAL				+	+	+
COMMUNICATIONS				+	+	+
BEHAVIORAL				+	+	+

Figure 14.3. Relative emphasis of different approaches to marital therapy.

Viewing therapy from this perspective allows the therapist to choose prescriptions from a number of approaches irrespective of modality (e.g., individual, couple, family), approach (e.g., structural, strategic), or method or technique (e.g., sculpting, symptom prescription).

The final consideration is the client's belief system regarding change. Every client has an implicit theory of how people change or fail to change. Some clients are pessimistic about change. They say, "People just don't change," or "I can't change." Others believe change occurs when they are told to do something or when they are given information. Others believe change comes from faith, choice, an emotional experience, moral training, crisis, clear thinking, unconscious processes, reward, punishment, trying harder, trust, hope, manipulation, and on and on. The one point on which all would agree is that change cannot be forced. It must be voluntary and it must be something attributable to the person. Even in the most extreme case of the recovered alcoholics who say they turned their life over to God, it was *they* who *chose* to accept God. Individuals may paradoxically appear to place the focus of change outside of self, but it is they who let "it" happen.

The choice of the prescription for change should be congruent with the client's view of how change occurs. If the couple share a common belief system, then the problem of matching is much easier. If they see change in different ways, a mix of prescriptions may be needed.

The client's view of change may evolve as therapy unfolds. The therapist can have a significant impact in influencing the client's implicit theory of change. With time, the therapist should be able to alter the client's view while maintaining the congruence needed to work effectively.

Ultimately, change results from the therapist's ability to change the direction of control in a relationship. A prescription is required which will change the control strategy used in the relationship without leading to supremacy or surrender. A sense of self-control *and* mutual control is the aim. Symptomatic behavior involves the denial of both self-control (I can't help my behavior) and mutual control (I am not trying to tell you how to be). When more appropriate control strategies are found, there is no longer a reason for symptomatic behavior.

The second way to change control is to place the other partner in charge of the symptom. This strategy redirects the power of the symptom to control the other, because the one being controlled by "it" is now in control of "it." The willingness of the other partner to accept responsibility for the symptom changes the impression of the other to that of someone trying to be helpful. The person exhibiting the symptom has no choice but to relinquish the symptom for another behavior. The change in behavior appears to be spontaneous. The new behavior which was not prescribed enhances the client's sense of having chosen a better way of relating.

CONCLUSION

This chapter has proposed a new approach for the integration of marital therapies. The Intersystem Approach allows us to integrate the individual, interactional, and intergenerational dimensions of understanding relationship dynamics and treatment. These dimensions are integrated through a social psychological model which has an empirical foundation rather than systems theory. In fact, the use of systems theory is strikingly absent in this chapter. Although systems theory provided the original metaphor for marital and family therapy, its usefulness as a metaphor is limited.

The integration of individual, interactional, and intergenerational dynamics and treatment techniques in this approach was accomplished through the use of three integrational constructs. All techniques of change were first reduced to either affirmation or negation paradoxes. It was argued that paradox is a universal element of psychotherapy. Because all psychotherapy is paradoxical, the basic problem is how to create the therapeutic condition of spontaneous compliance. Once the therapist understands how to increase compliance and create conditions of spontaneous compliance, the third construct comes into play.

This construct deals with the understanding of the marital system. A model of social psychology was used which has six key concepts: relationship definition, interpretation, prediction, congruence, interdependence, and attribution and impression management. These concepts all have some empirical foundation in social psychology. They direct our attention to six concurrently operating dimensions of relationship functioning. The understanding which comes through these dimensions allows the therapist to understand the marriage in a multidimensional fashion and design interventions around them. This third construct provides more direction for the content or substance.

The Intersystem Approach can be successful only when it is understood as a whole. The Intersystem Approach should continue to evolve as the constructs on which it is built are better articulated and as work in the different therapies progresses.

REFERENCES

Alexander, J., & Parsons, B. (1982). *Functional Family Therapy.* Monterey, CA: Brooks, Cole.

Andolfi, M. (1979). Redefinition in family therapy. *American Journal of Family Therapy, 7*, 5-15.

Bandler, R., & Grinder, J. (1982). *Reframing: Neuro-linguistic Programming and the Transformation of Meaning.* Moab, UT: Real People Press.

Bateson, G. (1979). *Mind and Nature: A Necessary Unity.* New York: Bantam Books.

Beisser, A. (1970). The paradoxical theory of change. In J. Fagan & I. L. Shepherd (Eds.), *What is Gestalt Therapy* (pp. 110-116). New York: Harper & Row.

Berman, E., Lief, H., & Williams, A. (1981). A model of marital interaction. In M. Scholevar (Ed.), *The Handbook of Marriage and Marital Therapy* (pp. 3-34). New York: S. P. Medical and Scientific Books.

Bopp, M., & Weeks, G. (1984). Dialectic metatheory in family therapy. *Family Process, 23*, 49-61.

Bowen, M. (1978). *Family Therapy in Clinical Practice.* New York: Free Press.

Deissler, K. (1985). Beyond paradox and counterparadox. In G. Weeks (Ed.), *Promoting Change through Paradoxical Therapy* (pp. 60-99). Homewood, IL: Dow-Jones.

Feldman, L. (1982). Dysfunctional marital conflict: An integrative interpersonal-intrapersonal model. *Journal of Marital and Family Therapy, 8*, 417-428.

Haley, J. (1973). *Uncommon Therapy: The Psychiatric Techniques of Milton H. Erickson.* New York: Ballantine.

Haley, J. (1976). *Problem-solving Therapy.* San Francisco: Jossey-Bass.

James, W. (1907). *Pragmatism.* New York: World Publishing.

Jones, W. (1986). Frame cultivation: Helping new meaning take root in families. *American Journal of Family Therapy, 14*, 57-68.

Kaslow, F. (1981). A dialectic approach to family therapy and practice: Selectivity and synthesis. *Journal of Marital and Family Therapy, 7*, 345-351.

Kelly, G. (1955). *The Psychology of Personal Constructs, Vol. 1, A History of Personality.* New York: W. W. Norton.

L'Abate, L. (1976). *Understanding and Helping the Individual in the Family.* New York: Grune & Stratton.

L'Abate, L., Ganahl, G., & Hansen, J. (1986). *Methods of Family Therapy.* Englewood Cliffs, NJ: Prentice Hall.

L'Abate, L., & McHenry, S. (1983). *Handbook of Marital Interventions.* New York: Grune & Stratton.

Lebow, J. (1984). On the nature of integrating approaches to family therapy. *Journal of Marital and Family Therapy, 10*, 127-138.

Lebow, J. (1987). Developing a personal integration in family therapy: Principles for model construction and practice. *Journal of Marital and Family Therapy, 13*, 1-14.

Minuchin, S. (1974). *Families and Family Therapy.* Cambridge, MA: Harvard University Press.

Omer, H. (1981). Paradoxical treatments: A unified concept. *Psychotherapy: Theory, Research, and Practice, 18*, 320-324.

Palazzoli, M., Cecchin, M., Prata, G., & Boscolo, L. (1978). *Paradox and Counterparadox.* New York: Jason Aronson.

Pinsof, W. (1983). Integrative problem-centered therapy. *Journal of Marital and Family Therapy, 9*, 19-35.

Sager, C. (1976). *Marriage Contracts and Couple Therapy.* New York: Brunner/Mazel.

Seltzer, L. (1986). *Paradoxical Strategies in Psychotherapy: A Comprehensive Overview and Guidebook.* New York: Wiley.

Singer, E. (1970). *Key Concepts in Psychotherapy.* New York: Basic Books.

Stanton, M., Todd, T., & Associates (1981). *The Family Therapy of Drug Addiction.* New York: Guilford.

Strong, S., & Claiborn, C. (1982). *Change Through Interaction. Social Psychological Processes of Counseling and Psychotherapy.* New York: John Wiley.

van Kaam, A. (1969). *Existential Foundations of Psychology.* New York: Basic Books.

Viaro, M. (1980). Case report: Smuggling family therapy through. *Family Process, 19,* 35-44.

Watzlawick, P., Weakland, J., & Fisch, R. (1974). *Change: Principles of Problem Formation and Problem Resolution.* New York: W. W. Norton.

Weeks, G. (1977). Toward a dialectical approach to intervention. *Human Development, 20,* 277-292.

Weeks, G. (1986). Individual-system dialectic. *American Journal of Family Therapy, 14,* 5-12.

Weeks, G., & L'Abate, L. (1979). A compilation of paradoxical methods. *American Journal of Family Therapy, 7,* 61-76.

Weeks, G., & L'Abate, L. (1982). *Paradoxical Psychotherapy: Theory and Practice with Individuals, Couples, and Families.* New York: Brunner/Mazel.

Name Index

Abelsohn, D., 216
Abt, L. E., 282
Alapack, R. J., 292
Alberti, P. E., 204–205
Alexander, J., 330
Andolfi, M., 329

Bach, G., 205
Baer, J., 205
Bandler, R., 329
Barker, P., 137, 140
Barnard, C. P., 120, 138, 139
Bateson, G., 330
Beach, S. R., 170, 171
Beavers, W. R., 173
Beisser, A., 322
Bell, A. P., 241, 242, 243
Benedek, T., 293
Bepko, C., 244, 247
Berg, B., 259, 269, 272
Bergman, I., 163, 188
Berman, E., 6, 50, 57, 173, 293, 295, 317
Bishop, D. S., 137
Bloch, D., 216, 223, 226
Bloom, B. L., 258, 259, 264
Blume, J., 216
Blumstein, P., 164, 165
Bograd, M., 209
Bopp, M. J., 290, 319
Boscolo, L., 330, 331
Boszormenyi-Nagy, I., 31
Bowen, M., 336
Breit, M., 180
Burch, B., 244, 247
Burns, D., 12
Buunk, B., 187

Cardell, M., 243
Carter, E. A., 18, 62, 291, 293, 295
Cecchin, M., 330, 331
Ching, J. W. J., 272
Chiraboga, D., 293
Claiborn, C., 322, 323, 324, 325, 326, 327, 331, 333
Clinebell, C. H., 7

Clinebell, H. J., 7
Colangelo, N., 6
Constantine, L. L., 167, 180, 187
Cornell, C. P., 194
Cuber, J. F., 167

Dayringer, R., 205
Deissler, K., 320
Deschner, J. P., 197
Deutsch, F., 293
Deutsch, H., 239
Deutsch, M., 216, 218
DiCaprio, N. S., 301
Doherty, W. J., 6
Dreen, K., 194, 195
Dwyer, B. J., 165n

Egan, G., 11, 14
Eidelson, R. J., 12
Elbaum, P. L., 180
Ellis, A., 167, 205
Emmons, M. L., 204–205
English, O. S., 167
Epstein, N., 12, 137
Erikson, E., 290, 293, 309

Fair, P. H., 272
Farber, L. H., 179
Faust, D., 72
Feldman, L., 16, 17, 173, 317
Fensterheim, H., 205
Fincham, F., 106
Finn, S., 243
Fisch, R., 103, 329, 330
Fischer, J., 243
Framo, J. L., 177, 222
Freud, S., 237, 238
Frey, J., 11, 14
Friedman, D., 192, 193, 212
Friedman, H., 216

Ganahl, G., 330, 331, 332
Gardner, R. A., 259
Gartrell, N., 244, 245, 247
Gelles, R. J., 194

341

Subject Index

344